Wellbeing

What produces a happy society and a happy wellbeing, we can now answer this question usin̺ ____ ̺̺ al evidence. This transforms our ability to base our decisions on the outcomes that matter most, namely the wellbeing of us all including future generations. Written by two of the world's leading experts on the economics of wellbeing, this book shows how wellbeing can be measured, what causes it and how it can be improved. The findings of the book are profoundly relevant to all social sciences, including psychology, economics, politics, behavioural science and sociology. This is the first field-defining text on a new science that aims to span the whole of human life. It will be an invaluable resource for undergraduate and graduate students, as well as policymakers and employers who will be able to apply its insights in their professional and private lives.

Richard Layard is a leading British economist, who thinks society's goal should be the wellbeing of the people. His landmark book *Happiness: Lessons from a New Science* has influenced policymakers worldwide. He is cofounder of Action for Happiness, of the World Happiness Report and of the World Wellbeing Movement. In 2020, he was awarded the Lifetime Achievement Award by Britain's Economic and Social Research Council.

Jan-Emmanuel De Neve is a Belgian economist and professor at the University of Oxford where he directs the Wellbeing Research Centre. He is best known for his research on the economics of wellbeing, which was selected among 'The Management Ideas that Mattered Most' by *Harvard Business Review*, and he was awarded the Veenhoven Award for his contributions to the scientific study of happiness. He is an editor of the World Happiness Report and cofounder of the World Wellbeing Movement.

Wellbeing

Science and Policy

RICHARD LAYARD
London School of Economics and Political Science

JAN-EMMANUEL DE NEVE
University of Oxford

Illustrated by David Shrigley

CAMBRIDGE
UNIVERSITY PRESS

Shaftesbury Road, Cambridge CB2 8EA, United Kingdom

One Liberty Plaza, 20th Floor, New York, NY 10006, USA

477 Williamstown Road, Port Melbourne, VIC 3207, Australia

314–321, 3rd Floor, Plot 3, Splendor Forum, Jasola District Centre, New Delhi – 110025, India

103 Penang Road, #05–06/07, Visioncrest Commercial, Singapore 238467

Cambridge University Press is part of Cambridge University Press & Assessment, a department of the University of Cambridge.

We share the University's mission to contribute to society through the pursuit of education, learning and research at the highest international levels of excellence.

www.cambridge.org
Information on this title: www.cambridge.org/9781009298926

DOI: 10.1017/9781009298957

First published 2023

A catalogue record for this publication is available from the British Library.

ISBN 978-1-009-29892-6 Hardback
ISBN 978-1-009-29894-0 Paperback

To Molly and Aude-Line
and all others who create a happier world

Contents

WE MUST KNIT A NEW WORLD

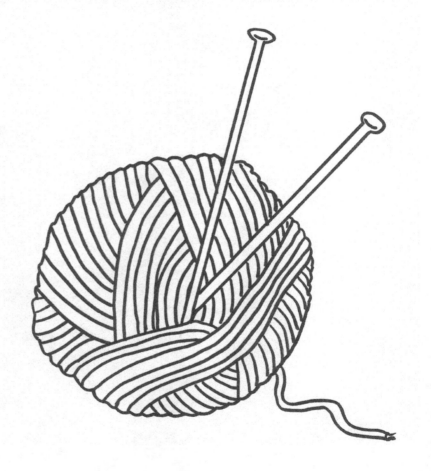

Introduction and Summary

Everyone wants to be happy.

The Dalai Lama

Let's begin with a thought experiment. Suppose you were not you, but someone not yet existing. Where would you want to be born? Would it be where people were richest, or healthiest or best educated, however happy or miserable they were. Or would you simply ask yourself, 'Where are people most enjoying their lives, most satisfied and most fulfilled?' If that was your approach, you would be part of a great tradition of thinkers (going back to the ancient Greeks and beyond) who believed that the best society is the one where people have the highest wellbeing.

By wellbeing we mean **how you feel about your life, how satisfied you are**. We do not mean the external circumstances that affect your wellbeing. We mean the thing that ultimately matters: your inner subjective state – the quality of your life as you experience it, how happy you are. We shall call this 'wellbeing' for short, but we always mean 'subjective wellbeing'.

Wellbeing, this book argues, is the overarching good and other goods (like health, family and friends, income and so on) are good because of how they contribute to our wellbeing. This idea is basic to the subject. It is illustrated in Figure I.1, which shows some of the more obvious causes of wellbeing.

So the key to a happier society is to understand how these various factors affect our wellbeing and how they can be altered for the better. Fortunately we have a whole new science to help us do that – the science of wellbeing.

For many people, the motivation for this science is the simple idea that the overarching goal for a society should be the wellbeing of the people. This philosophical idea is not new. In the eighteenth-century Anglo-Scottish Enlightenment, the central concept was that we judge a society by the happiness of the people. But, unfortunately, there was at the time no method of measuring wellbeing. So income became the measure of a successful society, and GDP per head became the goal. But things are different now. We are now able to measure wellbeing, and policy-makers around the world are turning towards measures of success that go 'beyond GDP'. This shift is really important because, as we shall see, income explains only a small fraction of the variance of wellbeing in any country.

Figure I.1 Some key causes of individual wellbeing

The movement to go beyond GDP brings together two main strands of thought. First, there are those who for over 50 years have argued for wider indicators of progress – the 'social indicators movement'. This has involved a range of social scientists including some economists like Amartya Sen. Then, second, are those who fear for the sustainability of the planet and for the lives of future generations. For all these groups, it has become natural to support the idea that the overall goal must be the wellbeing of present and future generations.

Fortunately, we can now see more clearly than ever before what is needed to increase our wellbeing. For over the last 40 years a whole new science has developed backed by major new sources of data.

Measurement

The simplest way to measure wellbeing is to ask people 'Overall, how satisfied are you with your life these days?'. Typically, people are asked to respond on a scale of 0 (not at all satisfied) to 10 (very satisfied). People's answers to this simple question about life satisfaction tell us a lot about their inner state. We know this because their answers are correlated with relevant brain measurements and with the judgements of their friends. They are also good predictors of longevity, productivity and educational performance (another reason for taking wellbeing seriously). And their answers predict voting behaviour better than the economy does – which is a good reason why policy-makers should take wellbeing very seriously!

There are two other ways to measure wellbeing. The first is usually called 'hedonic' and involves measuring a person's mood at frequent intervals. The second is called 'eudaemonic'. We shall describe both measures in Chapter 1 and explain why we think life satisfaction is the most helpful – how we feel about our life.

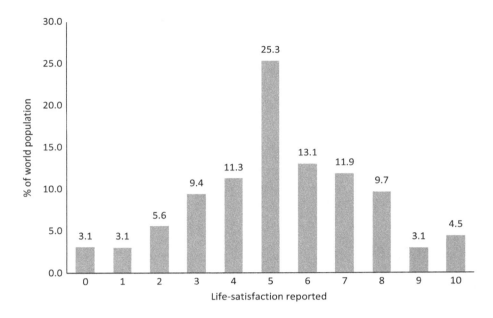

Figure I.2 Percentage of people in the world at each level of life satisfaction
Source: Helliwell et al. (2018a) Figure 2.1 Gallup World Poll 2015–17, Cantril ladder

If we focus on life satisfaction, there is a huge inequality of wellbeing in the world. A sixth of the people in the world report wellbeing of 8 or above (out of 10), while at the other end over a sixth report 3 or below (see Figure I.2). This is a huge difference, and, from the wellbeing perspective, this is the most important form of inequality that there is in the world. It is quite possibly the most important fact about the human situation.

So what does determine our life satisfaction? All human beings have similar deep needs – for food and shelter, safety, love and support, respect and pride, mastery and autonomy. How far these are satisfied depends on a mixture of what we ourselves do and what happens to us – a mixture of us as 'agents' and of our 'environment'. This determines the structure of the book.

So in this introduction we shall first describe the structure of the book. And then, to whet your appetite, we shall set out some of the findings in summary form. But don't worry if they are a bit condensed – all will become clear, chapter by chapter.

This Book

- The book begins with two general chapters (Chapters 1–2) on fundamental concepts.
- Then Chapters 3–5 describe what we contribute to our wellbeing as 'agents' through
  o our behaviour,
  o our thoughts and
  o our genes and our physiology.

- Next, Chapters 6–17 describe how we are affected by our environment – what happens to us:
  - o our family, our schooling and our experience of social media
  - o our health and healthcare services
  - o having work
  - o the quality of our work
  - o our incomes
  - o our communities
  - o our physical environment and the climate of the planet
  - o and our system of government.
- Finally, Chapter 18 shows how policy-makers can use this knowledge to choose policies that create the greatest wellbeing for the people.

Our Behaviour

But why do we need policy-makers and governments at all? In the traditional economic model, people do whatever is best for their own wellbeing, and the process of voluntary exchange leads to the greatest possible wellbeing all round (subject to some qualifications – see below). On this basis, laissez-faire will solve most problems. But modern behavioural science challenges this view of the world, and a founder of behavioural science, Daniel Kahneman, was awarded the Nobel Prize in Economics for his challenging work.

There are two main problems. First, people are not that good at pursuing their own best interests. Many people overeat or take little exercise. Some become addicts. Others make changes that they think will improve their lives, without realising that they will soon get used to the new situation and feel no better than before (the process of 'adaptation'). Moreover, people are hugely affected by how choices are presented to them (like the choice over saving for a pension) – so their preferences are often not well-defined. And in the short term, people are loss-averse – which can lead to greater losses in the long term.

The second key issue is that everybody is hugely affected by how other people behave (in ways other than through voluntary exchange). This is a case of what economists call 'externality' – things that happen to you that do not arise from voluntary exchange. Economists have always been explicit that 'externality' calls for government action, but they have not always realised how pervasive externality is in human life:

- It really matters to us what the pool of other people we live amongst is like – are they trustworthy; are they unselfish?
- Other people (society at large) influence our tastes, for good or ill.
- If other people or colleagues get higher pay, this reduces the wellbeing we get from a given income.

For all these reasons, there is a major role for governments and for educators in affecting the context in which we live and thus our wellbeing.

Our Thoughts

But there is also a huge role for us as individuals: in determining how our experience of life affects our own feelings. It matters how we think. For our thoughts affect our feelings. The reverse is also true of course – our feelings affect our thoughts. But the way to break into this cycle is by managing our thoughts. The importance of 'mind-training' was stressed in many ancient forms of wisdom (such as Buddhism, Stoicism and many religious traditions). But in the West, its importance has been re-established in the last fifty years and proved by state-of-the-art randomised experiments.

In this story of discovery, the first step was cognitive behavioural therapy (CBT) – for people with depression or anxiety disorders (led by Aaron T. Beck). These ideas were then expanded into things we can all do, by positive psychology (led by Martin Seligman). In addition, for many people, mind-training is increasingly learned from Eastern practices like mindfulness and compassion meditation.

Our Bodies and Our Genes

Striking new research shows how these mental states affect the workings of the body. At the same time of course, the reverse applies: physical interventions (like psychiatric drugs or exercise) can also affect our minds.

But who are we? An important part of who we are is determined by our genes. Evidence of their importance comes from two sources. The first are twin studies. These show that identical twins (who have the same genes) are much more similar to each other than non-identical twins are. For example, the correlation in wellbeing between identical twins is double what it is between non-identical twins. Any parent who has produced more than one child can see how children differ, even if they are brought up in exactly the same way. Our genes matter and now we are beginning to be able to track down which specific genes are important for wellbeing.

But our environment (social and physical) is also crucial. Moreover, in most cases a person's development depends not on two separate processes (genes and environment) but on the joint interactive effect of genes and environment. So it is not possible to identify separately which part of a trait is due to genes and which part to environment. And crucially, problems that arise due to genes are often as treatable as those which arise due to experience.

The Inequality of Wellbeing

So how does our experience affect us? The most general way in which to investigate this is by looking at the wide differences in wellbeing across people and finding what factors best explain them.

Of the huge variance of wellbeing in the world, nearly 80% is within countries. And within a country the main **'personal factors'** explaining the variance are (in rough order of explanatory power):

- mental and physical health,
- relationships at home and at work,
- relationships in the community,
- income and
- unemployment.

These factors are also the main ones that are responsible (in the same order) for the prevalence of misery (measured by a low level of life satisfaction). So we need a new concept of deprivation. It cannot be based on poverty alone. It must include everything that stops people from enjoying their lives.

However, our wellbeing also depends on broader features of our society, things that do not vary between people but do vary between societies. We can uncover these factors by comparing wellbeing in different countries. These factors include the social norms of trust, support and generosity and the degree of personal freedom. So, if we look across countries, the main **'societal factors'** that explain the differences in average wellbeing are (in order of explanatory power):

- income per head,
- healthy life expectancy,
- social support,
- personal freedom,
- trusting social relations and good government,
- generosity and
- peace.

These two sets of factors (personal and societal) provide the framework for the second half of the book. We look first at the more personal aspects of life (family, school, health, work, income) and then we move to the more societal aspects (community, environment and government). Here are some key findings.

Families and Schooling

Much of our adult life can be predicted from our childhood, and the best childhood predictor of a happy adult life is not good academic performance but a happy childhood. So what then determines whether a child is happy? Obviously parents matter, but it also makes a huge difference which school you go to and which teacher you are taught by.

At home, a child's key need is unconditional love from at least one adult – together with firm boundaries. The mental health of parents (especially the mother) is the most important measurable factor affecting the wellbeing of children. Children are also profoundly affected by how their parents get on with each other. Fortunately, there are now good evidence-based methods for helping parents who are in conflict and for reducing the likelihood of conflict in the first place.

Schools also have a major effect on children's wellbeing – as much as all the measurable characteristics of the children's parents. So it is crucial that schools have child wellbeing as an explicit, measurable goal. And, as many experiments have shown, the life-skills of children can be significantly improved if these skills are taught by trained teachers using well-tested materials.

Mental and Physical Health

However, at present at least a third of the population will have a diagnosable mental health problem at some time in their life. For severe mental illness, medication is required. But all mental illness should also be treated by the relevant psychological therapy. Modern evidence-based therapies for depression and anxiety disorders have at least 50% recovery rates, and they are quite short and inexpensive. But shockingly, even in the richest countries, under 40% of people with mental health problems receive treatment of any kind (including simply medication on its own). This is true of both adults and children.

By contrast, in rich countries at least, most physical illness is treated. But chronic physical pain continues to be very common, with a quarter of the world's population reporting a lot of physical pain yesterday. It is an important determinant of life satisfaction.

Though modern medicine cannot always eliminate pain, it has been extraordinarily successful at extending the length of life. A comprehensive measure of social welfare takes this into account: by multiplying average wellbeing by life expectancy. This measure provides an estimate of the average Wellbeing-Years (or WELLBYs) per person born. If we use this as a measure of the human condition, we can see just how much the human condition has improved over the last century and over the last decade.

Unemployment

Another key aspect of the human condition is work. The relationship between work and wellbeing is crucial and complex. One of the most robust findings to emerge from wellbeing science is the profound cost of unemployment. Workers who lose their jobs suffer declines in life satisfaction comparable with the death of a spouse. In some cases, those affected fail to recover back to baseline levels of happiness years later, even after returning back to work. The wellbeing consequences of unemployment are about much more than lost wages. Work can provide us with a sense of meaning in life, a source of human connection, social status and routine. When we lose a job, we lose much more than a pay check. As a result, for policy-makers interested in promoting and supporting wellbeing, reducing unemployment ought be a top priority (and finding ways to do this without increasing inflation).

The Quality of Work

However, having a job is not all that matters. How we spend our time at work can be just as important. Despite the overall importance of employment for life satisfaction, working turns out to be one of the less enjoyable activities for most people on a day-to-day basis. While pay is certainly important, the extent to which we enjoy our work proves to be even more dependent on a number of other conditions. Bad working relationships (especially with managers) can profoundly undermine wellbeing at work – for the average person, the worst time of day is when you are with your line manager. In addition, being unable to work the hours we want to work or finding little meaning in our jobs are central threats to wellbeing.

For companies and policy-makers, improving the quality of the workday may be important not only as a matter of principle but also a matter of business. Happier workers are more productive and less likely to quit or call in sick, while happier companies have happier customers and earn higher profits. The potential benefits of supporting wellbeing at work are therefore immense. To this end, a number of companies have begun experimenting with flexible work schedules and family-friendly management practices. We'll walk through the various methods researchers use to implement and assess these initiatives and what they may tell us about the future of work.

Income

This said, a major motivation for work is income. So a central issue is, To what extent does higher income lead to higher wellbeing? In 1974, Richard Easterlin set out what he argued was an important paradox:

(1) When we compare individuals at a point in time, those who are richer are on average happier.
(2) But, in the long term over time, greater national income per head does not produce greater national happiness.

The first statement is certainly true: in rich countries, a person with double the income of another person will be happier by around 0.2 points (out of 10). This is not a large effect but a worthwhile one. Moreover, the gain in wellbeing from an extra dollar is much more for someone who is poor than for someone who is rich – which is the central argument for the redistribution of income.

But the second statement is still a subject of dispute. At a point in time richer countries are certainly happier than poorer countries. But the effect of economic growth over time seems to vary widely between countries. In some countries, there is a clear positive effect. But there are other countries where there has been strong economic growth but wellbeing is no higher now than it was when wellbeing records first began. These latter countries include the United States, West Germany and China.

There is one obvious reason why extra income might do more for an individual (in a given context) than it would do for a whole population (when everyone gets richer at the same time). This reason is that people compare their own incomes with the incomes of other people. There is abundant evidence (including experimental evidence) that people are less satisfied with a given income the higher the income level of other people. This is an important negative externality – when others work harder and earn more, this reduces my wellbeing. Just as with pollution, the standard way to counter this negative external effect is by a corrective tax. So taxes on income or consumption may be less inefficient than most economists believe – they help to discourage a rat-race that reduces everybody's wellbeing.

Wellbeing research also reveals something important about the business cycle. Wellbeing is cyclical. When income grows in the short run, people become happier and, when it falls, they become less happy. But the negative effect of the slump is double the size of the positive effect of the boom. So business cycles are bad, and policy-makers should aim to keep the economy stable. This would be true even if greater stability somewhat slowed the long-term rate of economic growth.

The broad conclusion on income is this. Increases in absolute income are desirable, especially in poor countries. But we do not need higher long-term economic growth at any cost, since income is just one of many things that contribute to human wellbeing.

Community

As we have seen, the most important personal factors affecting wellbeing are health and human relationships – at home, at work and in the community. Communities provide vital forms of social connection. Some of this comes from voluntary organisations of all kinds, ranging from sports clubs to faith organisations. The evidence shows that countries are happier when more people belong to voluntary organisations. Moreover, these organisations depend mainly on the work of volunteers, and, as research shows, individuals are happier when they do some voluntary work.

Social norms are also crucial. In a well-functioning community, people have a high degree of trust in their fellow-citizens – people are happier in societies where lost wallets are more likely to be returned and where crime rates are low. Such societies also tend to have less inequality of wellbeing, which is also a powerful predictor of high average wellbeing. (It is also a better predictor of average wellbeing than income inequality is.)

Immigration is a challenge to social harmony, but there is no clear evidence it has so far damaged the average wellbeing of existing residents, and there is clear evidence that it has greatly increased the wellbeing of the immigrants.

In every community, some groups are less happy than others. Minority ethnic groups tend to be less happy (though in the United States at least the gap has been falling). Young people tend to be happier than people in middle age and than people at older ages (except in North America and Europe). But both men and women are almost identical in their average happiness in nearly every country.

The Physical Environment and the Climate of the Planet

Ultimately, human life depends on our physical environment. The evidence shows clearly how people's wellbeing is improved by contact with nature. But the majority of us now live in cities and work at some distance from our home. The evidence suggests that long commutes reduce wellbeing, since the lower house prices that commuters enjoy are not low enough to compensate for the pain of commuting. Similarly, air pollution and aircraft noise reduce wellbeing (and house prices do not adjust enough to compensate).

But our biggest assault on the environment is our impact on the climate. The world's average temperature is already over 1°C above its pre-industrial level and, if it exceeds the 1.5°C mark, scientists predict major increases in floods, droughts, fires, hurricanes and sea levels.

It will be future generations who bear the brunt of this. But in the wellbeing approach, everybody matters equally, regardless of when or where they live. So if we follow this approach, we have to maximise the total WELLBYs per person born in present **and** future generations. Because the future is uncertain, future WELLBYs should be discounted slightly relatively to present ones but by no more than 1.5% a year. (By contrast economists typically discount future real income by around 4% a year – which makes the future much less important.)

Climate change matters so much because we care about the wellbeing of future generations. So there is a natural alliance between those who care about wellbeing and those who care about climate change. And there is another reason for this: both groups agree that what matters is not just income but the overall quality of life, both now and in the future.

Government

Much of what determines the variation in wellbeing around the world relates to individual differences – genes, health, employment, family, income etc. Yet the quality of our lives is also shaped by the country in which we live. For better or for worse, governments play crucial roles in determining our life outcomes and opportunities. Understanding the relationship between governance and wellbeing is therefore essential to understanding differences in wellbeing around the world.

This relationship can be assessed at different levels. First, we can consider what types of governments are more or less conducive to wellbeing. Perhaps unsurprisingly, we find that governments that are able to perform certain essential functions well – (1) enforce the rule of law, (2) deliver good services, (3) pass effective regulation and (4) control corruption – are much more likely to have happier citizens. Democracy and wellbeing are similarly linked. Increasing opportunities for democratic participation in decision-making has been shown to improve wellbeing, regardless of the actual decision made. However, this relationship tends to be stronger in richer countries.

Along similar lines, we can consider the link between wellbeing and political ideology. If we analyse political projects on a spectrum from left to right, which set of policies is most likely to improve wellbeing? Given the impressive diversity of political opinions, the story here gets very complicated very quickly. Nevertheless, some consistent findings have begun to emerge from the empirical literature. The results of these endeavours suggest that reducing inequality, expanding social safety nets and limiting economic insecurity in particular are best positioned to promote and support wellbeing.

We can also flip the script and look at the extent to which wellbeing itself is predictive of political outcomes. Happier voters are more likely to support and vote for incumbent parties. Indeed, in some studies, national happiness levels predict the government's vote share better than leading economic indicators including GDP per capita and unemployment. This observation provides a strong reason for elected politicians and governments to care about the wellbeing of their constituents.

Similarly, dissatisfaction can provoke political protest. Even in the midst of increasing economic opportunities, declining levels of wellbeing in countries like Egypt and Syria have preceded and predicted uprisings and political protests. In some Western countries too – most notably France and the United States – dissatisfied voters are significantly more likely to support populists, to distrust the political system and to devalue democracy than their happier counterparts.

How to Select Good Policies

So, if wellbeing is the overarching goal, it is what should govern the choices of all policy-makers. This is true whether they are finance ministers, local government officers or leaders of NGOs. And they should take into account the effect of policies upon not only wellbeing but also how many years people live to enjoy that wellbeing. So the key measure of success is the total amount of wellbeing that each person born experiences over their lifetime. This means adding up their wellbeing score for each year that they live. We call the resulting score their Wellbeing-Years (or WELLBYs).

So, any budget-holder would be choosing those policy options that give the highest number of WELLBYS (suitably discounted) for each dollar of cost. That would be the proper meaning of the best 'bang for the buck'. Benefits would be measured in units of wellbeing and not of money. And monetary benefits would be converted into well-being benefits, using an estimate of how money affects wellbeing.

But many policy-makers will of course be keener to reduce misery than to increase wellbeing that is already high. For them the search for new policies could focus especially on those aspects of life that now account for the greatest inequality of wellbeing – and therefore account for the greatest amount of misery. That is a good starting point; and then, when we evaluate specific policies, we could use sensitivity analysis to give extra weight to the wellbeing of people who currently have little of it.

More and more governments are becoming interested in this way of making policy. New Zealand already has an annual Wellbeing Budget, and it is likely that the wellbeing approach will quite quickly become standard practice in many countries. In the meantime, public interest in wellbeing has escalated (see Figure I.3). This has been hugely helped by the annual World Happiness Report, launched annually at the United Nations.

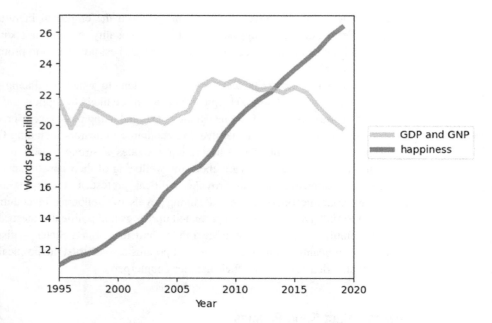

Figure I.3 Recent trends in word frequency in English language books
Source: Barrington-Leigh (2022)
Note: The darker trace shows the relative frequency of occurrence of the word 'happiness' among all English-language books published in each year, as tabulated by Google Books' n-grams database. The lighter line is the same thing but summed over occurrences of 'GDP' and 'GNP'.

Methodology

In conclusion, wellbeing science is about everything that is most dear to us. But it has to be pursued in a rigorously quantitative way. To explain wellbeing we have to have equations. But to identify what causes wellbeing is not easy. Cross-sectional equations are vulnerable to the problem of omitted variables. Longitudinal panel studies using 'fixed effects' help us to deal with this problem. But the most convincing way to establish causal effects is through experiments. In this book, we use all three methods, and (for people not already familiar with these methods) we explain them from the bottom up.

Learning Objectives

So in this book you will learn many things.

- First, you will reflect on what is the proper goal for our society and on the idea that the best goal is the wellbeing of the people.

- Second, you will learn the state of knowledge about the determinants of wellbeing and the policies that can improve it.
- Third, you will become familiar with many different ways of studying causal relationships in social science – and you will also learn to do your own research. For each chapter there are exercises on the book's website.
- Finally, you will see how different disciplines (especially psychology, sociology and economics) can each contribute usefully to understanding how we can produce a happier world.

The science of wellbeing is new and extremely ambitious. It brings together the insights of many disciplines. Its results are as relevant to how we conduct our own lives as to how we want policy-makers to conduct theirs. But there can be no more important way to think about the future of humanity. If we want a happier world, the science of wellbeing is there to help us.

Part I

The Case for Wellbeing

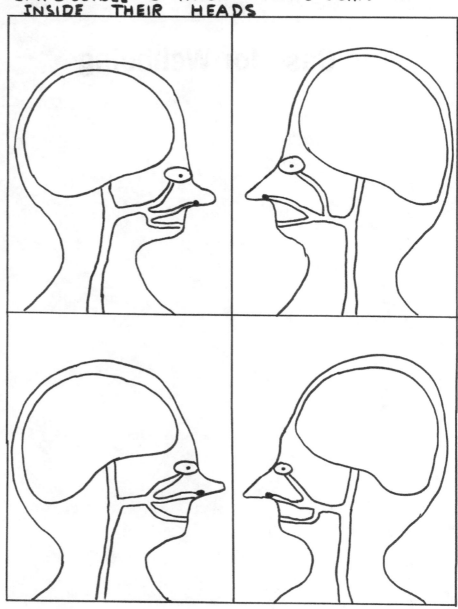

1 What Subjective Wellbeing Is and Why It Matters

The gross national product measures everything except that which makes life worthwhile.

Robert Kennedy

Subjective Wellbeing as the Overarching Good

The idea of wellbeing as the ultimate good is not new. But now it is coming to the fore, for many reasons. One is the new science of wellbeing. But another is the growing disbelief that higher incomes alone will solve all our problems.

The movement in favour of going '**beyond GDP**' has taken many forms. For the last fifty years, there has been a strong movement of scholars producing 'social indicators' in addition to GDP. In parallel with this, the Nobel-prize-winning economist Amartya Sen has set out the many 'capabilities' that a person needs to function well.[1] Following this, the OECD has developed a range of 'wellbeing indicators' for member countries, which include not only standard measures of education, health and so on but also psychological measures.[2] This work has inspired the New Zealand government to adopt wellbeing as its goal and to join a multi-country alliance known as Wellbeing Economy Governments.[3]

At the same time, the world has been shocked by the climate emergency, which has underlined the short-sightedness of maximising current GDP, without regard to the more distant future. To deal with this problem, the UN's 17 Sustainable Development Goals for 2030 look firmly to the future but they also enshrine a much broader view than the purely economic of what it is to be human.

There is, however, one central problem that still faces every policymaker. If you have multiple goals, how do you choose between alternative policies? Policy A may be better than Policy B in terms of one objective and worse in terms of another. How are you to choose?

Coherent choice is only possible if you have a single objective, in terms of which all alternative policies can be ranked. We need a '**common currency**' for decision-making. One way to have one is to construct an index that is a weighted average of all

---

[1] Nussbaum and Sen (1993); Sen (1999).   [2] OECD (2013).
[3] As of writing, Finland, Iceland, New Zealand, Scotland and Wales.

the different objectives. But you still have to choose the weights. They can only be found by having a single objective that can determine the weights.

What might that single objective be? The most obvious answer is '**how people feel about their lives**'. This is what we mean when we talk about '**subjective wellbeing**' (sometimes called SWB).

However, say some critics, feelings can't be that important because they are 'only subjective'. Are they right? There are of course many other things that are good, including health, income, freedom, respect and peace. For each of these things, you can ask people what makes it good, and people can generally give answers. For example, health matters because people feel awful when they are sick. Similarly, most other goods are good because of how they affect our felt experience. But why does it matter how people feel? No reason can be given – it **self-evidently** does. So when people advocate wellbeing, they are thinking of it as the ultimate good, with other things being good if they are instrumental in contributing to wellbeing. This basic idea was illustrated in Figure I.1 in the Introduction.

So the wellbeing approach builds upon the approaches where people specify multiple objectives – the 'dashboard' approach.[4] But it goes a lot further. It offers a vision of a society where the ultimate touchstone is the quality of people's lives as they themselves experience them. It says that the wellbeing of the people should be the goal for a society, for its policymakers and for us as individuals. If you find this idea problematic, you might try to think of a better alternative goal.

One further point. In the wellbeing approach, what matters is the overall wellbeing of everyone. So this approach is not saying that people should pursue only their own wellbeing. On the contrary, it is saying that each individual and each organisation should do what it can to produce the greatest overall wellbeing in society.

How Should We Measure It?

But how should wellbeing be measured? There are three main conceptions of wellbeing that have been measured:[5]

- Evaluative (life satisfaction),
- Hedonic, and
- Eudaimonic.

Evaluative measures: The life satisfaction approach

In the first of these, people are asked how they feel about their life these days. The most common question is 'Overall, how satisfied are you with your life

---

[4] The leading advocate of this approach is Sen (1999). But many other distinguished writers also follow the dashboard approach, including Pinker (2018) (health, happiness, freedom, knowledge, love and richness of experience); Seligman (2018) (positive emotion, engagement, relationships, meaning and accomplishment); and Skidelsky and Skidelsky (2012).

[5] On this section, see Helliwell (2021).

nowadays?'[6] To answer it, individuals have to choose a score between 0 and 10, where 0 means 'Not as all satisfied' and 10 means 'Very satisfied'. This is a question on **life satisfaction**. Alternatively (which gives very similar answers), people are offered a continuous line with the same answers at either end, and they are asked to mark where their answer lies in between. The results of using a 'visual analogue scale' like this are very similar to those from whole-number answers between 0 and 10 – both in terms of the score recorded and the factors that explain it.[7] The results are also similar when, the phrase 'satisfied with your life' is replaced by the phrase 'happy with your life'.[8]

In another variant, people are asked the following question, known as the **Cantril ladder** question:

Please imagine a ladder, with steps numbered from 0 at the bottom to 10 at the top. The top of the ladder represents the best possible life for you and the bottom of the ladder represents the worst possible life for you. On which step of the ladder would you say you personally feel you stand at this time?

The World Happiness Report uses the answers to the Cantril ladder question given when people reply in the Gallup World Poll.[9] This poll covers over a thousand people a year per country, in nearly every country. In surveys where people were asked both about life satisfaction and the Cantril ladder they were very highly correlated.[10] So for ease of language we shall describe the results of the Cantril ladder as 'life satisfaction'.

The Gallup World Poll shows the huge spread of life satisfaction both within countries and between countries. For illustration, Figure 1.1 gives the spread in the United States and in India. Some key facts emerge:

- In each country there is a very wide spread of life satisfaction. This corresponds to our own experience, across the range of people we meet.
- The average of life satisfaction is much higher in the United States than in India.

There is indeed a huge variation of life satisfaction **within any country**, and this within-country variation actually accounts for 78% of the overall variance in life satisfaction across the world's population.[11] Exploring the within-country variation provides key information about the **personal factors** that matter most in human life (see Chapter 8). For example, as we shall see, income differences explain some 2% of the variance of life satisfaction within countries – much less than the 20% explained by mental health, physical health and human relationships. (Somewhat surprisingly, average life satisfaction in most countries is very similar for men and women.)

There are, however, also huge differences in average life satisfaction **across countries**. This is shown in Table 1.1,[12] which reveals the extraordinary variation in

---

[6] This is the version used by the United Kingdom's Office for National Statistics (ONS).
[7] Couper et al. (2006). But see also Cowley and Youngblood (2009). Neither of these surveys was measuring life satisfaction.
[8] Helliwell and Wang (2012) p. 14.
[9] We are using Gallup data a lot in this book because it covers almost every country. But in many cases, similar findings were obtained earlier from sources like Eurobarometer and the World Values Survey.
[10] Helliwell and Wang (2012).   [11] Helliwell and Wang (2012) p. 16.
[12] A comparable ranking of life satisfaction among 15-year-olds can be found in Table 6.1.

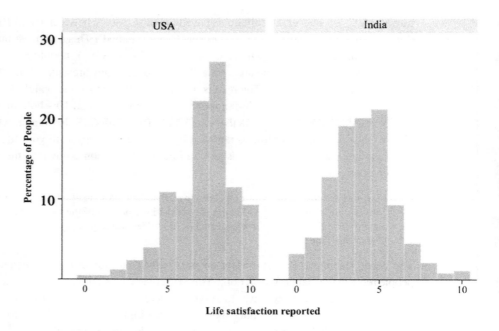

Figure 1.1 Percentage at each level of life satisfaction (0–10): United States and India
Source: Gallup World Poll 2016–2018, Cantril ladder

the human condition around the world. Average wellbeing is evaluated at 7.5 or above in four Scandinavian countries and at 3.5 or below in war-torn countries like Syria, Yemen, Afghanistan, the Central African Republic and South Sudan. Explaining this variation provides many clues to the **social factors** that matter most in human life (see also Chapter 8).

One obvious question is, 'Has wellbeing increased over time, as living standards have risen?' The answer is in some cases yes and in others no. For the world as a whole, average wellbeing rose between the 1970s and 2007.[13] Since then, however, it has stagnated.[14] And in some countries wellbeing has not risen since research began. This is true of the United States (since the 1950s), West Germany (since the 1970s) and China (since 1990).[15] Figure 1.2 shows the figures for the United States.

If only we knew more about trends in wellbeing in earlier periods.[16] There is certainly strong evidence that most of the external conditions of life are now better than in most of human history. As Stephen Pinker has shown,[17] there is less violence, better human rights and so on. So in most parts of the world, life is probably as good now as it has ever been.

---

[13] A. E. Clark et al. (2012); Figure 3.4.   [14] Helliwell et al. (2020); Figure 2.2.
[15] See Layard et al. (2010); and Easterlin et al. (2017) supplemented by Helliwell et al. (2020).
[16] For an attempt at this see Hills et al. (2019).
[17] Pinker (2018). However, in studies of the Masai and Inuit (both Old Stone Age cultures), surveys registered quite high levels of positive affect. Biswas-Diener et al. (2005).

Table 1.1 Ranking of countries by their average life satisfaction (0–10)

Rank	Country	Score	Rank	Country	Score	Rank	Country	Score
1	Finland	7.8		Philippines	6.0		Niger	4.9
	Denmark	7.6		Hungary	6.0		Laos	4.9
	Switzerland	7.6		Thailand	6.0		Albania	4.9
	Iceland	7.5		Argentina	6.0		Cambodia	4.8
	Norway	7.5		Honduras	6.0		Bangladesh	4.8
	Netherlands	7.4		Latvia	5.9		Gabon	4.8
	Sweden	7.4		Ecuador	5.9		South Africa	4.8
	New Zealand	7.3	60	Portugal	5.9	110	Iraq	4.8
	Austria	7.3		Jamaica	5.9		Lebanon	4.8
10	Luxembourg	7.2		South Korea	5.9		Burkina Faso	4.8
	Canada	7.2		Japan	5.9		Gambia	4.8
	Australia	7.2		Peru	5.8		Mali	4.7
	United Kingdom	7.2		Serbia	5.8		Nigeria	4.7
	Israel	7.1		Bolivia	5.7		Armenia	4.7
	Costa Rica	7.1		Pakistan	5.7		Georgia	4.7
	Ireland	7.1		Paraguay	5.7		Iran	4.7
	Germany	7.1		Dominican Republic	5.7		Jordan	4.6
	United States	6.9	70	Bosnia and Herzegovina	5.7	120	Mozambique	4.6
	Czech Republic	6.9		Moldova	5.6		Kenya	4.6
20	Belgium	6.9		Tajikistan	5.6		Namibia	4.6
	United Arab Emirates	6.8		Montenegro	5.5		Ukraine	4.6
	Malta	6.8		Russia	5.5		Liberia	4.6
	France	6.7		Kyrgyzstan	5.5		Palestinian Territories	4.6
	Mexico	6.5		Belarus	5.5		Uganda	4.4
	Taiwan Province of China	6.5		North Cyprus	5.5		Chad	4.4
	Uruguay	6.4		Greece	5.5		Tunisia	4.4
	Saudi Arabia	6.4		Hong Kong S.A.R. of China	5.5		Mauritania	4.4
	Spain	6.4	80	Croatia	5.5		Sri Lanka	4.3
	Guatemala	6.4		Libya	5.5	130	Congo (Kinshasa)	4.3

Table 1.1 (*cont.*)

	Country	Score		Country	Score		Country	Score
30	Italy	6.4		Mongolia	5.5		Swaziland	4.3
	Singapore	6.4		Malaysia	5.4		Myanmar	4.3
	Brazil	6.4		Vietnam	5.4		Comoros	4.3
	Slovenia	6.4		Indonesia	5.3		Togo	4.2
	El Salvador	6.3		Ivory Coast	5.2		Ethiopia	4.2
	Kosovo	6.3		Benin	5.2		Madagascar	4.2
	Panama	6.3		Maldives	5.2		Egypt	4.2
	Slovakia	6.3		Congo (Brazzaville)	5.2		Sierra Leone	3.9
	Uzbekistan	6.3	90	Azerbaijan	5.2	140	Burundi	3.8
	Chile	6.2		Macedonia	5.2		Zambia	3.8
40	Bahrain	6.2		Ghana	5.1		Haiti	3.7
	Lithuania	6.2		Nepal	5.1		Lesotho	3.7
	Trinidad and Tobago	6.2		Turkey	5.1		India	3.6
	Poland	6.2		China	5.1		Malawi	3.5
	Colombia	6.2		Turkmenistan	5.1		Yemen	3.5
	Cyprus	6.2		Bulgaria	5.1		Botswana	3.5
	Nicaragua	6.1		Morocco	5.1		Tanzania	3.5
	Romania	6.1		Cameroon	5.1		Central African Republic	3.5
	Kuwait	6.1	100	Venezuela	5.1	150	Rwanda	3.3
	Mauritius	6.1		Algeria	5.0		Zimbabwe	3.3
50	Kazakhstan	6.1		Senegal	5.0		South Sudan	2.8
	Estonia	6.0		Guinea	4.9		Afghanistan	2.6

Source: Helliwell et al (2020) Gallup World Poll 2017–2019, Cantril ladder

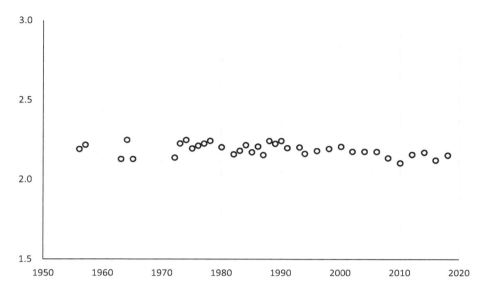

Figure 1.2 Average happiness in the United States (on a scale of 1–3)
Source: AIPO (1956–1970); NORC (1963–1976); GSS (1972–2018) grafted together onto the GSS scale based on overlapping years (see online Annex 1.1)

Hedonic measures based on 'affect'

Our findings so far are based on people's replies to a single question about how respondents evaluate their life 'nowadays'.[18] But some people prefer a different approach to the study of human wellbeing – where we study more directly how people feel at the time. By comparison with this, the evaluative measures cover a longer unspecified period of time and involve an element of judgment (although they are generally completed within a few seconds).[19]

The alternative measures are known as **hedonic measures** (from the Greek word *hedone* meaning pleasure). Psychologists use the word 'affect' to describe feelings of different sorts. Some types of affect are positive (happiness, enjoyment, laughter) and some are negative (worry, sadness, anger and stress). There are three main ways to capture these feelings. One is in real time by beeping people and asking how they are feeling just now (**Ecological Momentary Assessment**). The second is to sit people down a day later and have them record how they felt on the previous day hour by hour – and what they were doing and who they were with (the **Day Reconstruction Method**). The third, also used by the Gallup World Poll, is to ask them to summarise their different feelings over

[18] There is an obvious issue of what time period people have in mind when they answer this question. Benjamin et al. (2021) investigate this issue asking people whether they are 'evaluating their situation' as it is right now or also as it was in the past or will be in the future. Clearly, how people feel now is affected by things that have happened or may happen. But their answers may still be reflecting their current state of feeling.

[19] Frijters and Krekel (2021).

Table 1.2 Happiness in different activities

Activity	Average happiness	Average hours a day
Sex	4.7	0.2
Socialising	4.0	2.3
Relaxing	3.9	2.2
Praying/worshipping/meditating	3.8	0.4
Eating	3.8	2.2
Exercising	3.8	0.2
Watching TV	3.6	2.2
Shopping	3.2	0.4
Preparing food	3.2	1.1
Talking on the phone	3.1	2.5
Taking care of my children	3.0	1.1
Computer/email/internet	3.0	1.9
Housework	3.0	1.1
Working	2.7	6.9
Commuting	2.6	1.6

Source: Kahneman et al. (2004) Table 1. 900 Texan women
Note: Day Reconstruction Method. Average happiness is measured by the difference between positive affect (0–6) and negative affect (0–6). For similar studies on the United States, see Krueger (2009) and on the United Kingdom, see Bryson and McKerron (2017). For further evidence of the effects of sex on happiness, see Blanchflower and Oswald (2004).

the previous day by asking Yes/No questions like 'Yesterday did you experience a lot of happiness?'

How people feel when they are doing different things is hugely interesting. A team led by Daniel Kahneman used the Day Reconstruction Method to investigate the feelings of around 900 Texan women during the course of the previous day.[20] Table 1.2 shows what they enjoyed most and what they enjoyed least.

Such information is highly relevant to how each of us can improve our daily life.[21] And, in principle, hedonic measures could be used to produce a single measure of wellbeing over a period of time. You could either pick a single question (such as How happy are you right now, or yesterday) or you can calculate an 'affect balance' by adding up all the positive scores and subtracting all the negative ones.[22] Or, altogether novel, you can analyse people's social media activity (especially Twitter) and calculate the balance between positive and negative words or remarks.[23] Or you can analyse Google searches.

Comparison of evaluative and hedonic measures

So which of the two preceding criteria is best for use as a guide to the choice of policies? As we argued at the beginning of the chapter, it self-evidently matters how

---

[20] Kahneman et al. (2004).   [21] Dolan (2014).   [22] Bradburn (1969).
[23] Jaidka et al. (2020). Metzler et al. (2022) show a good intertemporal correlation between text-based and questionnaire-based estimates of SWB. For an interesting analysis of emotions during the COVID-19 pandemic, based on Google searches, see Brodeur et al. (2021).

people feel. This is extremely obvious when it comes to pain versus contentment/ enjoyment (the 'hedonic' dimension of experience). But it also applies to how people 'feel about their life' (the 'evaluative' dimension).

As a measure of wellbeing, life satisfaction has many good features. First, it covers more than a day or two.[24] Second, researchers and policymakers know what it means – it is based on a single question that they themselves could answer. Third, it is democratic – it does not require analysts to compile a list of indicators and then use their own arbitrary weights to produce an overall index.[25] Instead, each citizen applies her own weights and tells us the result – how she feels about her life. And fourth, policymakers are used to asking people how satisfied they are with their services, so why not ask people how satisfied they are with their lives?

Hedonic measures are an even more direct measure of experience, but they are much more difficult to collect over a long enough period to be relevant to many basic social issues. They are, however, essential in analysing brief experiences – like a country walk or a game of tennis or a gig. And, as science develops, they will become easier and easier to measure (including via the use of biomarkers – see Chapter 5). So, in this book, we use both life satisfaction and hedonic measures but mainly life satisfaction. When possible, we report where the two approaches yield different results.[26]

Eudaimonic measures

The third wellbeing measure in common use is usually called '**eudaimonic**' after the word '*eudaimonia*' used by the Greek philosopher Aristotle. *Eudaimonia* is difficult to translate but it means literally having a 'good demon', which Aristotle understood, roughly, as having a rounded and virtuous character.[27] So it includes the idea that

---

[24] Answers on life satisfaction are similar on weekdays and weekends, while those on happiness yesterday give higher scores at weekends.

[25] Hedonic measures are usually subjected to some form of weights, e.g., to produce a measure of affect balance.

[26] When philosophers discuss wellbeing, they generally consider there to be three main theories of what wellbeing is: (i) desire-fulfilment theories, where wellbeing consists in getting what you want; (ii) hedonism, where wellbeing consists in happiness, that is, how good you feel; and (iii) objective list theories, where wellbeing might consist in happiness or desire fulfilment but also consists in some 'objective' goods, perhaps achievement, love, knowledge or virtue.

For reasons we have given, we do not accept (iii) – it does not solve the problem of multiple objectives. Our 'hedonic' measure is (ii) and so is life satisfaction (unless we consider people to have an overarching desire to be satisfied with their lives).

As regards (i) there is the empirical issue of what people **really** desire. Surveys show that, when asked to make choices, people most commonly, but not always, choose what will make them happy (see, for example Benjamin et al. 2012; and Perez-Truglia 2015). In another study, people were asked to make choices that required pitching happiness against other outcomes like income, health, etc. (Adler et al. 2017) – happiness came top except for health (but in this study there was no distinction between health as quality of life and health as a factor affecting survival). We do not however accept the desire-fulfilment approach since people often make choices which have bad effects.

Thus, we opt for (ii) how people feel, because of its **self-evident** value (i.e., that no further reason can be given for its importance).

[27] For a modern empirical definition of eudaimonia see Ryff (1989).

Box 1.1 Different concepts of wellbeing

Type of wellbeing	Typical question(s)
Evaluative	Overall, how satisfied are you with your life nowadays? (0–10)
Hedonic	How happy were you yesterday?
	Or
	An hour by hour reconstruction of yesterday recording how you felt (the Day Reconstruction Method)
	Or
	Regular real-time bleeping to record your feelings (Ecological Momentary Assessment)
Eudaimonic	Do you feel that the things you do in your life are worthwhile? (0–10)

---

virtue ought to be included in any measure of wellbeing. A typical question is 'Do you feel that the things you do in your life are worthwhile?'

There are, however, two objections to this approach. First, virtue is difficult to measure. If you want to know whether someone is virtuous, you cannot find out by asking that person – the Nazis felt that what they did was positive and worthwhile. Second, in the wellbeing approach, virtue is a means to an end.

We want people to be virtuous for two reasons: it will raise the wellbeing of others, and it will often (though not always) raise the wellbeing of the virtuous person. So, for example, in Figure I.1, my wellbeing is higher if

(i)   the people I meet – my 'social connections' – are virtuous, and
(ii) I myself have good altruistic 'values'.

But these are just some of the many things that determine wellbeing – they are not part of the wellbeing outcome itself. To include virtue in the outcome is to confuse means with ends. We should study virtue deeply, but we should not include it in the measure of wellbeing.[28] So, in this book, we do not use the eudaimonic concept of wellbeing.[29] We rely mainly on evaluative and hedonic measures of wellbeing, which we also sometimes call happiness. As an aide memoir, Box 1.1 summarises the preceding discussion.

Can we believe self-reports?

As time passes, we shall undoubtedly get better at measuring wellbeing. Neuroscience will improve, and we shall also use more and more big data from sources like Twitter and Google. But do the questionnaires we currently use really supply any useful information? When we ask people these questions, are their answers accurate? Do they really mean anything, or do different people interpret the question and the scales

---

[28] We do urgently need to know how to produce virtuous people (see Chapter 3). But this is a different issue from the definition of wellbeing.

[29] It is in fact highly correlated with evaluative wellbeing. See Keyes et al. (2002), Model 4; and Ryff and Singer (2003).

so differently that their answers cannot really be compared? In other words, are the measures 'reliable' and 'valid' evidence on the thing they purport to measure.

On **reliability**, the question is 'Do people give consistent answers when retested?' In one study, the correlation between the two sets of answers two weeks apart was 0.55 for life satisfaction and 0.64 for net affect.[30] This is not bad, but it shows that there is some noise in the data.

A quite different issue is whether the scale is a **'valid'** representation of what we want it to represent, including whether different people use the scale in the same way[31] There are at least four reasons to believe that people's answers provide significant objective information about how their subjective wellbeing compared with that of other people in the same country.

Correlation with brain activity

First, how people score their subjective wellbeing is correlated with objective meas- ures of electrical activity in certain parts of the brain (see Chapter 5). The same is true of their reporting of physical pain. In a fascinating experiment, researchers applied an equally hot pad to the legs of all the people being studied. People were asked to rate the pain, and the resulting scores were then correlated across people with the electrical activity in the relevant part of the pre-frontal cortex. The correlation was good.[32] In addition, over time within the same individual over time, there is a good correlation between the wellbeing she reports and objective measurement of her brain waves.[33]

Correlation with third-party reports

Second, we can ask the friends or colleagues of the individual to rate the person's happiness. These ratings are quite well-correlated with the individual's own self-reports.[34] Another study investigated the relationship between smiling and life satisfaction. Researchers rated the positive affect displayed in the most recent Facebook profile photo of those being studied, and this was quite well correlated with their self-reported life satisfaction.[35]

Predictive power

Next, these self-reports are good predictors of many aspects of future behaviour, like quitting a job, divorce or voting behaviour. They are even a good predictor of individual life expectancy. These findings are so important that we describe them in more detail at the end of the chapter.

Explicability

And, finally, we can explain a good part of the variation in these measures by precisely the kind of things one would expect to matter. That is what makes the study of wellbeing so exciting.

---

[30] Krueger and Schkade (2008). See also Fujita and Diener (2005).
[31] For an economist's discussion of the issue of comparability, see Sen (1970).
[32] Coghill et al. (2003); and Coghill (2010).   [33] Davidson (2004).   [34] Diener and Suh (1999).
[35] Seder and Oishi (2012) r = 0.38. The correlation with life satisfaction 3 years later was even higher (r = 0.57).

So we have good evidence that different people in the same country report their feelings in a similar way. We also have evidence that the same person reports her feelings in a similar way over time. However, do people in **different countries** report their feelings in the same way or are international comparisons highly unreliable? After all, people are reporting in different languages and many words do not have exact equivalents in other languages. There are, however, three reasons to believe that the country rankings do indeed correspond to real differences out there.[36]

- The rankings are similar across a whole range of words – like happiness in life, satisfaction with life and position on the Cantril ladder.
- Within a country, people speaking different languages (e.g., in Switzerland) give very similar answers, and these differ from the average of other countries using the language (e.g., the French compared with French-speaking Swiss).
- Which language-group a country belongs to adds little to a standard explanation of the wellbeing in that country.

The reporting scale

A different issue is exactly how people use the reporting scale they are offered (0,1, ... ,9,10). Do they treat it like a metre rule, where the difference between 3 and 4 centimetres is the same size as the difference between 8 and 9 centimetres? This practice would make the scale an '**interval scale**' (or what economists call a '**cardinal scale**'). Or do the points on the scale simply reflect a **ranking** of different mental states (making it an '**ordinal scale**')?

So what would it mean to say the scale is cardinal? If we want to measure differences in the level of a sensation, the standard basic unit of difference is one that is just noticeable by the person experiencing it. In other words, the natural unit for sensations is the **just-noticeable difference (JND)**.[37] So we would call a scale an interval scale (or cardinal) if the number of JNDs between the answer 3 and the answer 4 were the same as the number of JNDs between 8 and 9.

Are they? There is a simple empirical test of whether the scale is cardinal: when people are asked and then re-asked to record their life satisfaction (0–10), the average absolute difference in replies should be similar at all points on the scale. It is.[38] So there is good reason to suppose that people use the scale in a cardinal way, as we have defined it – apparently, respondents naturally reply as though the difference between 3 and 4 is as noticeable as the difference between 8 and 9.

We have already mentioned another relevant fact. Sometimes people are asked to score a variable not by selecting an integer but by selecting a point on a continuous scale (the 'visual analogue' method). Studies of the kind give very similar regression results to those using integer scales.[39]

---

[36] Veenhoven (2012). See also Diener et al. (1995). It is sometimes suggested that people re-norm the scale in the light of experience. Evidence against this is presented in Odermatt and Stutzer (2019).

[37] See, for example, Stevens (1986), chapter 1 (not an easy read).   [38] Kruger and Schkade (2008).

[39] See footnote 7.

Box 1.2 'Reporting functions' in psychology

The study of sensations assumes that humans report their sensations in a cardinal fashion. It then addresses the question: How does their sensation relate to the intensity of **external** phenomena – like brightness? In other words, what is the 'reporting function' that relates the reported sensation to the external stimulus (measured in its own units)? For example, how does the reported brightness of light relate to its actual brightness measured in lumens per square metre of receiving surface?

In this case, the just-noticeable difference (JND) in brightness corresponds to a given proportional change in actual brightness (measured in lumens per square metre). Thus the 'reporting function' for brightness is

$$\text{Sensation} = a \log \text{Brightness}$$

This is known as the Weber–Fechner effect. Similar 'reporting functions' have been found for the intensity of sound and indeed for many other things that can vary over a huge range from 0 upwards. But when the range of variation is narrow relative to the average (as with human height), the reporting function becomes roughly linear.[40]

These reporting functions are telling us how people report on an **external** phenomenon. When it comes to wellbeing, we are talking about something quite different – how people record an **inner** state. There is no obvious reason why they would not do this in the cardinal way we have described, and the science of psychophysics assumes they do so.

So, when psychologists study sensations, they generally assume people treat the scale as cardinal (see Box 1.2 for further details). By contrast, it is difficult to see how respondents could use the scale (0–10) in an ordinal fashion. There would have to be a ranking of all their possible states of wellbeing, and they would then somehow divide this up into eleven ranges (0–10). However, since there is no concept of distance between one state and another, it is extremely difficult to see how they would undertake this process in any way that is consistent over time or across people.[41]

So we shall assume throughout this book that different individuals use the scale in the same way, that the scale used is stable from period to period and that the scale is a normal one (like a metre rule).

What causes wellbeing?

So what determines their wellbeing? If we want to improve wellbeing (for ourselves or others), we have to know what affects it and by how much. To find this out we have

---

[40] Oswald (2008).

[41] For a different view on all this, see Bond and Lang (2019). And for a response to Bond and Lang, see Kaiser and Vendrik (2020).

two main sources of **evidence**. The first is **surveys** in which people are asked about their wellbeing – but also about many other aspects of their life. The relationship between wellbeing and these other things tell us how much different things matter to people. But precise causality is always difficult to establish from such surveys, nor do they tell us in any detail what we can do to make things better. For this, we need evidence from **experiments** where some people have received a particular treatment and their change in wellbeing can then be compared with that of a control group. In the last 40 years, evidence of both types has developed at such a rate that we now have the new science of wellbeing, whose findings are the subject of this book.

What Use Is This Knowledge?

This knowledge gives us the power to produce huge improvements in human wellbeing. It helps us as individuals to manage our external life and our own inner experience. It gives new purpose to organisations like schools and businesses. And it provides a whole new framework for the conduct of government.

In each case it works in two stages. First, it helps to set **priorities** by providing an overall goal against which to test out various options. This goal is the greatest wellbeing possible in ourselves and those around us. Secondly, the evidence provides detailed information about which **specific actions** work best in terms of wellbeing.

(i)   For **individuals** it offers a perspective on what matters most. Though individuals differ, it shows how we all make systematic mistakes based on the excessive reliance on some issues (like money). It shows how we all suffer from excessive comparisons with others and how we can educate our own mind-sets to generate more compassion for ourselves and for others. Armed with these tools, we can contribute more to the lives of others both in our private lives and through our work. For we now have a moral compass and knowledge about how to use it.

(ii) For **organisations** like schools and businesses, it provides a test of whether they are performing the functions that justify their existence. For example, it shows how most schools need to give more attention to the wellbeing of the children relative to their exam results – and provides experimental evidence on how to produce happier children. For business, more and more CEOs now consider that business exists to promote the wellbeing not only of shareholders but also of workers, customers and suppliers.[42] There is now good experimental evidence on how to do this.

(iii) For **governments**, it provides for the first time a coherent objective. For too long, countries have talked as though economic growth was their overriding objective, though in truth they had multiple objectives that they could not compare. Now for the first time there is a coherent and measurable overall objective – the wellbeing of the people. This is not a new idea. As Thomas Jefferson said, 'human life and

[42] US Business Roundtable (2019). On work and wellbeing, see Chapter 12.

happiness is the only legitimate object of government'.[43] But until recently, the information to apply this principle was not available. Now it is, and as we shall see, countries are increasingly applying it. And there are now more and more experiments to test which policies are the most cost-effective in terms of their impact on wellbeing. For those who believe that wellbeing is the ultimate objective, this is an exciting prospect, bringing hope to millions and new and worthwhile career opportunities.

Wellbeing helps us achieve other valuable objectives

There are, however, many people who question the idea of wellbeing as the objective. We shall discuss this issue in Chapter 2. But even people who do not value wellbeing for its own sake should value wellbeing because it is an important means to many other objectives that they do value. Here are some striking examples.

- **Education.** Making children happier makes them learn better.[44]
- **Health.** Your wellbeing has a powerful effect on your longevity.[45]
- **Productivity.** Greater wellbeing increases productivity and helps with problem-solving.[46]
- **Family/Social cohesion.** Happy people create more stable families, and happy people are more pro-social.[47]
- **Political stability.** Wellbeing affects election outcomes more than the economy does. And unhappy people tend to support populist parties.[48]
- **Charitable giving.** Happy people give more to others.[49]

These consequences of wellbeing are of major importance. So throughout this book we shall discuss the two-way relation between wellbeing and the different aspects of human life.

To re-cap, the two relations are these:

- One relation is the effect of each aspect of life on overall wellbeing. This was displayed in Figure I.1, with the arrows pointing towards wellbeing.
- The other relation is the effect of wellbeing on each aspect of life. This involves a diagram just like Figure I.1 but with the arrows pointing in the opposite direction.

In this book, we look at both sets of effects, but our strongest interest is in the first relation: how wellbeing itself is determined.

---

[43] Jefferson (1809).

[44] The best evidence comes from interventions to improve wellbeing. See Durlak et al. (2011); Hanh and Weare (2017); Adler (2016); and Frederickson and Branigan (2005).

[45] For UK data, see Steptoe and Wardle (2012). On the United States, see Lee and Singh (2020).

[46] Bellet et al. (2020); Edmans (2012); Isen et al. (1987).   [47] Idstad et al. (2015).

[48] Ward (2020) and Ward et al. (2020) show that incumbent governments do worse when people are less happy. On populism, see Nowakowski (2021).

[49] Kessler et al. (2021).

Human needs

So let's examine some basics about how wellbeing is determined and use this to explain the structure of the book. There is evidence that all human beings have similar **fundamental needs**[50] and that their wellbeing can be (at least partly) explained by how well these needs are met.

A typical list of these needs includes:

- Food and shelter,
- Safety from attack,
- Love and support,
- Respect and pride,
- Mastery of what you do,
- Autonomy in what you choose to do.

Since 2005, the Gallup World Poll has surveyed representative samples of people in every country in each year. It asks about their life satisfaction and also whether their different needs are met.[51] The analysis confirms that satisfaction with life increases when more of these needs are met – and people are more satisfied both when their own needs are met and those of their fellow citizens. This confirms a common finding that wellbeing is contagious.[52]

But are some of these needs prior in importance to others? For example, if your life is physically hard, how important is it to experience respect and pride? According to Maslow,[53] there is a hierarchy of needs (proceeding upwards from Physiological to Safety, Love and Belonging, Esteem and ultimately Self-actualisation): and the best strategy is to satisfy the needs by progressing up the sequence. Thus 'respect is a disposable luxury when compared with food or safety'. Though hugely famous, there is little supporting evidence for Maslow's hierarchy. The evidence from the Gallup World Poll is that when each need is satisfied, wellbeing improves. But having one need satisfied has little effect on the value of satisfying another need.[54]

How people interact with their environment

This book is about what determines how far our needs are satisfied. A first answer to that question is that it depends on the interaction between our genes (with which we enter the world) and our external environment – meaning by external environment the whole social and physical world outside ourselves. This is illustrated in Figure 1.3.

---

[50] Brown (1991).

[51] See Tay and Diener (2011). The questions are binary (Yes/No). For food and shelter: enough money for food and shelter and did not go hungry. For safety: safe walking alone, nothing stolen nor assaulted in the last 12 months. For love and support: experienced love yesterday and have someone to count on. For respect and pride: treated with respect and proud of something. For mastery: did what you do best at work, learned something. For autonomy: chose how best to spend your time, and experienced freedom. These are similar to the basic needs identified by Maslow (1954); Deci and Ryan (2000); Ryff and Keyes (1995); and Sen (1999).

[52] See, for example, Fowler and Christakis (2008).   [53] Maslow (1948).   [54] Tay and Diener (2011).

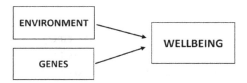

Figure 1.3 How genes and external environment determine wellbeing

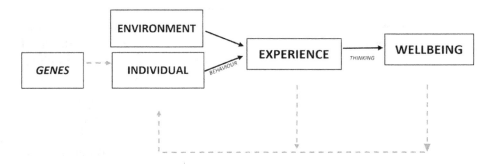

Figure 1.4 How the individual and the external environment interact to produce wellbeing

But this gives the impression that the individual herself is a passive player in the drama, with the environment simply interacting with the person's genes to produce the outcome. Yet in fact every human being has some degree of **agency**. We influence our own wellbeing in two key ways:

- By our **behaviour**, we significantly influence the situations we experience and the behaviour of others towards us.
- By our **thoughts**, we influence how these experiences affect us – both through our attitudes and how we think about our life.

Figure 1.4 tries to capture some of this. Outside us there is a given social environment, but how we experience it is hugely affected by what we bring to it. So the individual's behaviour interacts with the environment to produce the individual's experience. This experience then affects the individual's wellbeing – but how much depends also on how she thinks. This process is repeated over and over again. At each phase, the person's wellbeing feeds back into her character and behaviour in the next phase of her life (as shown in the dotted lines).

From this analysis it is clear that our wellbeing does not only depend on our social environment. It also depends on what we bring to the table, in particular

- our behaviour,
- our thinking and
- our genes.

In Chapters 3–5, we discuss each of these processes, before we discuss the details of the environment in Part III of the book.

What kind of a subject is wellbeing science?

Finally, what kind of a subject is wellbeing science? It is a new, emerging field, which is totally interdisciplinary. Many of the most important subjects that have emerged in recent years are interdisciplinary – subjects like molecular biology or human geography. But this one is rather special, because it provides a rationale for each of the separate social sciences: they are only important because they help to explain wellbeing. If you look at Figure I.1, you will see what we mean. For example, international relations are important because of how they contribute to human wellbeing, and so on. In this sense, wellbeing science could be the queen of the social sciences: it gives a role to each science by showing quantitively how its own outcomes contribute to the overall good.

But, as we shall see in the chapters that follow, there are four key disciplines that are most central to the study of wellbeing: psychology, sociology, economics and statistics.

- **Psychology.** The study of wellbeing started in psychology.[55] Psychologists study how human nature works at the individual level, using both surveys and experiments. They study how individual personality, family experience and education affect wellbeing. They also study how to make things better for individuals (clinical psychology) and at work (occupational psychology). However, except for social psychology, psychologists tend to ignore the role of social norms and social structures upon human wellbeing.
- **Sociology.** That is where sociologists come in. They study, above all, the way people interact in groups and how that affects their wellbeing.
- **Economics.** Economics brings four main contributions. First, economists have always focused on wellbeing as the overarching outcome (calling it 'utility'), even though they often have a rather narrow view of it and what causes it. Second, they discuss policy in terms of maximising that single outcome. Third, they distinguish clearly between the things people choose and the things that just happen to them (which they call 'externalities'). And fourth, they bring understanding of markets, income and unemployment.
- **Statistics.** This is central to the preceding disciplines. When it is used to analyse the distribution of characteristics in a population, it is sometimes called epidemiology.

There are three other fields of study, which, though relevant, are not the same as the science of wellbeing.

- **Behavioural science.** In recent years, economists have been developing, jointly with psychologists, a deeper understanding of how people actually behave – a subject sometimes known as behavioural economics. But the study of wellbeing is a different endeavour. It does not study how to get people to behave in a certain way. It studies the results of behaviour and thus which behaviours would maximise social wellbeing.

---

[55] Some key figures were Hadley Cantril (1906–1969) and Angus Campbell (1910–1980) – see Cantril (1965) and Campbell, Converse and Rodgers (1976).

- **Health and wellbeing.** This phrase, increasingly used, signifies a welcome extension of health science to include mental states as well as physical conditions. But it does not typically view wellbeing as the overarching good, with health as just one of many influences upon it. Wellbeing science, in contrast, studies the effects of everything in life upon the wellbeing of the population.
- Finally, **philosophy.** 'What is wellbeing?', 'Is it all that matters?', 'How should it be distributed?', and so on, are, of course, philosophical issues. We turn to these issues in Chapter 2. After that, the rest of the book is about the science of what causes wellbeing and how it can be improved.

Conclusions

(1) For many people, the reason to study wellbeing is the belief that it is the only thing that ultimately matters.
(2) In this view, many other things are good, like health, freedom, income and so on, but they are good because (and only because of) how they affect wellbeing.
(3) By wellbeing we mean subjective wellbeing – how people feel. This can be measured in three different ways:
  - Evaluative: how people feel about their life nowadays
  - Hedonic: how people feel at each moment
  - Eudaimonic: whether people believe their life is worthwhile
  The most commonly-used measure is evaluative, for example, 'satisfaction with life', but we shall also use hedonic measures where these are relevant.
(4) Evaluative wellbeing differs hugely across countries and within countries, while hedonic wellbeing also varies across activities.
(5) There is good evidence that these measures are reliable and valid. They are correlated with objective brain measurements, with third-party reports, with many consequences (like longevity, voting, productivity and learning) and with many plausible causes (which is mainly what the book is about).
(6) Most human beings have similar fundamental needs and their wellbeing varies with how well these needs are met. However, people are not passive agents, simply affected by their environment. Their own behaviour affects what they and others experience. And their own thoughts mediate how these experiences affect their wellbeing.

So Chapters 2–5 deal with

- The overall objective for society
- The role of behaviour
- The role of thoughts
- The role of genes and the working of our bodies.

These are all issues of basic human nature.

Then in Part III we turn to the hugely different experiences that different people have and how they affect our wellbeing – the role of family life and schools, healthcare, employment, the quality of work, income, social connections, the physical environment and climate and government. We look at their effect and at how wellbeing could be improved in each of these dimensions. Finally, we look at the techniques of policy-making and show how every policy-maker could use wellbeing data to produce a better world.

Questions for discussion

(1) Is there anything more important than how we feel? Is wellbeing the overarching goal? If not, what is, and how should we weight multiple goals?
(2) What is the best way to measure wellbeing? Are these measurements 'cardinal'?
(3) How does wellbeing science relate to other subjects you have studied?

Further Reading

Coghill, R. C., McHaffie, J. G., and Yen, Y. F. (2003). Neural correlates of interindividual differences in the subjective experience of pain. *Proceedings of the National Academy of Sciences*, 100(14), 8538–8542.

Helliwell, J. F. (2021). Measuring and using happiness to support public policies. In Lee et al. (Eds.). *Measuring Well-Being: Interdisciplinary Perspectives from the Social Sciences and the Humanities* (pp. 29–49). Oxford University Press.

Sen, A. (1999). *Development as Freedom*. Alfred Knopf.

Tay, L., and Diener, E. (2011). Needs and subjective well-being around the world. *Journal of Personality and Social Psychology*, 101(2), 354.

World Happiness Report, New York: Sustainable Development Solutions Network. Chapter 2 of the latest report.

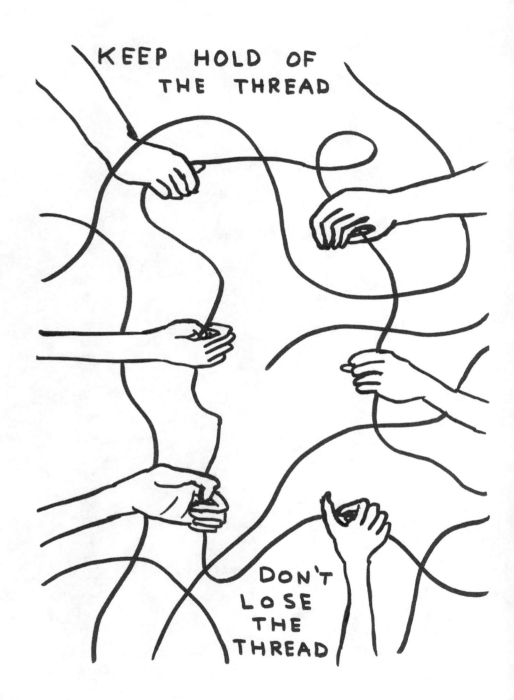

2   Wellbeing as the Goal for Society

Create all the happiness you are able to create: remove all the misery you are able to remove.

Jeremy Bentham

Some History

How would we recognise a good society? The idea that it is defined by the wellbeing of the citizens goes back at least to the ancient Greeks.[1] In this chapter, we shall see how this idea developed from then until now. We shall then provide a rigorous modern formulation of the idea. And finally, we shall discuss some of the main objections that people have made to it.

Greece and Rome

We can begin with the great Greek philosopher **Aristotle** (384–322 BC). He, more than anyone, is responsible for the idea that there must be some ultimate end that we should aim at – with other things like wealth, health and good relationships being good because of how they contribute to that end. That is the hierarchical idea we already displayed in Figure I.1. The ultimate end he called 'eudaimonia', which he envisaged as a balanced, rational and virtuous state of being. He especially emphasised virtue, which he considered essential if your experience of life is to be truly fulfilling. He did not define virtue exactly as this book does, but he had a realistic modern empiricist view on how it should be acquired – by constant repetition and habit-formation.

Greek philosophers who came after Aristotle emphasised different aspects of his message. Epicurus (341–270 BC) emphasised the importance of a simple life, focused on things you really enjoy, like friendship and family life. Zeno the Stoic (333–264 BC) emphasised civic virtue and the ability to calm your mind whatever adversity befell you. The ideas of these two thinkers spread widely through the Roman world.

---

[1] We discuss the contribution of the Buddha in Chapter 4.

Eventually, it was Stoicism that became the philosophy of much of the Roman middle class – and of the emperor Marcus Aurelius (AD 121–180), who wrote much about the secrets of happiness. Similar ideas had already been developed in China by Confucius and in India by the Buddha.

However, in the centuries that followed, Christianity brought in a quite different perspective. Happiness was still to be sought but only in the afterlife. In this world, the aim was virtue alone and this would bring happiness after death.[2]

The eighteenth-century Enlightenment

It was only in the late seventeenth century that philosophers dared to re-establish happiness on earth as the goal of life. The great English philosopher John Locke (1632–1704) took it as axiomatic that people wanted to feel good and that to acquire that feeling was their principal motivation. But it was a Scotsman, Francis Hutcheson (1694–1746), who took the first huge step towards establishing happiness as the goal for society, rather than just for the individual. He taught that the moral thing to do was whatever produced 'the greatest happiness for the greatest number'[3] – or, more precisely, what produced the greatest total happiness. And he argued that this is what any 'impartial spectator' would think.

From the wellbeing point of view, this idea was probably the greatest idea of modern times. It has three key implications.

(1) **For judgements**: If we want to compare two different situations and to say which is better, we should use the happiness of the people as the test. This would be so, for example, if we were asking which country is doing better, or whether the present is better than the past or which is the best way to spend public money.
(2) **For individual action**: If we ask, 'What is the ethical thing to do?', the answer is, 'Whatever produces the greatest overall happiness'.
(3) **For government policy**: When we ask, 'What should the government be trying to achieve?', the answer is, 'The greatest possible happiness for the people'.

As the eighteenth century progressed, these ideas took a firm hold among the educated classes in the English-speaking world, including in North America.[4] Thomas Jefferson, who drafted the US constitution, would write, 'The life and happiness of the people is the first and only object of good government.' But the writer who immortalised these ideas was the Englishman **Jeremy Bentham** (1748–1832) in *The Principle of Morals and Legislation*. In this book, Bentham argued that all actions should be judged by their consequences – by their impact on the happiness of everyone. In other words, actions should be judged by their 'utility'. Thus

---

[2] Of course, Christianity also forecast a new world on earth but only after the Second Coming.
[3] Raphael (1969).
[4] There were also supporters on the continent of Europe but not so numerous. Notable contributors included the Italian jurist Cesare Beccaria (1738–1794) and the French philosopher Claude Adrien Helvétius (1715–1771).

Bentham's concept of ethics, which is so humane, became known as 'utilitarianism', which makes it sound quite the opposite. (Similarly economics, which was founded by Adam Smith (1723–1790) to study the economic conditions for the greatest happiness, chose the word 'utility' to describe individual wellbeing rather than the word 'happiness').

During the nineteenth century, the principle of the greatest happiness inspired many major social reforms. It was forcefully presented by John Stuart Mill (1806–1873) in his book *Utilitarianism* and in his essay 'The Subjection of Women'. However, he also proposed that some pleasures are intrinsically better than others (for example, poetry was better than the game of pushpin). This was in our view a confusion of means with ends. You will certainly be happier in general if you have a clear purpose in life (as we show clearly in Chapter 4). And you will make others happier if you are virtuous. But the ultimate test of a society is how happy people are (irrespective of how they became so).

During the nineteenth century, economists continued to focus on happiness as the ultimate test of economic arrangements, and the economist Edgeworth (1845–1926) foreshadowed the modern science of wellbeing when he talked about the need for a 'hedonimeter' – a technique to measure happiness in a cardinal fashion. In the nineteenth century, most economists believed that an extra dollar gives more extra happiness to a poor person than to someone who is better off. Similarly, in psychology, the great psychologist William James was primarily concerned with life as people experienced it from the inside.

Behaviourism

But then in the twentieth century, psychology turned away from the study of wellbeing – to behaviourism. Scholars like Ivan Pavlov and John B. Watson argued that we could not know what occurred inside people or how they felt. One could only study how they behaved and how this was affected by external stimuli. This doctrine soon impacted on economics, and in 1932, the economist Lionel Robbins asserted that we could not compare the happiness of one person with another.[5] Even for the same person, he argued, we could only rank different situations, A, B and C, in order; we could not say whether going from A to B gave more (or less) extra happiness than going from B to C.

The consequences for economics were serious. It became impossible to evaluate any issue involving income distribution. We could not say whether it was better if two people had $50,000 dollars each **or** if one had $20,000 and the other had $80,000. All that could be claimed was that a change was good if some people gained and no one lost (a so-called Pareto improvement). When, as generally happens, a change involves some gainers and some losers, economists, according to Robbins, could say nothing. But in fact, this did not stop them from pronouncing in such cases, and John Hicks and

---

[5] Robbins (1932).

Nicholas Kaldor quickly provided what they considered a justification. They argued that, even if some people lose, a change is good if the gainers **could** have compensated the losers – even if they actually didn't.[6] This was the so-called **Hicks–Kaldor criterion** for a welfare improvement.

This criterion also justified a second dubious practice: the use of **national income (or gross domestic product, GDP)** as a measure of national wellbeing. GDP is a measure of the scale of economic activity, the things that happen for which people get paid. In the national income, everybody's dollars are added up regardless of who has them; and, if the national income increases, that is a Hicks–Kaldor improvement, even if many poor people have become worse off. But GDP was invented for a quite different purpose – by Simon Kuznets – as a way of analysing the business cycle and the fluctuations of unemployment. It was not meant to measure wellbeing. As Kuznets himself said, 'The welfare of a nation can scarcely be inferred from a measurement of national income.'[7] There are two obvious reasons for this view:

- GDP adds up the dollars of rich and poor as if they are of equal value.
- GDP fails to include any source of wellbeing other than things you can buy. As Robert Kennedy put it, 'GDP does not allow for the health of our children, the quality of their education, or the joy of their play.'[8]

But despite all this, GDP per head became the totem of national success in the post-WWII period.

In recent years, there has, however, been a massive pushback against the idea that GDP is an adequate measure of national progress. In 1974, the economist Richard Easterlin used psychological surveys to show that wellbeing in the United States had not risen since WWII, despite massive economic growth.[9] And subsequent research has shown that economic growth is no guarantee of increased wellbeing (see Chapter 13). So it is not surprising that even before the economic slowdown in the West from 2008 onwards, there was increased public demand for a wider goal than economic growth.

Taking feelings seriously again

But key to the demand for a new approach has been our increased ability to measure wellbeing and to understand its causes. The key figure here has been **Edward Diener** (1946–2021). Beginning in the early 1980s, he showed that wellbeing could be effectively measured and explained.[10] As time went on, more and more psychologists joined this enterprise, including Daniel Kahneman who in 2002 won the Nobel Prize for Economics. Economists also joined in, using large population surveys to throw light on the effect of different experiences upon individual wellbeing.

---

[6] Kaldor (1939); and Hicks (1940).   [7] Kuznets (1934).

[8] Robert Kennedy in a speech at the University of Kansas on 18 March 1968.   [9] Easterlin (1974).

[10] See Diener (1984). Important forerunners were Cantril (1965); Campbell, Converse and Rodgers (1976); and Andrews and Withey (1976). These books used the new wellbeing metric.

At the same time, ordinary **citizens** have become increasingly aware of their own mental states and interested in how to improve their own feelings. Two forces are at work here. The first is cognitive psychology (embodied in cognitive-behavioural therapy) and the second is mind-training techniques imported from the East. We discuss both at length in Chapter 4.

The Definition of Social Welfare

So it is time to lay out somewhat more formally a view of ethics based on the wellbeing of society as the goal.[11] The overall objective is called '**social welfare**' (**S**). Social welfare is the concept we use when comparing one situation with another, to find out which is best. Any formula for social welfare must obviously satisfy some basic principles including these:

- Everybody's wellbeing is of equal importance. So every person's wellbeing should be treated in the same way when we compute social welfare.[12]
- Social welfare must be higher if one person's wellbeing increases and no one else's falls.

But we need to be more specific than this. The measure of social welfare that Hutcheson, and then Bentham, proposed was the simple sum of wellbeing (W) across all the members of the population. In other words, if W_i is the wellbeing of the 'i'th person and $\sum$ means the sum across all members of the population, then at any point in time social welfare is

$$Current\ Social\ Welfare = S = \sum_i W_i \tag{1}$$

This is the classic utilitarian approach. Later in this chapter, we shall consider a more egalitarian or 'prioritarian' approach. But the classic utilitarian approach is a good starting point.

Wellbeing over time and WELLBYs

Of course, most decisions affect wellbeing over a period of time. For example, decisions affecting the climate will affect generations yet unborn. So we need a social welfare function that enables us to find the best path of wellbeing over the future and not just in the current period. So how should we value **future wellbeing**?

---

[11] There are some wellbeing scientists who would only use the social welfare function as a guide to the choice of political constitutions, not as a guide on individual policies (see Frey 2008).

[12] As we argue later, future wellbeing should be slightly discounted.

An obvious starting point is that the wellbeing of every human being in every year matters equally. However, since there is major uncertainty about the future, we should slightly discount the wellbeing that could be expected in future years – by multiplying wellbeing in t years hence by $(1 - \delta)^t$ where δ is the discount rate per annum. (In Britain, the official value of this 'pure time preference rate' is 1.5% per annum).[13] In proceeding in this way, we are assuming that a person's suffering in any one year is equally important, whether or not the rest of their life is happy.

On this basis, **intertemporal** social welfare (S^*) becomes simply the discounted sum of all future wellbeing, whoever is experiencing it:

$$Future\ Social\ Welfare = S^* = \sum_{i}\sum_{t} (1 - \delta)^t\ W_{it} \tag{2}$$

So if we want to decide whether a policy change is desirable, we should evaluate whether the following expression is positive:

$$\Delta S^* = \sum_{i}\sum_{t} (1 - \delta)^t \Delta W_{it} \tag{3}$$

To make this practical, we have to decide on the length of each period. If we take it as a year, ΔW_{it} would be the change in wellbeing for person i in year t. In other words, it is a change in **Wellbeing-Years (or WELLBYs)**. So when we come to methods of policy evaluation in Chapter 18, the key issue will be how a policy affects the number of (discounted) WELLBYs.

Sustainability and climate change

Thus the wellbeing approach provides a comprehensive framework for considering the future of our society from the smallest choices to the biggest. Of these, the biggest of all is the future of the planet. A central issue here is the **wellbeing of future generations**.[14]

Wellbeing science favours a low discount rate, so that what happens to future generations is really important when we decide what to do now. The only legitimate reason for discounting future wellbeing is 'pure time preference', based on uncertainty about the future. Typical rates of pure time preference are 1.5% a year. By contrast economists mainly analyse the future in terms of levels of real income. They generally assume that real incomes will rise steadily, which will reduce the impact of extra future income on future wellbeing. They therefore discount future income by at least 3.5% a year – making the future appear much less important relative to the present.[15] So it is not surprising that those who want everything analysed in terms of wellbeing find strong allies among those who want more attention to the future of the planet. For both groups, sustainability is crucial.

---

[13] HM Treasury (2020, 2021).   [14] Budolfson et al. (2021).   [15] HM Treasury (2020).

Length of life and the birth rate

There is one further issue – the issue of life and death. One way to increase future social welfare (as in equation 2) is to help people live longer. If someone lives longer and has wellbeing greater than zero, that increases social welfare.[16]

But can we also increase future social welfare by increasing the birth rate? If we could, it would be one of the least expensive ways of increasing future social welfare, and we would therefore choose to do it even if it decreased the number of Wellbeing-Years (or WELLBYs) per person born. John Stuart Mill rejected the idea that social welfare depended on the size of the population, and we shall focus instead on the **number of WELLBYs per person born**.

Today's medical policy-makers have adopted the same approach. Their aim is to produce the highest possible number of Quality-Adjusted Life Years (suitably dis-counted) for each person born.[17] We shall follow this approach. So when we use equation (3) to evaluate a policy change, we do not include in our evaluation any effect of the policy change upon the number of people born.

How egalitarian should we be?

We have thus far adopted the stand of classic utilitarianism – that all that matters is average lifetime wellbeing, regardless of how unequally it is distributed. This means that the following distributions of wellbeing are of equal value:

	Situation 1	Situation 2
Person A	8	5
Person B	2	5

But today many people are more egalitarian than Hutcheson and Bentham were and believe that it is more important to raise the wellbeing of the least happy people than to raise by an equal amount the wellbeing of those who are already quite happy.[18] In other words, the social value of i's wellbeing is not identical to W_i. Instead, it rises with W_i but it rises at a declining rate. So the social value of W_i is a 'function' of W_i, $f(W_i)$, which has the property we have just described.[19] And social welfare is the sum of $f(W_i)$ added up across all members of society. Thus,

$$\text{For egalitarians: } S = \sum_i f(W_i)(f' > 0, f'' < 0) \qquad (4)$$

---

[16] We are now measuring wellbeing on a '**ratio scale**' implying that we can say A is twice as happy as B. This is a further assumption that goes beyond (but does not contradict) the case for an interval scale which we made in Chapter 1.

[17] See Chapter 10.   [18] For example, Rawls (1971) – see equation (5) below.

[19] The symbol $f(W_i)$ means a magnitude that varies with W_i. The symbol f' means the increase in that magnitude as W_i increases by 1 unit. The symbol f'' means the increase in f' as W_i grows by one unit. If we assume that dead people have no social value, we have to choose a $f(W)$ function that has the property that $f(0) = 0$.

There are thus two alternative concepts of social welfare that we could use to decide whether one situation is better than another. Which of them should we use? In choosing between the Benthamite (or strictly **'utilitarian'**) view and the more egalitarian (or **'prioritarian'**) view, a good approach is the one pioneered after WWII by Jan Harsanyi and John Rawls.[20] In this approach, we imagine ourselves in an **'original position'** behind a **'veil of ignorance'**, not knowing which actual human being we are going to be. We then ask ourselves to choose between different situations, not knowing who we will be in each situation.

So how would we evaluate different situations? Egalitarians who use this framework believe that most individuals have a degree of risk-aversion. They would not therefore evaluate a distribution of possible levels of wellbeing entirely according to its average value. They would also look at the spread of the possible outcomes. And they would prefer prospects where the probability of experiencing low wellbeing was low. In other words, for any given average wellbeing in the population, they would prefer a more equal to a less equal distribution of wellbeing.[21] The simplest way to represent this set of values is by a concept of social welfare of the type we have already described, $\frac{\Sigma}{i} f(W_i)$ where the social value of additional W declines as W increases.[22]

If one accepts this argument, the issue is then 'How fast is the decline?'[23] The most extreme view is one inspired by the work of the Harvard philosopher John Rawls.[24] In this view, the decline is so sharp that the only thing that really matters is the wellbeing of the least happy person. So the social welfare equals the wellbeing of the least happy person.

$$\text{For followers of Rawls: } S = Min\ (W_1, \ldots,\ W_n) \tag{5}$$

A less extreme view is that the only thing that really matters is the number of people below some acceptable level of wellbeing.[25]

Choosing a social welfare function is not a scientific matter – it involves normative considerations, even if we try to solve the issue by 'positive' thought experiments or by surveying the population. This is why, however much the science of wellbeing improves, there will always be a spread of views on the exact definition of social welfare.

---

[20] Harsanyi (1953, 1955); Rawls (1971).   [21] Dolan (2014) p. 179.

[22] This is not contrary to the principle that future prospects should be valued according to their 'expected utility', as Harsanyi (1953, 1955) argued, i.e., according to $\Sigma\ \pi_i u_i$ where π_i is the probability of outcome i and u_i is the 'utility' of outcome i. This is because for every outcome i there is a value u_i such that the person is indifferent between the outcome i (experienced with certainty) and, alternatively, the probability u_i of the best outcome plus the probability $(1 - u_i)$ of the worst outcome. But Egalitarians would argue that if people are risk averse, u_i will be a concave function of true happiness, W_i: thus $u_i = f(W_i)$ $(f' > 0; f'' < 0)$.

[23] One formulation of this question is to assume $S = \Sigma \frac{1}{\lambda} W_i{}^\lambda$ $(\lambda \leq 1)$. We then debate the value of λ.

[24] Rawls (1971). (Rawls applied this judgement only to the distribution of 'primary goods').

[25] This approach has been called 'sufficientarian'. To encourage a focus on misery Kahneman and his colleagues devised a so-called **u-index**, which measures the proportion of the day in which a person is predominantly miserable (Krueger 2009).

Therefore, the most **practical** approach in any choice situation is to begin by first examining the difference in $\sum_i W_i$ and then seeing how far the result would be altered by varying assumptions about the form of $f(W_i)$.[26] A further practical step is to begin the search for new policies in those areas of life that account for the greatest amount of misery (on which Chapter 8 provides relevant evidence).

Criticisms

It is time now to face the music. For, despite its powerful approach, a philosophy based on subjective wellbeing has been subject to major criticisms. Here are some of the main criticisms, together with a typical reply from the advocates of wellbeing. It should be pointed out that many of these problems are extremely difficult to handle using any philosophical system, and the real issue is whether there is any other ethical system that is more defensible than that based on wellbeing.

Consequentialism and rights: The fat man

The first criticism is that we only take into account the consequences of actions (even though we do include in that the experiences that occur during the action itself). Critics often use the following example.[27] You are on a railway bridge. You see a train approaching from one side of the bridge, while down the line are five people on the track who will be killed by the train. However there is a fat man sitting on the bridge. Should you push the fat man to his death in order to save five others?

The calculus says there would be a net gain of four lives from this action (5 minus 1). So is it the right thing to do? Critics argue that the wellbeing approach says Yes, and this shows that the wellbeing approach is inadequate. However, how would millions of people in our society feel about their own lives if such actions became acceptable? Clearly, society has to have rules that make its members flourish. The philosophy of utilitarianism thus has two functions.[28] First, it helps us to choose the rules we should generally follow, and second, it helps us to decide when we should break the rule (for example, when we should lie to protect a Jew in hiding from the Nazis).

Some of the rules will be moral principles we teach our children, while others will be rights enshrined in law. We will teach our children to be kind because that makes other people feel better. But we also need legislated rights, especially for minorities. If we wish to prevent misery, we have to establish many legal rights. But these are deliberate legislative acts designed to promote social welfare; they are not the

---

[26] Some modern philosophers, like the leading utilitarian philosopher Peter Singer, argue that we should stop at $\sum W_i$ partly because going any further takes us too far from what could in principle be objectively measured. De Lazari-Radek and Singer (2017).

[27] Sen and Williams (1982). For a different view, see Smart in Smart and Williams (1973).

[28] Hare (1981).

recognition of some pre-existing 'natural rights'.[29] The only natural right is that each individual's feelings count equally.

The experience machine

But are good feelings the only things that matter? In 1974, the Harvard philosopher Robert Nozick questioned the primacy of feelings by posing the following hypothetical question: 'Suppose there was an "experience machine" you could link up to, which would make you feel anything you desire and which was equally available to other people. Would you link up to it?'[30]

Many people say No. They say it matters that the experience is real. But what if the real experience was awful and that we reverse the sequence of the question. So imagine you are having a lovely time in the experience machine and are offered instead the real experience of solitary confinement in a rat-infested cell. Which would you choose?[31]

A more likely possibility is that scientists come up with a drug that makes everybody feel better and has no bad side effects. This issue was raised in a striking form by Aldous Huxley in his book *Brave New World*. In it he has people taking soma to make themselves feel better. This was meant to appal the readers. But most people throughout history have used alcohol or other substances to improve their mood. The problem has been that all known substances of this kind also bring bad side effects. But it may be hard to object to a substance that improves mood without any bad side effects.

Adaptation

Then there is the issue that our feelings adapt (see Chapter 3). Most people adapt to hardship to a considerable extent, so that it causes less misery than might be expected.[32] If we take this fact into account, critics say, we shall do less to reduce hardship than we should.[33] But this does not follow, because people who are more fortunate also adapt to their good fortune. So if we take from the privileged and give to the deprived, the privileged will also suffer less than might be expected. Thus the case for redistribution is hardly affected by the fact of adaptation: the poor may gain less extra wellbeing from it than might be expected, but the rich also suffer less than might be expected.[34] The balance of the argument is thus unaffected.

However, adaptation does have important implications if some experiences are less subject to adaptation than others. It is therefore important to distinguish between hardships that cannot be adapted to and those that can be. Hardships that are hard or

---

[29] According to Bentham the doctrine of natural rights is 'nonsense on stilts'. See Bentham (2002).
[30] Nozick (1974).   [31] See Hindriks and Douven (2018).
[32] For the scale of adaptation to many types of experience, see A. E. Clark et al. (2018).   [33] Sen (2009).
[34] Actually, there is not much evidence of adaptation to income once social comparisons are taken into account – see Chapter 13.

Figure 2.1 How wellbeing is determined by behaviour

impossible to adapt to include mental pain, chronic physical pain, incarceration, torture, indignity and intolerable noise.[35] These types of hardship need high priority in public policy.

Selfishness is encouraged

Critics often complain that, if we accept wellbeing as the supreme goal, this means that individuals should simply maximise their own wellbeing. Far from it. For each person's wellbeing depends hugely on the benevolent behaviour of others. This is illustrated in Figure 2.1.

In this profoundly important diagram, the outcome we care about is the overall wellbeing of society, represented by the whole right-hand side of the diagram. How can it be maximised? The answer is: only if everyone chooses to behave so as to maximise the **overall** wellbeing of society. That is the fundamental ethical principle proclaimed by Bentham and by all other supporters of the greatest happiness principle. This aspiration should inform a person's whole life – both in private matters and also in the job they choose to do. In this view, morality is not just about what you should **not** do but also what you **should** do. For example, it is wrong to hurt someone but it is also wrong not to help them.

Some people say this is too 'demanding'[36] – it takes over too much of your life. As with all other moral theories, it is hard to specify exactly how far we should sacrifice our individual happiness for the sake of others. But, if we want to reduce suffering, we clearly have to avoid not only hurting people (sins of commission) but also failing to help them (sins of omission).

To encourage good lives, we have two key psychological traits we can build on. The first is the pleasure that people derive from helping others: doing the right thing is not always pleasurable but it often is (see Chapter 3). The second is the impact of norms on habit. If people are expected to behave well from an early age, it just becomes a habit. This was the route that Aristotle stressed.

Both of these routes are at variance with the doctrines of Immanuel Kant, the great philosopher of the German Enlightenment, which provide the main alternative system of ethics to that based on the maximisation of wellbeing.[37] In the Kantian system, the ethical rightness of a person's actions are judged by the person's motives and not by

---

[35] On noise, see Weinstein (1982).   [36] See Railton (1984).   [37] See, for example, Scruton (1982).

their consequences. A moral action has to be a conscious act of will, and pleasure and habit are considered antithetical to truly moral action. There is, however, one key feature on which both Kantian and Benthamite approaches are agreed: every individual is of equal ultimate importance. This is fundamental to any ethical theory based on reason.

The nanny state

Turning to political theory, critics of the wellbeing approach sometimes claim that, if the government concerns itself with how people feel, this will lead to excessive interference in people's lives. But wellbeing science itself shows the huge importance of freedom for personal wellbeing (see Chapters 8 and 16). So any government aiming at wellbeing will be constantly restrained by that consideration. Whenever possible, the government will provide opportunities that people can use or not, as they prefer.

It is, however, crucial to realise that many of the things that matter most to people are intensely personal (their mental health, their family relationships and their work situation) and failures in these dimensions are major sources of human misery. So a benevolent state is bound to offer help, if there are cost-effective forms of help that can be made available.

Social justice

A final problem is one that affects all ethical theories – how much weight to give to the interests of the least fortunate. Classic utilitarianism can be criticised because it gives equal value to more happiness whether it accrues to someone who is already happy or to someone who is miserable. But the 'prioritarian approach' we advocated earlier avoids this problem, and it provides a stronger basis for the legal creation of rights. It also asserts that income inequality is bad because an extra dollar is worth more to a poor person than a rich one. So a good society establishes rights (as a form of safety net) and it redistributes income.[38]

No ethical theory is without problems. If you find the wellbeing approach problematic, can you think of a better criterion for how to live or how to make policy?

We can end with a different question. Is wellbeing an experience that humans were designed for? The answer from '**evolutionary psychology**' is 'Partly yes and partly no'. The basic features of human nature were created by natural selection about 200,000 years ago in Africa. The genes that survived in the struggle for survival were those that maximised our 'inclusive fitness' – in other words, the genes that were most likely to produce successive generations carrying the same genes. So how conducive to wellbeing were the genes that got selected? We were certainly constructed to enjoy many of the things necessary for survival and reproduction – sex, food, drink and a capacity to cooperate (see Chapter 3). Moreover, as we have seen, wellbeing is

---

[38] Layard and Walters (1978) pp. 47–51 and references therein.

extremely good for many other things that are good for our survival – good for our physical health, for our productivity and for our creativity.[39]

There were, however, some traits that were essential for survival in the Savannah that are not particularly conducive to an enjoyable life. The most obvious of these is anxiety. If lions are about, it is a good thing to be anxious. But life today is a lot more safe, and most people would have a more enjoyable life if they were less anxious (see Chapter 4).

As this book shows, we have the knowledge to improve our own wellbeing and that of others – a noble cause.

Conclusions

(1) We are considering a very powerful idea – that social welfare depends only on the subjective wellbeing of the population. This is relevant to all aspects of life from public policy-making to personal behaviour. It is a concept with at least three uses.
   - It provides a measure for **comparing situations**, for example, comparing countries or comparing the same country at different periods in time.
   - It provides the fundamental principle of **moral philosophy:** that we personally should at all times do what we can to maximise social welfare.
   - It provides the fundamental principle of **political philosophy:** that governments should provide the conditions for the greatest possible social welfare.
(2) Wellbeing has been a central issue in philosophy from the earliest times.
(3) In the eighteenth century, Anglo-Scottish philosophers proposed the 'greatest happiness' of the people as the goal of moral and political action. Thus individuals should aim to be 'creators of happiness' and policy-makers should target the wellbeing of the people.
(4) In the early twentieth century, behaviourism postulated that we could not know how others feel. In consequence, economists abandoned the policy goal of maximising happiness and moved to maximising aggregate income (GDP).
(5) There is now a strong movement against using GDP as an indicator of wellbeing and in favour of some measure of the quality of life.
(6) One version of the 'social welfare function' is ΣW_i, where W_i is the wellbeing of the ith person. But most policies have impacts over a number of years. Thus forward looking social welfare is measured by $\sum_i \sum_t (1 - \delta)^t W_{it}$, the discounted sum of future Wellbeing Years (WELLBYS).

---

[39] See De Neve et al. (2013). On creativity, see Fredrickson (2000).

(7) The discount rate should be low. In this case the wellbeing of future generations is given the weight it deserves – making climate change and sustainability into hugely important issues.

(8) Egalitarians prefer to measure the social value of today's wellbeing not by ΣW_i but by $\Sigma f(W_i)$ where $f(W_i)$ rises at a diminishing rate as W_i increases. In policy evaluation, a practical approach is to start with ΣW_i and then test for sensitivity to different forms of $f(W_i)$. In addition we can mainly search for new policies in those areas of life which account for the greatest amount of misery.

(9) The wellbeing approach has been criticised on many grounds including rights, 'experience machine', adaptation, selfishness and the 'nanny state'. This book discusses these criticisms.

Questions for discussion

(1) Do you agree that coherent policy-making requires some single overarching criterion? Should this be wellbeing?

(2) Should the same idea govern our personal ethical choices?

(3) Should the social welfare function be the simple sum of wellbeing across people? Or should it give extra weight to the scale of misery?

(4) What is your view on the main criticisms made of the wellbeing approach to ethics and policy choice:

- Consequentialism, rights and social justice
- The experience machine.
- Adaptation
- Selfishness
- Nanny state

Further Reading

de Lazari-Radek, K., and Singer, P. (2017). *Utilitarianism: A Very Short Introduction*. Oxford University Press.

Layard, R., and Ward, G. (2020). *Can We Be Happier? Evidence and Ethics*. Penguin UK.

Mill, J. S. (1863). *Utilitarianism*. Parker, Son & Bourn, West Strand.

Nozick, R. (1974). *Anarchy, State, and Utopia*. Basic Books.

Smart, J. J. C., and Williams, B. (1973). *Utilitarianism: For and Against*. Cambridge University Press.

Part II

Human Nature and Wellbeing

LIFE ISN'T POINTLESS

3　How Our Behaviour Affects Our Wellbeing

To a psychologist it is self-evident that people are neither fully rational nor completely selfish, and that their tastes are anything but stable.

Daniel Kahneman

Individual Responsibility versus Collective Action

If social welfare is the objective – the thing that needs to be maximised – the next issue is Who is going to make that happen?

In traditional economics, a huge reliance is placed on the unfettered choices of individuals. As Adam Smith argued in the *Wealth of Nations*, people may be selfish; but, in order to get what they want, they do best by supplying what others need. The result of this process of voluntary exchange is an **efficient** situation where (on four assumptions) it would be impossible to make anyone better off without making someone else worse off. These assumptions are:

- no monopoly or oligopolies,
- no public goods (like roads or parks),
- full information for all,
- no one affects anyone else except through voluntary exchange (i.e. there are no 'externalities').

The classic example of a negative **'externality'** is air pollution. The pollution just comes my way whether I agree to it or not. So an externality is something that just happens to me without my choosing it. Psychologists and sociologists will immediately realise that externalities comprise a huge fraction of everything that happens – from how we learn our values to whether we are robbed.[1] Coping with externality is essential if we want an efficient society.

There is also another problem with pure laissez faire (where individual action is unfettered). This is the issue of **equity**. Even if the framework is efficient, it may leave

---

[1] There is no problem with so-called pecuniary externalities, where my action affects market prices enjoyed by others. Layard and Walters (1978) p. 226.

some people much less happy than others. People differ hugely in their talents, in the wealth they inherit and, most importantly, in their inner capacity to live an enjoyable life.

Thus pure laissez-faire is neither efficient (the four assumptions are not satisfied) nor is it equitable. So we need both society and the state to be active in promoting the wellbeing of the people and the prevention of misery. And for this they need well-being science.

There is also a further reason. People themselves differ hugely from what is assumed in traditional economics. On the one hand, they are much less good at promoting their own best interests than economists assume. And, on the other hand, they do often care a lot about the wellbeing of others. So we have to begin this book with a fundamental look at some of the basics of human behaviour.

In this chapter we shall investigate two questions.

- To what extent do people pursue their own best interests?
- In what ways are people affected by others' behaviour beyond voluntary exchange – in other words, what are key examples of externality?

Human Decision-Making

Clearly, people do to some extent pursue their own best interests. That is one reason why the human race has survived. People are 'attracted' to things that are good for survival – and feel happier when they achieve them (eating, mating etc.). And they 'avoid' things which are bad for their survival. This 'approach/avoidance' system is a basic part of human nature. But things are more complicated than that.

In 2002, the Nobel prize for economics was awarded for the first time to a psychologist. Some would say 'About time', since economics is based on a psychological theory about how people behave. But Daniel Kahneman's message was different from that of the economists. As Kahneman put it, economists typically assume that people 'are rational, selfish and their tastes do not change'.[2] After decades of research with his friend Amos Tversky, Kahneman believed otherwise.

Together they founded a new subject – called **behavioural economics** by some and **behavioural science** by others. Many others followed them, especially the economist/psychologist Richard Thaler (another Nobel laureate) and the lawyer Cass Sunstein. In their book Nudge,[3] they distinguished sharply between the people of traditional economic theory (who they called Econs) and real people (who they called Humans).

The two central issues are these: how effectively do people pursue their own wellbeing, and how do they impact on the wellbeing of others? There are at least five major ways in which humans do not maximise their own wellbeing:

- Addiction and lack of self-control,
- Unforeseen adaptation,

[2] Kahneman (2011) p. 269. This whole chapter draws heavily on this book.
[3] Thaler and Sunstein (2008). See also Thaler (2015).

- Framing,
- Loss-aversion,
- Unselfishness.

Addiction and self-control

People regularly decide to give up smoking, alcohol, drugs or gambling but then fail to do so. Frequently, they decide to do it next year, and when next year comes they decide to do it the following year. This is a case of 'dynamic inconsistency'. It is inconsistent because in the first year they have planned on the basis of their preferences in the first year; but, when the second year comes, their preferences for the second year have changed. More generally, as people look forward, many of them give a very high priority to the present over all ensuing periods: they use a very high discount rate between now and next year. But they use a much lower discount rate when they compare next year with the one that follows, and so on – and this is why they plan to give up next year rather than this year. Interestingly, neuroscientists have shown that decisions between this year and next are made in more primitive parts of the brain than decisions between more distant future years.[4]

Unforeseen adaptation/habituation

Another source of bad decisions is adaptation that is not foreseen. Human beings are generally pretty adaptable. They adapt to hardship – and they habituate to good experiences. In other words, the initial impact of a change on wellbeing eventually wears off, either partially or totally.[5] As we shall see in this book, **people adapt** (partly at least) to divorce, disability and poverty, and they also adapt to new houses, a new car, a new partner or a new child.[6]

If adaptation is **total**, the only way to change your wellbeing permanently is to experience continual change. Thus in 'total adaptation' we might have

$$W_t = b \left(X_t - X_{t-1} \right) \tag{1}$$

where X is anything that matters to you. So if you like X, your mood is higher when X is increasing. But, once X stops increasing, you return to your previous level of wellbeing. In other words, there is a 'set point' of wellbeing – neither good changes nor bad ones have any permanent effect.[7]

But if in fact we follow people through their lives, we find that their wellbeing often fluctuates a lot from one decade to another.[8] So, total adaptation is relatively

---

[4] Laibson (1998) and Rabin (1998).

[5] Addiction often arises from this source. At first the substance raises wellbeing, but over time, you need more and more of it to get the same good effect.

[6] See later chapters and A.E. Clark et al. (2018).

[7] Of course, if you can keep X growing every year, you will be better off but you are then on a '**hedonic treadmill**'.

[8] Headey (2006).

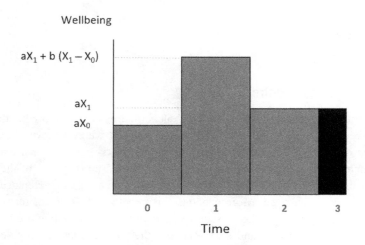

Figure 3.1 Partial adaptation of wellbeing to changes in X

rare – poorer people are, for example, less happy than rich people (other things being equal). But they also suffer less than you might imagine if you thought about how you would feel next year if you suddenly became that poor.

For the most common case in real life is '**partial adaptation**'. This is very common. When you move house, your next new house makes you feel great at first, but then gradually you take it for granted (you reduce your attention to it) and you return towards how you felt before the move.[9] The same happens with a new car or a rise in income. A typical case of partial adaptation is

$$W_t = aX_t + b\,(X_t - X_{t-1}) \tag{2}$$

So suppose we start from a position where X has equalled X_0 for some time, with

$$W_0 = a\,X_0$$

Then X rises to X_1 and stays there from then on. In response, wellbeing in the first time period is

$$W_1 = aX_1 + b\,(X_1 - X_0)$$

But in the following period, there is no further stimulating increase in X. So

$$W_2 = a\,X_1$$

This sequence is shown in the Figure 3.1, where X is taken to be desirable.[10] The key point is that the degree of adaptation is measured by the ratio of b to a. The higher b is relative to a the more adaptation occurs, and the further W moves back to its original

---

[9] Odermatt and Stutzer (2019).

[10] If more lagged terms appeared in equation (2), the decline to aX_1 would be more gradual.

position after its initial change. This kind of pattern applies to the effects of finding a partner, losing a partner, having children and many basic experiences.

If one looks deeper into the reasons for adaptation, it clearly has much to do with **attention**. When you attend to things, they become very important. When you do not, they become less so. As Kahneman puts it, 'nothing in life is as important as you think it is when you are thinking about it'. Things that are very salient and obtrusive like money can easily grab people's attention, although for much of the time most people don't actually think about them. For example, most people think that people in California are happier than people in the mid-west region of the United States. This is because, when they make the assessment, they are thinking about the difference in the weather. But in fact there is no difference in happiness because neither group actually spend that much time thinking about the weather.[11] Nor after a while do most people spend much time thinking about their car, unless someone draws their attention to it.

So what are the implications of adaptation for the wellbeing of the individual? The key question is whether or not individuals foresee their adaptation. If people foresee the adaptation, the decisions they take will be optimal. But in many cases, people clearly overestimate the gain in wellbeing they will eventually get from a change – a higher income, a new car, a new house or even a new partner. In such cases, people will put too much effort into acquiring the new situation, and in some cases they will come to regret the effort they made.[12] The Harvard psychologist, Daniel Gilbert, has called this a case of 'miswanting'.[13]

Framing

People's behaviour is also hugely affected by how a decision is presented to them. Every advertiser knows this – to sell a product you associate it with something attractive, however irrelevant. And you make sure people hear about it as frequently as possible.[14] Clearly advertising affects people's tastes. In particular it often makes them feel they need something that they did not formerly need. So, not surprisingly, there is some evidence that advertising reduces human happiness.[15]

But the clearest case of framing is the effect of the 'default'. For example, there are two ways in which people can be presented with the decision on whether to save for old age through a pension plan:

(1) you are asked if you want to opt in to the plan
(2) you are automatically enrolled unless you opt out ('auto-enrolment').

This can make a huge difference to what you do. For example, four US companies switched from opting in to opting out.[16] Under opting in, only 25–43% joined the

---

[11] Schadke and Kahneman (1998); Loewenstein, O'Donaghue and Rabin (2003).
[12] Loewenstein and Schadke (1999) p. 90.   [13] Gilbert and Wilson (2000).
[14] On the power of mere exposure, see Zajonc (1968).   [15] Michel et al. (2019).
[16] Choi et al. (2006).

company's pension plan, but once enrolment was automatic (unless you opted out) 86–96% joined the plan. This is extraordinary. A huge decision depends simply on whether you have to push a button or not. It is clear that, on a matter as important as this, people have no clear preferences, even though most economists would assume they do. Instead, many people let the framing of the decision determine what they do.

Similar behaviour is found in relation to how you can pre-donate your organs after death. In countries where you have to opt in to donate, donation rates can be as low as 4%; but, when you have to opt out, the rates approach 100%.[17] In all these cases, opting in appears to involve a psychic cost, but this cost disappears if someone else does it for you.

Because framing is so important, anyone wanting to influence people's behaviour must frame their approach to people carefully. This applies to government as much as to everyone else. This idea is central to the policy of **Nudge**, advocated by Richard Thaler and Cass Sunstein. They argue that, if we know how we want people to behave, we should if possible, make them do so by framing their choices right, rather than by dictating to them. This approach is known as **'libertarian paternalism'**.[18]

There are three key principles in framing the choices that people are offered:

(i)   Keep the message simple.
(ii) If you want someone to do something, point out that lots of other people are doing it.
(iii) Associate doing it with something positive rather than something negative.

The following experiment illustrates the last point. Two randomly selected groups (A and B) were offered the following choices:

Group A	Would you accept a gamble that offers a 10% chance to win $95 and a 90% chance to lose $5
Group B	Would you pay $5 to participate in a lottery that offers a 10% chance to win $100 and a 90% chance to win nothing

The majority of Group A refused to accept the gamble, while the majority of Group B agreed to participate in the lottery. And yet both these offers were identical (just check it out). The reason for the different answers was that Group A heard the word 'losing' while Group B did not.

Loss-aversion and the endowment effect

This leads directly to another key human characteristic: loss-aversion. Even for small things, people hate losing them by more than they would value gaining them. This is a

---

[17] Johnston and Goldstein (2003) p. 1338
[18] They particularly favour nudges where decisions are big, long-term and complicated.

deep psychological trait in all animals – their strongest impulse is to hold on to what they have. Just try removing food from your cat.

Richard Thaler calls this the **'endowment effect'**. So here is a remarkably simple experiment.[19] Students are randomly divided into two groups. The first group is shown a particular type of mug and asked how much they would be willing to pay for it. The average answer is $3.50. The other group are given the same mug for free. After a while they are asked how much money they would need to be paid in order to get them to part with the mug. The average amount is $7. So the same mug is worth $7 once you have it, but you are only willing to pay half that in order to get it. Thus there is no simple answer about the value of the mug, even to the same person: it depends whether she already owns it.[20] The value depends on the **'reference point'**.

Another clear example of loss-aversion is people's response to uncertainty, where Kahneman was awarded the Nobel prize for what he and Tversky called 'prospect theory'. So here is one simple experiment. You are asked whether to accept the following gamble:

- 50% chance of winning $150 and
- 50% chance of losing $100.

Someone who accepts this gamble can, on average, expect to win $25. Yet the majority of people decline the offer.[21] This cannot be explained by assuming that there is a smooth relationship between happiness and income, regardless of what the person's income was until now.[22] Instead, when people value their future income, they are comparing it with their present income. And they dislike losses more than they like gains. In other words, as Figure 3.2 shows, if a person started with an income of y_o, she would lose more happiness if she lost $100 than she would gain if she won $150.

Loss-aversion goes way beyond our attitude to income, and it affects behaviour in all sorts of ways.[23] For example, professional golfers are more likely to sink a putt if it is needed to avoid a bogey (a loss) than if the same shot would give them a birdie (a gain). Taxi drivers work longer hours on bad days, even though there is less work. Homeowners insist on selling their houses for a higher price when it involves a loss. And investors are more likely to sell stocks that have increased in value (since they were bought) than to sell stocks that have gone down: they hate to 'realise' losses. None of these attempts to avoid losses would be in the interest of a rational maximiser of expected outcomes.[24]

---

[19] Kahneman et al. (1990).

[20] Another striking example is when students are randomly given either a coffee mug or a chocolate bar (both of which cost the same). They are then offered a chance to trade. One would expect that 50% would prefer what they did not have. In fact it was 18%. List (2003).

[21] This is not of course true of traders who make hundreds of bets. For someone making this bet many times over would be almost certain to win a lot.

[22] As Rabin (2000) shows, a person with a smooth utility-of-income function who rejected a 50:50 chance to win $200 or lose $100 would also have to reject a 50:50 chance to win $20,000 or lose $200. This shows that a smooth utility-of-income function cannot be the reason for loss-aversion.

[23] Camerer et al. (1997); Odean (1998); Genesove and Mayer (2001); Kahneman (2011).

[24] This is one example of separate 'mental accounting' – we judge things in compartments, not in their overall context.

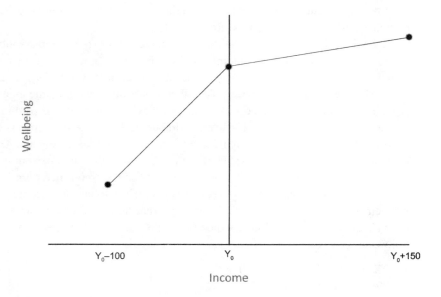

Figure 3.2 Loss-aversion

Many studies have attempted to measure the scale of loss-aversion, as measured by the slope of the wellbeing/income relationship for losses relative to that for gains. The typical finding is a ratio of 2:1. For example, suppose there was

- a 50% chance of winning $x and
- a 50% chance of losing $100

and you were asked what value of x would make you just willing to undertake the gamble. The typical answer is $200.[25]

A similar size of effect can be found at the level of the **whole economy** – this time in relation to actual wellbeing experienced rather than anticipated wellbeing. When incomes fall in a slump, the fall in national happiness is double the increase in happiness that occurs when incomes rise in a boom.[26] Once again the ratio is 2:1. Loss-aversion explains many forms of behaviour that standard economics cannot explain but that wise people have always noticed. One of these is wage stickiness in the downward direction. As Keynes pointed out, people fiercely resist a cut in the money value of their wage. If prices are falling enough, this may appear irrational since a person might gain in real income even though their money wage fell. But people do not see it that way, and a combination of loss-aversion and 'money illusion' stops wages falling and exacerbates the slump. This simple observation is central to Keynesian economics, but it is inconsistent with pure rationality.

---

[25] See, for example, Kahneman (2011).   [26] At least double – see De Neve and Ward (2017).

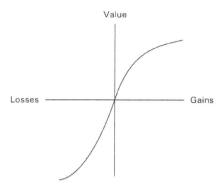

Figure 3.3 Loss aversion with diminished sensitivity
Source: Adapted from Kahneman (2011)

More generally, it is loss-aversion that makes many economic reforms so difficult to achieve. Even if 95% of the population would gain, a reform will often be defeated because of the 5% who lose. Examples abound in every country. In Britain in the 1930s, mass unemployment caused little political protest until the government reformed the unemployment benefit system in a way that benefitted most unemployed people but hurt a few.[27]

Before leaving loss-aversion, let's note one further fact: **diminished sensitivity**. One aspect of this is standard in economics – as you gain more and more, you value each additional gain less and less. But the same is true of losses – as you lose more and more, each extra loss causes less and less additional pain. For example, suppose once again that we look at gains and losses of money. The corresponding changes in wellbeing are shown in Figure 3.3.

This has remarkable results. Suppose people have to choose between the following alternatives:

- a 50% chance of losing $100
- the certainty of losing $50.

They will prefer the gamble since it offers at least a 50% chance of losing nothing. To retain the hope of avoiding loss, decision-makers worldwide are prone to risk a lot, even though it might be more rational to accept a much smaller loss and move on.[28]

The combination of loss-aversion and diminished sensitivity constitute what Kahneman and Tversky called 'prospect theory' and it was for this that Kahneman won the Nobel prize (Tversky having sadly died). Each prize-winner receives a personalised drawing, and the drawing on Kahneman's certificate was a more artistic version of Figure 3.3.

---

[27] Runciman (1966).
[28] There is also a well-documented tendency to exaggerate the **probability** of small risks, which is how insurers make their money. Tversky and Kahneman (1992).

Unselfishness

Finally, there is a key aspect of human behaviour that does not often appear in standard economics: **unselfishness**. People regularly do things for other people whom they will never see again and who could never return the favour. They return lost wallets to their owners and they are more likely to return wallets the more money they contain.[29] People give money in secret to charity; they dive into rivers to rescue drowning strangers. This behaviour can only be explained by the presence of a moral sense, partly learned and partly in our genes.[30] People of course vary in the strength of their moral sense. So what can account for this dual aspect of our human nature – the mixture of the selfish and the unselfish? You might think that at the individual level people who were more selfish would end up doing better in the Darwinian struggle for survival. And, if so, the genes for unselfishness would become less and less common. But this doesn't happen. Two things sustain the prevalence of cooperation.

The first is **social sanctions**. Your fellow citizens know that for many purposes co-operation is more efficient than competition. So they punish people who won't co-operate – such people get left out; people will not work with them. So, as the evidence shows, non-co-operators do worse on average than other humans.[31] The same happens among chimpanzees. In an impressive recent experiment with chimpanzees, there were five times more co-operative acts than non-co-operative ones – and the non-co-operators were either shunned or physically punished.[32] So one reason why people co-operate is to win the favour of others.

But there is a second reason: on average, pro-social behaviour makes us **feel good inside ourselves** – the 'warm glow'. In one experiment, students were randomly divided into two groups. One group were given money to spend on themselves, and the second group were given money to spend on other people. When asked about their happiness after the experiment, those who had given the money away were happier. This experiment has been repeated in four countries and a similar experiment with toddlers has produced the same results – they smile more.[33]

Neuroscience confirms this mechanism. When playing the Prisoner's Dilemma game (when you can either 'co-operate' or not), people who co-operated showed more activity in the standard brain area where other positive rewards are processed.[34] And this was even before they knew whether the other player would co-operate. In other words, if you want to feel good, do good.

---

[29] Cohn et al. (2019).   [30] Ricard (2015).

[31] For some evidence, see Schwartz (1970); and Lyubomirsky et al. (2005b). However, some cheats do also survive in the competitive struggle. Frank (1988) has a nice explanation of how in equilibrium both cheats and non-cheats can survive – by consorting with people like themselves. See also Fehr and Fischbacher (2003), who show how multiple equilibria are possible: if there are enough selfish people, even unselfish people will behave selfishly.

[32] Suchak et al. (2016).

[33] Otake et al. (2006); Dunn et al. (2008); Aknin, L. B. et al. (2012); Aknin et al. (2013, 2015, 2019); Lane (2017). As Helliwell et al. (2018c) show on page 10, helping behaviour gives more pleasure to the helper when it is done for the sake of the other person than when it is done for self-oriented reasons.

[34] Rilling et al. (2002). See also Harbaugh et al. (2007).

Externalities

The conclusion so far is that Humans do not always maximise their own wellbeing. In cases where this produces a bad outcome, good advice, nudges and even government intervention might help them do better.[35] But there is another reason for government intervention that also arises from human nature: the role of **externality**. Let us look briefly at three forms of externality: the trustworthiness of others, the sources of our social norms and social comparisons.

The trustworthiness of others

We are hugely affected by the ethical character of those around us (see Figure 2.1). A libertarian might argue that we can choose who to have around us. But this is not quite right. Only some people can choose. If they choose the most trustworthy, the rest of the population end up interacting with the less trustworthy. What matters for the population as a whole is the total pool of characters they can interact with. So the virtues and vices of our fellow citizens are huge external influences on our wellbeing. This has always been given as one reason for public education.

The sources of our social norms

Our own tastes and norms are things we absorb from the outside world – mostly in childhood and adolescence. They affect what we enjoy – and how we treat others. Libertarians like the Nobel prize-winning economists Gary Becker and George Stiglitz argue that no one set of tastes is better than any other (in Latin, 'de gustibus non disputandum est').[36] Wellbeing science offers a different view on this. As we have seen, our preferences have huge effects on other people. Our genes certainly have some effect on our tastes and norms of behaviour. But we are also hugely affected by our own parents, our schools, our peers and society as a whole. One has only to think about how tastes in fashion or music change from decade to decade or our attitudes to gender, race and smoking.

Basic human needs may not change much. According to one school of thought, our social needs can be summarised under three headings: autonomy, competence and relatedness.[37]

- **Autonomy.** We need a sense of agency – that we are in control of our lives.
- **Competence.** We need to feel able to do what is needed of us.

---

[35] Another issue is whether people do choose what they **think** will make them happy? Interesting research in this area shows that generally they do but not always. However, many of the contrary cases can be explained either by unselfishness or by people using a longer time horizon for their future happiness than the survey allows for (e.g., you take a less pleasant job to access a satisfying later career). See Benjamin et al. (2012); Fleurbaey and Schwandt (2015); Glaeser et al. (2016).

[36] Stigler and Becker (1977).   [37] Deci and Ryan (2000). Self-Determination Theory.

- **Relatedness.** We need to feel appreciated and to appreciate others – we need positive connections.

This may be true. But the specifics of what we desire depends hugely on the norms of the society in which we live.

Social comparisons

People are hugely affected by how they are doing compared with other people. They care about how their incomes compare with colleagues or how their children compare with other people's children. We discuss this further in Chapter 13. People also tend to imitate each other. This sort of herd behaviour is generally the result of safety-seeking behaviour among members of a herd.[38]

Conclusions

In the traditional economic model, people have well-defined preferences and pursue them consistently and selfishly. According to this model, wellbeing is efficiently promoted, in a laissez-faire world, except for various problems. The biggest of these problems is 'externality', which is the way in which people affect other people without their agreement.

However, there are in fact many other problems. Humans are different from the traditional economic model in many ways.

- They often lack self-control (e.g., over drugs, alcohol and gambling), and what they plan for tomorrow they often fail to execute.
- They often do not realise how much they will adapt to change, and they put effort into new acquisitions that make less difference to them than they expect.
- They are hugely affected by how decisions are framed – for example, many will adopt a pension plan when it requires effort to opt out of it, but they would not choose it if they had to opt in to it.
- People are hugely loss-averse, which often makes desirable changes much more difficult.
- And, on the other side, they often help each other without expecting anything in return.

These complexities mean that government intervention or nudges are often needed to produce efficient outcomes. These arguments become even stronger when we consider the many pervasive 'externalities' affecting our experience:

- We benefit if we live in a trustworthy society.
- We get many of our norms and tastes from society.
- Because of rivalry, we lose wellbeing if others are more successful.

---

[38] Hamilton (1971).

Thus, the simple economic model explains a lot about the behaviour of companies and workers. But it is a very incomplete account of how people often behave. Clearly we need to understand why people behave as they do. But to know what behaviours should be encouraged, we also need to know how behaviour affects wellbeing. That is the central feature of the rest of this book.

Questions for discussion

(1) If people fail to pursue their own best interest, should the government ever do more than nudge them?
(2) What is the right mix of competition and cooperation?
(3) Whose job is it to produce good citizens: (i) parents, (ii) schools, (iii) government, (iv) faith organisations, (v) others?
(4) How useful is traditional economic theory for thinking about public policy? What are its main short-comings?

Further Reading

Choi, J., Laibson, D., and Madrian, B. C. (2006). Saving for retirement on the path of least resistance. In E. McCaffrey and J. Slemrod (Eds.). *Behavioral Public Finance: Toward a New Agenda* (pp. 304–351). Russell Sage Foundation.

Gilbert, D. T., and Wilson, T. D. (2000). Miswanting: Some problems in the forecasting of future affective states. In J. P. Forgas (Ed.). *Studies in Emotion and Social Interaction, Second Series. Feeling and Thinking: The Role of Affect in Social Cognition* (pp. 178–197). Cambridge University Press.

Kahneman, D. (2011). *Thinking, Fast and Slow*. Allen Lane.

Layard, R., and Walters, A. A. (1978). *Microeconomic Theory*. McGraw-Hill.

Rilling, J. K., Gutman, D. A., Zeh, T. R., Pagnoni, G., Berns, G. S., and Kilts, C. D. (2002). A neural basis for social cooperation. *Neuron*, 35(2), 395–405.

Thaler, R. H., and C. R. Sunstein (2008). *Nudge: Improving Decisions about Health, Wealth, and Happiness*. Yale University Press.

I AM GOING TO TURN MY
LIFE AROUND

AND I WILL
START BY
IRONING MY
TROUSERS

4   How Our Thoughts Affect Our Wellbeing

People are disturbed not by things but by the view they take of them.

Epictetus

Our experiences affect our wellbeing but so does the way we think about our experience – and about our future. The best evidence about this process comes **when people are taught how to control their thoughts better.** So in this chapter we examine three types of mind-training:

- Clinical psychology (for people in distress),
- Positive psychology (for all of us),
- Meditation and mindfulness

The Experimental Method

In each area, we shall rely on evidence from **well-controlled experiments**. Such experiments are a vital part of wellbeing research. They are the surest way to establish causality in general and they are particularly important if we are trying to find out how to improve things. It is so easy to think that some method works – you see that those treated (the 'treatment group') improve. But would they have improved anyway? You can only answer this question if you had a 'control group' who were as similar as possible to the 'treatment group' but did not receive the treatment. The progress of the 'control group' then provides the 'counterfactual' with which you can compare the progress of the treatment group.

The gold standard for such a comparison is the randomised-controlled trial (or RCT). Here the treatment group and control group are drawn randomly from a single population. This does not guarantee that they are identical, but it hugely reduces the risk of conclusions that are biased because of pre-existing differences between the treatment and the control group.

The key issue with any intervention is the size of its effect. This is more important than whether the effect is or is not significantly different from zero (which also depends largely on the size of the sample).

The size of the effect can be measured in two ways. In the first, we measure it in units of the outcome being measured. For example, we could measure the effect in units of life satisfaction on a scale of 0–10 and find that an intervention raises life satisfaction by say 1 unit.

But it is also interesting to see how big this effect is, when compared with the overall spread of life satisfaction in the population. So suppose the standard deviation (SD) of life satisfaction is 2. Then this same intervention has increased life satisfaction by 0.5 standard deviations. This is the statistic known as the **effect size** (or Cohen's d).[1] So for an outcome variable Y, the effect size of an intervention is given by

Effect size = Effect (in units of Y)/SD(Y) = Cohen's d

Cognitive-Behaviour Therapy (CBT)

So, let us start with clinical psychology and ask, Are people in distress just victims of their past, who can only be helped by uncovering their past? Or can they improve their state of mind by changing their present pattern of thinking?

The leading exponent of the first view was the Austrian psychiatrist Sigmund Freud (1856–1939). According to Freud, our current feelings are largely the result of what happened to us in childhood. If our experience was bad, this has a lasting effect, especially if the memories of the bad experiences are 'repressed', buried deep in the 'unconscious' part of the mind. According to Freud, it is only if these memories are brought to the surface that the person can move forward. This is best achieved through psychoanalysis. Here the patient lies on a couch with the therapist behind him, while the patient practices 'free association'. And, through this free association, the repressed memories come to light and the patient's suffering is relieved.

Many people have been helped by Freudian treatment, though it is not easy to know how many, due to the paucity of controlled trials.[2] Freud was hugely influential on our culture, especially our greater openness about sex. But Freud's view of human possibilities lacked optimism. In *Civilisation and Its Discontents*, he wrote: 'The intention that man should be happy is not in the plan of creation.'

Most psychotherapists in the generation that followed Freud had a more optimistic view of human welfare. This was particularly true of Carl Rogers (1902–1987), who founded what he called humanistic psychology.[3] More than anyone, Rogers stressed the importance in psychotherapy of the therapeutic alliance between the therapist and

---

[1] The following other relations hold.

(1) If the effect size (denoted d) is below around 0.5, a treated individual who is initially at the median will rise up the distribution by about $40 \times d$ percentile points (assuming the distribution is 'normal').

(2) The correlation of the treatment dummy and the outcome variable is $d \sqrt{p(1-p)}$ where p is the proportion treated. For a randomised treatment, where one half the population are treated, this is $d/2$.

[2] For two of the controlled trials, see Fonagy (2015); and Leichsenring et al. (2009). There are now shorter Freudian treatments known as 'psychodynamic'.

[3] It is also true of Carl Gustav Jung (1875–1961), who first defined the concepts of extroversion and introversion and of a complex, and of Alfred Adler (1874–1937) who first defined the inferiority complex.

the client, which is so central to much of counselling today. But the main focus of such counselling (now face-to-face) continued to be on understanding the past and how it has influenced the present.

The cognitive revolution

However, in the 1970s a completely new approach was developed by Aaron T. Beck. This approach was based on the key facts that

- our thoughts affect our feelings,
- we can (up to a point) choose to think differently
- and therefore, we can directly affect our feelings.

This approach does not ignore the past (especially when it was traumatic). But it focuses on how our current thinking is maintaining the bad feelings that we have. These bad feelings are causing **'automatic negative thoughts'**. But we can observe these thoughts, question them (where relevant) and separate ourselves from them rather than being possessed by them. In this way, we can create space for more positive thoughts – for more appreciation of what we have and for better hopes and plans for the future. This will often involve a reassessment of our goals, since unattainable goals are one of the main causes of depression. We recover by 'reframing' our thinking.

Thus was born the **'cognitive revolution'**[4] – it was cognitive because it focused on cognition (i.e., thoughts). Beck's main interest was the problem of depression. Trained as a Freudian psychotherapist, he had been taught that people were depressed because of repressed anger, which they redirect against themselves. According to this theory, that anger is revealed in their dreams and, from uncovering the anger, patients can be relieved of their depression. Wishing to make psychoanalysis scientific, Beck therefore arranged with a team of colleagues to compare the dreams of depressed and non-depressed people. It emerged that depressed people had **less** hostile dreams than other people did. Instead, the dreams of depressed people mirrored quite closely their conscious thoughts while waking – thoughts of being victims, with the world against them and themselves tormented, rejected or deserted.[5]

So Beck altered his treatment. He got his patients to observe their 'negative automatic thoughts' and replace them with thoughts of a more constructive kind. In 1977, Beck published the first randomised controlled trial of cognitive therapy for depression, comparing it with the leading anti-depressant.[6] The results were striking – cognitive therapy was more effective. Since then there have been thousands of such trials, and the current wisdom is that cognitive therapy and anti-depressants are equally effective at ending a serious depressive episode.[7] But, after the depression ends, anti-depressants have no effect on the risk of subsequent relapse (unless you go

---

[4] Beck (1979). See also Beck and Beck (2011); and Layard and Clark (2014).   [5] Beck (2006).
[6] Rush et al. (1977).   [7] Roth and Fonagy (2005).

on taking them), while cognitive therapy (once experienced) halves the subsequent rate of relapse.[8]

The behavioural revolution in clinical psychology

Originally the 'cognitive revolution' in psychological therapy focused on depression. In the meantime, there was a **'behavioural revolution'** in progress, for the treatment of anxiety disorders. This was based on the ideas of the Russian physiologist Ivan Pavlov (1849–1936), who showed how dogs could be conditioned to respond to a stimulus, depending on the good or bad events associated with the stimulus. The South African doctor Joseph Wolpe (1915–1997) inferred from this that humans who were currently terrified of doing something could be progressively desensitised by the step-by-step experience that nothing bad resulted when they did that something (like public speaking or going out of the house). He founded behaviour therapy.

In the 1960s, Gordon Paul put this theory to the test by doing the first controlled experiment in clinical psychology. The aim was to cure the phobia of public speaking. Paul compared systematic desensitisation with two other approaches: insight-oriented therapy (based on Freud's ideas) and no treatment at all. Systematic desensitisation worked best.[9]

In the decades that followed, people found that anxiety disorders were helped not only by behavioural methods but also by better styles of thinking. Likewise, depression was helped not only by better thinking but also by behavioural activation. And so was born **Cognitive-Behaviour Therapy (CBT),** which focuses on helping people change unhelpful patterns of thinking and thus bring about changes in behaviour, attitude and mood.

But CBT is not actually one thing. It is a set of different therapies for different problems. For example, for post-traumatic stress disorder (PTSD), there has to be a detailed revisiting of the traumatic experiences. But the essential focus of CBT is on directly restoring people's control of their inner mental life and thus enabling them to move forward. If undertaken with fidelity in the field, CBT produces a recovery rate of at least 50% after around 10 sessions – and for anxiety disorders the subsequent rate of relapse is very small.[10]

Critics of CBT say, correctly, that it concentrates on dealing with the symptoms that are distressing the patient rather than on uncovering the causes of these symptoms. It is, therefore, they say, no more than a 'sticking plaster'. But the test is surely the outcome as experienced by the patient. There is nothing wrong in dealing with symptoms rather than causes – it happens all the time in medicine, especially in surgery. The encouraging thing is that it gives immediate hope – that humans can take control of their inner life by conscious activity, properly trained.

CBT is not the only form of effective psychological therapy. For anxiety disorders it is the best, but for depression, UK government guidelines also recommend interpersonal psychotherapy, brief psychodynamic therapy and a specific form of

---

[8] Hollon and Beck (2013).   [9] Paul (1966).   [10] Hollon and Beck (2013).

counselling.[11] And of course drugs also help for severe depression and some forms of anxiety. But we have focused on CBT because it illustrates the key point of how our thinking can influence our mood.

Positive Psychology

If thoughts influence moods for people in real distress, the same must surely be true of everyone else also. This was the insight of Beck's leading followers. In his presidential address to the American Psychological Association in 1998 Seligman proposed a new concept called **Positive Psychology**.[12] This applies the same principles as CBT to the lives of everybody. Everybody, it says, can be happier if they have better control of their mental lives and more sensible goals. The secret is to build on your strengths rather than to correct your weaknesses.[13] And to look for the best in any situation and the best in any person – to reach out and to feel grateful for what you have.

There are many good books on positive psychology[14] and there are many controlled trials of the procedures it recommends, such as

- a daily gratitude exercise and
- a daily extra act of kindness.

At this point it is enough to present the 10 Keys to Happier Living, distilled from this literature by the movement called **Action for Happiness**. The five items in the left-hand column (see Figure 4.1) are five recommended actions for every day – the psychological equivalent to the daily five fruit and vegetables recommended by the WHO.[15] The five items in the right hand column are the main long-term dispositions we should cultivate in ourselves. To promote the 10 Keys, Action for Happiness has offered an eight-session course, which has been subjected to a randomised control trial. This showed that, two months after the course ended, the treatment group had gained over 1 point in life satisfaction (on a scale of 0–10), which is more than occurs when someone gets a job (after being unemployed) or finds a partner to live with.[16]

A key issue in positive psychology is **attention**. What we focus on affects not only what we do (as in Chapter 3) but also how we feel. As we have seen, when humans evolved in the Savannah, there was a daily risk of being killed. So a high level of anxiety was functional, and it became embedded in our genes. As the psychologist Rick Hanson has put it 'the mind is like Velcro for the negative and like Teflon for the

---

[11] See latest guidance from NICE.

[12] A forerunner of this approach was the concept of Emotional Intelligence popularised in Goleman (1995).

[13] Seligman (2002) offers techniques for identifying your strengths.

[14] Seligman (2002); Ben-Shahar (2007); Lyubormirsky (2008); Gilbert (2009); Dolan (2014); and King (2016).

[15] These were originally developed by the New Economics Foundation – see Foresight Mental Capital and Wellbeing Project (2008) p. 24.

[16] Krekel et al. (2020). The course is now six sessions, either online or face-to-face. Another course is available online through Corsera called 'The Science of Wellbeing', based on the highly successful course at Yale University taught by Laurie Santos.

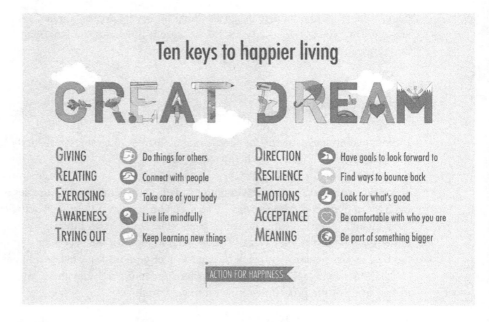

Figure 4.1 10 Keys to Happier Living
Source: Action for Happiness, 10 Keys to Happier Living

positive'.[17] But in most of today's world, people are much safer from violence than they have ever been.[18] So most people are more anxious than is good for them – they devote excessive attention to what goes wrong. The way to be happier is to devote more attention to what goes right.

Positive thinking has been subject to considerable criticism by those like Barbara Ehrenreich, author of *Smile or Die*, who says it encourages a Pollyanna attitude. According to these critics, it makes us overlook the bad stuff that is going on. Instead, these critics advocate 'realistic thinking'. Obviously when it comes to other people, realism is vital – we should attend to their suffering. We need to notice it and help them – and the evidence shows that happier people are more helpful to others.[19] But, for ourselves, it is we who can, in part, create our own reality. The glass may be both half-empty and half-full: but how much better to think of it as half-full!

Meditation and Mindfulness

The habits encouraged by CBT and positive psychology have much in common with those advocated by Eastern wisdom, especially Buddhism.[20] The East has developed a

---

[17] Hanson (2016).   [18] Pinker (2011).   [19] Huppert (2009).
[20] The teaching is also similar to that of the Stoics in the Roman Empire, but the Stoics did not recommend any particular spiritual practice.

more effective method of mind-training than is common in the West.[21] It is **meditation**. There are many forms of meditation, but the most common and the most studied is mindfulness.[22]

Mindfulness means focusing on the present in an open, aware and non-judgemental frame of mind. You set aside the past and the future and you simply observe the present moment. You choose what you will attend to, and then attend to it. If your mind drifts off, you gently bring it back.

At first, the most natural object of attention is your breathing (where simple breathing exercises are also very useful).[23] But you can then move on to different parts of the body (including a full 'body scan'), and then you can observe your thoughts, be they happy or sad. You do not push sadness or anxiety away, but you observe it from outside in a friendly way, so that it no longer possesses you. And you practice compassion towards yourself. If you feel you have done something stupid or wrong, you think, What would I say to a friend who was in this state? And you say just that to yourself.

Much mindfulness meditation in the West is based on Jon Kabat Zinn's eight-session course of Mindfulness-Based Stress Reduction (MBSR) developed at the University of Massachusetts. This was originally a course for people in chronic pain, but it has proved very beneficial to many other people. For adults, MBSR has been found to have beneficial effects on mood and sleep, on substance abuse and on concentration and empathy.[24] It also affects the body. Mindfulness has been found to increase the amount of grey matter (critical for learning) and the regulation of emotion, and to increase telomerase, which increases longevity.[25] In one randomised trial, four months after the MBSR course was over, members of the treatment group and the control group were given a flu jab. The meditators produced more antibodies.[26]

For children, comparable courses in mindfulness have been evaluated in a meta-analysis of 33 separate studies. They were found to have significant positive effects on depression ($d = .22$), anxiety ($d = .16$) and social behaviour ($d = .27$).[27] Some studies have also found good effects on academic learning.[28]

---

[21] There has of course been meditation in every religious faith (see below).

[22] For a practical self-help guide, see Williams and Penman (2011). The best informal introductions to mindfulness are by the Vietnamese master Thich Nhat Hanh (Hanh [2001], [2008]). For a scholarly introduction, see Williams and Kabat-Zinn (2013).

[23] An effective and immediate way to reduce stress is to breathe in deeply and hold for 20 seconds before breathing out and then to repeat this two more times. See Zaccaro et al. (2018).

[24] Baer (2003).

[25] Holzel et al. (2011); and Jacobs et al. (2011). Note, however, that Kral et al. (2021) found no changes in grey matter.

[26] Davidson et al. (2003).

[27] Dunning et al. (2019). In one trial, mindfulness training was also shown to reduce depression and burnout in teachers (Jennings and Greenberg [2009]). But see also Kuyuken et al. (2022) for the effects when there is no organised practice once the course has ended.

[28] Bakosh et al. (2016); and Bennett and Dorjee (2016).

Mindfulness meditation is totally non-judgemental. But there is another powerful strand in Eastern wisdom: the importance of compassion. A different form of Buddhist meditation focuses on developing compassion for others. In this, the meditator wishes first for her own wellbeing, then that of a loved one, then of an enemy and finally of all humankind. In a meta-analysis of 21 studies, this practice was found to increase wellbeing as well as compassion and to reduce depression and anxiety – all with effect sizes around 0.5.[29] Compassion meditation has also been found to increase levels of the feel-good hormone oxytocin and to improve the tone in the vagus nerve, which controls the heart rate.[30]

Even so, there are some people for whom meditation does not work particularly well. But everyone can find some way of regulating their thoughts to improve their wellbeing.

All religions offer some way of doing this, but we leave the discussion of religion to Chapter 14. We can end this chapter with the Dalai Lama, who of all Eastern teachers has been the most influential in the West. He was until recently the head of the Tibetan government in exile but practices the life of a monk. He has also travelled and taught widely in the West. His many books teach ways to achieve happiness that may or may not include meditation. But at every stage the Dalai Lama, who has a strong scientific sense, stresses the unity of mind and body.[31] This is the theme of Chapter 5.

Conclusions

As we have seen, there are many interventions that can make us feel better through influencing our patterns of thinking and our reactions to the world around us. But these interventions tell us more than that. They show (through experiments) a more general truth: that how we think has a major effect on how we feel. Of course the opposite is also true: our feelings affect our thoughts, but it is mainly through our thoughts that we can manage our feelings.

Questions for discussion

(1) If a person is suffering, is it sufficient to ameliorate the symptoms, even if you cannot uncover or remove the cause?
(2) Is it ultimately dangerous to look on the bright side of things?

---

[29] Kirby et al. (2017). The effect sizes were as follows: compassion 0.55, wellbeing 0.51, depression 0.64 and anxiety 0.49 – large effects.
[30] Frederickson (2013); Kok et al. (2013). See also Goleman and Davidson (2017).
[31] He is co-founder of the Mind and Life Institute, which produces a series of scientific books on mind-body interaction.

Further Reading

Goleman, D. (1995). *Emotional Intelligence*. Bantam Books.

Greenberger, D., and Padesky, C. A. (2015). *Mind over Mood: Change How You Feel By Changing the Way You Think*. Guilford.

Lyubomirsky, S. (2008). *The How of Happiness: A Scientific Approach to Getting the Life You Want*. Penguin Press.

McManus, F. (2022). *Cognitive Behavioural Therapy: A Very Short Introduction*. Oxford University Press.

Seligman, M. E. P. (2011). *Flourish: A Visionary New Understanding of Happiness and Well-Being*. Free Press.

Williams, J. M. G., and D. Penman. (2011). *Mindfulness: A Practical Guide to Finding Peace in a Frantic World*. Piatkus.

WHAT I USED TO BE

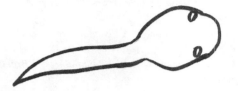

WHAT I AM NOW

5 Our Bodies, Our Genes and Our Wellbeing

I have chosen to be happy because it is good for my health.

Voltaire

Our thoughts, feelings and behaviour do not occur in disembodied space – they occur in our bodies. This chapter investigates four big questions about the relationship between mind and body:

- Can we locate our feelings in the brain?
- How does our mental wellbeing affect the rest of our body?
- How in turn does our body affect our mental wellbeing?
- How do our genes affect our mental wellbeing?

Feelings and the Brain

Neuroscience is still in its infancy. But we can already locate **areas in the brain** where people experience their mental wellbeing and their distress. The method is to ask many people how they feel and then to correlate their answers with the electrical activity in different parts of their brains. The best method of measuring electrical activity in different parts of the brain is by functional Magnetic Resonance Imaging (fMRI).[1] Using fMRI, significant correlations have been found between measures of wellbeing and electrical activity in a number of different brain areas. For example, Richard Davidson and his colleagues at the University of Wisconsin have found a strong relationship with activity in the ventral striatum (and within it the nucleus accumbens).[2] The relationship holds both over time for the same person (as when a mother is shown a picture of her child) and also, more importantly, across people. Thus people with higher sustained activity in the ventral striatum report higher psychological wellbeing (see Figure 5.1). Their adrenal glands also produce less cortisol – another positive sign of wellbeing (see below).

---

[1] This measures the rate of glucose metabolism (which is related to the firing of the neurons).
[2] Davidson and Schuyler (2015).

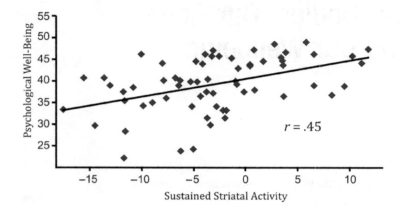

Figure 5.1 Sustained activation of the ventral striatum predicts psychological wellbeing
Source: Heller et al. (2013)

The ventral striatum is a subcortical area that humans share with other mammals. But neuroscientists have also found correlation between wellbeing and activity in different parts of the pre-frontal cortex (including the ventro-medial and the dorso-lateral).[3] Researchers have also identified a Default Mode Network in the brain that takes over when nothing much else is going on. It is focused on the self, and people where the network is more active report themselves to be less happy.[4]

So there are objective measurements that correlate with reports of subjective experience, and this confirms that there is some objective information content in the reports of subjective wellbeing. But our understanding of the neural correlates of wellbeing is still quite partial.

More advanced is the neuroscience of pain. The main area where people feel distress when they are in pain is the anterior cingulate cortex (ACC), which is another subcortical area. **Physical pain** has two components – the 'sensory' aspect and the 'emotional' aspect. The sensory aspect informs us where the pain comes from (back, leg etc.) and its nature (e.g., pulsating, continuous, hot, cold), and it is recorded in the somatosensory cortex. But the emotional distress felt as part of the pain is located in the ACC.[5]

So too, is the emotional distress resulting from **social pain**.[6] So it is not surprising that the pain-killing drug paracetamol (Tylenol in the United States) has the same

---

[3] Volkow et al. (2011).   [4] Raichle et al. (2001).
[5] Strictly, it is in the dorsal ACC (the top part, the dACC). If the dACC is somehow severed from the rest of the brain, the distress from physical pain disappears but the sensation of disturbance continues. Equally, if the somatosensory cortex is disconnected, the nature of the pain becomes unclear but the distress is still experienced.
[6] Eisenberger et al. (2003); and Lieberman (2013). With social pain, if this is induced (e.g., by a rejection in an online game) the dACC is stimulated. If Tylenol is taken, this dACC response does not occur, nor do people report as much distress. For qualifications to this analysis, see Ferris et al. (2019).

dulling effect on the experience of both physical pain and social pain. In each case, the drug is moderating the electrical activity in the same part of the ACC.

So we already know something about where our conscious feelings of wellbeing and pain are experienced. But how does our mental life affect the rest of our body?

How the Mind Affects the Body

The clearest effect of the mind on the body is its effect on **longevity**. In September 1932, the mother superior of the American School Sisters of Notre Dame decided that all new nuns should be asked to write an autobiographical sketch. These sketches were kept, and much later psychologists independently rated them by the amount of positive feeling they revealed. These ratings were then compared with how long each nun lived. Remarkably, the amount of positive feeling that a nun revealed in her twenties was an excellent predictor of how long she would live. Of the nuns who were still alive in 1991, only 21% of the most cheerful quarter died in the following nine years, compared with 55% of the least cheerful quarter of the nuns.[7] This shows how happiness can increase a person's length of life.

More recently, a random sample of English adults over 50 were asked questions about their happiness, and they were also asked whether they had been diagnosed with any long-term physical illness, such as heart disease, lung disease, cancer, diabetes or stroke.[8] They were followed for nine years to see if they died. The crude results are shown in Figure 5.1. The least happy third of them were three times more likely to die than the happiest third. And, even when controlling for all their initial physical illnesses, the least happy third were still some 50% more likely to die. Another study traced everybody in a Norwegian county over a six-year period. At the beginning, they were all diagnosed for their mental state and also asked other questions, such as whether they smoked cigarettes. Over the next six years, it turned out that diagnosed depression was as powerful a predictor of mortality as smoking was (Figure 5.2).[9]

What explains this effect of mood upon physical health? The clearest channel is through the effects of **stress**. The body has a mechanism that responds to stress in a similar way whether the stress is physical or mental. This is sometimes called the **'fight or flight'** response: our heart rate, blood pressure and breathing rate increase; we sweat more and our mouths go dry.

This response begins in the brain, which is linked to the rest of the body by two main sets of nerves. One set includes the sensory nerves and the motor nerves, which give conscious instructions to our limbs about what to do. But the other set is the 'autonomic nervous system', which is largely outside our conscious control and regulates the workings of all our internal organs.

The autonomic system has two main branches: the sympathetic and the para-sympathetic. It is the **sympathetic nervous system** that initiates the fight or flight

---

[7] Danner et al. (2001), Table 3, rows 5 and 8.   [8] Steptoe and Wardle (2012).
[9] Mykletun et al. (2009) Tables 1 and 2.

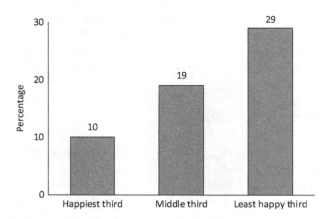

Figure 5.2 Percentage dying over the next nine years (People originally aged 50 and over)
Source: Andrew Steptoe. See also Steptoe and Wardle (2012)

response. It immediately instructs the adrenal gland to produce what Britons call **adrenaline** and Americans call **epinephrine**. This is a hormone (Greek for messenger) that enters the bloodstream and galvanises the whole body for action. It also mobilises the immune system to produce pro-inflammatory cytokines in case they are needed to handle possible infections. The **parasympathetic nervous system**, in contrast, calms the body. When it is active, the body's organs become less active. For example, in meditation or breathing exercises the vagus nerve is active in reducing the heart rate. But, so long as stress is maintained, it is the sympathetic system that is most active.

At the same time, a second hormone is produced in another part of the adrenal gland: **cortisol**. A message goes from the brain's hypothalamus to the pituitary gland to the adrenal gland, which releases cortisol into the bloodstream, and this then stimulates the muscles by releasing their store of glucose.

The stress response is totally functional when the stress is brief. But when the stress is persistent, it can lead to **over-activity of the immune system** (especially of C-reactive protein and IL6) and to persistent **inflammation** around the body, which eventually reduces life expectancy.[10] It also leads to more fibrinogen in the blood – intended to cause blood clots in a wound but unwanted in the longer term. In Western countries the most common sources of prolonged stress are psychological, and increased inflammation has been observed as a result of marital conflict, caring for demented relatives, social isolation, social disadvantage and depression.[11]

Another cause of stress with long-lasting effects is **child abuse**. One study followed children born in Dunedin, New Zealand. Those who had been abused in the first ten years of life had increased markers of inflammation twenty years later.[12]

---

[10] Murabito et al. (2018).   [11] Wilson et al. (2018).

[12] Danese et al. (2007). The inflammation index is based on an aggregate of high-sensitivity C-reactive protein, fibrinogen and white blood-cell count. See also Steptoe et al. (2007).

These findings on child abuse are confirmed in a meta-analysis of many comparable studies.[13] By contrast, optimism and purpose in life protect against coronary heart disease and stroke.[14]

Perhaps the simplest evidence of the effect of mind on body comes from a simple experiment. In it people were given a small **experimental wound**. Those who were depressed or anxious took the longest to recover.[15] In another experiment, people were given injections, and people in the greatest psychological distress developed the fewest antibodies.[16] Since we can affect the mind by psychological intervention, we can also affect the body that way. For example, mindfulness meditation reduces the level of pro-inflammatory cytokines.[17] It also increases the production of telomerase, which increases life-expectancy.[18]

Perhaps the most striking effect of the mind on the body is the **placebo effect**. For many diseases, up to 30% of people given a placebo pill (with no active ingredient) will recover.[19] People recover because they believe that they will.

So the mind has profound effects on the body. These are a major part of how our wellbeing is generated, and the different chemicals involved provide useful **biomarkers** of how our wellbeing is developing.

How the Body Can Affect the Mind

But there is also a stream of causation going in the opposite direction – from our body to our wellbeing. Bodily events can alter our mental state. Healthy living is vital for our mental wellbeing and this means plenty of exercise, enough sleep and good sense in drinking and eating.[20] Equally, physical illness and dementia reduce our wellbeing.

But one of the clearest examples of the effect of the body on the mind is the power of **drugs**, be they recreational or psychiatric. These work by affecting the operation of chemical **'neurotransmitters'**, which are crucial to the working of the brain. The brain consists of about 100 billion brain cells or neurons, and each neuron is connected to thousands of other neurons. Messages travel round the brain one neuron at a time. When that neuron 'fires', an electrochemical impulse travels from one end of the neuron to the other. But then it reaches a gap between that neuron and the next neuron. This gap is called a 'synapse' and the message is carried across the gap from the sending neuron to the receiving neuron by a chemical neurotransmitter.[21]

---

[13] Baumeister et al. (2016).

[14] Kubzansky et al. (2018) and references therein. See also Steptoe, Wardle and Marmot (2005) on the correlation of positive affect with reduced levels of neuroendocrine, inflammatory and cardiovascular activity.

[15] Kiecolt-Glaser et al. (1995). See also Cole-King and Harding (2001).   [16] Cohen et al. (2001).

[17] Cresswell et al. (2016).   [18] Schutte and Malouff (2014).   [19] Evans (2003).

[20] See Chapter 14. There is also growing evidence that the microbiome in our gut affects our mood. See Michels et al. (2019).

[21] The receiving neuron has 'receptors' designed to receive the neurotransmitter.

Table 5.1 Some recreational drugs and their effects

Effect	Drug	Effect on main neurotransmitters
Stimulant	Ecstasy (MDMA)	Increases serotonin
	Cocaine, amphetamines	Increases dopamine
	Nicotine	Mimics acetylcholine
Sedative/relaxant	Alcohol, barbiturates	Increases GABA
	Cannabis	Increases endocannabinoids*
Pain relief	Opiates (heroin, morphine)	Mimics endorphins**

* Can also increase dopamine, acting as a stimulant. **Endorphins are endogenous morphines, hence their name.

Table 5.2 Some psychiatric drugs and their effects

Problem	Drug	Neurotransmitter action
Depression	Prozac	Increases serotonin
Schizophrenia	Chlorpromazine	Reduces dopamine
ADHD	Ritalin	Increases dopamine
Anxiety	Diazepam	Increases GABA

So the different circuits in the brain are operated by different neurotransmitters:

- Serotonin produces a good mood.
- Dopamine and acetylcholine are neurotransmitters that stimulate (and can heighten) mental activity. (A 'high' feeling is generally associated with a rush of dopamine).
- GABA (gamma aminobutyric acid) and endocannabinoids reduce mental activity.
- Endorphins reduce pain.

Drugs affect the operation of a neurotransmitter. Some stimulate production of a neurotransmitter, others reduce its production, while others bind to the same receptors as some neurotransmitters and thus have a similar effect as the neurotransmitter that they mimic. Table 5.1 shows how the main **recreational drugs** alter our mental state, through the way in which they alter the operation of the neurotransmitters. Unfortunately, all these drugs can be addictive.[22]

There are, however, other drugs that can make people feel better: **psychiatric drugs**. These are generally less addictive. Table 5.2 shows some of the psychiatric drugs recommended for different psychiatric conditions. Take one example, Prozac. This is a psychiatric drug that increases the flow of serotonin and thus activity in the circuits that it serves. It does this by inhibiting the reuptake of serotonin, thus increasing the supply of serotonin and improving mood. In other words, it is a selective serotonin-reuptake inhibitor (SSRI). In many depressed patients, Prozac improves mood. Clearly dopamine is a tricky neurotransmitter: increasing it can be

---

[22] Whether they should therefore be banned is a separate issue. For one view on this, see Layard and Ward (2020) pp. 156–58.

stimulating, but an excess of dopamine leads to schizophrenia (and a deficiency of dopamine to Parkinson's disease). Like psychological therapy, psychiatric drugs do not always work. They are, however, strongly recommended for severe depression, where they achieve 50% recovery rates. But they have no effects on relapse unless they continue to be taken.

A key fact about the brain is the ease with which it can be altered by experience[23] – in other words, there is a high level of '**neuroplasticity**'. Blind people use part of their visual cortex to hear. And London taxi drivers have to remember so many streets and routes that they develop abnormally large hippocampal areas in their brains.[24] There are many places in this book where we shall report the effect of wellbeing interventions on brain activity.

How Our Genes Affect Our Wellbeing

The one part of our body that never changes is our **genes**. They were determined at the moment of our conception and, apart from mutations, we keep the same genes throughout our life. The same genes are present in the nucleus of nearly every cell in our body. It is the continuity in our genes that explains much of the continuity in our personality, our appearance and our behaviour over our life.

But how do we know this, and how far do differences in our genes explain the differences in wellbeing in the population? To explore these questions, we shall proceed this way.

(1) We shall examine twins and show that identical twins (with the same genes) are much more similar to each other in wellbeing than non-identical twins are (with many different genes).
(2) We shall look at adopted children and show that they still resemble their biological parents in many ways.
(3) We shall show that the genes and the environment do not have independent effects on our wellbeing – they interact. Therefore, it is not possible to say in any meaningful way how much of the spread of wellbeing is due to differences in genes and how much to differences in environment.
(4) We shall describe the pioneering search for the specific genes that affect wellbeing.
(5) Finally, we shall examine the inter-relation between genes, personality and wellbeing.

Evidence from twins

To see that genes matter we have only to look at the following data on Norwegian middle-aged, same-sex twins (see Table 5.3). Some of the twins are **identical**: both

---

[23] Dahl et al. (2020).   [24] Maguire et al. (2000).

Table 5.3 Correlation in life satisfaction between each twin and his/her co-twin (Norwegian adults in mid-life)

Identical twins	0.31
Non-identical twins	0.15
Difference	0.16

Source: Roysamb et al. (2018)

come from the same egg. They therefore have the same genes and look more-or-less identical. The other sets of twins are **non-identical**: each twin comes from a separate egg. So half her genes are the same as her co-twin's but half are different (just as is the case with any other pair of siblings).[25] And what a difference that makes! As Table 5.3 shows, if the twins are identical, their life satisfaction is fairly similar (with a correlation across the 2 twins of 0.31). But if the twins are non-identical, their enjoyment of life is much less similar (with an across-twin correlation of only 0.15).

What could account for this difference? Clearly it must be because the identical twins have genes that are more similar. Even though both sets of twins were raised together, their final wellbeing was very different. This suggests that the family environment has a smaller influence than many people suppose.

Countless twin studies testify to the effect of our genes not only on our wellbeing but also on our mental health. For example, if you are bipolar and you are an identical twin, then the chance that your co-twin is also bipolar is 55%. (That is the degree of 'concordance'.) But, if your co-twin is not identical, the chance is only 7%.[26] Thus if someone has bipolar disorder, the risk to the co-twin is a huge 48 points higher (55%–7%) if the co-twin is identical rather than non-identical. Figure 5.3 gives comparable numbers for many other types of mental illness. In every case, the difference is substantial. That is an astonishing testimony to the power of genes.

Evidence from adopted children

A different approach to the same issue is to look at **adopted children** and ask, Are they more similar to their adoptive parents or to their biological parents? Until the 1960s it was assumed (largely due to Freud) that mental illness was chiefly caused by how our parents behaved. But in 1961, Leonard Heston of Oregon University

---

[25] At each gene locus, I have 2 representations of the gene (2 'alleles'). One came from my father and 1 from my mother. For the same reason my father also had 2 alleles at that locus. But I only got 1 of my father's 2 alleles. Which of the 2 I got was randomly determined. The same is true of my sibling. Thus if I got any particular allele, the chance that my sibling also got it was ½. So we have half our father's alleles in common. The same is true of the alleles we got from our mother. Thus ordinary siblings 'have roughly half their genes in common'. But identical twins come from the same egg and have all their genes in common. (This analysis applies to those genes that differ between people, the so-called polymorphic genes. These genes comprise about a quarter of all our genes; the other three-quarters are the same for all humans.)

[26] Plomin et al. (2013) p. 246.

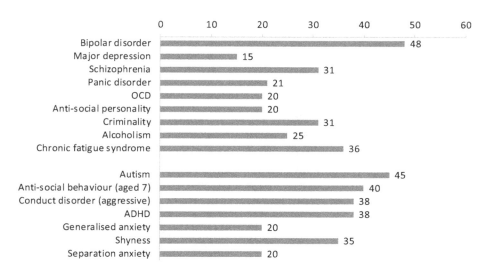

Figure 5.3 Difference between identical and non-identical twins in the concordance between twin and co-twin
Source: Plomin et al. (2013) pp. 245, 249, 251, 252, 259, 265, 290
Note: For each condition, we calculate the concordance for identical same-sex twins and for non-identical same-sex twins and report the difference. For OCD, alcoholism and all childhood conditions except autism, we give the difference in co-twins' correlation (on a continuous measure). For rare binary conditions, the concordance and the correlation are very similar

published his classic paper on schizophrenia. Heston studied adopted children and what he found was remarkable. One per cent of these adopted children became schizophrenic (the same as other children) – unless their biological mother was schizophrenic. But in that case 10% became schizophrenic. So it was the mother's genes that made the difference rather than the behaviour of their live-in adoptive parents. And in fact, if you had a mother with schizophrenia, you were no more likely to become schizophrenic if you lived with her than if you did not.[27] Not all adoptive studies are as striking as Heston's. For depression and anxiety disorder, they yield less striking results. But they are not inconsistent with the evidence from the twin studies that we have just looked at.[28]

When studying wellbeing, a key source of evidence has been the Minnesota Twin Registry, which includes twins who were raised together and twins who were raised apart (as adoptees). The study showed that identical twins raised apart were much more similar in wellbeing (r = 0.48) than non-identical twins brought up by their biological parents (r = 0.23).[29] This again underscores the importance of genetic factors.

---

[27] Layard and Clark (2014).   [28] Plomin et al. (2013) chapter 6.

[29] Tellegen et al. (1988). Wellbeing was measured by indicators of positive affect. For identical twins raised together the correlation was 0.58 – not much higher than for identical twins raised apart.

Heritability

A natural question now is to ask What fraction of the variance of wellbeing across individuals is due to the genes?[30] In other words, what is the **heritability** of wellbeing? Questions on heritability are usually answered using some strong assumptions, which we will question later.

We assume an additive model with (in its simplest form) two components – G for the genetic component and E for the environmental component. Thus wellbeing (W) is determined by $W = G + E$. It follows that the variance of wellbeing equals the variance of the genetic component plus the variance of the environmental component plus twice the covariance of the genetic component and the environmental component:

$$\text{Var}\ (W) = \text{Var}\ (G) + \text{Var}\ (E) + 2\ \text{Cov}\ (G, E)$$

Crucially, in behavioural genetics this **covariance is considered to be due to the genes**. But in truth, it can be as much due to the environment as to the genes. For while it is certainly true that people with good genes are skilful at finding good environments, it is equally true that in most societies good environments are more receptive to people with good genes.[31] So the first arbitrary assumption in behavioural genetics is that individual outcomes related to genes are caused by genes. The second arbitrary assumption (to which we shall return) is that there are **no gene-environment interactions**.[32]

But if we wish away these two problems, we can show that the heritability of a trait (like wellbeing) equals twice the difference between the correlation of the trait across identical twins and its correlation across non-identical twins.[33] So if we use the numbers in Table 5.1, the heritability of life satisfaction is 2 (0.31−0.15) = 32%. This is a typical estimate of the heritability of life satisfaction obtained from twin studies worldwide.[34]

Genes and environment

So the genes really matter. But so does the environment that we experience. In fact, the environment is generally more important. Even with the most heritable mental trait that we know of (bipolar disorder) only just over a half of the co-twins of bipolar people also have the condition. And for most conditions it is much less.

Moreover, genes do not operate on their own, with the environment just adding further effects. Rather, the genes and the environment interact, with the genes

---

[30] This clearly depends on the structure of the environment. For example, when educational opportunity improved in Britain after WWII, the heritability of school performance increased dramatically (Haworth et al. 2016).

[31] Wootton et al. (2017).

[32] See Plomin et al. (2013) p. 401 for an explanation of how difficult the concept of heritability then becomes.

[33] For derivation, see Annex 5.1 (from Layard and Clark 2014).

[34] Bartels (2015); Roysamb et al. (2018); Van der Weijer et al. (2020). By contrast, the heritability of height is some 90% and of Body Mass Index 70% (Plomin et al. [2013]).

Table 5.4 Chances of onset of major depression within the month following a severely stressful life event

Condition of co-twin	Chances of depression within the month(%)
Co-twin depressed and identical	14
Co-twin depressed and non-identical	12
Co-twin non-depressed and non-identical	8
Co-twin non-depressed and identical	6

influencing the effect that the environment has on us and vice versa. This we can see clearly in the following study of the impact of negative life events on a sample of twins in Virginia.[35] Negative life events included the death of a loved one, divorce/separation and assault. And the issue was how frequently did those people who had a negative event experience a major depression in the subsequent month?

Therefore, for each individual the study measured

(i)   what negative events they experienced,
(ii) whether major depression followed within a month and
(iii) the mental health and relatedness of the individual's co-twin.

As Table 5.4 shows, a person was **more** likely to experience a major depression if their co-twin was depressed (especially an identical twin who was). And they were **less** likely to be depressed if their co-twin was non-depressed (especially if it was an identical twin). This is a clear case where people have bad experiences but the effect depends also on how far their genes predispose them to depression.

Evidence of such interaction is ubiquitous. For example, in one study of adopted children anti-social behaviour was more common in adolescents if their adoptive parents were anti-social. But the effect was greater still when the biological parents were also anti-social.[36]

There is however some encouraging news. As we have seen, people with unfavourable genetic predispositions respond worse to bad events than other people do, but they also **respond better** to good events.[37] For example, children who carry the unfavourable variant of the gene most closely related to depression can respond better to CBT than other children do.[38]

The interaction between genes and environment in determining wellbeing should not come as a surprise. For such interactions are also common in physical health. A classic case is the disease known as phenylketonuria (which produces mental retardation). To get the disease requires two things:

- First, you need the unfavourable gene.
- Second, you have to eat phenylalanine, which is present in many foods.

[35] Kendler et al. (1995).   [36] Cadoret et al. (1995).
[37] On the 'differential sensitivity' hypothesis, see Belsky (2016); and Pluess (2015).
[38] The serotonin gene. See Eley et al. (2012).

If you avoid the foods, you don't get the disease.[39] So, even for people with unfavourable genes, we can greatly improve their lot by improving the environment.

Evidence from DNA

The previous discussion does not rely on any actual data on genes – you just compare the wellbeing of different pairs of twins or adoptees. But today we can sequence the actual **DNA** that each individual carries. There are millions of positions on the string of genetic material, and at each position, one of three variations is present. These variations are known as **Single Nucleotide Polymorphisms** (or SNPs, pronounced Snips). With the aid of this information we are able to get more direct evidence on the roles of genes.

For wellbeing, a comprehensive study of 11,500 unrelated people and over half a million SNPs assessed the genetic similarity of every possible pair of people in the sample. By relating this to the difference in their wellbeing, it showed that people's genes (treated as additive) explained 5–10% of the variance in their wellbeing. This is a minimum estimate since it omits the effect of any interaction between different genes.[40]

A different and potentially important endeavour is to discover which specific genes make the most difference, through **genome-wide-association studies** (GWAS), which look for the effects of each gene upon the trait in question. The first pioneering study was able to find three SNPs that passed the test of significant effects on wellbeing.[41] Each SNP explained 0.01% of the variance of wellbeing. A more recent study has been able to identify 148 significant SNPs, which together explain 0.9% of the variance. This is partly due to larger sample size and precise measurement of the outcome, and further work will then further increase our understanding.[42]

The conclusion is that there is no single gene for happiness, or even a small number of genes. Instead, thousands or more genes are involved, interacting in complicated ways with each other and with the environment. Taken together, these genes predispose people to more or less happy lives.

Personality and Wellbeing

As we have seen, an important way in which genes affect our wellbeing is through our mental health. But a more general way is through all aspects of our personality.

---

[39] Plomin et al. (2013). One particular form of gene-environment interaction is epigenetics. This occurs when environmental factors determine whether a gene gets 'expressed' or not (e.g., methylation in a gene's promoter region prevents the gene having any effect).

[40] Rietveld et al. (2013). This is equivalent to the share of explained variance in a multiple regression of wellbeing on all the SNPs. After allowing for measurement error the estimate rises to 12–18%.

[41] Okbay et al. (2016). The test of significance is demanding because it has to take into account the problem of multiple testing.

[42] Baselmans et al. (2019). A meta-analysis by Jamshidi et al. (2020) estimates heritability based on GWAS to be between approximately 0.5% and 1.5%.

Table 5.5 Correlation between twins and their co-twins in various aspects of personality (Norwegian adults in mid-life)

	Identical twins	Non-identical twins
Neuroticism	0.56	0.27
Extraversion	0.46	0.27

Source: Roysamb et al. (2018)

Psychologists find that much of the variation in character that we experience in those we encounter can be described by five dimensions. These are Openness, Conscientiousness, Extroversion, Agreeableness and Neuroticism (which spell **OCEAN**). Some of these dimensions appear to be poorly correlated with our life satisfaction. But two are highly correlated with life satisfaction. These are neuroticism (as you might expect from our earlier analysis) but also extroversion. So, if we revert to the mid-life Norwegian twins we discussed at the beginning of the chapter, personality overall explains about a third of the variance in wellbeing. And personality itself is partly determined by our genes (see Table 5.5). So a significant part of the heritability of wellbeing comes from the heritability of personality.

This said, it is crucially important to recognise that personality (like wellbeing) varies substantially over the life course. Not only do we on average become more conscientious, agreeable and emotionally balanced over time, but we also become less open and less extrovert. And we also change a lot relative to our contemporaries – due to differences in how life treats us.[43] Genes are important, but from now on we concentrate on the effect of what policy-makers **can** affect – namely our experience of the environment in which we live.

Conclusions

(1) Self-reported wellbeing is correlated with activity in a number of brain areas. The sensation of pain is most clearly experienced in the anterior cingulate cortex (ACC), which registers both physical pain and social pain.
(2) The mind affects the body. Wellbeing predicts mortality as well as smoking does. Prolonged psychological stress leads to excessive production of adrenaline/ epinephrine and cortisol, over-activity of the immune system and excessive inflammation in the body. Mindfulness meditation reduces these effects and increases life-expectancy.
(3) The body affects the mind. The most obvious effects are those of drugs, recreational and psychiatric.

---

[43] Specht et al. (2011).

(4) Genes have important effects on our wellbeing. We know this in two ways.
- Identical twins (who have identical genes) are much more similar to each other in their wellbeing than are non-identical twins (who share only 50% of their genes).
- Adopted children are more similar in mental health to their biological parents than to the parents who raised them.
  It is important that parents and professionals realise the importance of these genetic effects and do not automatically blame parents' behaviour for the problems of their children.
(5) It is, however, not possible to neatly separate the effects of the genes and the environment for two reasons:
- Genes and environment often interact in their effects on wellbeing.
- Genes and the environment are correlated, and there is no simple way to apportion that part of the variance of wellbeing that comes from the covariance of genes and the environment.

And we should never assume that, because a problem is partly genetic in origin, it cannot be treated as effectively as one that is primarily environmental.[44]

This completes our review of some basic processes common to all humans – our behaviours, thinking styles, physical processes and genes. It is time to turn to the impact on us of specific features of our experience.

Questions for discussion

(1) Does the evidence from the brain make people's self-reports any more credible?
(2) How important is the mind in explaining physical health?
(3) How far can drugs of all kinds improve our wellbeing?
(4) Does it help to know how far a person's wellbeing is affected by their genes? In what ways might it help?
(5) What does it mean to say that for most purposes genes and environment interact to determine character?
(6) Why is it so difficult to say what proportion of the variance of wellbeing is due to the genes?
(7) If something significantly influenced by genes, is it automatically more difficult to change than something mainly due to the environment?

---

[44] Haworth and Davis (2014).

Further Reading

On Brain Measurement

Eisenberger, N. I., Lieberman, M. D., and Williams, K. D. (2003). Does rejection hurt? An fMRI study of social exclusion. *Science*, 302(5643), 290–292.

On Effects of Mental Wellbeing on the Body

Kiecolt-Glaser J. K., Marucha P. T., Malarkey W. B., Mercado A. M., and Glaser R. (1995). Slowing of wound healing by psychological stress. *Lancet*, 346 (8984), 1194–1196.
Steptoe, A., and Wardle J. (2012). Enjoying life and living longer. *Archives of Internal Medicine*, 172(3), 273–275.
Wilson, S. J., Woody, A., and Kiecolt-Glaser, J. K. (2018). Inflammation as a biomarker method in lifespan developmental methodology. In Braddick, O. (Ed). *Oxford Research Encyclopedia of Psychology*. Oxford University Press.

On Brain Plasticity

Dahl, C. J., Wilson-Mendenhall, C. D., and Davidson, R. J. (2020). The plasticity of well-being: A training-based framework for the cultivation of human flourishing. *Proceedings of the National Academy of Sciences*, 117(51), 32197–32206.

On Genes

Røysamb, E., Nes, R. B., Czajkowski, N. O., and Vassend, O. (2018). Genetics, personality and wellbeing. A twin study of traits, facets and life satisfaction. *Scientific Reports*, 8(1), 1–13.
Van de Weijer, M., de Vries, L., and Bartels, M. (2020). *Happiness and Wellbeing: The Value and Findings from Genetic Studies*. Mimeo.

Part III

How Our Experience Affects Our Wellbeing

INEQUALITEA

6 The Inequality of Wellbeing
Some Basic Facts

Facts do not cease to exist because they are ignored.

Aldous Huxley

It is time to move on to the central issue of this book: how our experience affects our wellbeing. The starting point is the huge inequality that exists in wellbeing – both within countries and between them. This is the most fundamental inequality there is – the inequality in the overall quality of life as people experience it. So we begin with the key facts about the level and distribution of wellbeing in the world.

The Level and Inequality of Wellbeing in the World

The best evidence we have on the **worldwide distribution of wellbeing** comes from the Gallup World Poll. This remarkable survey happens every year and covers nearly every country in the world. Around a thousand adults are surveyed in each country each year. They are selected to be as representative as possible of the population in each country, and, when necessary, the results are re-weighted to be as representative as possible. The interviews are conducted face to face in the poorer countries (at least before COVID-19) and by telephone in the richer ones.

The main wellbeing question is what is known as the 'Cantril ladder' that we described in Chapter 1.[1] In the years when Gallup also asked about life satisfaction, the answers to both questions were very closely correlated.[2] So we can think of the Cantril ladder as a standard evaluative question about wellbeing.

In Chapter 1, we already showed the averages for the different countries. But more important than differences between countries are differences between people. So Figure 6.1 shows the worldwide distribution of individual adult wellbeing before COVID-19, each individual being given equal weight. The spread is very wide – over

---

[1] 'Please imagine a ladder with steps numbered from zero at the bottom to ten at the top. Suppose we say that the top of the ladder represents the best possible life for you and the bottom of the ladder represents the worst possible life for you. On which step of the ladder do you feel you personally stand at the present time?' The response categories range from 0 (Worst possible life) to 10 (Best possible life).

[2] Across countries the correlation of average Cantril rank and average life satisfaction rank is r = 0.94. See Helliwell and Wang (2012) p. 14.

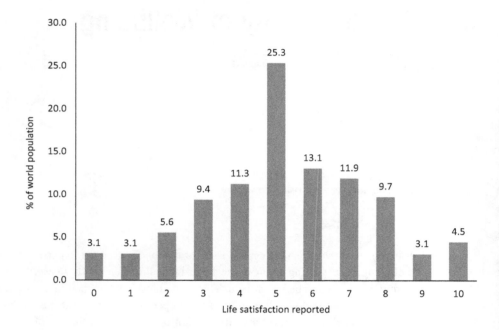

Figure 6.1 Percentage of people in the world at each level of life satisfaction
Source: Helliwell et al. (2018a) Figure 2.1 From Gallup World Poll 2015–17, Cantril ladder

a sixth of the world's population answer 3 or below, while over a sixth answer 8 or above. This must be one of the most basic facts about the human condition on earth today.

There is also another way of showing this huge spread of wellbeing – the same facts laid out differently. In Figure 6.2, we break the population down into ten groups of equal size, starting with those who are the least happy on the left of the graph and ending on the right with those who are happiest. As the graph shows, the least happy have an average wellbeing of 1.1 points and the happiest have a wellbeing of 9.2 points. It is a world with many lives that are limited and a few that are truly flourishing. The average wellbeing in the world before COVID-19 was 5.3 points (out of 10) but the spread, as measured by the standard deviation, was 2.3 points.[3]

But how much of this huge spread of wellbeing in the world is due to the spread between countries, and how much of it occurs within countries? The neatest way to answer this question is by taking the square of the standard deviation, known as the variance. We can then partition the variance of individual wellbeing worldwide into two elements:

- differences within countries and
- differences between countries.

---

[3] The standard deviation of a variable X_j with N observations is $\sigma_j = \sqrt{\frac{\sum(x_{ij}-\bar{x}_j)^2}{N}}$ in other words it is the square root of the mean squared deviation from the mean (or 'the root mean squared deviation'). The variance is σ_j^2. For country data on wellbeing inequality see Annex 6.1.

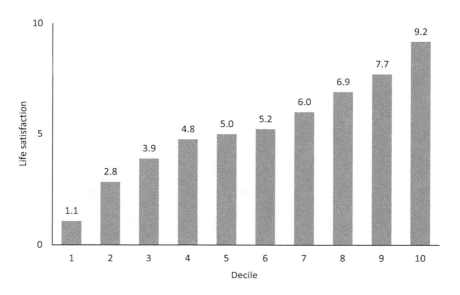

Figure 6.2 Life satisfaction (0–10) of people at each decile of life satisfaction
Source: Gallup World Poll 2015–17, Cantril ladder

It turns out that the difference between countries contributes only 22% of the overall variance and the main variation (78%) is within countries.[4] Thus the standard deviation of average wellbeing across countries is about 1.1, while the average of the standard deviation inside a country is about 2.3.

Changes Over Time

It is easy to think that we live in a peculiarly dreadful time. But this is not so, judged by the criterion of wellbeing. There are indeed some countries in which wellbeing declined between 2005–2008 and 2016–2018.[5] These include the United States, India, Egypt, Brazil, Mexico, Venezuela, South Africa and those affected by civil war. But there are as many countries where wellbeing has risen since 2005–2008 as where it has fallen. Countries where wellbeing rose include both China and most of the countries that were once Communist. Earlier on, between 1980 and 2007, wellbeing

---

[4] Helliwell and Wang (2012) p. 16. If W_{ij} is the wellbeing of the ith person in the jth country, the variance is the mean squared deviation from the overall mean. It is given by

$$\sum\sum \left(W_{ij} - \bar{W}\right)^2 = \sum\sum \left(W_{ij} - \bar{W}_j + \bar{W}_j - \bar{W}\right)^2$$

all divided by the number of people. Since the first and second terms are independent of each other, this equals $\sum\sum \left(W_{ij} - \bar{W}_j\right)^2 + \sum\sum \left(\bar{W}_j - \bar{W}\right)^2$, both divided by the number of people.

[5] Helliwell et al. (2019) figure 2.8.

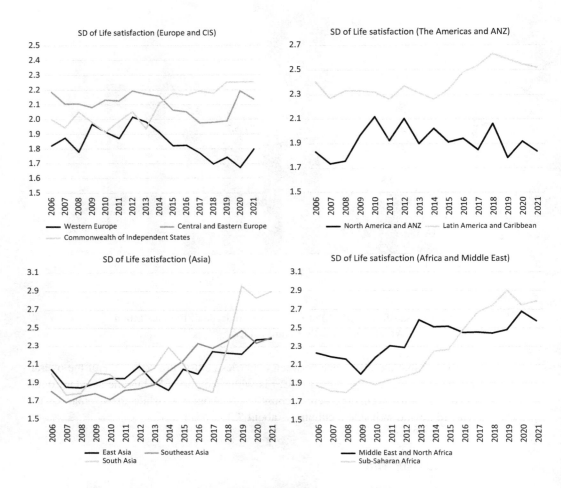

Figure 6.3 Trends in the inequality of life satisfaction (0–10) (Standard deviations)
Source: Helliwell et al. (2019) figure 2.6 Gallup World Poll 2006–18

rose in more countries than not.[6] On balance, therefore, the world as a whole is probably as happy as it has ever been.[7]

But progress in wellbeing is by no means automatic, and it is noteworthy that in some important countries, wellbeing is now no higher than it was when records began. In the United States, that means in the 1950s; in West Germany, it means in the 1970s; and in China, it means 1990. We shall discuss this issue more fully in Chapter 13.

By contrast, if we look at short-term changes in wellbeing over the business cycle, wellbeing generally fluctuates up and down around its trend – higher in the boom and lower in the slump. We shall also discuss this issue at length in Chapter 13.

---

[6] Sacks et al. (2010) figure 8.
[7] For powerful discussions of some of the reasons for progress in human happiness, see Pinker (2018); and Rosling (2019).

Meanwhile, how has the inequality of wellbeing been changing over time? In most countries, it rose between 2006 and 2018 with especially sharp rises in North America and Sub-Saharan Africa, which now have the highest levels of regional inequality (see Figure 6.3). However, wellbeing inequality fell in Europe, which now has the lowest levels of wellbeing inequality in the world.

Hedonic Measures of Wellbeing

The analysis so far is based on the Cantril ladder. The Gallup World Poll also asks questions about people's **emotions** – the hedonic measures of wellbeing that we discussed in Chapter 1. These questions give useful information about changes over time. At the world level, one can construct an index of positive and negative emotion, based on the question 'Did you experience X during a lot of the day yesterday?' For positive emotions, X includes separate questions about happiness, enjoyment, and smiling or laughing. These can be combined into a single index by taking the average proportion of people who said Yes to each question. Similarly for negative emotions – where the questions relate to worry, sadness and anger. Figure 6.4 shows trends at the world level for both positive emotion and negative emotion. As the figure shows, positive affect and the Cantril ladder have been trending down slightly. But negative affect has increased greatly – especially worry. This is confirmed by an additional question on stress where we reproduce the answers for the United States, Western Europe and the world as a whole in Figure 6.5. These findings are deeply troubling. But for the rest of this chapter, we shall revert to measures based on the Cantril ladder.

Differences Between Groups

So how does average wellbeing differ between groups?

Men and women

Remarkably, the distribution of wellbeing in the world is almost identical for **men and women**. Women are on average slightly happier than men but the difference is only 0.09 points (out of 10) – one fiftieth of the difference between the happiest and least happy country. Moreover, in almost every country the average wellbeing of men and women is nearly the same, even though wellbeing differs so hugely between countries (see Figure 6.6).[8]

But what about trends in the relative happiness of men and women? Over the last 50 years, women's rights in the workplace have been transformed in many countries by legislation requiring equal pay and equal job opportunities. At the same time,

---

[8] For the underlying numbers see online Annex 6.2. For further details see Fortin et al. (2015).

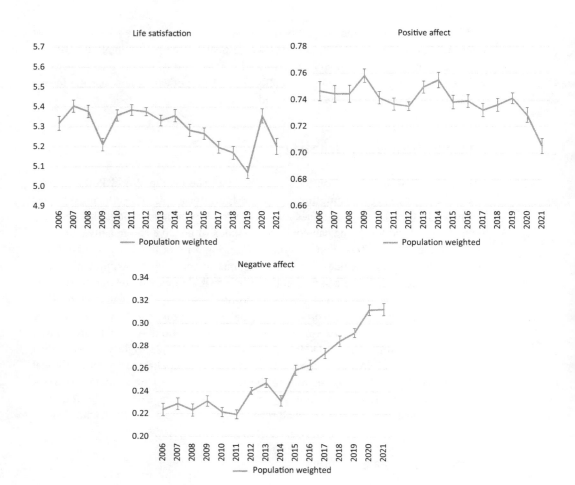

Figure 6.4 Trends in average wellbeing in the world
Source: Helliwell et al. (2019) p. 14, Gallup World Poll 2006–18; life satisfaction = Cantril ladder; for definition of positive and negative affect, see text

women have made huge educational advances relative to men, and through the contraceptive pill have achieved unprecedented control over their fertility. So one might expect that women's wellbeing would have risen relative to men's. But has it?[9]

In the United States since the 1970s, both men and women have become less happy, and this has been especially true of white women. In Europe, the situation has been different. Both women and men have become on average more satisfied with their lives, but European women's happiness has fallen relative to men's – and this has happened in all 12 countries for which the time series go back as far as the 1970s.

[9] This analysis is based on Stevenson and Wolfers (2009); and Blanchflower and Oswald (2019b).

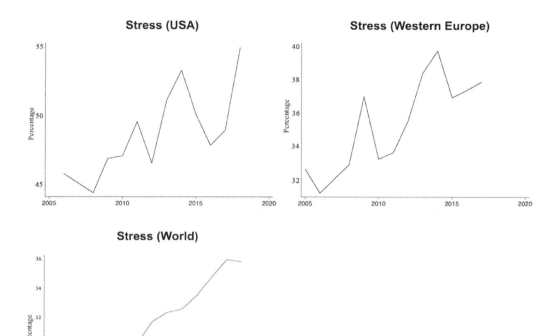

Figure 6.5 Trends in stress (Percentage saying 'I experienced a lot of stress yesterday')
Source: Gallup World Poll 2006–18

Why is this?[10] Empirical work has so far failed to produce an explanation. The most likely one (so basic to humans) is social comparisons. As more and more women work, they may increasingly compare themselves with their male colleagues (rather than with other women). And at work women are still frequently at a disadvantage. Another possibility is that women now experience a greater conflict of roles (as compared with men). The US evidence suggests that (up to 2005 at least) there was no change in women's total work relative to men's (total time spent in paid work, housework and childcare).[11] But that is not the same as the sense of responsibility. Women still do more work at home than men, and to that has been added much greater responsibilities at work. Another possibility is family conflict. In the United States, both men and women have become less satisfied with their marriages – and to an equal extent. But satisfaction with marriage affects women's happiness more than men's,

---

[10] For a fuller discussion, see Stevenson and Wolfers (2009).
[11] Krueger (2007). For multi-country evidence see Gimenez-Nadal and Sevilla (2012).

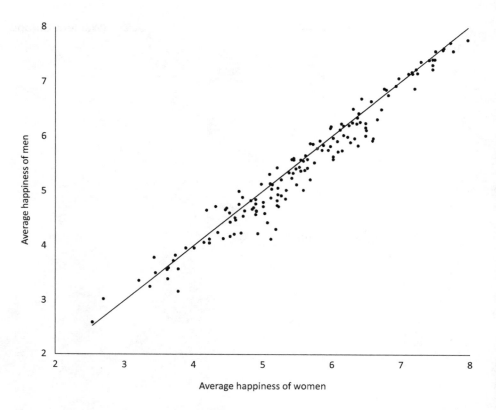

Figure 6.6 Average wellbeing of men and women: By country (the line represents equality)
Source: Gallup World Poll 2017–19, Cantril ladder

and increased dissatisfaction with marriage therefore helps to explain the increased gender gap in US happiness.[12] Finally, there is the enduring fact of male chauvinism. Though this may have diminished over time, the experience of it may have become more intolerable – as the #MeToo movement testifies.

Age

The next issue is Do we become happier as we get older? The effects of aging involve many factors but social factors are among them. As we move into adult life, we take on more responsibility, both in family life and at work. But after some time, we become more established, and any children we had leave home. We relax more. But eventually our health declines. So what is the overall effect of our journey through life?[13]

---

[12] Stevenson and Wolfers (2009).
[13] This whole section is based on Fortin et al. (2015). What we report comes from cross-sectional data. But longitudinal data typically confirm it (e.g. Cheng et al. 2017).

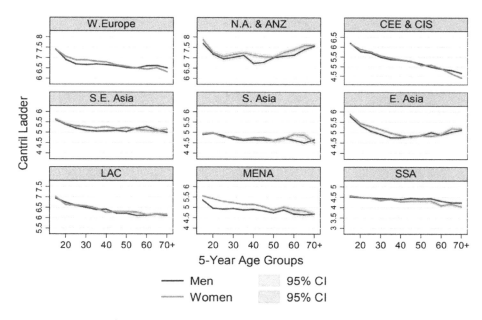

Figure 6.7 Average life satisfaction: by age, gender and region
Source: Fortin et al. (2015) Gallup World Poll 2004–14, Cantril ladder
Note: NA & ANZ = North America, Australia and New Zealand. CEE & CIS = Central and Eastern Europe and former Soviet Union. LAC = Latin America and Caribbean. MENA = Middle East and North Africa. SSA = Sub-Saharan Africa

In most countries, people on average become progressively less happy from their late teens up to their 40s. But then in some countries (including the United States and the UK), they become happier again up to their 70s (before a final decline). Figure 6.7 shows how wellbeing changes over life in each of the world's regions. Everywhere happiness declines up to around age 40. It then recovers in North America and to a lesser extent in East Asia; in Western Europe, it remains stable; but elsewhere, there are some further declines. (In the former Soviet Union and Warsaw Pact countries the old are markedly less happy, but this is the legacy of the transition and may not continue in future decades).

So what explains these patterns of **wellbeing over the life-course**? If age affects wellbeing, it must be through some mediating variables.[14] But what are they? The first step is to look at the standard variables explaining wellbeing, which we shall consider in Chapter 8. From 20 to 40 years old, most of these variables are moving in the direction that would produce higher wellbeing. So they provide little insight into variation across the life-course.[15]

---

[14] Somewhat differently, Blanchflower and Oswald (2019a) argue that there is intrinsic interest in the pattern of age differences after the effect of all observables has been removed.

[15] See Frijters and Beatton (2012).

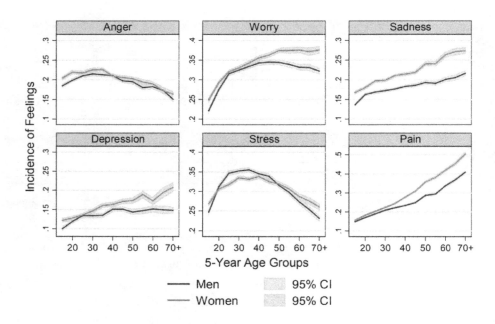

Figure 6.8 Negative Experiences: By age and gender (World)
Source: Fortin et al (2015) Gallup World Poll 2004–14; for questions, see text

More light can be found by looking at the Gallup World Poll's evidence on affect. As we have mentioned, this provides data on negative and positive affect. Beginning with negative emotions (Figure 6.8), stress rises sharply up to middle age and then declines. So does anger, though less markedly. These declines after middle age are especially marked in North America and Western Europe. By contrast, worry, sadness, depression and pain rise steadily through life, but as time passes they become balanced by declining stress and anger. Turning to positive emotions (Figure 6.9), happiness, enjoyment, smiling and interest fall steadily throughout life. In addition, as people age, they are less likely to report that they have someone they can rely on in times of need. People do however feel more rested.

Ethnic differences

What about the differences between **ethnic groups**? In every society, most minority ethnic groups have lower average wellbeing than the majority group. But these differences can be reduced or even eliminated by policy action, such as

- reducing gaps in education and income,
- banning discrimination in employment and housing,
- punishing severely both racially motivated crime and incitement to racial hatred and
- improving the respect shown to all (by citizens, by the police, and by the law).

With such action, things can change. For example, the United States has seen substantial improvement in the wellbeing of ethnic minorities, while at the same time

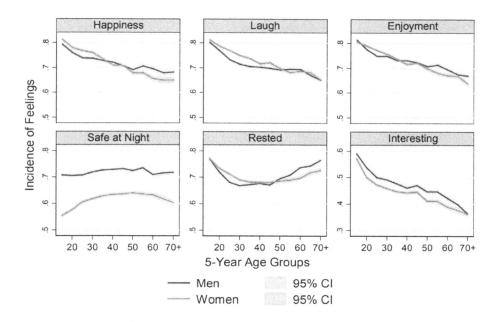

Figure 6.9 Positive Experiences: By age and gender (World)
Source: Fortin et al (2015) Gallup World Poll 2004–14; see text; 'laugh' means 'laugh or smile'

the average wellbeing of whites has declined.[16] This is shown in Figure 6.10, which is based on the General Social Survey. (The happiness scores used are very happy – 3; pretty happy – 2; not too happy – 1.) As Figure 6.10 shows, the gap in happiness between white and black citizens has fallen sharply.[17]

However, America still has serious ethnic problems, as the Black Lives Matter movement testifies. And so have most other countries, though the groups involved differ widely. In some countries, ethnic tensions lead to civil war.

The Wellbeing of Children

So much for adults; but what about **children**? In both 2015 and 2018, the OECD surveyed the wellbeing of 15-year-olds in their regular Programme for International Student Assessment (PISA). The question asked was on life satisfaction (0–10) and the survey covered most OECD countries and a number of others. The results by country are in Table 6.1.

As can be seen, among the OECD countries the lowest levels of satisfaction were in Turkey, the UK and Japan. The United States was also near the bottom of the list. As

---

[16] In the last decade, the same is true of the gap in life expectancy, see Case and Deaton (2020).
[17] The improvements from the 1970s to 2010 cannot be explained by changes in objective circumstances, see Stevenson and Wolfers (2008).

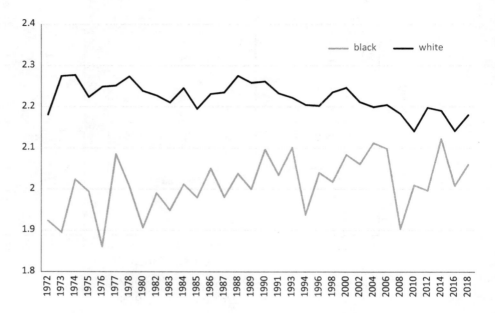

Figure 6.10 Average wellbeing (1–3) of different racial groups in the United States
Source: Blanchflower and Oswald (2019b) updated; General Social Survey

so often found, Finland was near the top. Among non-OECD countries, satisfaction was noticeably high in Latin America and post-Communist countries. In most countries, 15-year-old boys were on average happier than 15-year-old girls, with 72% reporting scores of 7 or above compared with only 61% for girls. In most countries, satisfaction was higher among young people from advantaged backgrounds and slightly higher for people from non-immigrant households.

Over time, between 2015 and 2018, young people became less satisfied in every country surveyed (except South Korea). This is a remarkable fact. The average fell by 0.3 points (from 7.3 to 7.0). But the fall was particularly striking in the UK (0.8 points) and in the United States, Japan and Ireland (0.6 points).

Life Expectancy and WELLBYs

Finally, we need to bring into play a completely different dimension – the length of life. As we argued in Chapter 2, the ultimate test of a society's success is not only the wellbeing that people experience but also the number of years for which they experience it. In other words, what we care about is the number of Wellbeing-Years (or WELLBYs) per person born.[18]

There is, of course, no direct and meaningful way of measuring, at a point in time, the length of people's lives. But statisticians measure life-expectancy at a

---

[18] For a given individual, this equals $\sum W_t = \bar{W}Y$ where $\bar{W}$ is average wellbeing per year and Y is years of life.

Table 6.1 Average life satisfaction of 15-year-olds (0–10)

OECD Countries		Other countries	
Mexico	8.11	Kazakhstan	8.76
Colombia	7.62	Albania	8.61
Finland	7.61	Kosovo	8.30
Lithuania	7.61	North Macedonia	8.16
Netherlands	7.50	Belarus	8.10
Switzerland	7.38	Dominican Republic	8.09
Spain	7.35	Ukraine	8.03
Iceland	7.34	Costa Rica	7.96
Slovak Republic	7.22	Saudi Arabia	7.95
Estonia	7.19	Panama	7.92
France	7.19	Romania	7.87
Latvia	7.16	Bosnia and Herzegovina	7.84
Austria	7.14	Croatia	7.69
Portugal	7.13	Montenegro	7.69
Hungary	7.12	Moldova	7.68
Luxembourg	7.04	Thailand	7.64
Chile	7.03	Serbia	7.61
Germany	7.02	Georgia	7.60
Sweden	7.01	Uruguay	7.54
Greece	6.99	Indonesia	7.47
Czech Republic	6.91	Vietnam	7.47
Italy	6.91	Russia	7.32
Slovenia	6.86	Peru	7.31
United States	6.75	Argentina	7.26
Ireland	6.74	Baku (Azerbaijan)	7.24
Poland	6.74	Philippines	7.21
Korea	6.52	Bulgaria	7.15
Japan	6.18	Brazil	7.05
United Kingdom	6.16	Malaysia	7.04
Turkey	5.62	Morocco	6.95
		Jordan	6.88
		United Arab Emirates	6.88
		Qatar	6.84
		Lebanon	6.67
		China	6.64
		Malta	6.56
		Chinese Taipei	6.52
		Hong Kong (China)	6.27
		Macao (China)	6.07
		Brunei Darussalam	5.80

Source: OECD PISA 2018 Volume III, figure III.11.1

point of time as the years a person born now would live if age-specific mortality rates remained as they are now. So a natural measure of the current success of a society is given by

Current social welfare = Average current wellbeing × Life expectancy

Table 6.2 Trends in wellbeing, life expectancy and social welfare

	Average wellbeing per year		Life expectancy (in years)		Social welfare (WELLBYs per person)		
	2006/8	**2017/19**	**2006/8**	**2017/19**	**2006/8**	**2017/19**	**Change**
World	5.4	5.2	68.7	72.4	369	373	4
N America	7.3	7.0	78.6	79.5	576	556	−21
S America	6.2	6.1	73.4	75.3	455	463	8
W Europe	6.9	6.8	80.3	82.2	550	561	11
C+E Europe	5.4	6.1	74.6	77.4	402	488	66
Former Soviet Union	5.2	5.4	67.5	72.2	352	393	41
S E Asia	5.1	5.4	69.4	72.5	354	391	37
E Asia	4.9	5.2	74.8	77.8	369	408	39
S Asia	5.1	4.0	65.7	69.5	334	278	−56
M E + N Africa	5.3	4.9	71.9	74.6	380	364	−16
Sub-Saharan Africa	4.5	4.5	53.6	60.7	240	271	31

Source: Layard and Oparina (2021)

This is not, of course, an appropriate maximand for policy, which should also involve the future wellbeing of those alive and those not yet born. But it is an interesting measure of where we are now.

Table 6.2 provides this assessment for each region of the world for 2017/19 (before COVID-19) and also for 2006/8 (the first available date). As the table shows, average current wellbeing fell slightly between the two periods, especially in South Asia, the Middle East/North Africa and North America. But life-expectancy rose everywhere, above all in Sub-Saharan Africa where it rose by an astonishing seven years. Thus the average WELLBYs per citizen born in the world rose from 369 (5.4 × 68.7) to 373 (5.2 × 72.4). The increase was especially large in the post-Communist regions. But in South Asia, the Middle East/North Africa and in North America there was a fall in current social welfare.

Conclusions

(1) Wellbeing varies hugely in the human population. Over a sixth of the world's population has wellbeing of 3 or below (out of 10) – a condition of serious misery. And another sixth has wellbeing of 8 or above.

(2) About 80% of this variance of wellbeing worldwide is within countries and about 20% is between countries.

(3) Between 1980 and 2007, average wellbeing rose in more countries than where it fell. But since 2008, wellbeing has fallen in roughly the same number of countries as where it has risen. Notable falls in wellbeing have been in India, the United States and the Middle East/North Africa. In the US average wellbeing is no higher

than it was in the 1950s and the inequality of wellbeing is one of the highest in the OECD.

(4) In most countries, the inequality of wellbeing has increased since 2008, except in Europe, which now has lower inequality than any other region.

(5) Since 2006/8 there has been a large increase in negative affect and in stress.

(6) Average wellbeing is very similar for men and women in almost every country. It declines with age in most parts of the world but in North America and Europe it improves after mid-life. Average wellbeing is below average for most ethnic minorities in most countries.

(7) Children's wellbeing fell substantially between 2015 and 2018 especially in the UK, the United States and Japan, countries where the wellbeing of 15-year-olds is lower than in most other OECD countries.

(8) Meanwhile, adult life-expectancy has risen in all regions of the world, especially in Sub-Saharan Africa. So the Wellbeing-Years (WELLBYs) that a person now born can expect have increased since 2006–2008 in all regions of the world except South Asia, the Middle East/North Africa and North America.

The rest of Part III of this book attempts to explain some of these facts – both the level of wellbeing and its inequality in the human population. But first we have to sort out the tools we need for this purpose.

Questions for discussion

(1) Do you believe the patterns of wellbeing portrayed in this chapter?
(2) You may want to develop hypotheses about what causes these facts.

Further Reading

Fortin, N., Helliwell, J. F., and Wang, S. (2015). How does subjective well-being vary around the world by gender and age. In Helliwell, J. F., Layard, R., and Sachs, J. (Eds.). World Happiness Report 2015, 42–75.

Stevenson, B., and Wolfers, J. (2009). The paradox of declining female happiness. *American Economic Journal: Economic Policy*, 1(2), 190–225.

World Happiness Report (latest version). De Neve, J. E., Helliwell, J. F., Layard, R., and Sachs, J. (Eds.). World Happiness Report New York: UN Sustainable Development Solutions Network.

LIFE IS LIKE A BOWL OF NOODLES

I WILL GIVE NO FURTHER EXPLANATION

7 Tools to Explain Wellbeing

There are three kinds of lies: lies, damned lies, and statistics.

Mark Twain

To explain the level and inequality of wellbeing, we use the standard tools of quantitative social science. These are mainly the techniques of multiple regression. In this chapter, we shall show how multiple regression can address the following issues.[1]

(1) What is the effect of different factors on the level of wellbeing (using survey data)?
(2) What problems arise in estimating this and how can they be handled?
(3) How far do different factors contribute to the observed inequality of wellbeing?
(4) How can experiments and quasi-experiments show us the effect of interventions to improve wellbeing?

So suppose that a person's wellbeing (W) is determined by a range of explanatory variables ($X_1, \ldots, X_N$) in an additive fashion. But in addition there is an unexplained residual (e), which is randomly distributed around an average value of zero. Then the wellbeing of the ith individual (W_i) is given by

$$W_i = a_0 + a_1 X_{i1} + \ldots + a_N X_{iN} + e_i,$$

which we can also write as

$$W_i = a_0 + \sum_{j=1}^{N} a_j X_{ij} + e_i. \qquad (1)$$

In this equation, wellbeing is being explained by the X_js. So wellbeing is the 'dependent' variable (or left-hand variable) and the X_js are the 'independent' or (right-hand) variables. These right-hand variables can be of many forms. They can be continuous like income or the logarithm of income or like age or age squared. Or they can be binary variables like unemployment: you are either unemployed or not unemployed. These binary variables are often called dummy variables and they take

---

[1] The treatment is introductory and some readers will already know it all. If not, it will help you understand what you are doing when you use statistical software. For fuller expositions, see one of the excellent textbooks such as Angrist and Pischke (2008).

the value of 1 when you are in that state (e.g., unemployed) and the value of 0 when you are not in that state (e.g., not unemployed).

If we want to explain wellbeing, we have to discover the size of the effect of each thing that affects wellbeing. In other words, we have to discover the size of the a_js. For example, suppose

$$W_i = a_0 + a_1 \ \log \ \text{Income}_i + a_2 \ \text{Unemployed}_i + e_i. \tag{2}$$

From Chapter 8, you will find as benchmark numbers that $a_1 = 0.3$ and $a_2 = -0.7$. This means that when a person's log Income increases by one point, her wellbeing increases by 0.3 points (out of 10). Similarly, when a person ceases to be unemployed, her wellbeing increases by 0.7 points (ignoring any effect of a simultaneous change in income). And, if both things happen together, wellbeing increases by a whole point (0.3 + 0.7).

Estimating the Effect of a Variable

But how are we to estimate, as best we can, the true values of these a_j coefficients? The best unbiased way of doing this is to find the set of a_js that leaves the smallest sum of squared residuals e_i^2, across the whole sample of people being studied.[2] This is known as the method of Ordinary Least Squares (OLS). Standard programmes like STATA will do it for you automatically. However, there are 4 possible problems with such estimates when obtained from a cross-section of the population.

Omitted variables

Suppose that equation (2) is not the correct model but that another X variable should also be in the equation. Suppose, for example, that the right model is

$$W_i = a_0 + a_1 \ log \ \text{Income}_i + a_2 \ \text{Unemployed}_i + a_3 \ \text{Education}_i + e_i \tag{3}$$

where Education means years of education. Clearly education and income are positively correlated. So if a_1 and a_3 are positive, people with higher income will be getting higher wellbeing for 2 reasons:

the direct effect of income (a_1) and
the effect of education in so far as it is correlated with income.

Thus, equation (2) will give an exaggerated estimate of the direct effect (a_1) of income on wellbeing.[3] To leave out education is to leave out a confounding variable. And any such **confounding variable** must have two properties:

it is causally related to the dependent (LHS) variable and
it is correlated with an independent (RHS) variable.

---

[2] This is the best unbiased estimation system (with least standard errors on the estimated a_js), provided the errors are homoscedastic.

[3] The sign of the bias in a_1 equals the sign of a_3 times the sign of the correlation of X_1 and X_3.

If we lack data on the confounding variable, the classic way to overcome this problem is to use time-series panel data on the same people. Provided the omitted variable is constant over time, it can cause no problem, since we can now estimate how changes in income within the same person affect changes in her wellbeing. Thus, if we use time-series data, we cease to compare different individuals at the same point of time and we compare the same individual at different periods of time. Algebraically, we do this by expanding equation (2) to include multiple time periods (t) and adding a fixed effect dummy variable (f_i) for each individual. This picks up the effect of all the fixed characteristic of the individual (which for most adults will include education). Thus, we now explain the wellbeing of the ith person in the tth time period by

$$W_{it} = a_0 + a_1 \, log \, \text{Income}_{it} + a_2 \, log \, \text{Unemployed}_{it} + f_i + e_{it}. \tag{4}$$

There are standard programmes for including fixed-effects. A similar method to this is used for analysing the effect of experiments, but we shall come to this later.

Reverse causality

However, there is another problem. Suppose we are interested in the effect of income on wellbeing. But suppose that there is also the reverse effect – of wellbeing on income.[4] How can we be sure that, when we estimate equation (2), we are really estimating the effect of income on wellbeing rather than the reverse relationship or a mixture of the two? In other words is equation (2) in principle '**identifiable**'?

For an equation to be identifiable, it must **exclude** at least one of the variables that appears in the second relationship (the one that determines income).[5] But, even if it is identifiable, there is still the problem of getting a causal estimate of the effects of the endogenous variable.

The aim has to be to isolate that part of the endogenous variable that is due to something exogenous to the system. A variable that can isolate that part of the endogenous variable is called an **instrumental variable.** For example, if tax rates or minimum wages changed over time, these would be good instruments. Instrumental variables can also be used to handle the problem of omitted variables. In every case a good instrument

(i)   is well related in a causal way to the variable it instruments and
(ii) should not itself appear in the equation, (i.e., it is not correlated with the error term in the equation).

There are programmes for the use of instrumental variables (IVs).

---

[4] For evidence on the reverse relationship (the effect of adolescent wellbeing on later earnings), see De Neve and Oswald (2012).

[5] In a three-equation system, it would need to exclude two variables from the rest of the system and so on.

Another way to isolate causal relationships is through the **timing** of effects. For example, income affects wellbeing in the next period rather than the current period. We can then identify its effect by regressing current wellbeing on income in the previous period. Similarly with unemployment. This gives us

$$W_{it} = a_0 + a_1 \log \text{Income}_{i,t-1} + a_2 \text{Unemployed}_{i,t-1} + f_i + e_{it}. \qquad (5)$$

Measurement error

Another source of biased estimates is measurement error. If the **left-hand** variable has high measurement error, this will **not** bias the estimated coefficients a_j. But, if an **explanatory** variable X_j is measured with error, this will bias a_j towards zero. If the measurement error is known, this can be used to correct for the bias. But, if not, an instrumental variable can again come to the rescue, provided it is uncorrelated with the measurement error in the variable it is instrumenting.

Mediating variables

A final issue is this. A multiple regression equation such as (3) shows us the effect of each variable upon wellbeing **holding other things constant**. But suppose we are interested in the **total** effect of changing one variable upon wellbeing. For example, we might ask What is the total effect of unemployment upon wellbeing?

The total effect is clearly

- a_2, plus
- a_1 times the effect of unemployment upon log income.

That is one way you could estimate it. An alternative way is to take equation (2) and leave income out of the equation, so that the estimated coefficient on unemployment includes any effect that unemployment has on wellbeing via its effect on income.

In a case like this, income is a **mediating** variable. If we are only interested in the total effect of unemployment, we can simply leave the mediating variable out of the equation. Or we can estimate a system of structural equations consisting of (2) and the equation that determines income. This discussion brings out one crucial point in wellbeing research. We should always be very clear what question we are trying to answer. We should choose our equation or equations accordingly.

Standard errors and significance

All coefficients are estimated with a margin of uncertainty. Each estimated coefficient has a 'standard error' (se) around the estimated value. The true value will lie within 2 'standard errors' on either side of the estimated coefficients in 95% of samples. Thus the '95% confidence interval' for the a_j coefficient runs from $\widehat{a}_j - 2se_j$ to $\widehat{a}_j + 2se_j$, where $\widehat{a}_j$ means the estimated value of a_j. If this confidence interval does not include the value zero, the estimated coefficient is said to be 'significantly different from zero at the 95% level'.

For many psychologists, this issue of **significance** is considered crucial. It answers the question 'Does X affect W at all?' But for policy purposes the more important question is 'How much does X affect W?' So the coefficient itself is more interesting than its significance level. For any sample size, the estimated coefficient is the best available answer to the question of how much X changes W. And, if you increase the size of the sample, the expected value of the estimated a_j does not change but its standard error automatically falls (it is inversely proportional to the square root of the sample size). So in this book we focus more heavily on the size of coefficients than on their significance (though we sometimes show standard errors in brackets in the tables).

The question we have been asking thus far in this chapter is How does wellbeing change when an independent variable changes? In algebraic terms, we have been studying dW/dX_j? This is the type of number we need in order to evaluate a policy change. For example, suppose we increased the income of poor people by 20%, how much would their wellbeing change (on a scale of 0–10)? If $a_j = 0.3$, it would increase by 0.06 points (0.3×0.2). A quite different question is In which areas of life should we look hardest in the search for better policies?

The Explanatory Power of a Variable

If our main aim is to help the people with the lowest wellbeing (as we discussed in Chapter 2), then our focus should be on what explains the inequality of wellbeing. To see why, suppose first that wellbeing depends only on one variable X_1, with $W = \alpha_0 + \alpha_1 X_1$. Then the distribution of W depends only on the distribution of X_1. If W is unequal, it is because X_1 is unequal and α_1 is high. The higher the standard deviation (σ_1) of X_1 and the higher α_1, the greater the inequality of W. This is illustrated in Figure 7.1. For high variance of W, the numbers in misery correspond to the areas A and B. But for the low variance of W the numbers in misery correspond only to the area B.

A next natural step is to compare the standard deviation of $a_1\sigma_1$ with the standard deviation of wellbeing itself. Obviously, if they were equal in size, the spread of X_1 would be 'explaining' the whole spread of wellbeing σ_w – in other words, the two variables would be perfectly correlated. The correlation coefficient (r) between W and X_1 is therefore $a_1\sigma_1/\sigma_w$:

$$r = \frac{a_1\sigma_1}{\sigma_w} = \text{Correlation coefficient}$$

However, this can be either positive or negative depending on the sign of a_1. So a natural measure of the **explanatory power** of a right-hand variable is *the* squared value of r (which is also often written as R^2):

$$r^2 = \frac{a_1^2\sigma_1^2}{\sigma_w^2} = \text{Share of variance explained}$$

Since the denominator is the variance of wellbeing, this shows what proportion of the variance in wellbeing is explained by the variance of X_1.

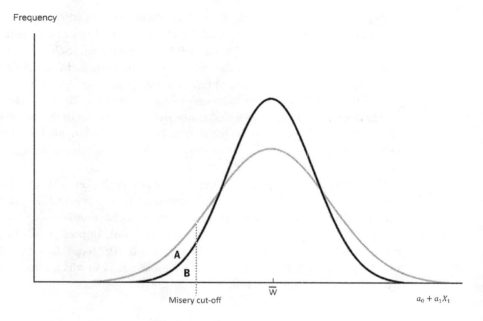

Figure 7.1 How the numbers in misery are affected by $a_1\sigma_1$

In the real world, wellbeing depends on more than one variable (see equation [1]). The policy-maker may then ask Which of these variables is producing the largest amount of misery?[6] For this purpose, we need to compare the explanatory power of the different variable. This is done by computing for each variable its partial correlation coefficient with wellbeing. This partial correlation coefficient is normally described as β_j where

$$\beta_j = \frac{a_j\sigma_j}{\sigma_w} = \text{Partial correlation coefficient.}$$

This β-coefficient will appear frequently throughout this book.[7]

These β-coefficients are hugely interesting, as we shall see via two steps. First, starting from equation (1) we can readily derive the following equation.[8]

$$\frac{W_i - \bar{W}}{\sigma_w} = \sum \beta_j \frac{(X_{ij} - \bar{X}_j)}{\sigma_j} + \frac{e_i}{\sigma_w} \tag{6}$$

---

[6] As discussed in Chapter 18, the policy-maker can then develop policies in these areas and target them at those individuals least favoured in these variables. This is reasonably practical, while it is not really practical to identify the individuals with the lowest wellbeing and then target them with the best policies (though that would be the most logical approach).

[7] Sociologists often call it the 'path coefficient, p'.

[8] (i) Divide both sides by σ_w. (ii) Multiply and divide X_j by σ_j. (iii) Derive the average equation for the whole population and subtract it from the original equation (to eliminate a_0/σ_w).

Here we have **standardised** each variable by measuring it from its mean and dividing it by its standard deviation. These standardised equations appear many times in this book.[9]

But, to see the importance of these βs, we move on to a second equation, which is derived from (6).[10] This says

$$r^2 = \sum \beta_j^2 + \sum \sum \ \beta_g \beta_k \ r_{gk} \ (g \neq k); \tag{7}$$

r^2 is the proportion of the variance of W that is explained by the right-hand variables. And r_{gk} is the correlation coefficient between X_g and X_k.

Thus, the left-hand side is the share of the variance of wellbeing that is explained. The right-hand side consists of $\Sigma \beta_j^2$, which includes all the effects of the independent variation of the X_js, plus the effects of all their covariances. Thus β_j (or the partial correlation coefficient) measures the explanatory power of a variable (just as the correlation coefficient does in a simple bivariate relationship).

But some readers may wonder if this approach can handle independent variables that are binary. It can, because the standard deviation of a binary variable is simply $\sqrt{p\,(1-p)}$, where p is the proportion of people answering Yes to the binary question. For example, the standard deviation of Unemployed is $\sqrt{u(1-u)}$ where u is the unemployed rate. Thus, if X_j is Unemployed, its β coefficient is $a_j \sqrt{u(1-u)}/\sigma_w$.

Binary dependent variables

The matter is more complicated when it is the dependent variable that is binary. For example, suppose we divide the population into those who are in misery (with wellbeing below say 6) and the rest. How can we handle this? The most natural approach is, as normal, to regress the binary variable on all the other variables. This is what we often do in this book and, since it provides statistics of the standard kind, it is easy to understand.[11]

Box 7.1 Odds ratios

In analysing the effect of one binary variable on another binary variable, psychologists and sociologists often use the concept of an '**odds ratio**' rather than the values of a_j and β_j we have been discussing. Suppose, for example, we ask: How much more likely are unemployed people to be in misery, compared with people who are not unemployed? Imagine 100 people were distributed as follows (Table 7.1):

---

[9] The standardised value of a variable is often called its z-score. In other words, $\frac{X_{ij} - \bar{X}_j}{\sigma_j}$ is individual i's z-score for the variable X_j.

[10] To derive this, (i) square both sides of equation (6) and (ii) add up the equations, for all the individuals. (iii) Note that $r^2 = 1 - \Sigma e_i^2 / \sigma_w^2$.

[11] This linear probability model (LPM) has the problem that whereas the left-hand variable is either 1 or 0, the regression equation predicts all kinds of values for different individuals including some which are greater than 1 or less than 0. Thus, there is an alternative approach to binary dependent variables which assumes that a person has a given probability of being 1 or 0 as a function of the X_js and then chooses that function which makes what actually happened to appear as likely as possible. Depending on the functional form, this type of analysis is called either **Logit or Probit** analysis which is again available in STATA.

Box 7.1 (*cont.*)

Table 7.1 Distribution of 100 people by unemployment status and misery status

	In misery	Not in misery	Total
Unemployed	2	8	10
Not unemployed	9	81	90
Total	11	89	100

In this situation, the chance of an unemployed person being in misery is much higher than the chance of a non-unemployed person being in misery. The odds-ratio is

$$\frac{2}{8} / \frac{9}{81} \simeq 2.25.$$

But odds ratios do not answer either of the main questions we are addressing in this chapter. First, if we are interested in the effect on wellbeing of reducing unemployment, the proper measure of this effect is not the odds ratio but the **absolute difference** in the probabilities of misery between unemployed and non-unemployed people, that is, $0.2 - 0.1 = 0.1$. Second, if we are interested in the power of unemployment to **explain the prevalence** of misery, the correct statistic is the correlation coefficient between the two. So we shall not be showing odds ratios in this book, though the reader is able to compute them, given the necessary information.

Effect size of a binary independent variable

We have so far considered two ways in which to report regression results. One is to report the absolute effect of say unemployment on wellbeing in units of wellbeing. The other is to look at the relationship when both variables are standardised. However, there is the third approach that is often useful. This is to measure only the dependent variable in a standardised fashion. For example, we might ask 'When a person becomes unemployed, by how many standard deviations does his wellbeing go down?' This is a measure known as the **effect size** of the independent variable (sometimes knows as Cohen's *d*):

$$\text{Effect size} = \frac{\text{Absolute effect}}{\text{SD of depdendent variable}} = \text{Cohen's } d.$$

This is particularly useful when reporting the effect of an experiment.[12]

---

[12] Much less useful is the odds ratio (see Box 11.1). It is also useful to know that, if someone started at the median of a normal distribution and experienced a treatment with a given effect size, the resulting rise in the person's position in the distribution would be given approximately by

Change in percentile points = 40 × Effect size

unless the effect size is very large.

Experiments

So far, we have been discussing the use of **naturalistic** data – mainly obtained by surveys of the population. As we have mentioned, it is often difficult to establish the causal effect of one variable on another from this type of data. The simplest way to establish a causal relationship is through a properly controlled experiment. Moreover, if you want to examine the effect of a policy that has never been tried before, it is the best way to get convincing evidence of its effects.

So how do we estimate the effects of being 'treated' in an experiment? Let's begin with a simple example. Suppose we want to try introducing a wellbeing curriculum into a school. Our aim is to see whether it makes any difference to those who receive it. So we would select two groups of pupils who were as similar to each other as possible. Then we would give the wellbeing curriculum to the treatment group (T) but not the control group (c). We would also measure the wellbeing of both groups before and after the treatment. So we would have the following values of wellbeing for each of four situations (Table 7.2).

To find the average effect of the treatment, we would compare the change in wellbeing experienced by the treatment group (T) with that experienced by the control group (C). Thus, the 'average treatment effect on the treated' (ATT) would be estimated as

$$ATT = (W_{T1} - W_{T0}) - (W_{C1} - W_{C0}). \tag{8}$$

In other words, the ATT is the '**difference in differences**', or for short the 'diff in diff'.

There may of course be many ways in which both groups changed between periods 0 and 1 – they will become older, they may experience a flu epidemic or whatever. But those changes should be similar for both groups. Thus the only observable thing that can produce a different change in wellbeing is the fact that Group T took the course and Group C did not.

Of course, there may also be some unobservable difference in experience, which means that the ATT is always estimated with a standard error. So, to put things into a more general form, let's imagine we have observations over a number of years. We then estimate

$$W_{it} = a_0 + a_1 T_{it} + v_t + f_i + e_{it}. \tag{9}$$

Here T_{it} is a variable which takes the value 1 in all periods after someone has taken the course, v_t is a year dummy, f_i is a person fixed effect and e_{it} is random noise.

Table 7.2 Average wellbeing of each group before and after the experiment

	Before	After
Treatment group (T)	W_{T0}	W_{T1}
Control group (C)	W_{C0}	W_{C1}

So far, we have assumed that in our experiment we can easily arrange for the treatment group and the control group to be reasonably similar. This is never in fact completely possible. But the method that gets us closest to it is '**random assignment**'.[13] In this case, we select an overall group for the experiment and then randomly assign people to either Group T or Group C (e.g., by tossing a coin for each individual). In this way, the groups are more likely to be similar than in any other way. Of course we can then check whether they differ in observable characteristics (X) and we can then allow in our equation for the possibility that these variables affect the measured ATT. Our equation then becomes

$$W_{it} = a_0 + a_1 T_{it} + a_2 T_{it} X_{it} + a_3 X_{it} + v_t + f_i + e_{it}. \tag{10}$$

Estimating equations like this are quite common.

However, randomisation between individuals is often not practicable. For example, suppose you wanted to test whether higher income transfers raised wellbeing enough to justify the cost. You could not randomly allocate money within a given population – it would be considered unfair since the transfer clearly benefits the recipient. You might, however, choose to transfer money to all eligible people in some **areas** and not in others, with the allocation between areas being random. This might not be considered unfair. Similarly, suppose you wanted to test the effects of improved teaching of life-skills in schools. Within a school it might be organisationally impossible to give improved teaching to some children and not others – or even to some classes. But you could use random assignment across schools. Or you could even argue that it is 'quasi-random' whether a child is born in Year t or Year $t - 1$; in this case, you could use children born in year t as a control group in the trial of a treatment applied to those born in year $t + 1$ (see Chapter 9). So all experiments should, if at all possible, use randomisation to reduce the unobservable differences between the treatment and control groups.

Selection bias

But suppose an innovation is made without an experiment and we then want to know its effects. For example, an exercise programme has been established, which some people have decided to adopt. Has it done them any good?

The only information that we have is for the period after the innovation. But we do also have information on people who did not opt in to the programme. So, can we answer our question by comparing the wellbeing of those who took the programme with those who didn't? Probably not, because the people who opted into the programme may have differed from those who didn't: they may well have started with higher wellbeing in the first place. So, if we just compared their final wellbeing with those of non-participants, the difference could be largely due to 'selection bias'.

---

[13] For the limits of this method, see Deaton and Cartwright (2018).

One method to deal with this is called Propensity Score Matching. In it we first take the whole sample of participants and non-participants and do a logit (or probit) analysis to identify that equation that best predicts whether they participate or not. From this analysis, we can say for every participant what was the probability they participated. We then find, for each participant, a non-participant with the same (or nearly the same) probability of participating. It is those non-participants who become the control group and we now compare their wellbeing with that of the treatment group. This gives us our estimate of the average treatment effect on the treated:

$$ATT = \tilde{W} \text{ of treated} - \bar{W} \text{ of matched sample.} \qquad (11)$$

Summary

(1) If $W = a_0 + \sum a_j X_j + e$, then the best unbiased way to estimate the values of the a_js is by Ordinary Last Squares (choosing the a_js to minimise the sum of squared residuals e^2).

(2) Omitted variables are confounders that can lead to biased estimates of the effect of the variables which are included.

(3) Time series estimation can eliminate any problem caused by omitted variables which are constant over time. Time series can also help to identify a causal effect if this takes place with a lag, so that for example X_{t-1} is affecting W_t.

(4) If a right-hand variable is endogenous, it should if possible be instrumented by an instrumental variable that is independent of the error in the equation. Instrumental variables can also help with omitted variables and measurement error.

(5) If an explanatory variable is measured with error, its estimated coefficient will be biased towards zero. This problem can again be solved by using an instrumental variable uncorrelated with the original measurement error.

(6) All regression estimates are estimated with 'standard errors' (se). The 95% confidence interval is the coefficient ± 2 se. Provided this interval does not include zero, the coefficient is 'significantly different from zero at the 95% level'. But the coefficient estimate is more interesting that its significance.

(7) To find the explanatory power of the different variables, we run the equation using standardised variables, that is, the original variables minus their mean and divided by their standard deviation. The resulting coefficients (β_j) – or partial correlation coefficients – reflect the explanatory power of the independent variation of each variable X_j. They are equal to $a_j \sigma_j / \sigma_w$ where w is the dependent variable.

(8) The surest way to determine a causal effect is by experiment. The best form of experiment is by random assignment. We then measure the wellbeing of the treatment and the control group before and after the experiment. This difference-in-difference measures the average treatment effect on the treated.

(9) Where random assignment is impossible, naturalistic data can be used and the outcome for the treatment group compared with a similar untreated group chosen by Propensity Score Matching.

(10) If the measured effect of a treatment is a (in units of the outcome variable W), the 'effect size' is a/σ_w.

We can now put these tools to work.

Further Reading

Angrist, J. D., and Pischke, J. S. (2008). *Mostly Harmless Econometrics*. Princeton University Press.

LIFE CAN ONLY BE UNDERSTOOD BACKWARDS
BUT IT MUST BE LIVED FORWARDS

8 Explaining Wellbeing
A First Exploration

Happy the man who has learned the cause of things ...

Virgil

We can now put these tools to use in explaining the huge inequalities that exist in wellbeing. These inequalities are interesting in themselves. And they also provide naturalistic evidence that helps us to predict how policies of different kinds would change people's wellbeing.[1] So this chapter applies the tools presented in Chapter 7 to explain and learn from the differences in Chapter 6.

We proceed as follows:

- First, we outline a framework for how adult wellbeing is determined within a country.
- Next, we take adult wellbeing differences within a country and see how these are explained by differences in adult characteristics.
- Then we go back to childhood and see how well the child predicts the adult.
- Finally, we look at the role of social norms and institutions and study their effects by looking at differences between countries.

This chapter is very important in setting the framework for the rest of Part III of the book – which looks at each influence in much more detail.

Wellbeing and the Life Cycle

Our adult wellbeing is the product of our whole life to date (see Figure 8.1). Our early development is affected first by our parents (including their genes) and then by our schooling. These are the main factors that determine our outcomes up to the end of childhood. These outcomes then help to predict our adult outcomes, which in turn determine our adult life satisfaction. In what follows, we shall work backwards, looking first at the role of adult outcomes, then at the role of child outcomes and finally (in Chapter 9) at the role of family and schooling.

---

[1] This also requires evidence on the immediate effects of the policy, preferably from experiments.

Figure 8.1 How adult wellbeing is determined
Note: Earlier factors also influence later outcomes directly

Personal Determinants of Adult Wellbeing

There have been thousands of studies of the personal causes of adult wellbeing. But they are difficult to compare because they use different measures of wellbeing and they study the effect of different sets of determinants. We shall therefore focus in this chapter on one study that used a single measure of wellbeing (life satisfaction) and looked at all the main influences simultaneously.[2] The main influences included were:

- Health
  Physical health (number of illnesses)
  Mental health (has ever been diagnosed with depression or an anxiety disorder)
- Work
  Is unemployed (versus employed)
  Quality of work (index)
- Family
  Has partner (versus single)
  Is separated (versus single)
  Is widowed (versus single)
- Income (log of household income per equivalent adult)
- Education (years)

Many studies of wellbeing do not include mental health as an explanatory factor, since it is itself a feeling. But this is why we do not include self-reported feelings as measures of mental health – instead, we include an objective diagnosis by a third party. The question used is 'Have you ever been told by a doctor, nurse of other health professional that you had an anxiety disorder and/or depressive disorder?' Since most

---

[2] A.E. Clark et al. (2018). In Chapter 13, we report results for the full range of countries using the Gallup World Poll.

Table 8.1 How different factors affect life satisfaction (0–10) of adults over 25 (Britain) (Pooled cross section) ($R^2 = 0.19$)

	Effect on life satisfaction (0–10)
Physical health problems (No. of illnesses)	−0.22 (0.01)
Mental health problems (0,1)	−0.72 (0.05)
Unemployed (versus employed; 0,1)	−0.70 (0.04)
Quality of work (effect of 1SD)	+0.40 (0.04)
Partnered (versus single; 0,1)	+0.59 (0.03)
Separated (versus single; 0,1)	−0.15 (0.04)
Widowed (versus single; 0,1)	+0.11 (0.08)
Income (log)	+0.17 (0.01)
Education (years)	+0.03 (0.00)

Source: A. E. Clark et al. (2018) Table 16.2 Mainly Britain (Understanding Society) 1996–2014 but see text
Notes: Control variables include comparators' income, education, unemployment and partnership, as well as gender, age and age squared and year fixed effects. Standard errors in brackets.

such experiences are prior to being surveyed, they are essentially measuring something exogenous. Besides, it would be quite wrong not to include mental illness as an explanation for wellbeing, when this is such an important issue for so many people, independently of the other right-hand variables. As the equations that follow show, **low wellbeing is not the same as mental illness** and can be caused by many other factors besides mental illness.

So the task is to estimate equation (1) in Chapter 7, with current life satisfaction as the dependent variable and the variables listed above as the independent variables. The equation estimated is cross-sectional – a point to which we shall return. The study covered Britain, Germany, Australia and the United States, with broadly similar results from all four countries. The results we report in Table 8.1 come mainly from a British survey (Understanding Society). But the mental health coefficient is from the United States and Australia (where the measure of mental health is more exogenous and the results are very similar). And the quality of work result comes from a different study using the European Social Survey.[3]

Table 8.1 shows, for example, that people ever diagnosed with mental illness are currently (other things equal) less satisfied with their life by 0.72 points.[4] Unemployment has a similar effect, as does not having a partner. A unit increase in log income increases wellbeing by 0.17 points, which means that the doubling of income raises wellbeing by 0.12 points.[5] Note that the standard error (in brackets) of

---

[3] For the quality of work, see A. E. Clark et al. (2018) p. 74. On mental health, the British measure (being less exogenous) attracts a higher coefficient than the US measure.

[4] In the Gallup World Poll analysis reported in annex 13.1, there is a similar coefficient on the self-reported question 'Yesterday did you experience a lot of depression'.

[5] $Log_e 2 = 0.7$. Note that we always use logarithms to the base e.

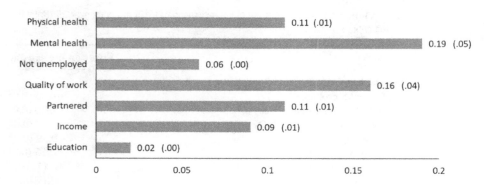

Figure 8.2 What explains the variation of life satisfaction among adults over 25? (Britain) Partial correlation coefficients (β) ($R^2 = 0.19$).
Source: A. E. Clark et al. (2018) Table 16.1; otherwise see Table 8.1; 'partnered' means partnered versus any other relationship status
Notes: For quality of work see their chapter 4. Standard errors in brackets

these coefficients are small relative to the coefficients themselves, so the estimates are fairly well defined and significantly different from zero at the 95% level.

From Table 8.1, we learn the effect of each variable upon wellbeing. But this does not tell us how far the inequality of that variable explains the inequality of wellbeing. For that purpose, we have to multiply the effect of each explanatory variable by its own standard deviation – and then divide it by the standard deviation of wellbeing. This gives us the β_j measure discussed in Chapter 7 – recall that $\beta_j = a_j \sigma_j / \sigma_w$.

In Figure 8.2, we give these β values in graphical form. To simplify the display, we have treated every variable as if it had a positive β – by, for example, relabelling Unemployed as Not unemployed.

Notice first that the whole equation has an R^2 of 0.19 – we are only explaining 19% of the total variance. It is very important not to over-claim explanatory power.[6] And it is also quite wrong to label the unexplained residual as 'luck'. It is quite simply the variation in wellbeing that we have not been able to explain or is due to measurement error. Nevertheless, what we do know is that health is extremely important (especially mental health). Work is also important – having it (if you want it) and its quality. Family life also matters.

So does income, but its explanatory power is no higher than many other variables. In Figure 8.2 it explains under 1% of the variance of life satisfaction, since its β^2 value is under 0.1^2. But as we shall see in Chapter 13, the figure can rise to 3% in some countries – but still no higher than some other influences.

Before we accept this conclusion, we have to ask some of the questions we discussed in Chapter 7. First, is there a problem of **measurement** error? This is unlikely to affect the ranking of income in Figure 8.2 since income is measured more accurately than many of the other variables. Second, are there important omitted

---

[6] A well-known device for over-claiming is the odds ratio. See Chapter 7.

variables or problems of endogeneity? To investigate these problems, we can use the panel data to perform a fixed-effects analysis as in Equation (7.4). In panel regressions, all the coefficients are reduced, partly because the problem of measurement error becomes more acute. The coefficients on income fall more than most, though this may be partly because the exact timings are not well caught by the data. For this chapter, we stick to cross-sectional results; but in Chapter 13 we also give the results of fixed effects regressions.

It is important to stress that for all the variables in Table 8.1 and Figure 8.2, the coefficients reflect the effect of the variable, **other things constant.** If we wanted to investigate the **total** effect of income on wellbeing, we would also have to include its effects through other 'mediating' variables like having a partner. This is quite difficult to compute. But it is easy to compute a **maximum** value for the total coefficient on income (or any other variable). It is the simple bivariate coefficient, which in this case is about double the coefficient holding other things constant.

Another obvious question is this: Doesn't income explain more of the prevalence of **low wellbeing** than is implied by Figure 8.2? To investigate this, we construct a new variable. This is a simple binary variable for misery (M), which is constructed as follows:[7]

M equals 1 if wellbeing is 5 or below
M equals 0 if wellbeing is above 5

Misery (thus defined) affects the bottom 10% or so of the British population – so it is a good measure of deprivation. We can then run the following simple equation:

$$M_i = a_0 + \sum a_j X_{ij} + e_i.$$

If we take averages across all individuals, this equation predicts the proportion of people in misery, which is given by

$$\bar{M} = a_0 + \sum a_j \bar{X}_j.$$

In an analysis for Britain, Australia and the United States, mental health problems accounted for more of the misery than any other factor.[8] In Britain and Australia, this was followed by physical illness, and in the United States by low income. Unemployment, though devastating to those affected, came in lower than health and poverty, because of the smaller numbers affected.

A slightly different question is What best explains **who** is in misery and who is not? In other words, what are the most important elements in the following relationship:

$$R^2 = 1 - \frac{\sigma_e^2}{\sigma_M^2} = \sum \beta_j^2 + \sum \sum \beta_k \beta_s r_{ks} (k \neq s).$$

---

[7] In the original Understanding Society survey, life satisfaction is measured on a scale of 1–7. We have here transformed it to a scale of 0–10. Note that the multiple regression approach can be used to examine binary outcomes, with easy-to-interpret coefficients. Logit and probit analysis can also be used, but usually deliver equivalent results but in a form that is more difficult to understand.

[8] A. E. Clark et al. (2018) Table 6.1.

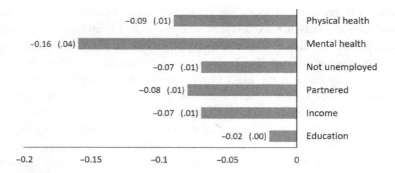

Figure 8.3 What explains the variation of misery among adults over 25? (Britain) Partial correlation coefficients (β) ($R^2 = 0.14$)
Source: A. E. Clark et al. (2018) Table 16.1 Mainly Britain (Understanding Society) but see text
Note: See Figure 8.2

In Figure 8.3, we show the values of the β coefficients where this time Misery is the dependent variable. As can be seen, these coefficients are slightly smaller than when we are explaining the full continuous range of Life–Satisfaction (in Figure 8.2). This is to be expected. But, strikingly, the relative importance of the different factors is the same whether we are explaining low wellbeing or the whole spread across the spectrum.

Childhood Predictors of Individual Wellbeing

So much for the adult causes of adult wellbeing. But aren't many of the adult influences we have looked at caused by how we were in childhood? They are indeed. There are three main dimensions of **child development**: intellectual, emotional and behavioural. A big question for schools is 'Which of these is the best predictor of whether a child will have a satisfying adult life?'

The following analysis is based on a follow-up of all British children born in a week in 1970 (the British Cohort Study 1970). The measures of child development that we use are these:

- Intellectual: highest qualification ever obtained
- Behavioural: behaviour measured at age 16 (by 17 questions asked to the mother)
- Emotional: emotional health measured at age 16 (by 22 questions asked to the young person and 8 to the mother).

As Figure 8.4 shows, **the best predictor of a satisfying adult life is not your qualifications but a simple measure of your emotional health at 16**. This is an important finding for educational policy since, as Chapter 9 shows, schools have such a huge influence on the wellbeing of their children. Qualifications also matter of course and are by far the best predictor of an adult's income. But, as we have seen,

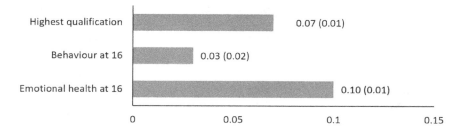

Figure 8.4 How adult life satisfaction is predicted by child outcomes (Britain) Partial correlation coefficients (β) ($R^2 = 0.035$)
Source: See A. E. Clark et al. (2018) Figure 1.2 British Cohort Study (BCS)
Note: Adult life satisfaction is average at ages 34 and 42. Controls include family variables. Standard errors in brackets

income is less important for adults than their mental health, which is best predicted by their emotional health in childhood.

As we argue in Chapter 9, child wellbeing is important in itself – childhood is a substantial part of our whole life experience. But wellbeing as a child is also the foundation for wellbeing as an adult.

The Effects of Social Norms and Institutions

We have focused so far on what explains the differences in wellbeing between people within the same country. But what explains the differences between countries? There are important **social norms and institutions** that everyone in a country shares. While we cannot identify these effects by studying people in one country only, we can do it by comparing one country with another. The Gallup World Poll data enable us to do just that – to study the effect of

- ethical standards (trustworthiness and generosity),
- networks of social support and
- personal freedom.

We measure these by the answers in each country to the following questions:

Trust	Proportion who say Yes to the first half of 'In general, do you think that most people can be trusted, or alternatively that you can't be too careful in dealing with people?'
Generosity	Proportion who say Yes to 'Have you donated money to a charity in the present month?'
Social Support	Proportion who say Yes to 'If you were in trouble, do you have relatives or friends you can count on to help you whenever you need them?'
Freedom	Proportion who say Yes to 'Are you satisfied or dissatisfied with your freedom to choose what you do with your life?'.

Table 8.2 How national life satisfaction (0–10) is affected by country-level variables ($R^2 = 0.77$)

	Change	Effect on average life satisfaction (0–10)
Trust	100% v. 0%	1.08 (.45)
Generosity	100% v. 0%	0.54 (.41)
Social support	100% v. 0%	2.03 (.61)
Freedom	100% v. 0%	1.41 (.49)
Income	Doubling	0.23 (.06)
Health	Years of healthy life	0.03 (.01)

Source: Gallup World Poll, Cantril ladder; average data for 2009–2015 except for trust (mostly 2009); analysis by John Helliwell; standard errors in brackets

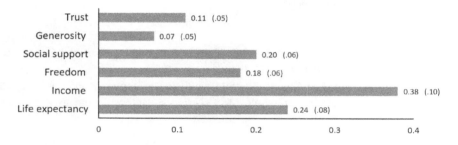

Figure 8.5 How differences in national life satisfaction are explained by country-level variables – partial correlation coefficients (β) ($R^2 = 0.77$)
Source: See Table 8.2

We also include the effect of average GDP per head and healthy life expectancy (measured in years).

In the cross-sectional analysis in Table 8.2, we show for each of these variables how average life-evaluation changes when the percentage who say Yes rises from 0 to 100. All four factors have substantial effect. So does healthy life-expectancy – for example, an increase of 10 years raises life evaluation by 0.3 points. And the effect of income across countries is similar to its effect within many countries – a doubling of income raises average life-evaluation by 0.23 points (out of 10).

It is also interesting to see how far the different factors contribute to the actual dispersion of life satisfaction across countries. Here income plays a more conspicuous role due to the huge income differences between countries. Health differences also come through as very important. This can be seen in Figure 8.5, which gives the β_j coefficients corresponding to the a_j coefficients in Table 8.2. The social norms are also very important. For example, what distinguishes the eight countries with the highest life satisfaction in the world is not their income but their high levels of trust, social support, freedom and generosity.[9] These are the five Nordic countries as well as the Netherlands, Switzerland and New Zealand (see Table 13.1). The countries at the

[9] See Helliwell et al. (2019) Table 2.2.

bottom are mainly the war-torn countries of sub-Saharan Africa and the Middle East (Afghanistan, Syria and Yemen), which not only have poor income and healthcare but are low on the social features that wellbeing requires.[10]

Conclusions

This concludes our brief initial overview of the main causes of high and low wellbeing – and of the huge variation in wellbeing in the world. All the findings are cross-sectional, with time series and experiments left to later chapters. The findings of this chapter provide the framework for the rest of Part III of the book – starting with personal factors and working outwards to those relating to whole communities.

- Within a country (if it is advanced), the main factors explaining the variance of wellbeing (and the prevalence of misery) are in rough order of importance:
  mental illness,
  physical illness,
  having work and the quality of that work,
  having a partner,
  family income and
  education
- The variation of wellbeing across countries is largely explained (in rough order of importance) by:
  income,
  health,
  social support,
  personal freedom,
  trusting social relations and
  generosity
- Predicting whether a child will become a happy adult is not easy. But the child's wellbeing is a better predictor of satisfaction in adult life than the child's academic success is. And as Chapter 9 shows, both schools and parents have big effects on children's wellbeing.

Questions for discussion

(1) Are the findings about income in Figure 8.2 credible? Could problems of measurement error have produced incorrect rankings?
(2) Is Figure 8.5 informative?

---

[10] If the Global Peace Index is added to a fixed effects regression of average life satisfaction on the 6 variables, a 1 standard deviation of the Index raises average live-satisfaction by 0.15 points (Helliwell et al. [2019] p. 40).

Further Reading

Clark, A. E., Flèche, S., Layard, R., Powdthavee, N., and Ward, G. (2018). *The Origins of Happiness: The Science of Wellbeing over the Life Course*: Princeton University Press. Especially chapters 1, 2, 6 and 16.

World Happiness Report (latest version). Helliwell, J. F., Layard, R., Sachs, J., and De Neve, J. E. (Eds.). World Happiness Report. New York: Sustainable Development Solutions Network. Chapter 2.

I FELL OUT OF MUMMY'S POUCH AND INTO THE MUD

9 Family, Schooling and Social Media

Don't be too hard on parents. You may find yourself in their place.

Ivy Compton Burnett

We begin our lives in families. After a while we go to school. And eventually most of us form families of our own. How do these experiences affect us?

The Effect of Parents

How our parents treat us makes a huge difference. For humans, we cannot prove this experimentally, but we can for animals – by allocating them randomly to be brought up by different parents. A classic study of rats by Michael Meaney took the offspring of mother rats who were bad at licking their offspring and allocated some of them to foster mothers who were good at licking.[1] These offspring grew up to be much less stressed, and they also became much better at licking their own offspring. Similarly, a classic study of rhesus monkeys by Stephen Suomi took the offspring of overactive mothers and randomly allocated some of them to calmer foster mothers.[2] These offspring became much calmer than those who stayed with their biological mothers.

However, we cannot do such experiments on humans. So we have to rely on data thrown up by people's actual experiences of life. Fortunately, there are now a number of longitudinal studies, which follow the same person from the cradle into adult life, and most of our understanding of the impact of families and schooling comes from these surveys. In each of them, the wellbeing of the children is measured initially by questions to their parents and teachers and then (after about 10) to the children themselves as well. Here are some key findings.

Every child needs unconditional love. The basic need is for a secure emotional tie to at least one specific person. This experience of **'attachment'** is the basis for an inner security that can last throughout life.[3] Sixty years ago, the importance of attachment was identified by John Bowlby;[4] and his idea has stood the test of time quite well. In meta-analyses, early attachment is correlated with later social

---

[1] Anisman et al. (1998).　[2] Suomi (1997).　[3] Groh et al. (2014).　[4] Bowlby (1969).

competence (r = .18), pro-social behaviour (r = .15) and inner wellbeing (r = .08),[5] and these correlations are undoubtedly underestimates because attachment is so difficult to measure precisely.

A striking illustration of the importance of caring relationships comes from a tragic 'natural experiment'. After the end of Communism, some Romanian orphans were randomly assigned to foster-care in Western families; the unlucky ones remained in the orphanage. On average, the children were 21 months old when they were assigned one way or the other, and they were assessed again at 4 ½ years of age. If they had been assigned for foster-care, the children's mental and cognitive wellbeing at 4 ½ was over one half of a standard deviation higher than if they had stayed in the orphanage.[6] And the younger the age at which the fostering began the better the outcome.

So the love of caregivers is essential. But so too is **firmness** – the ability to set boundaries. If combined with warmth, this is known as 'authoritative' parenting, and it is the most widely recommended approach. In this approach, compliance with rules does not come from fear, but children learn to internalise the parent's response and thereafter act to please their own 'better selves'.[7]

Abusive parents can change their children for life, and abuse includes psychological neglect as well as sexual or physical abuse. Though most abused children develop normally, a minority experience long-lasting damage. On average, there are marked brain differences between people who have and who have not been maltreated as children.[8] Maltreatment also affects behaviour,[9] but the long-term effects on internal wellbeing are even stronger.[10]

So for a child the relationship to her parents is crucial. But so is the **relationship between the parents themselves**. At present, 50% of 16-year-olds are in separated families in the United States, and in Britain it is over 40%. How much does this matter?

The literature on child development is large.[11] However, most of the main findings can be illustrated from within one study, which makes the findings on different influences easier to compare. This is the famous ALSPAC survey of all the children born in or around Bristol, England in 1991/2. Table 9.1 shows how their parents affected the wellbeing of their children – and also their behaviour and their academic performance (all measured at age 16).

As the table shows, **family conflict** is bad for all three of these outcomes. And, incidentally, for any given level of family conflict, a break-up of the family causes no additional damage, except to academic performance. But ongoing conflict between the parents after they break up increases the risk that the children will become depressed or aggressive. By contrast, seeing more of the absent parent reduces that risk.[12]

[5] Fearon and Roisman (2017).   [6] Nelson et al. (2007).   [7] Layard and Dunn (2009).

[8] Lim et al. (2014).   [9] Caspi et al. (2002).

[10] Danese and Widom (2020), based on a sample of abusive parents taken to court in the Mid-West USA 1967–71, matched to otherwise similar non-abusive parents. Their children were followed up, on average at age 29.

[11] Goodman and Scott (2012).

[12] Pleck and Masciadrelli (2004). On the effects of separation, see Amato and Keith (1991).

Table 9.1 How child outcomes at age 16 are affected by family and schooling – partial correlation coefficients (β)

	Wellbeing at 16	Behaviour at 16	Academic score at 16
Conflict between parents	−0.04	−0.14	−0.02
Mother's mental health	0.16	0.17	0.03
Father's mental health	0.04	–	–
Family income (log)	0.07	0.08	0.14
Mother's involvement with child	0.04	0.05	0.02
Mother worked (% of 1st year)	–	–	−0.02
Mother worked (% of other years)	–	−0.05	0.04
Father unemployed (% of years)	–	–	−0.03
Parents' education (years)	–	0.04	0.17
Mother's aggression to child	−0.03	−0.12	–
All parental variables	0.27	0.31	0.35

Source: A.E. Clark et al. (2018) Table 16.4 ALSPAC data; for questionnaires, see online Annex 9.1
Note: Wellbeing is the average of mother's and child's replies to the Short Mood and Feelings Questionnaire. Behaviour is mother's replies to Strength and Difficulties Questionnaire. Academic score is the General Certificate of Secondary Education (GCSE). Control variables include gender, ethnicity and the name of the primary and secondary school. For questionnaires see Annex 9.1.

Closely related to family conflict is the **mental health** of the parents. In the Bristol study, the single most important family variable predicting a child's wellbeing at 16 was the mental health of the mother.[13] The father's mental health also mattered but less so – probably because the mother is still, generally, the primary care giver. Clearly poor mental health can lead to family conflict, and vice-versa, but what emerges clearly is that both matter, holding the other constant.

There are three other causal factors that are much discussed. The first is **family income**. This is much less important for child wellbeing than it is for exam performance. The Bristol study showed that a 10% rise in family income would increase a child's wellbeing by only 0.007 standard deviations. Similar findings emerge from other studies.[14] A second important influence is **parental involvement** in the life of the child. This is important in early life, but in the Bristol study it had few lasting effects. And the third issue is whether the **mother works** and for how long. In the majority of studies, this has no negative effect on child wellbeing, once the positive effect of the mother's earnings is taken into account.[15]

---

[13] A. E. Clark et al. (2018).

[14] Duncan and Brooks-Gunn (1999). For the United States, see Yeung et al. (2002); and Mistry et al. (2002). For the UK, see Washbrook et al. (2014). In addition, using the national survey of the Mental Health of Children and Young People in Britain, 2004, Ford et al. (2004, 2007), showed that, cet. par., family income had no effect on child mental health either in a cross-section of children **or** in explaining their changes in mental health over time.

[15] For example, A. E. Clark et al. (2018) pp. 162–163 and references therein.

As the last row of Table 9.1 shows, the overall effect of all the observed parental characteristics upon the wellbeing of the child is a β-coefficient equal to 0.27.[16] It is time to compare this with the contribution of schooling.

The Effect of Schools

The Bristol study covered all the children who were born in that area over a 2-year period. As a result, each school in the area taught many children who were in the study. This enables us to see how much difference it made which school a child went to. The results showed that it made a very great difference – the schools really did affect the wellbeing of the children, as well as their behaviour and their exam performance.

The study estimated the following equation for wellbeing (W), as well as similar equations for behaviour and academic score:

$$W_i = \sum_s a_s D_{si} + \sum b_j X_{ij} + c\, W_{i\,\text{lagged}}. \tag{1}$$

Here W_i is the wellbeing of the ith child, and the X_{ij}s are the characteristics of the parents. There is also a 1/0 dummy variable D_s for each school (which takes the value 1 when the school is the one the individual attended and otherwise zero). So the coefficient a_s tells us what difference it made that a pupil went to school s.[17]

We can now ask: How far did these different effects of the different schools contribute to the overall spread of wellbeing in the child population? The answer can be found by looking at the standard deviation of the a_s coefficients (weighted by pupil numbers) relative to the standard deviation of W. The answers are in Table 9.2. In the first row, the table examines how much difference secondary schools make to children at age 16, holding constant not only all the measured family variables but also the child's measurement on the same outcome when she entered the school at age 11. The second row does the same for primary schools, showing their effects at age 11 holding constant the measurement of the same outcome at age 8. And the third row shows their effects at age 8 holding constant the measurement of the same outcome at age 7. As Table 9.2 shows, schools make a remarkably huge difference to the wellbeing of their pupils – almost as much a difference as they make to their academic performance. And, looking back at Table 9.1, schools are making as much difference to child wellbeing as parents do (in so far as we can measure parents' characteristics).

For primary schools, we can go a lot further and isolate the effect of individual **teachers**. This is possible because each child has only one main teacher in any one year. So we use the same methodology as shown in equation (1), but we replace individual schools by individual teachers. Table 9.3 shows the average results for the

---

[16] 0.27 is got by first estimating equation (1) below and then estimating $W_i/\sigma_w = \gamma_0 + \gamma_1(Z_i/\sigma_Z) + etc$, where $Z_i = \sum b_j X_{ij}$. The resulting estimate of γ_1 is 0.27.

[17] The lagged wellbeing is the wellbeing the pupil had when entering the school (or class).

Table 9.2 Standard deviation of school dummy coefficients for different standardised outcomes

		Wellbeing	Behaviour	Academic performance
Secondary school	Age 16	0.26	0.21	0.29
Primary schools	Age 11	0.24	0.19	0.27
	Age 8	0.19	0.20	0.30

Source: A. E. Clark et al. (2018) Tables 14.1 and 14.3, ALSPAC data
Note: Academic performance was measured at 16 by GCSE score; at 11 by KS2 Maths, English and Science; and at other ages by local data on Maths, Reading and Writing.

Table 9.3 Standard deviation of primary school teacher impacts on different standardized outcomes over the year

Ages	Wellbeing	Behaviour	Maths score
11 and 8 (pooled)	0.22	0.09	0.14

Source: A. E. Clark et al. (2018) Table 14.5, ALSPAC data; note: Wellbeing and Behaviour based on parents' reports

children aged 11 and aged 8 (averaged). Strikingly, the teachers have a more differential effect on the wellbeing of their children than they have on their maths score. It is also possible to follow the long-term effects that primary school teachers have on their pupils right into their 20s. It turns out that a teacher who is good at raising children's wellbeing also makes her children nearly 4 percentage points more likely to go to university.[18] And a good teacher reduces their likelihood of becoming depressed, antisocial or alcoholic in their early twenties.This type of analysis shows clearly that schools and teachers make a big difference to the wellbeing of their children. But exactly **how** do they make that difference? This is a much more difficult question to answer. Some negative findings are fairly well established:

- Smaller class sizes have no well-established advantages, in terms of their impact on wellbeing (or on intellectual development).[19]
- Larger schools have no well-established advantages in terms of wellbeing.

But we have little naturalistic evidence on what things do make a difference. There is, however, one way to discover: by experiment. There have been many outstanding experiments that tell us a lot about how we can produce happier children.

---

[18] This is the effect of 1 standard deviation in the skill of raising children's wellbeing at age 11. See Fleche et al. (2021).

[19] See A. E. Clark et al. (2018) chapter 14. On wellbeing, see also Jakobsson et al. (2013) but also Dee and West (2011); Fredriksson et al. (2013). On test scores, see also Hanushek (1999) and Hoxby (2000) but also Angrist and Levy (1999) and Krueger (2003).

Can we teach happiness?

In the earliest (and most famous) experiments, the wellbeing of the children was not measured as such, but many other important outcomes were. Most of these early experiments were conducted with young pre-school children (though there is no convincing evidence that early intervention is more cost-effective than later intervention).[20] Two well-known **pre-school interventions** are the Perry Pre-School project and the Abecedarian Project.[21] Perry Pre-School was a randomised trial on high-risk African-American children aged three and four. They spent two years in school for half the day, and their mothers were also visited at home each week. The children in the programme behaved better in subsequent life and were half as likely to be arrested than those in the control group. They also studied better, and a calculation of the project's real rate of return to society was 7–10% per annum – better than the real return on equities.[22] The Abecedarian Project provided all-day play-based care for deprived children from birth to the age of 5. By age 21, the treatment group were less criminal and also earned more than the control group.[23]

A less expensive project for **children of school age** was the Good Behaviour Game, played in schools in a deprived area of Baltimore. In the treatment group, each first-year primary class is divided into three teams, and each team is scored according to the number of times a member of the team breaks a rule. If the team has fewer than five infringements, a reward goes to all members of the team. Children who played (or did not play) the game were followed up to ages 19–21, and those in the treatment group used fewer drugs, less alcohol and less tobacco, and fewer had anti-social personality disorder.[24]

However, one should be careful about generalising from individual experiments, since once in a while an intervention will, by chance, appear effective even if it is really not so. To see what can be achieved we really need a **meta-analysis** that summarises the results of a large number of experiments on children of school age.

CASEL (the Collaboration for Academic, Social and Emotional Learning) has provided just such a meta-analysis (see Table 9.4). It has analysed 200 programmes aimed at the whole range of children in a school and covering the basic topics in social and emotional learning (SEL), namely

- understanding and managing your own emotions and
- understanding and responding well to other people.

[20] The case for earlier intervention has been argued most carefully for cognitive outcomes, rather than for wellbeing (see, for example, the work of James Heckmann). But brain research stresses the plasticity of the brain right into early adulthood (Dahl et al. [2020]) and in 1 training exercise people aged 16–30 learned better than those aged 11–16 (Blakemore [2018] pp. 92–94).

[21] The UK's Sure Start Programme, begun in 1999, had much less structured ways of working than most interventions. There was also no randomised evaluation. However, comparing Sure Start with similarly deprived non-Sure Start areas suggested that Sure Start significantly improved 5 out of 14 outcomes at age 3 (Melhuish et al. [2008]). By age 7, rather fewer significant effects were observed (DfE [2012]).

[22] Parks (2000); and Heckman et al. (2010).   [23] Wilson (2011) p. 215.

[24] Kellam et al. (2011); and Ialongo et al. (1999).

Table 9.4 Effects of programmes of social and emotional learning (SEL)

	Average gain (in standard deviations)	(Number of programmes)
Effect of programme on		
Emotional wellbeing	0.23	(106)
Behaviour	0.23	(112)
Academic performance	0.28	(35)

Source: Durlak et al. (2011)

The overall findings were encouraging and some key lessons emerge.

- **Programmes that improve wellbeing also improve academic performance**. These objectives do not conflict with each other. This is a vital and quite general point.[25]
- Most programmes improve wellbeing more for the children whose wellbeing was initially **low**. But this does not argue for targeting because the programme works partly through changing the overall ethos of the class, and it is also important to avoid stigma.
- Programmes work better if they are '**manualised**' (i.e., use detailed manuals and related materials for each lesson) and if the teachers using them have been trained in how to use them.[26]
- Programmes are more likely to succeed if they **focus on what is worth doing**, rather than on what **not** to do. Most programmes fail if they are focused exclusively on the dangers of sex, drugs, alcohol, tobacco, gambling or crime.[27] In general, children and adolescents respond better to the prospect of a positive reward rather than the threat of a negative outcome.[28]
- The effects of most programmes **fade over time**. This is largely because they are too short – typically less than 20 hours in total.

The conclusion is therefore that, if we want to improve the wellbeing of our children, we need a more ambitious approach.[29] This could include the following:

- The school makes wellbeing an explicit **goal** of the school and measures the wellbeing of pupils each year to see how they are improving or falling behind. Good tests exist.[30] In the Dutch secondary schools, this is required to be done by

---

[25] See also Frederickson and Brannigan (2005); Adler (2016); Fleche (2017); Hanh and Weare (2017).

[26] Humphrey et al. (2010) gives this as 1 reason why Britain's secondary school Social and Economic Aspects of Learning (SEAL) programme failed. (There is however good evidence within the group of schools doing SEAL that good implementation produced better results, Banerjee et al. [2014]). As regards primary SEAL, there has been no controlled experiment involving children's outcomes – but see Hallam et al. (2006); and Gross (2010).

[27] Layard and Clark (2014) p. 228 　[28] Blakemore (2018) p. 155.

[29] See Education Endowment Foundation, Moore et al. (2019).

[30] See, for example, annex 6.2 of Layard and Ward (2020), available online at: http://cep.lse.ac.uk/CWBH/annexesCWBH.pdf. For wellbeing (as for academic achievement), the school should be looking at its 'value-added' – compared with a national reference norm. Some organisation from outside a school

law and the government provides the logistics for the measurement and also processes the results.[31] In Southern Australia, the system is similar, but participation by the school is voluntary.[32]

- This goal of wellbeing is reflected in **all** aspects of school life including how teachers, parents and pupils behave to each other.[33]
- There is specific **weekly** teaching of life-skills. This does not depend on inspired teachers. It is normally manualised. The race is therefore on to produce a curriculum that can cover the whole age-range in schools. One major trial was recently completed in Britain of a 4-year curriculum for ages 11–15 called Healthy Minds, which raised life satisfaction at 15 by 0.25 standard deviations (or 10 percentile points) – see Box 9.1.

Box 9.1 The Healthy Minds Experiment[34]

This provided the curriculum for a weekly lesson over four years, with detailed materials for the teacher and pupils for each lesson and professional training for teachers. The topics covered were emotional resilience, self-management, relationships with others (including sex), healthy living, managing social media, handling mental illness, becoming a parent and the practice of mindfulness. Teachers received 19 days of training over the 4 years for the experiment.

Thirty-four schools were involved, randomly divided into Groups A and Group B. Group A schools taught the curriculum to the cohort of children aged 11 in 2013 and measured their wellbeing at age 11, at age 13 and at age 16. Group B schools did the same for the cohort of children aged 11 in 2014; but they also measured the wellbeing of the cohort of children aged 11 in 2013. Thus the older group B cohort acted as the control group both for the Group A cohort and the later Group B cohort. The overall effect of the course was estimated by the following equation (analogous to equation (9) in Chapter 7):

$$W_{ist} = a_0 + a_1 T_{ist} + v_t + f_i + u_s + e_{ist}$$

where W_{ist} is the wellbeing of student i in school s in year t and T_{ist} means 'Have completed the course'.

The findings showed that at the end of the final year 'global health' (the primary outcome designated before the trial) was raised by 0.25 standard deviations, and life satisfaction by a similar amount.

The teacher training and teaching materials are available through Bounce Forward, https://bounceforward.com/healthy-minds-research-project/.

---

should organise the measurement (typically online). In addition, the scope for gaming will be reduced if secondary schools judge themselves by how they augment pupils' wellbeing beyond the level already measured by some other body, that is, at primary school.

[31] See www.onderwijsinspectie.nl/onderwerpen/sociale-veiligheid/toezicht-op-naleving-zorgplicht-sociale-veiligheid-op-school.

[32] The Government of South Australia runs the online administration of the questionnaire and tabulation of the results. No individual is identified but schools and classrooms are provided with benchmark data for comparison. Further information, see www.education.sa.gov.au/wellbeing-and-engagement-census/about-census.

[33] Weare (2000).   [34] See Lordan and McGuire (2019).

Bullying and school discipline

We can end this review of schooling with two specific topics: bullying, and school discipline. **Being bullied** is a major problem for many children. Bullying means repeated aggressive behaviour by a child or a group of children against a victim who cannot easily defend him/herself. Bullying can mean physical violence (pushing or hitting), name-calling and taunting, rumour spreading, public exclusion or obscene gestures. It can also be done online (cyber-bullying). On average across OECD countries 23% of 15-year-olds report being bullied at least a few times a month.[35] The correlation between life satisfaction and being bullied is substantially negative (r = 0.26).[36] There is also clear evidence that children who are bullied experience subsequent falls in mental health.[37] The more extreme the victimisation, the more extreme the deterioration. And many of these effects persist into adulthood.[38]

Most schools have a policy about bullying. But perhaps the most successful has been the KiVa programme, which is now virtually universal in Finland.[39] The basic idea is to train pupils how to behave when they see someone being bullied: they are trained to support the person being bullied, not the bully. When this approach was first trialled, it reduced the rate of bullying (reported by victims) by 30%. In the national roll-out the effect was around 15%.

In almost every country, **school discipline** is a problem, at least in some classrooms. In a British survey of 11- and 14-year-olds in large cities, 29% said that every day other pupils disrupt their lessons.[40] Teachers' reports corroborate this. Yet the skill of keeping order can be trained. For example, the Incredible Years course for teachers takes 3–5 days in college with occasional follow-up. Teachers are taught how to (1) keep calm, (2) give as much praise as possible and (3) give small immediate punishments. In a large trial, the programme improved children's mental health in the first year (especially that of the least happy children) but in the following years the effect had disappeared.[41]

Social Media

Another huge influence on young people's lives (and those of adults) is **social media**. Clearly, this brings huge possibilities for disseminating information and reducing isolation. But social media also has one major disadvantage: it exacerbates the

---

[35] OECD (2017) p. 136.

[36] Przybylski and Bowes (2017). There is also a strong correlation between bullying and being bullied (Veldkamp et al. [2019]).

[37] Moore et al. (2017) shows clear evidence of causality.   [38] Wolke et al. (2013).

[39] Salmivalli and Poskiparta (2012); and Menesini and Salmivalli (2017).

[40] Wilson et al. (2007). In a national survey, 'Understanding Society', children aged 10–15 were asked how often other children misbehaved in class. Some 27% said 'in most classes' and 47% said 'in over half of all classes' (Knies [2012] appendix 1). This significantly reduced their life satisfaction (Knies [2012] appendix 2).

[41] Ford et al. (2019).

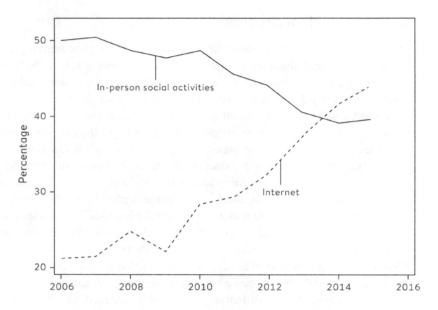

Figure 9.1 Percentage of 18-year-olds spending 10 or more hours per week on the internet and percentage undertaking 4 face-to-face social activities in a week (United States)
Source: Twenge (2017)

problem of social comparisons. People put the best of their life on social media, and others feel inferior or left out. It is notable that at the same time as social media has soared, adolescent depression has too (compare the changes since 2010 in Figures 9.1 and 9.2). And so has the number of people who say 'I often feel left out of things' or 'A lot of times I feel lonely'.[42]

However, correlation does not prove causality. Experiments are the clearest method of establishing causality. There have been about a dozen **controlled experiments** where participants abstain from using Facebook. The majority of these show positive effects of abstention on subjective wellbeing.[43] In the most elaborate of them, a sample of US citizens were asked how much they would have to be paid to stop using Facebook for a month.[44] The researchers then selected those 1,700 or so with the lowest values and randomly assigned them to the treatment group (paid \$102) and the control group. The treatment group did not use Facebook for a month. In consequence, the subjective wellbeing of the treatment group was higher during the month by 0.12 points (out of 7) than it would otherwise have been. Three months after the

---

[42] Twenge (2017) pp. 96–99.

[43] Allcott et al. (2020) conducted the experiment about to be described. They also list in an appendix all the randomised experiments done so far – on college students and on older people. See especially Deters and Mehl (2013); Tromholt (2016); and Shakya and Christakis (2017). By contrast, simple studies of the effects of time online show no clear effect on wellbeing (Orben [2020]).

[44] Allcott et al. (2020).

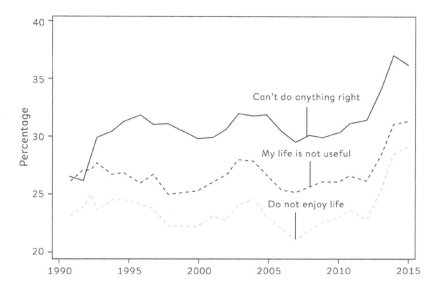

Figure 9.2 Percentage of 13–18-year-olds experiencing various negative thoughts in last 12 months (United States)
Source: Twenge (2017)

end of the experiment the treatment group were using Facebook 22% less than the control group – a partial vote of no confidence.

However, clearly Facebook has positive uses as well as negative. In some discussions, a distinction is made between active use (posting things on to Facebook), which is considered positive for the actor, and passive use (just reading other people's posts), which is considered negative – because it often induces unfavourable comparisons of oneself with others and sometimes involves cyberbullying.[45] Passive use takes up ¾ of the time so the combined effect of active and passive is negative. But people will always use social media and the central issue is how to promote the positive use while reducing the negative.

Family Conflict

Sometime after adolescence, most people start forming families of their own. As we have seen, **having a partner** is on average very beneficial to one's wellbeing. In the British Household Panel Survey, people with partners are on average happier than others by a large amount (other things equal). Compared with people without a partner, they are on average happier by 0.6 points (out of 10). Similar results are found in other countries though they are reduced by about 0.2 points in fixed-effects regressions.[46]

[45] Verduyn et al. (2017). See also Birkjær and Kaats (2019).   [46] A. E. Clark et al. (2018).

We have already seen how family conflict and separation can damage children. But it can also be terrible for the adults. Roughly 12% of all partnered men and women in the United States engage in physical aggression, with more violence usually coming from the men.[47] There can also be psychological violence – denigration, dominance or extreme withdrawal.

These behaviours often reflect chauvinistic attitudes, which society needs to change, and the law needs to be enforced. But there are also services that can help to stop conflict developing in the first place. A key moment is when the first child is born. From that point couples become, on average, less satisfied with their relationship. But this can be averted if both parents take ante-natal classes that cover not just the physical and emotional care of children but also the sustaining of love between the parents.[48] There are many courses of this kind. One of the most successful is Family Foundations, which involves eight group meetings with the parents. Compared with a control group, parents who take the course were less stressed and more cooperative by 6 percentile points.[49]

But even with these courses, many couples will still fight. They need help and, as Chapter 10 shows, there are good treatments that can be provided.

Conclusions

- The way our parents behave affects our wellbeing.[50] Warm love and firm boundaries are good for wellbeing. However, many children survive severe abuse without major changes. The mental health of parents (and especially mothers) is important for the wellbeing of their children.
- Schools have more effect on children's wellbeing than is usually appreciated, and so do individual teachers.
- If they wish to improve child wellbeing, schools will make that a major goal of the school and will measure it regularly.
- Life skills will also be taught at least weekly using evidence-based materials.
- In adulthood, family life is on average beneficial to wellbeing. But the quality of relationships often deteriorates after the birth of the first child. This problem can be reduced if both parents take ante-natal classes covering not just childcare but the impact of the child on their relationship.
- If, despite this, the mental health of the children or their parents deteriorates, it is vital that professional mental health support is available.

So let us turn now to the issue of health – of mind and of body.

---

[47] Epstein et al. (2015).
[48] Layard and Ward (2020) pp. 168–170. See WHO (2009) for useful community and school-based interventions.
[49] Feinberg et al. (2010).
[50] Low estimated effects of 'shared environment' can be because parents treat different children differently (even if they are identical twins).

Questions for discussion

(1) How big is the true influence of parents on children's wellbeing at age 16, compared with the effect of school experience? Given the scale of measurement error is it possible to answer this question?

(2) Can life-skills be taught effectively in schools?

(3) Is social media making children happier or less happy? Is it improving the quality of communication or reducing it?

Further Reading

Allcott, H., Braghieri, L., Eichmeyer, S., and Gentzkow, M. (2020). The welfare effects of social media. *American Economic Review*, 110(3), 629–676.

Bowlby, J. (1969). *Attachment and Loss: Attachment*. Basic Books.

Clark, A. E., Flèche, S., Layard, R., Powdthavee, N., and Ward, G. (2018). *The Origins of Happiness: The Science of Wellbeing over the Life Course*. Princeton University Press.

Heckman, J. J., Moon, S. H., Pinto, R., Savelyev, P. A., and Yavitz, A. (2010). The rate of return to the HighScope Perry Preschool Program. *Journal of Public Economics*, 94(1–2), 114–128.

Lordan, G., and McGuire, A. J. (2019). Widening the high school curriculum to include soft skill training: impacts on health, behaviour, emotional wellbeing and occupational aspirations. CEP Discussion Paper 1630, Centre for Economic Performance, LSE.

Moore, D., Benham-Clarke, S., Kenchington, R., Boyle, C., Ford, T., Hayes, R., and Rogers, M. (2019). Improving Behaviour in Schools: Evidence Review.

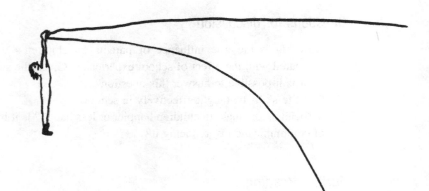

I'M HANGING ON
QUITE COMFORTABLY

10 Health and Healthcare

The vast majority of people in the world (92%) view mental health as being equally important to overall wellbeing as physical health is, if not more so.

Wellcome Global Monitor[1]

We all get sick at one time or another in our lives. All of us get physically sick, and at some point at least a third of us experience diagnosable mental illness.[2] Both types of illness cause us pain, disrupt our lives and can shorten them. As we mentioned in Chapter 5, both mental and physical pain are experienced in the same brain areas (the anterior cingulate cortex and the anterior insula). And mental illness can cause physical illness and vice versa.

Yet the healthcare system responds quite differently when our illness is mental rather than physical. If we are sick in body, we normally get treated. If we are sick in mind, we most commonly do not – even in the richest countries. This is a major cause of unnecessary suffering.

So in this chapter we shall begin with mental illness and consider:

- how prevalent it is,
- why we should take it more seriously and
- what cost-effective treatments exist and how they can be deployed.

Then, after looking at physical pain, we consider the length of life. The remarkable increase in this shows the power of medical science to improve the human lot.

How Much Mental Illness?

There is a difference between low wellbeing and diagnosed mental illness. Low wellbeing can be due either to current external circumstances (poverty, unemployment, recent bereavement and so on) or it can be due to something more internal, something that is partly or wholly psychological in origin.[3] Of course, nearly everyone

---

[1] The Role of Science in Mental Health
[2] For the United States, Kessler et al. (2005a) Table 2 estimate 46%.
[3] This could of course be due to **previous** experience. It could also be psycho-physical in origin.

has some psychological hang-up or other. But to be defined as mental illness, the problem has to be severe enough to cause major distress and impaired ability to function.[4]

So to know the scale of the problem there has to be first a clear diagnostic definition and then a survey to see how many people it applies to. There are two main systems for diagnosing mental illness. One is the US Diagnostic and Statistical Manual **(DSM5)** and the other, broadly similar, is the WHO's International Classification of Disease **(ICD-11)**. Diagnosis is vital to ensure that people get the treatment that is most effective for their problem.

But to know the scale of the problem, we cannot rely on people coming for treatment. We have to have a household survey, ask people the diagnostic questions and then apply DSM or ICD to determine whether they count as mentally ill – in England, for example, there is a regular official survey of this kind.[5]

The most common mental disorders are either depression or they are anxiety disorders (like Post-Traumatic Stress Disorder (PTSD), Obsessive-Compulsive Disorder (OCD), panic attacks, phobias and generalised anxiety). In England, 17% of all adults are suffering from at least one of these so-called **common mental disorders** – with depression and anxiety disorders being equally common. In addition, 0.7% of people are suffering from the more serious 'psychotic' mental illnesses like schizophrenia. There are also other serious mental health problems like bipolar disorder, addiction and Attention Deficit Hyperactivity Disorder (ADHD), but these to a large extent overlap with the other disorders we have already described. Thus, in broad terms, some 20% of the adult British population suffer from diagnosable mental illness (excluding dementia). The same is true in the United States.[6] And in poorer countries, rates of mental illness are similar to those in richer ones.[7]

These are the numbers of people who are ill at a moment in time. But many more people experience mental illness at some point in their lives – at least a third of us do so. Much mental illness begins in childhood. At any one time at least 10% of children aged 5–16 have a diagnosable mental health problem – mainly anxiety disorders or conduct disorder (both of which can begin quite early in life).[8] Depression does not generally begin till the teens, and schizophrenia begins in the late teens or later. By the early 20s, rates of mental illness are higher than at any other age, and then they decline steadily as people age. The majority of people who experience mental health problems in childhood also experience them as adults, unless the problems are tackled early.[9]

---

[4] Similarly, for much physical illness, diagnosis requires cut-offs, e.g., 'high' blood pressure is defined as the level that causes an unacceptable risk of heart attack or stroke.

[5] For the latest survey of adults in England (in 2014), see McManus et al. (2016). For the United States, see 2019 National Survey of Drug Use and Health run by SAMSHA.

[6] The US figure is 20.6% – see 2019 National Survey of Drug Use and Health run by SAMSHA, Table 8.7B.

[7] Ayuso-Mateos (2010); and WHO (2017).   [8] On England, see Sadler et al. (2018).

[9] Kim-Cohen et al. (2003); and Kessler et al. (2005b).

There is some evidence that mental health problems have become increasingly common, especially among young women (adolescents and young adults).[10] But mental illness has always been a serious issue.

There are at least four reasons why mental health should be taken more seriously than it often is:

- its impact on wellbeing
- its impact on physical health
- its impact on the economy
- the existence of cost-effective treatments.

The Effects of Mental Illness

On wellbeing and suicide

As we saw in Chapter 8, diagnosed depression or anxiety disorder is one of the biggest factors explaining the dispersion of happiness in advanced countries – and the biggest single cause of misery. Mental illness also has huge implications for other members of society, especially the person's family.[11]

It is a major factor in most **suicides**. Some 1.3% of all deaths in the world are from suicide[12] – and so are roughly 1% of deaths in the advanced world (see Figure 10.1). And about 90% of people who kill themselves are mentally ill when they do it.[13] Though a half of those who kill themselves are also physically ill, it is generally the mental pain that drives them to suicide: suicide is rare among physically ill people who are not also mentally ill.[14] Successful suicide is more common among men than women, but attempted suicide is the other way around. Almost every suicide is a tragedy – a life lost and a terrible blow to family and friends. And so are the other 'deaths from despair' that are now so common in the United States – the deaths from drug overdose or alcoholic liver disease.[15] There are many resources available to people in despair which they are encouraged to contact.

On physical illness

Mental stress and illness can also shorten life in other ways than suicide. Mental illness makes you more likely to contract all the main **physical diseases**.[16] And people

---

[10] For English data, see McManus et al. (2016); and Sadler et al. (2018).
[11] See A. E. Clark et al. (2018) Table 6.4.
[12] World Health Organization (2014). https://apps.who.int/iris/bitstream/handle/10665/131056/9789241564779_eng.pdf.
[13] Barlow and Durand (2009) p. 251; Blumenthal (1988); Barraclough et al. (1974). Sixty per cent of them have depression.
[14] Williams (2001) p. 36.   [15] Case and Deaton (2020).
[16] Patten et al. (2008) Table 1. Mentally ill people were also more likely to die. (But the authors warn against possible bias, since positive findings are more likely to get published.) On stroke, see also Pan et al. (2011) Figure 3. On cancer, see also Chida et al. (2008).

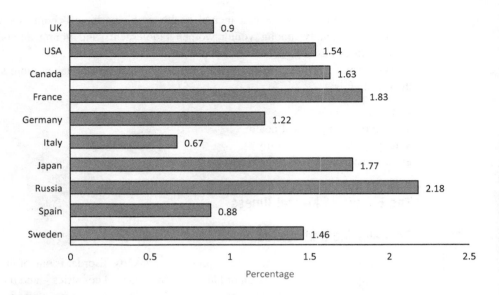

Figure 10.1 Suicide as a percentage of all deaths
Source: Global Burden of Disease Collaborative Network; Global Burden of Disease Study Results (2019); Seattle, United States: Institute for Health Metrics and Evaluation (IHME), http://ghdx.healthdata.org/gbd-results-tool

who are already physically ill are more likely to get worse, if they are also mentally ill.[17] Why is this? There are some obvious channels. Mentally ill people are more likely to smoke and drink, take drugs, overeat and under-exercise. But a huge effect still remains on top of these factors. And the reason for this is that chronic stress changes the body in so many ways, as we saw in Chapter 5.

On the economy

Mental illness also imposes significant **economic costs**. This is because mental illness is mainly a disease of working age, while physical illness mainly occurs in old age. Figure 10.2 shows the percentage reduction in the average quality of life at each age due to mental and physical illness in advanced countries. As the figure shows, among people under 60, one half of all morbidity is due to mental illness.

These facts have huge economic implications.[18] First, disability. In OECD countries, nearly half of all the disabled people who are not working are suffering from mental rather than physical illness. Second, absenteeism. Among people who do have jobs, between a third and a half of all days off sick are due to mental illness. Third, 'presenteeism'. Even if they turn up at work, many mentally ill people are not fully

---

[17] Satin et al. (2009). See also meta-analyses by Nicholson et al. (2006) for depression and by Roest et al. (2010) for anxiety. For hospital consultations by patients with asthma, see Ahmedani et al. (2013).

[18] On what follows see Layard and Clark (2014) pp. 72, 73, and 86.

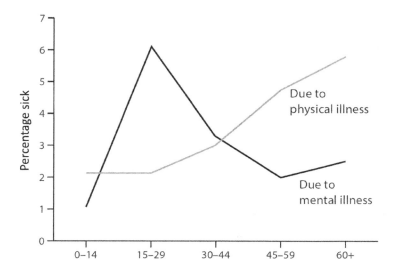

Figure 10.2 Rate of morbidity in different age groups
Source: A. E. Clark et al. (2018) Figure 6.2; based on WHO (2008); Analysis by Michael Parsonage

'there', and this is estimated to cost their employers at least as much as absenteeism. So the economic loss due to mental illness is, according to the OECD, at least 4% of GDP, of which one half is borne by the taxpayer. It follows that, if we treat more mental illness and more people return to work, we can save much money both for taxpayers, businesses and the workers themselves.

The Treatment of Mental Illness

But can we really treat these conditions and help people to recover? The answer is Yes. We now have appropriate treatments for every type of mental health condition, based on the evidence of thousands of randomised controlled trials. The recommended treatments can be found in the **Cochrane Reviews** or in the official guidance produced by England's National Institute for Health and Care Excellence, otherwise known as **NICE**.[19]

Recommended treatments include drugs (for some conditions) and psychological therapy (for all conditions). **Drugs** are recommended for

- schizophrenia (e.g., chlorpromazine)
- bipolar disorder (e.g., lithium)
- severe depression (e.g., Prozac)
- some anxiety disorders (e.g., a benzodiazepine)
- alcoholism (a benzodiazepine to facilitate withdrawal, and naltrexone to reduce craving)

[19] See Layard and Clark (2014), chapters 10 and 13.

Table 10.1 English government's recommendations for the psychological treatment of depression, anxiety and eating disorders

Condition	Treatment
Depression: moderate to severe	CBT or Interpersonal psychotherapy, each with antidepressants
Depression: mild to moderate	CBT (individual or group)
	Interpersonal psychotherapy
	Behavioural activation
	Behavioural couples therapy
	Counselling for depression
	Short-term psychodynamic therapy
Panic disorder	CBT
Social anxiety disorder	CBT or Short-term psychodynamic therapy
Generalised anxiety disorder	CBT
Obsessive-compulsive disorder	CBT
Post-traumatic stress disorder	CBT, EMDR*
Bulimia	CBT
	Interpersonal psychotherapy
Anorexia	In-patient weight-gain programme
	CBT
	Interpersonal psychotherapy
	Cognitive analytic therapy

*EMDR= eye movement desensitisation reprocessing therapy (considered by many to be a form of CBT).
Source: NICE recommendations

- heroin addiction (e.g., methadone replacement therapy and naltrexone)
- ADHD (Ritalin).

But **psychological therapy** is also recommended to be offered for every condition, Table 10.1 shows the most effective treatments for anxiety disorders and depression. Mental health problems are at the root of many other problems in society – for example, family conflict is often a mental health problem and effective psychological treatments exist, such as Cognitive Behavioural Couple Therapy (CBCT).

Some people argue that it does not matter much which form of therapy is provided – what matters is the skill and character of the **therapist**. But the evidence given in support of this view is not based on randomised trials – it is based on cases selected by therapists.[20] By contrast, when a given therapy is given by a range of different therapists with different characters but all using the same methods and trained to a high standard, the success rates of different therapists are remarkably similar.[21] What makes a large difference is how well the therapists are trained and whether they use the right therapy for each condition.[22] If this is done, at least 50% of patients will recover from most anxiety disorders or depression, after an average of some 10 sessions. For depression, this is the same recovery rate as with drugs, but the relapse rate after psychological therapy is one half that after drugs, unless the drugs continue to be taken.

[20] See Layard and Clark (2014) pp. 125–126.   [21] D. M. Clark et al. (2006).   [22] D. M. Clark (2018).

Economic benefits of treatment

So what are the economic costs and benefits of making psychological therapy more widely available? The average cost of therapy per patient is around a half of the average monthly wage in a country. To set against this, the benefits come from two sources. The first is the effect of the therapy on peoples' **ability to work**. The evidence suggests that in a typical group of patients there are at least 4% who would not otherwise have worked but who will now work for at least an extra 25 months.[23] Thus, for the average patient who is treated, the result will be an extra month of work (4% times 25 months). Even if the patient earns only half the average national wage, this is enough to repay the initial cost of the treatment – since, as we have seen, that was also half the average monthly wage. So the overall economic balance is impressive (but the balance for different groups in society, like taxpayers, will be different – depending on how healthcare is financed).

There is also a second major economic benefit – the savings on **physical health-care**. As we have already seen, mental health affects physical health. And it also affects the amount of physical healthcare a person actually receives. On average, people with given physical symptoms get 50% more physical healthcare if they are also mentally ill.[24] This applies equally to people with breathing problems, heart problems and diabetes. So, if their mental health improves, there are huge savings on their physical healthcare. In all these cases, psychological interventions have been shown to pay for themselves, through the large savings in physical healthcare costs.[25]

The shortfall in mental healthcare

Since treatment produces such large economic savings, one might expect that most people with mental health problems would receive treatment. This is of course what happens when people are physically ill – most of them get treated, at least in rich countries (over 90% of people with diabetes are in treatment). But most people with mental illness are not treated. In England, only 40% of adults with clinical levels of depression or anxiety disorder are in treatment,[26] and in most advanced countries it is less than this.[27] In low- and middle-income countries the **treatment gap** is even worse, with under 10% in treatment. The situation is worse for children: in England only 30% of diagnosable children get specialist treatment,[28] and in poor countries hardly any do so.

Moreover, for adults, the main form of treatment is medication – drugs of one sort or another. Few get evidence-based psychological therapy. For example, in England in

---

[23] Proudfoot et al. (1997); Wells et al. (2000); Rollman et al. (2005); D. M. Clark et al. (2009); Fournier et al. (2014); Toffolutti et al. (2019).
[24] Katon (2003); Hutter et al. (2010); Naylor et al. (2012) p. 11.
[25] Chiles et al. (1999); Chisholm et al. (2016); D. M. Clark (2018); Gruber et al. (2019).
[26] McManus et al. (2016).   [27] Chisholm et al. (2016).
[28] Sadler et al. (2018) give a figure of 25% for 2016 but more up-to-date information suggests 30%. For the United States, the Center for Disease Control report a figure of 20%.

2014 only 12% of adults with depression or anxiety were receiving any. Yet psychological therapy is what the majority of them would prefer.[29]

Many celebrities, including sports stars and the British royal family have drawn attention to the low rate of treatment for mental illness. So what accounts for it? There are three main reasons. The first is **stigma** and the nature of the illness itself. People are often ashamed of having mental health problems, and so are their family. They frequently feel is it their fault. By contrast, most people feel that physical illness is something that just happens to you. So, there is much more public pressure for better cancer care than for better mental health care.

Second, most people do not realise what effective treatments we now have for most mental health problems. This is a case of **technological lag**. This lag is also one reason for the stigma – if you cannot be cured, many people will avoid you. But as people come to realise that effective treatments exist, the stigma will be reduced.

And there is a third reason for under-treatment – the slothful response of healthcare providers and insurers. Insurance companies often offer to pay for only 6 sessions of treatment – like paying for half a surgical operation. There is a simple principle that should apply to both mental and physical illness, which is '**parity of esteem**'. This means that a person who is mentally ill should be as likely to receive state-of-the-art treatment as someone who is physically ill.

Effective mental health services

How to achieve this ambition will depend on each country's system of providing healthcare. But in any system, there are four essential ingredients:

(1) clear decisions about which treatments are to be offered for which conditions,
(2) a system of training therapists to deliver these treatments,
(3) a network of services where the treatments are provided and
(4) monitoring of each patient's progress in order to guide treatment and to know what the service is achieving.

Good examples of such systems exist around the world. For example, in England, the **Improving Access to Psychological Therapies (IAPT)** programme began in 2008.[30] By 2021, it employed some 9,000 psychological therapists, mostly trained within the system, and it treated over 640,000 people a year for depression or anxiety disorders.[31] Over half of them recovered after an average of 7–8 sessions of treatment. Its system is now being copied in at least six other countries.

Another model bases most of the treatment in primary care – closer to the family doctor. A good example of this is Chile's **National Depression Detection and**

---

[29] See, for example, Chilvers et al. (2001); van Schaik et al. (2004); Deacon and Abramowitz (2005); McHugh et al. (2013). In England, NICE guidelines say that psychological therapy should be offered for all types of mental illness.
[30] D. M. Clark (2018).
[31] NHS Digital (2021). https://digital.nhs.uk/data-and-information/publications/statistical/psychological-therapies-annual-reports-on-the-use-of-iapt-services/annual-report-2020-21.

Treatment Program. Here treatment is organised by the family doctor and includes medication as well as psychological therapy. In poorer countries, the most feasible approach is to train general healthcare staff in the rudiments of diagnosing and treating mental health problems.[32] Trials show that such an approach can deliver good results, and this is the approach pursued in six poorer countries belonging to the EMERALD consortium.[33]

Clearly similar principles should apply to the treatment of **children** as of adults. There are good evidence-based treatments for all the main conditions in childhood, and it makes no sense if people with mental health problems have to wait until adulthood to get their treatment. For example, social phobia generally starts in childhood. But in the United States, half the people with it never get treated, and those who do get treated have already lived with the problem for, on average, 25 years.[34]

Up to now, most psychological treatment has been delivered face to face. But this is changing rapidly, due to the **digital revolution** and the experience of COVID-19. One change is the use of online video platforms like Zoom to conduct one-on-one therapy. This is often more convenient[35] but it leaves the economics of the therapy unchanged. A more revolutionary innovation is computerised treatment – supported by brief telephone or Zoom contacts with a live therapist. For example, there is a face-to-face treatment for social phobia with an 80% recovery rate. But it has also now been put into an audio-visual form online (supported by much less time of telephone assistance from a live therapist). The recovery rate is not significantly lower.[36] As more and more therapies are put online, the prospects for mentally ill people worldwide will be transformed – especially if the programmes are free.

Physical Illness – Pain and Shortened Lives

Let us turn to **physical illness**. This reduces wellbeing by causing pain and restricting activity. And it shortens life.

A quarter of the world's population report (in the Gallup World Poll) that they experienced a lot of **physical pain** yesterday.[37] And the importance of pain is illustrated in a pioneering US time-use study.[38] A representative sample of American adults were asked to reconstruct the previous day into episodes, and then in each episode they were asked to say to what extent they experienced pain of any kind, on a scale of 0–6 (0 not at all, 6 very strong). This made it possible to compile for each person what percentage of time in the previous day they had spent in any sort of pain (and separately what percentage they had spent in serious pain at levels 4–6).

---

[32] Singla et al. (2017).   [33] Semrau et al. (2015).   [34] Wang et al. (2005) Figure 2.
[35] In IAPT, the total number of sessions given by the programme was undiminished during the COVID-19 lockdown, as was patients' recovery rate.
[36] See also Andersson (2016).   [37] Macchia and Oswald (2021).   [38] Krueger and Stone (2008).

Table 10.2 The experience of pain: By people with different levels of life satisfaction (United States)

Satisfaction with life	Average % of time in any pain	Average % of time in extreme pain
Very satisfied	22	8
Satisfied	29	12
Not satisfied	41	24
Not at all satisfied	54	36
All	29	11
Under 20	21	7
Age 80–89	35	15

Source: Krueger and Stone (2008)
Note: Extreme pain is levels 4–6 (on a scale of 0–6).

As Table 10.2 shows, people with high life satisfaction spent less time in pain, and vice versa. There is probably causation in both directions. But the table is important in showing the strong connection between high life satisfaction and the absence of pain.[39]

Physical health also affects how long you live. One of the greatest inequalities is the inequality in the length of life. The standard deviation of the age of death in England is now 14 years. But this compares with 29 years a century earlier. So the coefficient of variation (SD/mean) of length of life is about 0.17, which compares with the coefficient of variation of life satisfaction which is about 0.27.

Health Policy-Making

Clearly, to judge a situation we need to take into account the length of people's lives as well as the quality of their life. And when we evaluate a policy (such as a healthcare plan) we need to take into account both the length and quality of life. How?

This dilemma faces policy-makers on a daily basis. Suppose, for example, that a healthcare provider has enough money to treat either

(A) 100 cancer patients with a drug that will extend their lives by 1 year at a wellbeing level of 6 or

(B) 100 depressed patients with a therapy that will raise their wellbeing for 20 years from an average of 6 to an average of 6.5.

Which should she do?

The wellbeing approach says that what matters is the total effect on wellbeing. As we put it in Chapter 2 (and ignoring discounting), social welfare looking forward is

$$S = \sum_i \sum_t W_{it} \tag{1}$$

[39] Men and women experience similar levels of pain.

and the test of a policy is the size of its impact on social welfare, given by

$$\Delta S = \sum_i \sum_t \Delta W_{it}. \tag{2}$$

In our example, the impacts on social welfare from the two alternative policies are

A : $100 \times 1 \times 6 = 600$
B : $100 \times 20 \times 0.5 = 1000$.

The first policy produces 600 more Wellbeing-Years or WELLBYs. The second produces 1,000 more. It is therefore more desirable.

A similar approach to this has been used by health planners in many countries for many years. It is known as the 'QALY' approach. So the aim of the healthcare system is to produce the largest number of **'Quality-Adjusted Life-Years' (QALYs)**. This is very similar to the approach advocated in Chapter 2 where the aim of all public policy is to produce the largest number of Wellbeing-Years. But QALYs are generally limited to the so-called health-related quality of life.

The guidelines from England's NICE then recommend treatments for which the cost per QALY is less than about $40,000. In this analysis, the quality-of-life is measured on a scale of 0–1, with 1 corresponding to normal healthy life, whereas in our analysis, wellbeing is measured on a scale of 0–10, with 7.5 corresponding to a normal healthy life. But the basic approach is the same: once a person is dead, their score is 0. They contribute nothing to social welfare. The World Health Organisation has a similar approach. They talk in terms of **'Disability-Adjusted Life Years' (DALYs)**, but that means almost the same as Quality-Adjusted Life Years.

But how, you might ask, do NICE or the WHO actually measure the quality of life associated with each illness? WHO uses panels of doctors to determine the point between 0 and 1 corresponding to each illness. NICE asks members of the public the following 'time trade-off' question, 'Suppose you faced 10 years of life with this illness. How many years of healthy life would be of equal value to you as those 10 years of illness?' If the answer is 8 years, the QALY value for that condition (on the scale 0–1) is 0.8. Neither the WHO nor the NICE method is completely satisfying. Wellbeing science can provide a more direct approach by just asking people with each illness how satisfied they are with their lives.[40] This research has yet to be done but in this view health policy should ultimately be based on WELLBYs including impacts on the family.

Finally, let's return to the big picture of human progress. As we showed in Chapter 6, there has been little progress in average wellbeing worldwide since 2006/8. But there have been huge advances in life expectancy – from 68.7 back then to 72.4 in 2017/19. These gains in life expectancy have been particularly high in sub-Saharan Africa (7 years), the former Soviet Union (5 years) and Asia (3 years). Much of this is due to improved public health and physical healthcare.

---

[40] Dolan and Kahneman (2008).

Conclusions

- Mental and physical illness are intimately related. Both cause pain in the same area of the brain and reduce our ability to function normally.
- Some 20% of the population would be diagnosed as having a mental illness. But in most advanced countries under a third of them are in treatment (mostly medication).
- Though severe conditions require medication, evidence-based psychological treatment is recommended for all conditions. With recovery rates of at least 50%, these treatments are highly cost-effective, because they enable many more people to work productively and they also reduce the demand for costly physical healthcare.
- Physical pain is an important determinant of life satisfaction. Physical health also prolongs life.
- To evaluate any healthcare-intervention, its benefits should be measured in WELLBYs. These need to be high enough relative to the cost.

Questions for discussion

(1) Does the concept of mental illness make sense? How does it differ from low mood due to objective external circumstances?
(2) How important is the correct diagnosis of mental illness?
(3) Are online treatments likely to be of much use for mental illness or is the quality of the therapist crucial?
(4) Why is so much mental illness untreated?
(5) In this chapter, is it claimed that in a group of depressed or anxious people treated with psychological therapy, there will be 4% who would not otherwise work who will now work for at least an extra 25 months – or equivalently there will be an average increase in work of 1 month per person treated. Does the evidence cited in note 23 convince you of that?
(6) Do you agree with the WELLBY measure of social welfare as a good basis for policy evaluation?
(7) How important is it to keep people alive at very high cost if this will only provide a very low quality of life? Should it be legal to assist a terminally ill person in pain to end their own life?

Further Reading

Chiles, J. A., Lambert, M. J., AMD Hatch, A. L. (1999). The impact of psychological interventions on medical cost offset: A meta-analytic review. *Clinical Psychology: Science and Practice*, 6(2), 204–220.

Clark, D. M. (2018). Realizing the mass public benefit of evidence-based psychological therapies: The IAPT program. *Annual Review of Clinical Psychology*, 14, 159–183.

Layard, R., and D. M. Clark (2014). *Thrive: The Power of Evidence-Based Psychological Therapies*. Penguin.

OECD (2012). *Sick on the Job? Myths and Realities about Mental Health and Work*. OECD.

11   Unemployment

The insupportable labour of doing nothing.

Sir Richard Steele

Introduction

In the next two chapters, we turn to the issue of work: do people have it and do they like it? **Unemployment** is another major cause of low wellbeing (see Chapter 8). It damages the individual and it often damages their family. And a high unemployment rate causes anxiety throughout the population. It also reduces the aggregate income of the community. So in this chapter, we ask four main questions:

- How does unemployment affect the unemployed individual?
- Why is unemployment so painful?
- How does high unemployment affect the rest of the community?
- What policies can reduce equilibrium unemployment?

How Important Is Work?

To begin answering this question, we can look at average differences in wellbeing between people according to their employment status. In Figure 11.1, these differences are plotted for six large countries using data from the Gallup World Poll. Here, we consider differences in life satisfaction between adults employed full-time, part-time, self-employed, underemployed, unemployed, and out of the labour force. In this case, 'underemployed' means working part-time but wanting to work full-time, and 'out of the labour force' means not having a job and not actively looking for one. This last category is mainly composed of homemakers, early retirees, students and those unable to work due to disability.

As Figure 11.1, shows, unemployed people are less happy on average than employed people in every country. The crude difference is over 1 point (out of 10) in the United States and the UK and rather less in poorer countries. This is partly because employment

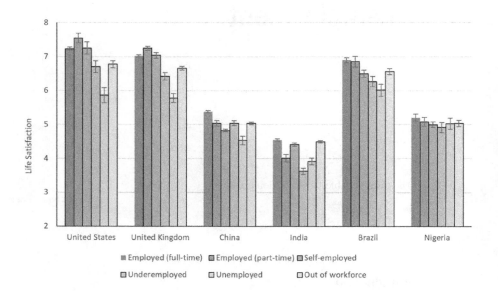

Figure 11.1 Average life satisfaction (0–10) by employment status
Source: Gallup World Poll 2005–2019, Cantril ladder, adults 18–65.
Note: 95% confidence intervals displayed.

classifications become less meaningful in lower-income countries. In Africa, 85% of all employment is informal. In Asia, this figure is roughly 70%.[1] In countries without welfare states or labour protections, the concept of unemployment itself becomes much harder to define. Yet even in these regions, wellbeing differences between working and non-working adults tend to remain statistically significant.

However, looking at raw differences alone can be misleading. Averages can tell us about the distribution of happiness in a population but much less about its underlying causes. There may be any number of **confounding variables** that complicate the story. Relative to those who work full-time, the unemployed are, for example, more likely to be young, female and without a college education.[2] All of these other differences can independently affect wellbeing. If we fail to account for them, we risk misattributing differences in happiness to differences in employment status rather than to other personal characteristics.

In the first wave of empirical wellbeing research, many researchers attempted to address this problem using **cross-sectional regressions**. These models typically take the form:

$$W_i = \alpha_0 + \alpha_1 \text{ Employment}_i + \alpha_2 X'_i + e_i. \tag{1}$$

Here, wellbeing is treated as a continuous variable and modelled as a function of employment status and a vector of controls. The coefficients α_2 represent average

---

[1] International Labour Organization (2018).   [2] Authors' estimations using Gallup World Poll data.

differences in wellbeing attributable to varying demographic characteristics including income, education, marital status, age and so on. The coefficient α_1 then estimates the extent to which any remaining variation in wellbeing can be explained by differences in employment status. In other words, α_1 measures the psychic impact of unemployment.

Using this approach, Helliwell analysed global data from the World Values Survey. In this case, jobless adults were found to be 0.6 points less satisfied with their lives than full-time employees on a 10-point scale, other things equal.[3] By contrast, a halving of income (which unemployed people might also experience) would have a smaller effect (see Chapter 13).

But cross-sectional estimates produced by OLS are still only capable of telling us about average between-person differences. Even with the addition of control variables, there are still two important potential sources of bias to consider:

- **Omitted variables:** For example, happiness can be influenced by unmeasured genetic or personality traits:[4] those who become unemployed may simply be predisposed to be unhappy.
- **Reverse causality:** Happiness itself affects labour market outcomes.[5] If unhappiness precedes unemployment, it would be a mistake to conclude that the latter causes the former.

To counter these biases, researchers look at changes in happiness experienced by workers before, during and after becoming unemployed using **fixed-effects regressions.** Instead of comparing adults with jobs to adults without them, fixed-effects regressions estimate the effect of unemployment by comparing people who become unemployed to their former selves. Running these types of analyses requires **panel data** in which the same people are surveyed multiple times over a given period of time. These models typically take the form:

$$W_{it} = \alpha_0 + \alpha_1 \text{Employment}_{it} + \alpha_2 X'_{it} + f_i + e_{it}. \tag{2}$$

Here, the wellbeing of an individual i at time t is modelled as a function of employment status and control variables. However, in this case, f_i is introduced to capture unobserved time-invariant individual effects, like genetic or personality traits. As a result, we are no longer considering between-person differences but rather **within-person changes.** The coefficients for all variables included on the right-hand side of the equation then represent the effect of transitioning from one state to another – for example, employed to unemployed, childless to parent, single to married. In this way, we can estimate the wellbeing impact of changes in life circumstances from one period to the next.

Early versions of this approach were presented by the economists Liliana and Rainer Winkelmann, using large-scale representative data from the **German**

---

[3] Helliwell (2003).

[4] For evidence, see Lykken and Tellegen (1996); Diener and Lucas (1999); Bartels and Boomsma (2009).

[5] For evidence, see Frijters et al. (2011); De Neve et al. (2012); Oswald et al. (2015).

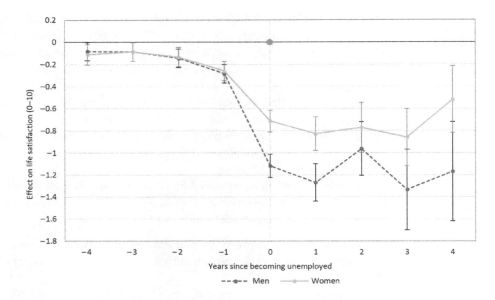

Figure 11.2 Effect of unemployment on life satisfaction (0–10) over time (Germany)
Source: De Neve and Ward (2017); SOEP data
Note: Estimated using fixed-effects (within-person) regressions. Controls included for age, nationality, education, income, number of children, health and marital status. Levels are normalised relative to the baseline happiness level recorded five years before becoming unemployed; 95% confidence intervals displayed.

Socio-Economic Panel (SOEP).[6] The authors found that unemployment lowered life satisfaction by roughly 1-point on a scale from 0 to 10. To put this effect into context, it is roughly analogous to the drop in happiness associated with becoming widowed.[7]

To see how this works over time, the effect of unemployment on life satisfaction is plotted for German workers using SOEP data in Figure 11.2.[8] These effects are estimated using fixed-effects regressions controlling for age, nationality, level of education, income, number of children, health and marital status. Measures of life satisfaction are then normalised relative to a baseline level recorded five years prior to workers losing their jobs. For both men and women, unemployment substantially reduces life satisfaction on top of the effect through lost income. The negative effect of unemployment is roughly 30% larger for men than women, a trend generally reflected

---

[6] Winkelmann and Winkelmann (1995, 1998).

[7] The effects of unemployment were generally stronger for men than for women. Frijters et al. (2004) replicated these results and showed that unemployment was found to have worse effects for East German women than West German women.

[8] The regression is performed for people who had at least one spell of unemployment. It estimates the effect of becoming unemployed and of continuing to be unemployed 1, 2, 3 and 4 years later.

in the literature.[9] Importantly, workers who remain unemployed for longer periods of time struggle to improve their happiness. Even after four years, men and women who lose their jobs are still as unhappy as when they first became unemployed.

Broadly similar results have been found in Britain, the United States and Australia[10] – as well as Russia,[11] South Korea[12] and Switzerland.[13] The **psychic** effect of unemployment is large and there is little adaptation. Given the high degree of adaptation observed in response to many other life events, the lack of adaptation to losing a job is notable.[14] In fact, when the passage of time is taken into account, the cumulative negative effect of long-term unemployment is greater than the long-term impact of becoming married, divorced, widowed or having children.[15]

But does the impact of unemployment differ between workers who choose to leave their jobs and those who become unemployed for reasons outside their control? While quitting is an **endogenous** driver of unemployment, redundancy is **exogenous**. So it is interesting to look at the two groups separately. An analysis of this type in Germany found that workers who lost their jobs due to company closures experienced declines in wellbeing (0.8 points) that were larger than those who resigned from their jobs (0.6 points), although the effect for both groups was statistically significant.[16] At the same time, self-employed workers who had to shut down their business experienced the largest declines overall (1.5 points).

Given this weight of evidence, the substantial negative impact of unemployment on wellbeing is widely regarded to be one of the largest and most robust findings to emerge from empirical happiness research.

Scarring

But is that all, or do unemployed people continue to have reduced wellbeing even after finding new jobs? In some studies, unemployment has been shown to have lingering effects on wellbeing after returning to work. In a seminal analysis, a team of researchers examined the effect of the fraction of the previous five years that had been spent in unemployment. For every year that a person had been unemployed in the previous five years, people were on average 0.1 points (out of 10) less happy.[17] Taking a longer-term perspective, two studies of British workers in the United Kingdom find that spells of youth unemployment predict lower levels of life satisfaction well into adulthood.[18] These results again remain significant after controlling for a host of personal, parental and childhood characteristics. Along similar lines, young people who come of age

---

[9] For example, Theodossiou (1998); A. E. Clark (2003); A. E. Clark and Georgellis (2013). Also see Figure 11.2. In contrast to these results, Frijters et al. (2006); and N. Carroll (2007) find similar effects of unemployment for men and women in Russia and Australia , respectively.

[10] See A. E. Clark et al. (2018) p. 43.   [11] Frijters et al. (2006).   [12] Rudolf and Kang (2015).

[13] Anusic et al. (2014).   [14] A. E. Clark and Georgellis (2013).

[15] A. E. Clark and Georgellis (2013).   [16] Hetschko (2016).

[17] A. E. Clark et al. (2018). The results were similar in Britain, Germany and Australia.

[18] Bell and Blanchflower (2011); and Clark and Lepinteur (2019).

during a recession (rather than a boom) care more highly in later life about their financial security.[19]

What are we to make of these effects? One possible interpretation is that workers who spend longer periods of time unemployed become more insecure about losing their jobs in the future. By this account, it would be job insecurity itself that drives down wellbeing. Some authors have noted that once feelings of job insecurity are accounted for, the effect of past unemployment on wellbeing does become much weaker.[20] However, in a more recent test, a team of researchers have studied retired people, for whom job insecurity is not an issue. They found that people who retired from a position of involuntary unemployment are more dissatisfied with their lives than those who retired straight from work.[21] This effect goes beyond what may be expected from losses in retirement income and looks like a direct effect on mood and outlook.

Why Is It So Painful To Be Unemployed?

But why is unemployment so painful? One obvious answer might be the loss of income. But we have already taken this into account. And in fact we can easily compare the size of the non-pecuniary effects with those of the pecuniary effects.[22] These comparisons have been done by a number of authors, all of whom found the non-pecuniary effects to be more than the pecuniary effects. For example, one widely cited analysis found them to be twice as large, and this is a typical estimate.[23] So the costs of unemployment go far beyond the income loss.

The seeds of this realisation were planted in the academic literature as far back as 1933. That year, a team of sociologists led by the husband-and-wife team of Paul Felix Lazarsfeld and Marie Jahoda published the findings of an extensive field experiment in the Austrian town of Marienthal, following a plant closure that left most of town unemployed. At the time, Austria offered generous unemployment insurance, providing workers who lost their jobs with considerable financial benefits. Yet rather than experiencing gains in wellbeing as a result of more leisure time, affected workers became increasingly despondent. Social and community life in the town quickly disintegrated. The researchers concluded that employment is not simply a pathway to income but rather something that 'imposes a time structure on the waking day, implies regularly shared experiences and contacts with people outside the nuclear family, links individuals to goals and purposes that transcend their own, enforces activity, and defines aspects of personal status and identity'.[24]

---

[19] Cotofan et al. (2021a).   [20] Knabe and Rätzel (2011).   [21] Hetschko et al. (2019).

[22] Suppose we have a regression, $W = a_1 + a_2$ UNEMP $+ a_3 \, log$ Income; we just compare a_2 with $a_3 \, \Delta$ log Income.

[23] Knabe and Rätzel (2011). The implications are remarkable. Suppose that, typically, unemployed people lose one half their income. Then the psychic cost is equivalent to being reduced to ¼ of your original income. It could only be compensated by a 4-fold increase in income.

[24] Jahoda (1981) p. 188. Quoted from Hetschko et al. (2021).

Many decades later, modern theoretical understandings of employment continue to focus on three related channels through which work relates to wellbeing: (1) identity, (2) social network and (3) routine.[25] We will dive into the empirical evidence for these channels in greater detail later in Chapter 12.

Spillovers on the Community

The family

If unemployment changes the unemployed individual, it also damages the rest of the family and the wider community. **Partners of workers** who lose their jobs suffer declines in wellbeing. One early study observed significant declines in female partner's life satisfaction following their spouse's job loss – of the order of 0.5 points (out of 10) – although similar effects were not observed for male partners.[26] More recently, a study looking at unemployment following plant closures in Germany again found that cohabiting partners of unemployed workers experienced significant declines in wellbeing. On average, the spillover effect of unemployment for partners was roughly one fourth of the direct effect on the worker. These negative impacts were largely similar for men and women – roughly 0.3 points on a 0 to 10-point scale.[27] Related studies in the United Kingdom,[28] Australia[29] and Germany[30] have found analogous declines in the mental health of spouses following partners' entry into unemployment

Spells of parental unemployment can also have negative effects on the **children's wellbeing**. These effects are generally small but tend to be particularly significant when parental unemployment is experienced when you are in your teens. In one of the first studies conducted along these lines in the United Kingdom, the authors found mostly insignificant effects of parental unemployment on happiness for children under 12 years of age. But the effects turn significant for older children – among 15-year-olds, father's unemployment produces a decline in happiness of 0.4 points (out of 7), while mother's unemployment produces a decline of 1 point.[31]

What about the longer-term effects of parental unemployment? Only a few studies have investigated this. One noted that 18- to 31-year-olds who experienced spells of parental employment as a result of plant closures as young children (0–5) or in adolescence (11–15) reported lower levels of life satisfaction than counterparts whose parents remained employed, controlling for other factors. The magnitude of this effect was about 0.6 points (out of 10).[32] Similarly, another study found that adult wellbeing

---

[25] For a short summary of the relevant theoretical models in psychology and organisational behaviour, see Suppa (2021).

[26] Winkelmann and Winkelmann (1995).   [27] Nikolova and Ayhan (2019).

[28] A. E. Clark (2003); Mendolia (2014).   [29] Bubonya et al. (2014).   [30] Marcus (2013).

[31] Powdthavee and Vernoit (2013). See also Kind and Haisken-DeNew (2012). A. E. Clark et al. (2018) find similar effects of father's unemployment (but lack data on mother's unemployment).

[32] Nikolova and Nikolaev (2021).

Table 11.1 How life satisfaction (0–10) is affected by your own unemployment and by the regional unemployment rate (Household data, cross-section)

	Own unemployment rate (1 or 0)	Regional unemployment rate (0–1)
Britain	−0.71 (.09)	−1.38 (.56)
Germany	−0.96 (.07)	−1.58 (.36)
Australia	−0.35 (.11)	−0.37 (.42)
USA	−0.45 (.06)	−1.44 (.47)

Source: A. E. Clark et al. (2018) Table 4.4; slightly adapted; Understanding Society (Britain), SOEP (Germany), HILDA (Australia) and BRFSS (United States); data for many years pooled with year dummies and usual controls

is lower for people whose parents were unemployed, especially if those parents were from more privileged backgrounds (where the shock is greater).[33]

The community

The final – and most important spillover from unemployment – is on the population at large. High unemployment makes everyone feel less secure, even if they have a job. For, if unemployment is high and you lose your job, you will find it more difficult to get another one. Table 11.1 reports the results of a cross-sectional analysis of data from four countries. Life satisfaction of person i is regressed on:

- first, whether the individual person i is unemployed, and
- second, the regional unemployment rate (expressed as a proportion).

As can be seen, the coefficient on own employment is less than the coefficient on the regional unemployment rate.

So how does average wellbeing in a region change when average unemployment in the region changes? The wellbeing of individual i in region r is given by

$$W_{ir} = a_0 + a_1 U_{ir} + a_2 \bar{U}_r + \text{etc} \tag{3}$$

and the average wellbeing in region r is therefore given by

$$\bar{W}_r = a_0 + (a_1 + a_2)\bar{U}_r + \text{etc.} \tag{4}$$

In all our countries $a_1 < a_2$. This means that, when unemployment rises, the **total** loss of wellbeing is higher among employed people than among those who are newly unemployed.[34]

---

[33] A. E. Clark and Lepinteur (2019).

[34] In a study of world unemployment using the Gallup World Poll, De Neve and Ward (2017) also find that $a_1 < a_2$. They also find evidence that the pain of being unemployed is slightly reduced if more others are unemployed. But the effect is tiny. If the local unemployment rate is 10% (rather than 0) – a huge difference – the pain caused by unemployment is reduced by only 6%.

Policy Implications

Clearly, we would like to reduce unemployment to the lowest level compatible with stable inflation.[35] There are two main practical issues.

- The approach to redundancy.
- Active labour market policy to stimulate employment.

Redundancy

As we have seen, a high unemployment rate reduces the wellbeing of the unemployed and of workers.[36] Moreover, worker wellbeing (and hence productivity) is increased by a sense of **job security**. This creates a presumption in favour of adjusting to shocks through reduced hours or furlough (where workers do not lose their jobs) rather than through redundancy. A test case of this choice arose in the COVID-19 pandemic.

Broadly speaking, high-income countries opted for one of two approaches to the downturn – either job retention or income replacement. Job retention policies aim to maintain employment contracts by subsidising firms to keep workers on the staff, while income replacement policies generally focus on providing financial relief for workers who lost their jobs.[37] Taking a wellbeing perspective, we may expect the former approach to be preferable to the latter. Unlike income replacement schemes, policies aimed at keeping workers in their jobs are better poised to keep the non-pecuniary benefits of work intact. While empirical research on the topic is still emerging, countries favouring job retention policies did in fact see both lower levels of unemployment and less severe declines in wellbeing in the first year of the crisis.[38]

A parallel issue arises even in terms of economic stability. Some countries have stricter laws to discourage redundancy than others. Clearly, such laws reduce the number of workers who get fired, but they also reduce the number of new hires that employers are willing to take on. On balance these effects probably cancel out, and employment protection has little effect on aggregate unemployment.[39]

Active labour market policies

But some people inevitably lose their jobs. What then becomes crucial is whether or not they drift into long-term unemployment, where their chances of re-employment deteriorate sharply. For a key issue of equity and efficiency is how to prevent long-term unemployment. It may thus be important to shorten spells of unemployment.

---

[35] Layard et al. (2005).

[36] An underestimated issue is how far worker wellbeing is affected by the flow into unemployment as opposed to the stock of unemployed.

[37] OECD (2020).   [38] OECD (2020); and Cotofan et al. (2021).

[39] Layard et al. (1991). With higher employment protection there is less short-term unemployment and more long-term unemployment.

To this end, **active labour market policies** (**ALMPs**) have shown effective macro-economic results.[40] ALMPs include (a) subsidised hiring of unemployed workers, (b) training programmes (on and off the job) and (c) job-search assistance for the unemployed. Many of these interventions have now been evaluated using properly controlled methods. A meta-analysis of these studies found that on average they raised the probability of being in employment after the end of the programme by 2 percentage points in the short-term, rising to 9 points in the long-run.[41] Subsidised employment was the most effective policy and those who benefitted most from this were those who were already long-term unemployed. But within each type of programme, there was a wide spread of results, depending on the effectiveness of the design. There is also the issue of whether helping unemployed people disadvantages other workers, through displacement or substitution effects. This has been little studied, with mixed results.[42]

In many cases, unemployed people who are offered subsidised employment are told that they can no longer continue to receive unemployment benefits if they refuse to accept the offer of employment. An alternative is 'workfare', which means working for your benefits (whereas most workers on ALMPs receive at least the minimum wage). Under both schemes there is an element of compulsion. So the question naturally arises 'Are workers on these schemes happier than they would have been if they had remained unemployed?' Only a handful of studies have addressed this issue. They find that, though workers on these schemes are less happy than workers in normal employment, they are more satisfied than those who remain unemployed.[43] This is because work provides important psychological and social benefits as well as income. But we should also remember the importance of not letting people become 'locked-in' to subsidised activity, rather than moving on as quickly as possible to regular employment.[44]

Conclusions

- The unemployed are generally significantly and substantially less satisfied with their lives than the employed. This relationship tends to be stronger in high-income countries where there are sharper differences between employment and unemployment.
- In studies that look at within-person changes over time, unemployment typically reduces wellbeing by at least 0.6 points (out of 10).
- Studying plant closures allows researchers to distinguish between endogenous and exogenous effects of unemployment. Workers who lose their jobs due to reasons

[40] Layard et al. (1991).   [41] Card et al. (2018) Tables 2 and 3.
[42] Blundell et al. (2004) pp. 569–606; Crepon et al. (2013); Gautier et al. (2018).   [43] Knabe et al. (2017).
[44] In some studies, workfare programs have been found to have minor effectiveness at reducing overall unemployment (see Card et al. [2018]). But such analyses of workfare programmes are also likely to suffer from selection bias, since workers who join these programmes are those least likely to have found work before having to enroll in the programme.

outside of their control are generally more dissatisfied, although the effect of job loss remains negative and statistically significant for both groups.

- Longer periods of unemployment can have scarring effects with long-lasting negative implications for wellbeing even after those affected have returned to work.
- Aggregate unemployment also affects the wellbeing of people in work. This causes greater total losses of wellbeing than the loss of wellbeing on the part of the unemployed.
- The psychosocial effects of unemployment on wellbeing are greater than the effect of lost income. Policy approaches targeting unemployment are therefore likely to be most conducive to wellbeing if they are able to protect and provide for the psychological and social benefits of work, as opposed to simply providing income support.

Questions for discussion

(1) What are two benefits of using fixed-effects regressions to model the effect of unemployment relative to cross-sectional OLS regressions?
(2) What do you think explains the lack of adaptation to unemployment?
(3) Several countries around the world have begun debating proposals to provide citizens with an unconditional basic income. What do the results of this chapter suggest about the potential wellbeing impacts of these policies?
(4) Some programmes require welfare recipients to accept work in order to receive support. Do you think this is reasonable?

Further Reading

Clark, A. E. (2003). Unemployment as a social norm: Psychological evidence from panel data. *Journal of Labour Economics*, 21(2), 323–351.

Clark, A. E., and Georgellis, Y. (2013). Back to baseline in Britain: adaptation in the British household panel survey. *Economica*, 80(319), 496–512.

Kassenboehmer, S. C., and Haisken-DeNew, J. P. (2009). You're fired! The causal negative effect of entry unemployment on life satisfaction. *The Economic Journal*, 119(536), 448–462.

Knabe, A., and Rätzel, S. (2011). Quantifying the psychological costs of unemployment: The role of permanent income. *Applied Economics*, 43(21), 2751–2763.

Winkelmann, L., and Winkelmann, R. (1998). Why are the unemployed so unhappy? *Evidence from panel data*. *Economica*, 65(257), 1–15.

SUMMARY OF THE SERVICES

THAT YOU ARE
EXPECTED TO
PROVIDE

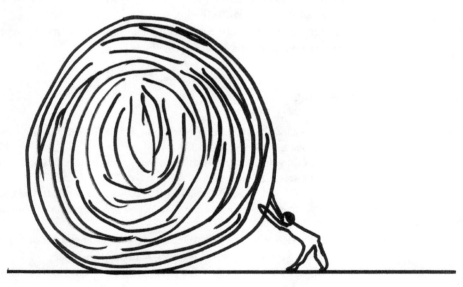

12 The Quality of Work

The best careers advice to give the young is 'Find what you like doing best and get
someone to pay you for doing it'.

Katherine Whitehorn

Introduction

The author Annie Dillard once wrote, 'How we spend our days is, of course, how we
spend our lives'. Well, for many of us, most of our days are spent at work. Today, the
average working adult spends roughly 30% of her waking hours at work, in some
countries almost 50%.[1] Understanding wellbeing at work is therefore essential to
understanding how most people experience their lives.

Despite the overwhelming importance of employment documented in Chapter 11,
and the relatively high levels of job satisfaction reported around the world, work turns
out to be one of the **least enjoyable** activities we engage in on a day-to-day basis. The
extent to which employees enjoy their work also proves to be highly dependent on
social and eudaimonic drivers, in some cases even more than income. After discussing
each of these issues in detail, we will conclude by looking at the links between
wellbeing and productivity/company performance.

Are We Satisfied With Our Jobs?

To better understand the relationship between work and wellbeing, we can begin by
surveying **job satisfaction** around the world. Similar to the evaluative dimension of
wellbeing, job satisfaction captures an individual's overall satisfaction with their
work. It belongs in the basket of so-called **domain satisfaction indicators** including
marital satisfaction, family satisfaction, satisfaction with residential area and others.[2]
While life and domain satisfaction measures are often highly interrelated, the latter can
be useful in eliciting more precise estimates of the effects of some aspects of life.

---

[1] Giattino et al. (2013).   [2] Delhey (2014).

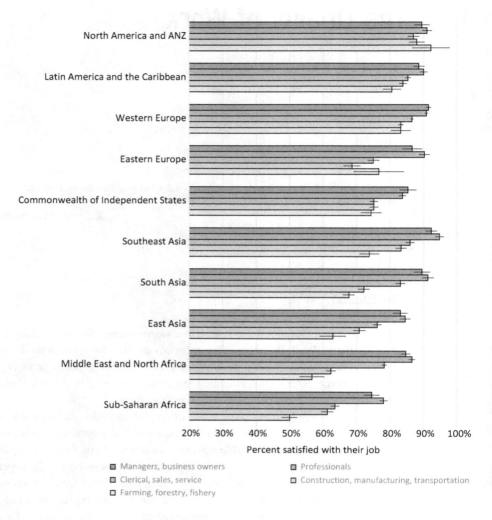

Figure 12.1 Job satisfaction by region and job type
Source: Gallup World Poll
Note: 'Would you say you are – completely satisfied, somewhat satisfied, somewhat dissatisfied or completely dissatisfied with your job?' The first two responses are coded as satisfied, while the latter two are coded as dissatisfied. Levels averaged from 2006 to 2013; 95% confidence intervals displayed. See Annex 12.1 for individual country rankings.

For example, even if life satisfaction is itself driven by job satisfaction, task variety at work may be more important to the latter than the former.[3] Without considering job satisfaction, we may only therefore arrive at a somewhat vague or incomplete picture of what really drives worker wellbeing.

One of the largest and most representative datasets on job satisfaction to date is provided by the **Gallup World Poll**. In Figure 12.1, we show job satisfaction broken

---

[3] In fact, this does seem to be the case. See Figure A12.1.

down by ten world regions and five different job types. Individual country rankings are also provided in Annex 12.1. There are several key points worth noting. The first is that overall job satisfaction levels differ considerably by region. Regardless of job type, workers in North America, New Zealand, Australia and Western Europe are generally more satisfied with their jobs than those in other regions. Nevertheless, job satisfaction levels do also differ significantly within regions. Managers, business owners and professionals tend to be more satisfied with their jobs than other groups. Forest, fishery and farm workers are among the least satisfied. At the same time, there are also large differences in the range of job satisfaction levels across countries. In richer countries, the gap between the most and least satisfied groups is substantially smaller than the gap in poorer regions. In sub-Saharan Africa, this gap is roughly 28 percentage points, while the analogous divide in North America is only about 4 percentage points.

At this stage, it may be tempting to conclude that the global distribution in job satisfaction can be attributed to differences in income. After all, workers in higher-income countries as well as those in higher-income professions do seem to be more satisfied with their jobs on average. However, while pay is certainly an important driver of wellbeing at work, it is by no means the only one. Upon closer analysis, other job characteristics including social support and job security prove to be just as, if not even more, important than income. We will explore these relationships in much more detail later on in the chapter.

Nevertheless, perhaps the most important takeaway from the analysis thus far is that, regardless of job type, the vast majority of workers around the world report feeling relatively satisfied with their jobs. At first glance, this may seem unsurprising given the close link between wellbeing and employment status documented in Chapter 11. In fact, being satisfied with one's job overall may even be considered somewhat of a low bar to clear, especially if workers compare themselves to those who are unemployed. Simply having a stable job that provides a reliable source of income may for many people provide enough reason to be sufficiently satisfied with it. However, as we will see in the next section, it would be a mistake to conclude that being satisfied with a job implies actually enjoying it. In fact, work turns out to be one of the least enjoyable activities we engage in on a daily basis.

Are We Happy While We Work?

Thus far in this book, we have primarily been concerned with **evaluative** measures of wellbeing. Most researchers generally place life satisfaction and job satisfaction in this category. Evaluative indicators are considered particularly useful for policy-making, as they remain relatively stable over time and tend to reflect objective conditions that can be targeted by policy.[4] However, in this section, as we turn our focus to happiness at work, we will be paying more attention to **affective** measures of wellbeing.

---

[4] Diener et al. (2013).

Indicators of affect – including joy, stress, boredom, interest, etc. – are designed to be more reflective of day-to-day moods and emotions. Unlike life satisfaction, affect varies considerably depending on the day of the week,[5] time of the day[6] and the activity we are engaging in.[7] For this reason, it can provide a useful lens by which to assess real-time effects of work on wellbeing. Here we will largely rely on the results of **experience sampling studies (ESM)**, which allow for reliable and contemporaneous measurements of affect.

In the largest study of its kind, Alex Bryson and George MacKerron employed an ESM design using the Mappiness app, compiling over a million datapoints on the emotional wellbeing of tens of thousands of adults in the United Kingdom from 2010 to 2011.[8] The main results of this analysis are presented in Figure 12.2. Because the impact of each activity on **momentary happiness** is assessed using fixed-effect regressions, estimated effects are taken to represent causal effects of engaging in each activity on happiness. In other words, because the study surveys the same people over multiple points in time, the researchers were able to isolate the change in happiness from engaging in any one particular activity compared to another. In doing so, individual time-invariant fixed effects are controlled for and the potential for reverse causation is limited.

The most important result for our purposes is the considerable consequence of work for emotional wellbeing. Out of 40 activities, paid work proves to be the worst activity for happiness, with the exception of being sick in bed. This effect held controlling for time of day, day of the week, month, year, number of prior survey responses, simultaneous activities and individual time-invariant fixed effects. This negative impact of work on emotional wellbeing has also been replicated in a series of related studies.[9] In one analysis conducted during COVID-19, time spent at work was again found to be the second worst activity for positive affect, the worst being reading news about COVID-19.[10]

Yet at this point we seem to have something of a paradox on our hands. How can work be so crucially important for how we evaluate our lives as a whole and yet so apparently unenjoyable on a day-to-day basis? It is worth noting that as surprising as this result is, it is not conceptually impossible. Evaluative judgements may be more likely to reflect personal narratives and social comparisons than affective reports.[11] When prompted to evaluate how satisfied we are with life, we may compare ourselves to a reference group or perhaps evaluate ourselves against social and cultural expectations. In many societies around the world, and particularly those in Europe and North America, having a job is of paramount financial, social and cultural importance. Viewed from this perspective, it may not be surprising that employed adults would judge their lives more favourably than the unemployed. Day-to-day emotions need not factor strongly in the equation.

---

[5] Helliwell and Wang (2014).   [6] Golder and Macy (2011).
[7] Kahneman et al. (2004); Bryson and MacKerron (2017).   [8] Bryson and MacKerron (2017).
[9] Ayuso-Mateos et al. (2013); Bureau of Labor Statistics (2014); Mellor-Marsá et al. (2016).
[10] Lades et al. (2020).   [11] Dolan (2019).

Effect of engaging in each activity on self-reported happiness

Figure 12.2 Effect of different activities on momentary happiness (0–10)
Source: Bryson and MacKerron (2017)
Note: Coefficient on each activity estimated using fixed-effects regressions. Happiness measured on a scale from 0 to 10 using the experience sampling method (ESM).

Another potential explanation has to do with the context by which we ought to understand our emotional experience at work. Physical exercise may be a useful analogy in this respect. If most runners were stopped and asked how happy they felt in the middle of a marathon, it seems hard to imagine they would report anything other than extreme distress. Yet it would obviously be a mistake to conclude that running is detrimental for wellbeing. Even if moments of physical exertion are particularly unpleasant, the overall experience of exercise can still be judged to be positive, especially in retrospect.[12] In the same way, even if the actual experience of work is often demanding and stressful, we may still evaluate the overall experience to be positive inasmuch as it contributes to our sense of achievement, purpose or belonging.[13]

Despite the intuitive appeal of both explanations, the existing evidence does not easily lend itself to conclusively accept or reject either one. The reason why employment should be so crucial for evaluative wellbeing and yet so apparently destructive for affective wellbeing is still very much an open question. Whatever the underlying reason, the apparent unpleasantness of work demands attention. As a matter of principle, and (as we shall see in the last section of this chapter) as a matter of good business, private and public institutions alike would be wise to improve the quality of the workday. How should they go about it? To help answer this question, in the next section we will present and evaluate the most important drivers of wellbeing at work.

What Drives Employee Wellbeing?

So far, we have found that the relationship between work and wellbeing is complicated. Having a job is both important for evaluative wellbeing, yet often unenjoyable. Need it be so? Despite the overall average negative relationship between work and emotional wellbeing revealed in the last section, there are of course some workers who do enjoy their work. While this group may be a minority, examining the features of work that are conducive to wellbeing can reveal important insights about how to raise employee happiness and engagement in other workplaces. At the same time, looking at workplace characteristics that are most likely to undermine wellbeing can be instructive for the same reason. In this section, we will consider both perspectives to better understand the most important drivers and threats to employee wellbeing around the world. While we will focus mostly on what may be considered 'individual' drivers of workplace wellbeing, including pay and personal relationships, at the end of this section we will also consider the effect of 'collective' drivers including union membership and other forms of organised representation.

To help frame our discussion, in Figure 12.3 we present associations between 13 workplace characteristics and job satisfaction using international data from the **International Social Survey Program (ISSP)**.

---

[12] Careful readers may object to this analogy given the high ranking of sports and physical exercise in Figure 12.2. Nevertheless, it seems reasonable to imagine that respondents would be more likely to respond to pings during rests or after finishing their workout than in the midst of physical exertion. In the study, the researchers incorporate all responses provided within one hour of receiving the notification, although they do not provide average response time data for each individual activity.

[13] Other research has shown that not all stressors are created equal, and challenge stressors may even be good for productivity and performance (LePine and LePine [2005]).

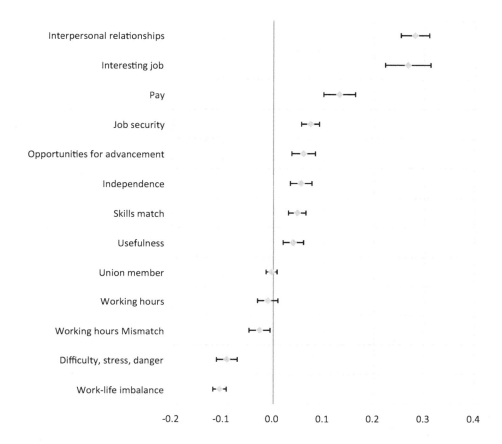

Figure 12.3 Effect of workplace characteristics on job satisfaction – partial correlation coefficients (β)
Source: De Neve (2018) using data from International Social Survey Program (ISSP).
Note: Partial correlation coefficients obtained from regressing job satisfaction on different domains of workplace quality using an OLS linear regression. All variables are standardised with mean zero and standard deviation one. Sample is restricted to all working adults. Control variables included for age, gender, marital status, education, number of children, and household size. Additional controls included for occupation, industry, and country fixed effects. Data from 37 countries across multiple geographic regions;[14] 95% confidence intervals displayed.

Pay

Pay seems like a good place to start. Some have even hastened to suggest that income itself ought to be considered a proxy for wellbeing. Throughout the history of economics, the idea that wellbeing is rooted in the ability of individuals to freely

---

[14] Australia, New Zealand, Russia, China, Japan, Taiwan, Austria, Belgium, Croatia, Czech, Republic, Denmark, Estonia, Finland, France, Georgia, Germany, Britain, Hungary, Iceland, Latvia, Lithuania, Norway, Poland, Slovakia, Slovenia, Spain, Sweden, Switzerland, Chile, Mexico, Suriname, Venezuela, Israel, United States, India, Philippines and South Africa.

satisfy their desires has been profoundly influential. Because higher levels of income presumably increase one's ability to satisfy desires, it has often been assumed that maximising income is the surest way to maximise wellbeing. If so, this section should be rather short. Want to increase workplace wellbeing? Pay people more. However, on closer inspection, the reality is a bit more complicated.

The relationship between income and happiness is one of the oldest and most well-researched topics in empirical wellbeing research. Chapter 13 will be entirely devoted to it. For the time being, it is worth making a few brief observations. The first is that when compared to other drivers of workplace wellbeing, income usually does score quite highly but rarely tops the list. In Figure 12.3, it ranks third. In online Annex 12.2 we present the results of a similar analysis of job satisfaction and workplace characteristics using data from the **European Social Survey (ESS)**. In this case, wages rank 9th of out 20 drivers of job satisfaction.[15] In yet another analysis of the American labour market using data from the international jobs site called Indeed, fair pay ranked fifth out of eleven drivers of workplace happiness.[16] All in all, while income is certainly important, it does not stand alone as the only or even most important driver of workplace wellbeing.

At the same time, there is evidence to suggest that it is not just what we are paid but also how we are paid that matters. One standard approach is to compensate workers individually according to their personal performance. This so-called **individual performance pay** can be entirely appropriate in jobs with highly individualised work and minimal team collaboration – for example, mechanics, plumbers and drivers. Most studies generally show that tying pay to performance in these contexts has positive effects on productivity[17] and no negative effects on life satisfaction.[18] However, an increasing share of the modern labour force works in jobs that require considerable amounts of teamwork. In this case, attempting to rate employees by their individual contributions to team projects can have deeply concerning implications for wellbeing.[19] In one study, researchers observed significant upticks in anti-depressant use in the months following the introduction of individual performance pay schemes in a Danish study of 300,000 workers.[20] In another experiment, researchers randomly assigned workers to receive flat daily wages or unequal wages depending on their individual productivity at an Indian manufacturing plant.[21] Those in the latter group became less productive and less likely to show up to work. However, these effects were minimised if the workers were more easily able to observe the productivity differences.

Other organisations have begun to experiment with alternative pay schemes in which workers get compensated depending on group or company performance in addition to a fixed wage. This approach – broadly defined as 'share capitalism' or more specifically as **'group-based performance pay'** – has shown promising results for wellbeing. In an analysis using three large datasets in Europe, the United Kingdom and a multinational private company, group-based performance pay was found to

[15] De Neve (2018). See Figure A12.1.   [16] Cotofan et al. (2021b).
[17] Lazear (2000); Bloom and Van Reenen (2010); Bandiera et al. (2017).   [18] Böckerman et al. (2016).
[19] Kruse et al. (2010); Böckerman et al. (2016).   [20] Dahl and Pierce (2019).   [21] Breza et al. (2018).

significantly increase job satisfaction for workers, after controlling for the level of wages.[22] In Europe and the United Kingdom, participating in schemes in which company profits are shared with employees predicted increases in job satisfaction of 0.07 points. A related study of the '100 Best Companies to Work For in America' from 2005 to 2007 found that employees in companies offering more extensive group-based incentive compensation schemes report more positive work experiences and higher levels of organizational trust.[23] The authors of both papers suggested that these sorts of pay schemes endow workers with a greater sense of ownership and agency within their companies, with positive downstream effects for motivation and wellbeing.

Working relationships

At this point, readers may not be surprised to learn that the quality of **social relationships** at work is generally the most important single predictor of workplace wellbeing. In Figure 12.3, interpersonal relationships tops the list out of eleven drivers of job satisfaction. In fact, the extent to which employees feel supported by colleagues is the most important driver of both job satisfaction and life satisfaction in Europe out of 20 workplace characteristics considered.[24] Even more important than what we do at work is often who we do it with.

In a number of studies, social relationships with colleagues have been found to be predictive of both individual and organisational outcomes. In one widely cited analysis, workers who reported having friends at work were found to be more productive, less likely to leave their jobs, more satisfied with their work and more engaged at work during the day than those without close friends at the office.[25] Other research has shown that friendships at work increase employee energy and vigour.[26] More recently, one of the largest studies on employee wellbeing during COVID-19 found that feeling a sense of belonging and inclusion at work was the most important driver of workplace happiness in the United States.[27] On the other hand, one study found that close relationships at work can also increase the propensity for distractions through the day.[28] Nevertheless, the authors still noted that the positive effects of strong working relationships on work outcomes far outweighed the downsides.

Relationships with **managers** are especially consequential. In Figure 12.3, the quality of interpersonal relationships is considered in terms of three dimensions: contact with others, relationships with managers and relationships with other co-workers. When each of these dimensions is considered separately, the effect of relationships with managers proves to be more than twice as important in predicting variation in job satisfaction as relationships with co-workers. These disaggregated effects are presented in Figure 12.4. Here, the quality of relationships with managers proves to be more than twice as important for job satisfaction as relationships with co-workers. Partial correlation coefficients for each domain are 0.22 and 0.09, respectively. Related research from Gallup has found that managers account for 70% of the

---

[22] Bryson et al. (2016).   [23] Blasi et al. (2016).   [24] De Neve (2018).   [25] Rath (2006).
[26] Dutton (2003); Dutton and Ragins (2007).   [27] Cotofan et al. (2021b).   [28] Methot et al. (2016).

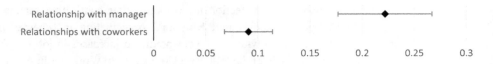

Figure 12.4 Disaggregated effect of relationships with managers and co-workers – partial correlation coefficients (β)
Source: De Neve (2018) using data from International Social Survey Program (ISSP)
Note: Partial correlation coefficients obtained from regressing job satisfaction on different domains of workplace quality using an OLS linear regression. All variables are standardised with mean zero and standard deviation one. Sample is restricted to all working adults. Control variables included for age, gender, marital status, education, number of children, and household size. Additional controls included for occupation, industry, and country fixed effects. Data from 37 countries across multiple geographic regions;[29] 95% confidence intervals displayed.

variation in employee engagement.[30] In a recent review of their largest study on quality of work to date, researchers from Gallup also reported that managers were the single greatest predictor of long-term organisational success and employee well-being.[31] These effects can be acutely felt even within the same organisational context. In two studies of healthcare workers in the United Kingdom, having supportive and competent managers significantly increased job satisfaction relative to those with bad managers working in the same hospitals.[32]

These types of dynamics can have crucial downstream consequences. Employees working under good managers are found to be both more productive and less likely to leave their jobs. In a five-year study of 23,878 workers and 1,940 bosses in a large service company, the best bosses (as judged by employee ratings) were found to increase team productivity by about 22% per hour.[33] Employees working under highly rated managers were also 12% less likely to leave the company. Another large-scale survey in the United States found that roughly one in two American workers had left a job at some point in their career to escape a bad manager.[34] As it turns out, the old adage that 'workers don't leave their jobs, they leave their managers' may not be so far from the truth.

Part of the reason managers are so important is the considerable influence they wield over employees' schedules, routines and relationships. A bad relationship with a manager can bleed over into almost every aspect of our working lives. The results of this section are particularly striking, given that good managers are also exceedingly hard to come by. Research from Gallup suggests that only one in ten eligible candidates actually possess the skills for successful management, and companies fail

[29] Australia, New Zealand, Russia, China, Japan, Taiwan, Austria, Belgium, Croatia, Czech, Republic, Denmark, Estonia, Finland, France, Georgia, Germany, Britain, Hungary, Iceland, Latvia, Lithuania, Norway, Poland, Slovakia, Slovenia, Spain, Sweden, Switzerland, Chile, Mexico, Suriname, Venezuela, Israel, United States, India, Philippines and South Africa.
[30] Harter and Adkins (2015).   [31] Clifton and Harter (2019).
[32] Artz et al. (2017); Ogbonnaya and Daniels (2017).   [33] Lazear et al. (2015) p. 841.
[34] Harter and Adkins (2015).

to pick the best possible candidate for managerial positions 82% of the time.[35] This can have worrying implications for employee wellbeing and company performance.

Hours and flexible working

Let's move on to **working hours**. Given the results of the first two sections, it would be logical to imagine that one way to raise wellbeing would be to minimise time spent working while still remaining employed. By this account, part-time workers should be the happiest of all. Some evidence does support this hypothesis. In Figure 12.1, we saw that part-time workers in the United States and United Kingdom were in fact slightly more satisfied with their lives than full-time workers. In another more detailed analysis using British panel data, the positive effects of work on wellbeing became significant after only 8 hours worked per week, after which point additional gains in wellbeing delivered by working more hours become insignificant.[36]

Several studies have also considered the relationship of wellbeing and working hours by exploiting the impact of **natural experiments** following changes in national labour market policy. After reforms were introduced in Japan and Korea reducing the workweek from 48 to 40 and 44 to 40 hours, respectively, the life satisfaction of affected workers and their spouses appeared to improve.[37] Other studies looking at similar policy changes in France and Portugal found positive effects of shorter work-weeks on both job satisfaction and leisure satisfaction,[38] as well as subjective health.[39] Several experiments conducted within organisations have also revealed positive well-being effects of shortening the workweek, with mostly negligible or even positive effects on aggregate productivity.[40]

So perhaps less work means more happiness after all. Unfortunately, other evidence complicates the story. In China and India, part-time workers actually have lower life satisfaction than full-time workers, while no significant differences are observable in Brazil and Nigeria (Figure 12.1). The effect of raw working hours on job satisfaction is also found to be insignificant in both global (Figure 12.3) and European data (online Figure A12.1). In other studies of Germany and the United Kingdom, longer working hours have even been associated with improvements in wellbeing.[41]

In fact, the relationship between working hours and wellbeing seems to be much more dependent on the extent to which employees are able to work the hours they want to be working. Both underemployment and overemployment can damage well-being.[42] In Figure 12.1, we saw that 'underemployed' workers who work part-time but want to work full-time are significantly less satisfied with their lives than voluntary part-time workers. In Figure 12.3, it is in fact working hours mismatch and work-life imbalance in particular that represent the biggest threats to job satisfaction. In online Figure A12.1, being too tired to enjoy activities outside of work damages both life

---

[35] Beck and Harter (2014).   [36] Kamerāde et al. (2019).   [37] Hamermesh et al. (2017).
[38] Lepinteur (2016): France and Portugal.   [39] Berniell and Bietenbeck (2017): France.
[40] Brough and O'Driscoll (2010).   [41] Schoon et al. (2005); Meier and Stutzer (2008).
[42] Angrave and Charlwood (2015).

satisfaction and job satisfaction in Europe more than any other workplace characteristic. And inability to dedicate enough time to family is found to be the second biggest threat to job satisfaction and third biggest threat to life satisfaction.

Giving workers more control over their schedules can therefore have substantial positive effects. In three related studies, introducing collaborative scheduling procedures – allowing employees to decide in coordination with each other when they work and for how long – significantly improved job satisfaction,[43] perceived work-life balance[44] and even sleep.[45] In another study, a large-scale randomised trial of 867 information technology (IT) workers in a Fortune 500 company was conducted to evaluate the effects of STAR – an 8-hour program designed to promote greater employee control over scheduling and support from managers for workers' personal lives. The program included supervisory training sessions for managers to better recognise and support employees' personal lives and job performance, and interactive sessions to identify and implement new practices for employees to exert greater control over their work-life balance. A careful analysis of its effects found significant reductions in stress and burnout and increases in job satisfaction and work-life balance.[46] Follow-up analyses revealed that treated workers were significantly less likely to leave their jobs. Affording workers opportunities to work from home has also shown promising results. In a large Chinese travel agency, one study documented the effects of randomising workers to work from home.[47] Those selected to work from home reported higher job satisfaction and were more productive than controls who stayed at the office. They were also less likely to leave the firm later on.

These results are reflected in a related literature suggesting that workers are willing to sacrifice portions of their salary for alternative working arrangements. In a large online field experiment, one study found that while most job seekers preferred an 8-hour standard workday, the average worker was willing to give up 20% of their income to avoid a schedule set by an employer on a week's notice.[48] Women, in particular, and especially those with young children, were also willing to give up 8% of their salaries to have the option of working from home. Along similar lines, another study using data for hourly service sector workers in the United States found that exposure to employer-driven schedule instability predicted higher levels of psychological distress, poor sleep and unhappiness.[49] These effects were largely explained by work-life conflicts.

Both of these studies were conducted before the COVID-19 pandemic began in 2020. At the time of writing in 2022, the most recent data suggests that more than 557 million adults worked from home during the second quarter of 2020, amounting to almost one-fifth the global workforce.[50] While the trendlines regarding alternative working arrangements were already increasing in the years leading up the pandemic,[51] the crisis itself served as a catalyst for even faster change. The recent proliferation of video-conferencing software and communication platforms including

---

[43] Pryce and Nielsen (2006).   [44] Pryce and Nielsen (2006); Albertsen et al. (2014).
[45] Garde et al. (2012).   [46] Kelly et al. (2014); Moen et al. (2016, 2017).   [47] Bloom et al. (2015).
[48] Mas and Pallais (2017).   [49] Schneider and Harknett (2019).   [50] Soares et al. (2021).
[51] Katz and Krueger (2019).

Zoom and Teams have contributed significantly to the feasibility of working from home arrangements.

The wellbeing implications of these developments are not immediately obvious. The results of this section suggest that certain groups of workers may value and benefit from flexible working arrangements, notably women and parents of young children. A wide body of evidence has also suggested that spending time commuting to work dramatically lowers wellbeing.[52] This would seem to imply that working arrangements limiting time spent working in a central office would improve wellbeing. However, other evidence points in a different direction. In the Chinese travel agency experiment, while employees who worked from home were more satisfied with their jobs, they were also less likely to be promoted than their peers as time went on. Social relationships with colleagues and managers are also crucially important for employee wellbeing. Inasmuch as these relationships become weaker or more difficult to manage from home settings, the transition to more flexible working arrangements could serve to decrease wellbeing. Examining and untangling these effects will be a central challenge for happiness researchers in the years to come.

Interesting work

So far we have considered the relevance of income, social relationships and working hours in explaining variation in workplace wellbeing around the world. Before moving on, it is worth mentioning two more, important channels. The first is how **interesting** we find our work. In Figure 12.3, the extent to which workers find their job interesting is the second most important predictor of job satisfaction. In online Figure A12.1, task variety at work ranks second. Perhaps as a result, so-called job crafting interventions allowing employees to have more autonomy and control over (a) the tasks they work on, (b) their daily interactions and relationships with others in the organisation and (c) their goals and mission as an employee, have been found to positively impact employee engagement and job satisfaction.[53]

Purpose

Along similar lines, feeling a sense of **purpose** or meaningfulness at work can be hugely beneficial for wellbeing. While the primary analyses discussed in this section do not capture meaning directly, an array of related studies have shown that meaningfulness at work can promote higher levels of job satisfaction, employee engagement and even productivity.[54] Job crafting interventions have also shown promise at increasing perceived meaningfulness at work, with positive knock-on effects for wellbeing.[55] All in all, believing that what we do matters not only for ourselves, but even more importantly for others, can help to ensure that work is not just something we tolerate but something we enjoy.

---

[52] See Chatterjee et al. (2020) for a review of relevant literature.
[53] Tims et al. (2016); Van Wingerden et al. (2017).   [54] For example, see Grant (2008).
[55] Berg et al. (2013).

Unions

Thus far we have largely focused on what can be understood as 'individual' drivers of employee wellbeing: job characteristics and circumstances experienced by individual workers that support or undermine workplace wellbeing. Yet it is also worth considering another class of 'collective' drivers of workplace wellbeing, of which **unions** are the most notable example.

The relationship between union membership and wellbeing has been widely studied, though not always with consistent results. Early influential analyses found negative relationships between union membership and job satisfaction.[56] These results, supported by a raft of smaller studies around the same time, contributed to the widely shared belief towards the end of the twentieth century that unions did not actually increase workers' wellbeing.[57] Relative to other drivers, union membership was also found to be an insignificant predictor of job satisfaction in Figure 12.3. While some of these effects have been attributed to differences in working conditions between union members and non-members,[58] a handful of studies have continued to find negligible or even negative effects of unions on wellbeing even after these influences are controlled for.[59]

However, an emerging body of research has begun to suggest that union membership may have begun to confer positive benefits on members in certain contexts in recent years. Using data from the first decade of the twenty-first century for the United States and for Europe, two related studies found *positive* correlations between union membership and wellbeing.[60] In Figure A12.1, trade union membership also appears to have positive effects on job satisfaction and life satisfaction. In one of the largest studies to date, David Blanchflower and Alex Bryson considered the effect of unions by looking at large-scale longitudinal data in the United States and Europe.[61] The authors again found negative relationships between union membership and job satisfaction in data from 1960 to 1990. However, after this point, the relationship turned positive. Controlling for other factors, between 2010 to 2018 in the United States, and 2006 to 2012 in Europe, unionised workers were significantly more satisfied with their jobs than non-unionised workers. The magnitude of these respective differences were roughly 0.2 points and 0.15 points. Union members were also less likely to experience stress, worry, sadness, depression and loneliness.

These results are also reflected in studies of worker **representation on company boards**. In an analysis of Finnish companies, researchers looked at the wellbeing effects of a policy reform that was introduced in 1991 requiring firms of more than 150 workers to include elected worker representatives on company boards.[62] By considering differences in wellbeing between the employees of firms just below and above this threshold of 150 workers, and controlling for a wide variety of individual,

---

[56] Freeman (1978); Borjas (1979).   [57] Freeman and Medoff (1984).
[58] See, for example, Pfeffer and Davis-Blake (1990); Bessa et al. (2020).   [59] Bryson and Davies (2019).
[60] Davis (2012); Donegani and McKay (2012).   [61] Blanchflower and Bryson (2020).
[62] Harju et al. (2021).

organisational and societal variables, the authors found that the policy reform led to slight improvements in workers' feelings of job security, health, subjective job quality and even their actual wages.

To briefly recap, throughout this section we have highlighted some of the important drivers of workplace wellbeing. While the effects of collective drivers including unions and other forms of worker representation have historically been rather mixed, recent results have seemed to suggest that they may be starting to have positive implications for wellbeing in certain contexts. Individual drivers including social relationships, work-life balance, interestingness, purpose and income also proved to be key determinants of employee wellbeing. While the first four of these are best understood as intrinsic drivers of wellbeing (benefits that arise directly from the work) income is an extrinsic driver (something provided from outside in return for the work). A large, related literature in psychology has demonstrated the crucial importance of intrinsic sources of motivation over extrinsic sources in explaining human behaviour. One of the most influential theories in this regard is Self-Determination Theory (SDT), which understands the most important intrinsic human drives to be autonomy, competence and relatedness.[63] In the context of work, more recent approaches have added a fourth driver, beneficence, to the pantheon.[64] All of these map closely onto the drivers of workplace wellbeing described in this section. As we have already begun to see, creating workplaces that are conducive to wellbeing can not only improve wellbeing but also have positive implications for productivity and performance. In the next section, we will turn our full attention to this latter issue.

Does Wellbeing Matter for Performance?

Sceptical readers may wonder whether worker wellbeing should really matter to management. After all, shouldn't businesses be concerned with making money first and foremost? Hardline neo-classical thinkers would argue that if businesses focus on profit, that will produce the highest level of social wellbeing. We have already questioned that. Moreover, business leaders and investors themselves are increasingly incorporating non-financial measures of company performance into decision-making procedures, especially those that gauge how a company rates on its Environmental, Social and Governance (ESG) dimensions. This movement is perhaps best captured by a 2019 statement released by the US Business Roundtable – a non-profit organisation whose members include executives of many of the most powerful companies in the United States, including Amazon, Apple, Microsoft and General Motors. In a statement signed by 181 CEOs, the group committed to redefine and redirect the purpose of their organisations from generating profit to 'creating value for all stakeholders, including customers, employees, suppliers, communities and shareholders'.[65] This represented a radical shift from corporate thinking that dominated the second half

---

[63] Deci and Ryan (1985); Ryan and Deci (2000).   [64] Martela and Riekki (2018).
[65] Business Roundtable (2019).

of the twentieth century and reflects a growing demand for companies to create and demonstrate social impact. In the coming years, the ability of firms to demonstrate social value is set to become an even more important driver of investment decisions. A fundamental part of this project will be to ensure that employee wellbeing is prioritised and supported. Companies that fail to support the wellbeing of their workers will face increased scrutiny from investors.

Even so, it is important to ask whether improving workers' wellbeing is good for profits. So, in the rest of this section, we will present the most important evidence and methods on the impact of wellbeing on performance.

The study of employee wellbeing and company performance dates back more than a century. Around the turn of the twentieth century, many business owners were beginning to take note of a new approach to scientific management. This approach, pioneered by the factory worker turned manager Frederick Winslow Taylor, sought to apply scientific and engineering methods to management practices in an effort to improve labour productivity. Then in the 1930s, the human relations movement was born out of a marriage between Taylor's ideas and the emerging field of social and organisational psychology. George Elton Mayo, the sociologist largely credited with founding the movement, argued for a reconceptualisation of workers as human beings with psychological wants and needs, rather than as interchangeable economic inputs. This gave psychological theories of motivation and attitudes a central role to play in our understanding of labour productivity. This led to the first experiments on the relationship between worker wellbeing and company performance at the Hawthorne plant of the Western Electric Company in the 1930s.[66] The apparent success and early notoriety of these experiments – spurred on by the endorsements and related initiatives of powerful business magnates including Henry Ford, George F. Johnson and Henry Bradford Endicott – led many to believe that they ought to provide for employee wellbeing not only as a matter of principle but also as a matter of good business.

All of this led to a flurry of experimentation throughout the mid-twentieth century. Organisational scholars and psychologists began putting these theories to the test. Was worker wellbeing really related to company performance? Or was the relationship contingent on other factors? Early studies produced mixed results. Two of the most influential reviews of the literature found that the relationship between job satisfaction and job performance was minor and negligible for practical purposes.[67] Yet both reviews were rather limited by the small number of reliable studies that had been published at the time they were written. As more evidence began to emerge in the 1980s and 1990s, the story began to change. In an influential meta-analysis, Timothy Judge and colleagues improved and expanded on the methodology of previous reviews by looking at 254 studies, comprising 312 unique samples with more than 54,000 unique observations.[68] The authors estimated the overall correlation between job satisfaction and job performance to be 0.3 and statistically significant.

[66] Muldoon (2012).   [67] Brayfield and Crockett (1955); Iaffaldano and Muchinsky (1985).
[68] Judge et al. (2001).

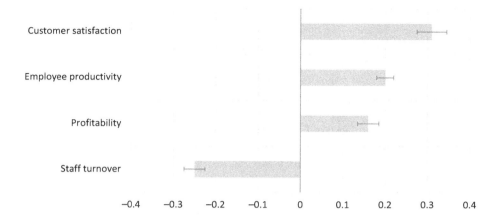

Figure 12.5 Job satisfaction and firm performance – correlation coefficients
Source: Krekel et al. (2019) using Gallup data
Note: The figure plots adjusted average correlation coefficients between job satisfaction and different performance outcomes from a meta-analysis of 339 independent research studies including observations on the wellbeing of 1,882,131 employees and the performance of 82,248 business units; 95% confidence intervals displayed.

More recent reviews have produced largely similar findings. One of the largest single studies to date analysed Gallup data collected from 339 independent research studies on 82,000 business units across 49 industries in 73 countries.[69] The results of this analysis are presented in Figure 12.5. Job satisfaction was found to be positively and significantly associated with customer satisfaction, employee productivity and profitability and negatively associated with staff turnover. In later specifications, these results proved to be consistent across four separate industries – finance, manufacturing, services and retail – and for both US and non-US companies. This type of evidence is now widely considered to be indicative of a significant relationship between employee wellbeing and firm performance.[70]

Yet we must remember not to confuse correlation for causation. The fact that job satisfaction and company performance are highly related does not necessarily mean the former causes the latter. The reverse could very well be true. It seems entirely plausible that employees would be happier in more successful companies, especially if the best companies are more likely to offer higher wages and better benefits. Or perhaps the relationship is more dynamic. Maybe job satisfaction and job performance interact and influence each other in a positive feedback loop. Parsing out these causal relationships can be complicated. Looking at correlations alone won't do the trick.

[69] Krekel et al. (2019).   [70] For other studies, see Tenney et al. (2016).

The question of causation in the literature on wellbeing and performance is not a new concern. Many researchers have adopted creative analytical techniques to shed light on it. Some of these will be familiar. The first strategy is to analyse longitudinal panel data (preferably using fixed-effect regressions) to determine whether or not increases in happiness precede increases in firm performance. In an early review of 16 studies adopting this approach, job attitudes did in fact significantly predict subsequent performance, although the effect was relatively small.[71] At the same time, job performance did not significantly predict later job satisfaction. A follow-up study replicated these results, using longitudinal data on 2,178 business units in 10 large organisations and found that employee engagement significantly predicted later retention, financial performance and customer loyalty, while the reverse relationships were insignificant.[72] Other studies using panel data in the United Kingdom[73] and Finland[74] also found that employee wellbeing predicted later workplace performance. In Finland, the gain in productivity associated with a one standard deviation increase in job satisfaction was estimated to be 6.6%. Yet another analysis using panel data on US companies found that firms considered to be most supportive of wellbeing generated 2.3% to 3.8% per annum higher stock returns than counterparts over a 27-year period.[75]

These results are encouraging but can still be hard to interpret. There is an issue of timing. High frequency panel data is quite rare. Given how expensive it can be, few large-scale surveys make an attempt to collect wellbeing data from the same respondents every month or every week, let alone every day. In the context of major life events like becoming unemployed or getting married, this may not be a problem. Events like these are expected to have impacts on wellbeing that remain observable many months later. In the context of work, predicting the effect of employee satisfaction in one year on individual productivity or company performance the next year can be much more difficult. The fact that longitudinal panel studies continue to find any effect at all may in fact be a testament to the strength of this relationship. Nevertheless, the largest effects of wellbeing on productivity are much more likely to observable in the short term. These are not easily captured by yearly or even monthly response data.

To address this concern, many researchers have turned instead to **experience sampling methods (ESM)**. One influential study assessed the relationship between positive affect and creativity by collecting daily and monthly wellbeing data from 222 employees in seven companies over the course of several months.[76] Using a total of 11,471 employee reports, the authors found that positive affect predicted increases in the production of creative ideas, as evaluated by peers. Importantly, increases in positive affect also preceded increases in creativity by up to two full days, providing evidence of a causal effect. Another analysis adopted a similar methodology to evaluate the impact of morning moods on the productivity and performance of call centre workers.[77] Employees who were in better moods handled incoming calls more

---

[71] Riketta (2008).   [72] Harter et al. (2010).   [73] Bryson et al. (2017).
[74] Böckerman and Ilmakunnas (2012).   [75] Edmans (2012).   [76] Amabile et al. (2005).
[77] Rothbard and Wilk (2011).

efficiently throughout the day – measured in terms of independently resolving issues without a supervisor and having more time available to customers. Though at the same time, workers who reported higher levels of negative affect made more calls overall.

A separate stream of research has looked at the effect of happiness on productivity in **laboratory experiments**. These studies generally try to induce positive affect in randomly selected groups of participants – often with funny or uplifting videos, music, expressions of praise or gratitude or gifts – and then compare their performance on particular tasks to a control group. The results of these endeavours constitute a sizeable literature, though most tend to point in the same direction.[78] Overall, inducing positive affect is generally found to improve productivity. One of the most widely cited studies in this regard comes from Andrew Oswald, Eugenio Proto and Daniel Sgroi.[79] In a series of three experiments, study participants were exposed to happiness-inducing treatments including watching ten-minute comedy videos or receiving free food. Control groups were shown placebo clips of neutral footage or nothing at all. Both groups then were asked to perform moderately complex tasks like adding up five two-digit numbers under time pressure. Increases in happiness were associated with a sizeable and significant 12% increase in productivity, demonstrating a causal effect of positive mood on performance. In a natural experiment, participants who had recently experienced family tragedies, (events that can presumably be attributed to random natural variation), were also both less happy and less productive than those who did not.

This type of experimental research is widely considered to be the gold standard for establishing causation. Yet reliability can often come at the cost of generalisability. There are two related concerns here. First, even if inducing happiness can increase performance in laboratory settings, to what extent can we be sure this result would hold in the real world? The controlled environment of a laboratory study is quite different from a typical workplace. Would happiness still increase productivity and performance in a company setting? A second related issue concerns the practical usefulness of these results. Showing employees comedy videos every hour of the day may not be a practically useful tool for organisations seeking to boost productivity.

One way to address these issues is to run **field experiments**. These are similar to laboratory experiments, although generally conduced at larger scales and implemented in real world settings. The results of some of these endeavours were already introduced in the last section. In the Chinese travel agency experiment, working from home led to a 13% increase in productivity, higher work satisfaction and lower attrition, but workers who worked from home were also less likely to be promoted later on.[80] The STAR program to promote family supportive behaviours in a Fortune 500 company also identified significantly subsequent reductions in employee turnover.[81]

These sorts of studies are invaluable tools to advance and qualify our understand of wellbeing and performance. However, they can be enormously complicated and expensive to carry out, requiring significant buy-in from companies. At the same time, if one group of workers is allowed to benefit from an intervention to improve

---

[78] For reviews, see Lyubomirsky et al. (2005); Tenney et al. (2016).   [79] Oswald et al. (2015).
[80] Bloom et al. (2015).   [81] Kelly et al. (2014). Also summarised in Moen et al. (2016, 2017).

their working lives, but another group within the same company is not, this can also raise ethical and practical concerns. Spill-over effects, where the treatment of one group influences the experience of another, can be very difficult to control for.

With these considerations in mind, some researchers have instead employed **quasi-experimental designs**. These are very much like field experiments in that they seek to analyse causal relationships in real world settings, although in this case treatment and control groups are not randomly assigned. Instead, researchers look for sources of **exogenous natural variation** by which to divide and compare group behaviour or performance. For example, if students in a particular school are divided into classes based on the first letter of their last name, we may be able to use this variation to estimate the causal impact of different teachers on students' test scores. The key assumptions here would be that both groups are similar enough that any observed differences in test scores could be causally attributed to differences in teacher performance. The role of this type of natural variation is to act as a substitute for random assignment.

In one of the largest studies of its kind, a team of researchers applied this technique to study the relationship between happiness and productivity among call centre workers at British Telecom, the largest internet and broadband provider in the United Kingdom.[82] The researchers collected weekly happiness reports from employees in eleven call centres over six months and matched these reports with productivity data – measured in terms of calls converted to sales, adherence to daily schedules and number of calls made per hour. Yet just comparing happiness and productivity data would not be sufficient to establish causation. In addition, the authors collected daily weather data surrounding each call centre and data regarding the window coverage of each call centre itself. The fundamental assumption here is that visual exposure to bad weather – presumed to be a natural and randomly occurring source of variation – is likely to influence workers' moods throughout the day, which in turn influences their productivity. Overall, the study found not only that gloomy weather predicted lower sales performance but that this relationship was also strongly dependent on visual exposure. In call centres with few windows, bad weather had no influence on performance. In call centres with more windows, visual exposure to bad weather predicted declines in happiness and subsequent declines in productivity and performance. The effect of a one unit increase in happiness (on a 0–10 scale) was found to increase sales per worker by 13.4%.

Taken together, the results discussed in this section – from fixed-effects analysis, experience sampling methods, laboratory experiments, field experiments and quasi-experiments – strongly suggest a causal effect of happiness on individual productivity and firm performance. Before bringing this chapter to a close, it is perhaps worth asking just one more question – why? Why should happier workers be better at their jobs and happier companies more successful? We have already hinted at a variety of potential mechanisms by which these relationships can operate throughout this chapter. In Table 12.1, we summarise the most important channels.

---

[82] Bellet et al. (2020).

Table 12.1 Pathways from wellbeing to performance

Subjective wellbeing				Individual and organisational performance
• Job satisfaction • Engagement • High positive affect • Low negative affect	→	**Better health** • Wellbeing predicts better mental and physical health.[a] This can lead to more energy on the job and fewer days out of work. **Greater self-regulation** • Happiness allows for greater control and regulation over mental and physical resources, while depression and stress can make it more difficult to focus on tasks and goals.[b] **Motivation** • Inducing positive affect in particular has been shown to increase intrinsic motivation to solve complex tasks.[c] **Creativity** • In line with Barbara Frederickson's (2001, 2004) broaden and build theory of positive emotions, happier people often have more mental resources to come up with creative ideas and solutions to problems.[d] **Positive relationships** • Better working relationships can foster more positive experiences at work, collaboration, and fewer voluntary exists.[e] **Lower absenteeism** • Job satisfaction predicts fewer absences from work.[f] Happier workers may be both more excited to come to work, and less likely to be unhealthy. **Lower turnover** • Workers who are less satisfied with their jobs are more likely to leave them.[g] This can cause slowdowns as well as additional hiring and training costs for firms. **Attract talent** • Organisations that are more supportive of wellbeing are more likely to attract the most talented workers.[h]	→	• Productivity • Profitability

Note: Adapted from Tenney et al. (2016). Category added for attracting talent. See Ward (2022).

[a] See Chapter 10.

[b] Heatherton and Wagner (2011).

[c] Oswald et al. (2015).

[d] Amabile et al. (2005).

[e] See, for example, the third section of this chapter on what drives employee wellbeing.

[f] Cooper and Dewe (2008).

[g] Tett (1993); Bouckenooghe (2013); Azeez et al. (2016).

[h] Ward (forthcoming).

Conclusions

Despite the importance of work for wellbeing, working turns out to be one of the least enjoyable activities we engage in on an hour-by-hour basis. To evaluate the effects of work on wellbeing, researchers often rely on experience sampling methods (ESM).

Social aspects of work often prove to be more important determinants of wellbeing than income. These include positive working relationships (particularly with managers), work/life balance, interesting work and purpose. The relationship between working hours and wellbeing also tends to be mediated by the extent that workers are able to choose the hours they work.

Workplace wellbeing affects individual productivity and company performance. To evaluate these dynamics and make causal inferences, researchers employ a variety of analytical strategies. These include fixed-effects regressions, laboratory experiments, natural experiments, field experiments and quasi-experiments. Each approach has its own unique advantages and disadvantages. Nevertheless, taken together, the findings of these endeavours generally suggest that happiness improves performance.

There are a number of possible pathways through which wellbeing can impact productivity. These include better health, greater self-regulation and more motivation at the individual level, as well as positive relationships, lower absenteeism, lower turnover and greater ability to attract talent at the firm level.

Questions for discussion

(1) Is work really a disutility after all?
(2) Keeping the discussion of workplace wellbeing drivers in mind, can you think of any interventions that companies could use to boost employee happiness? What is the effect of different criteria for paying workers?
(3) If you wanted to measure the impact of job satisfaction on, for example, the number of sick days taken, which methodology would you prefer to use: fixed-effects analysis, experience sampling methods or field experimentation? What could each approach tell you about the relationship?

Further Reading

Bellet, C., De Neve, J. E., and Ward, G. (2020). Does employee happiness have an impact on productivity? Saïd Business School Working Paper, 13.

Bloom, N., Liang, J., Roberts, J., and Ying, Z. J. (2015). Does working from home work? Evidence from a Chinese experiment. *The Quarterly Journal of Economics*, 130(1), 165–218.

Bryson, A., and MacKerron, G. (2017). Are you happy while you work? *The Economic Journal*, 127(599), 106–125.

Lundberg, U., and Cooper, C. (2010). *The Science of Occupational Health: Stress, Psychobiology, and the New World of Work*. John Wiley & Sons.

Oswald, A. J., Proto, E., and Sgroi, D. (2015). Happiness and productivity. *Journal of Labour Economics*, 33(4), 789–822.

GOING
NOWHERE

13 Income*

Money is like muck, not good except it be spread.

Francis Bacon

In 1974, Richard Easterlin published an important article. It was called 'Has economic growth improved the human lot?'.[1] In it he focused on two alleged facts that were not apparently consistent with each other:

(1) At a point in time, richer people are on average happier than poorer people, (though there is a huge overlap).
(2) Over time, increases in national income per head do not lead to increases in happiness.

This was the so-called **Easterlin paradox**. If richer people are happier than poorer people, you would think that, when a country becomes richer, it will also become happier. But, Easterlin claimed, this is not what happens. And his explanation was that, when national income increases, everyone increases the norm against which they compare their own income. The most obvious norm for comparison is the income of other people. If it is only their **relative** income that matters to people (rather than their **absolute** income), then that could explain why economic growth does not increase the nation's happiness.

In this chapter, we shall explore this hypothesis and much else besides.

- First, we shall look at individual happiness and how this is affected by a person's income. Similarly, we shall look at happiness and income across countries at a moment in time.
- Then we shall look at national happiness over time.
- Finally, we shall explore the role of relative income compared with absolute income and the policy implications of this difference.

---

* This chapter has benefitted greatly from help from Andrew Clark.   [1] Easterlin (1974).

Differences Between Individuals

As between individuals, three central findings of wellbeing research are these:

(1) In every country, richer people are on average happier than poorer people.
(2) This difference is quite small and explains around 2% of the variance of wellbeing within the population.
(3) The effect of additional income gets smaller, the richer you are.

Figure 13.1 shows the position in the UK. Each bar shows the average wellbeing of people at each level of income. As you see, richer people are on average happier than poorer people. But there is also a huge overlap. This is shown by the thin lines around each average figure. The lines span from 1 standard deviation below the average to 1 standard deviation above (i.e., they show the range of wellbeing for the middle two-thirds of people at each level of income). As the figure shows, there are many poor people who are happier than the average rich person.

The diminishing marginal utility of income

The diagram also shows something else. Extra income makes more difference to wellbeing at the bottom (left-hand) end of the scale than it does at the upper end of the scale. An extra $ of income produces a smaller and smaller amount of extra wellbeing the richer the person is. This old idea is now called '**the diminishing marginal utility of income**'; and before the behaviourist revolution (discussed in Chapter 2), it was a central belief of every economist. Indeed, it was why most economists favoured some redistribution of income – because, when $1 was transferred from a rich person to a poor person, the rich person lost less wellbeing than the poor person gained. So overall there was a net gain in wellbeing.

Until the last few decades, this was simply a speculative belief. But the new science now makes it possible to measure the quantitative effect with some accuracy. And, once we know how income affects wellbeing, we can compute by how much income inequality reduces average wellbeing, compared with a situation where everyone received the existing average level of income (see Box 13.1).

In investigating the effect of income on wellbeing, there are two issues:

(1) What is the functional form of the relationship?
(2) What is the actual size of the effect of income on wellbeing?

On the functional form, we can investigate this empirically, and it turns out that the semi-logarithmic linear relationship is a very good fit to the data in a whole range of surveys.[2]
Thus

$$W = \alpha \, log \, Y + etc \tag{1}$$

---

[2] Layard et al. (2008).

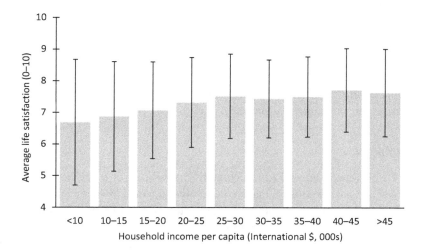

Figure 13.1 Average life satisfaction at different levels of income (Britain) (Bracketed range includes 2/3 of each income group)
Source: Gallup World Poll 2017–19, Cantril ladder

where Y is household income per equivalent adult. This fits in with the general law, known as the Weber–Fechner effect (discussed in Chapter 1), which says that, whether the experience is of light or sound, the perceived size of a change depends linearly on the proportional change in the thing that is changing. In a similar way, our feelings about a change in income depend linearly on the proportional change in income.

This gives us a direct measure of the marginal utility of income,[3] since

$$\frac{dW}{dY} = \frac{\alpha}{Y}. \tag{2}$$

So, a person's marginal utility of income is inversely proportional to her income: an extra $1 matters 10 times more to a poor person than to someone who is 10 times richer. If equation (2) is exactly right, the marginal utility of income will always be positive, even though it can be very low when a person's income is high; and there is some evidence that, in fact, marginal utility becomes zero at some point – the point of 'satiation'.[4]

The size of the effect of income on wellbeing

However, we still need to know the size of the coefficient α To find it, we could estimate a cross-sectional equation of the following form

---

[3] Prior to the science of happiness, economists tried to infer this from the degree of risk aversion or other indirect means.

[4] Jebb et al. (2018). Using the Gallup World Poll, they estimate satiation at around $100,000 per equivalent adult in advanced countries, China and the Middle East/North Africa and around $50,000 in other regions.

$$W_i = \alpha \log Y_i + \sum_j bjX_{ij} + u_i \tag{3}$$

where the X_js are the other things that determine wellbeing – acting in this case as control variables. These controls should obviously include age, age squared[5] and gender, but what else is not completely clear. For there are at least five problems that arise when estimating equation (3).

Problems

(1) If income is **measured** inaccurately, the estimate of α will be biased downwards.

(2) If we include controls that are themselves affected by income (and thus **'mediate'** its effect), we shall underestimate the total effect of income upon wellbeing.

(3) If, on the other hand, we omit variables that are positively correlated with both income and wellbeing, we shall overestimate the effects of income, by omitting these **'confounding'** variables.

(4) The relationship in equation (3) may not be properly identified, because there may also be a relation between income and wellbeing in which wellbeing is causing income. This is the problem of **reverse causality.**

(5) If people are affected by **other people's incomes**, we should include these in the controls.

We shall deal with these problems as follows.

(1) We measure income as **income per person** in the household (children being converted into 'equivalent adults'). This is a proxy for living standards. (Though consumption data would be preferable, they are not generally available in surveys where we also have data on wellbeing.) In most surveys, incomes are self-reported, but they are no less accurate than data on, for example, health.

(2) We shall show estimates **with and without** including mediating variables.

(3) To handle confounding variables that are omitted, we shall exploit the **panel** nature of the data, by including in each equation a person fixed effect f_i. This will remove the effect of any omitted variables that do not vary over time. It gives an equation

$$W_{it} = \alpha \log Y_{it} + \sum_j bjX_{ijt} + f_i + v_t + e_{it} \tag{4}$$

The estimate of α is now based on comparisons 'within-person' (rather than across persons). As we shall find, such panel equations tend to give very low estimates of α,[6] but this is partly due to enhanced effects of measurement error[7] and partly because the timing of effects may not be properly represented by the form of the equation.

---

[5] This needs to be included because in advanced countries happiness tends to follow a U shape – higher in youth and old age and lower in middle age (see Chapter 14).

[6] See Table 13.2.   [7] See any econometrics text.

(4) To deal with the problem of reverse causality,[8] we shall show the results of including an element of income that is completely random and therefore **exogeneous.** This is people's winnings in a lottery.

(5) We shall normally include the log income per head of a person's **comparator** group (people of similar age, gender and region). This is to estimate the role of relative income as compared with absolute income. However, we leave reporting these comparator effects till later in the chapter.

Results

We can begin with simple **cross-section** results for Britain, Germany, Australia and the United States. The data for the first three countries are from annual longitudinal household studies (UKHLS, SOEP and HILDA) and for the United States, they are from the annual cross-sectional BRFSS.

As Table 13.1 shows, the effects are not large. To take the US case, one additional point of log income, corresponding to nearly a tripling of income, will produce an extra 0.31 points of wellbeing (out of 10 points maximum).[9]

It is interesting to see how much of the variance of happiness is explained by income inequality. Remember that the partial correlation coefficient is

$$\beta = \frac{\alpha \, \text{SD} \, (log \, Y)}{\text{SD} \, (W)} = 0.31 \times \frac{0.82}{1.55} = 0.16. \tag{5}$$

So the share of the variance of W in the United States explained by income inequality is

$$\beta^2 = 0.16^2 = 0.0256 = 2.56\%.$$

This 2.56% compares with an R^2 of around 19% for the full set of influences shown in Figure 8.2. Yet, some economists claim that 'absolute income is the dominant fact determining wellbeing'.[10] That is clearly not correct. Income is one important influence but one among many.

Moving on to the issue of omitted variables, one possible solution is to use a fixed effects equation like that shown in Chapter 7 and thus exploit the panel nature of the data. As Table 13.2 shows, this produces smaller coefficients.[11] But we should probably ignore these time-series estimates due to the problems noted earlier.

A final way to handle omitted variables and reverse causation is to use data on lottery winnings. In the majority of studies, these are followed up over short periods

---

[8] De Neve and Oswald (2012) demonstrate that adolescent wellbeing affects subsequent income, using sibling fixed effects.

[9] These estimates hold other things constant. But some of these other things may be affected by income. To get a maximum estimate of the total impact of income we would hold nothing constant. In this case, the estimated cross-sectional coefficients tend to be very roughly double the estimates with controls of the kind we have shown.

[10] Sacks et al. (2013).

[11] This might suggest that the cross-sectional estimates may include an element of reverse causality.

Table 13.1 Effects of log income on life satisfaction (0–10) (pooled cross-sections)

Britain	Germany	Australia	United States
0.16	0.26	0.16	0.31
(.01)	(.01)	(.01)	(.01)

Source: A. E. Clark et al. (2018) Table 2.2; Britain, Understanding Society (1996–2014); Germany, SOEP (1984–2015); Australia, HILDA (2001–2015); United States, BRFSS (2006–14).
Note: Standard errors in brackets. 'Controls' include all those in Figure 8.1. Estimates omitting comparator income are very similar.

Table 13.2 Effects of log income on life satisfaction (0–10) (individual fixed effects)

Britain	Germany	Australia
0.04	0.08	0.06
(.01)	(.01)	(.01)

Source: A. E. Clark et al. (2018) Table 2.2; Britain, Understanding Society (1996–2014); Germany, SOEP (1984–2015); Australia, HILDA (2001–2015).
Note: Standard errors in brackets. 'Controls' include all those in Figure 8.1. Estimates omitting comparator income are very similar.

and are therefore difficult to interpret. But in a remarkable study, Lindqvist and others followed up people who played the Swedish lottery for a further 22 years after that.[12] Among the players, the winnings could reasonably be counted as random. And the size of the winnings had a similar effect on wellbeing over all the 22 years. If we convert these one-off winnings into an equivalent income stream, the effect of a unit change in log income is to raise wellbeing (0–10) by 0.38 points.

One further issue: are the effects of log income different in **poorer countries** to the effects in **richer** ones? We can examine this, using data from the Gallup World Poll. The results are shown in Table 13.3. The coefficients are remarkably similar in countries at all levels of income. This is less surprising than might appear since (due to the diminishing marginal utility of income) an extra dollar in the hands of a poor person is worth 20 times more than in the hands of someone who is 20 times richer. We should also note that for high income countries the coefficient is somewhat higher than those shown in Table 13.1, which makes sense since in Gallup data the Table 13.1 countries do have coefficients somewhat below the high-income country average.

It is helpful to have in mind a benchmark coefficient for the effect of log income on wellbeing. In picking one, we should also bear in mind the danger that the Table 13.3

---

[12] Lindqvist et al. (2020). Obviously, lottery winnings may have different immediate psychological effects from other types of income – but less so if spent over a long period.

Table 13.3 Effect of log income on life satisfaction (0-10): By income of country (Pooled cross-section)

High	Upper middle	Lower middle	Low	All
0.37	0.43	0.45	0.35	0.40
(.04)	(.04)	(.03)	(.04)	(.02)

Source: Gallup World Poll 2009–19, Cantril ladder; individual data; regressions include as controls: unemployed, degree, partnered, health problems, age, age^2, country by year fixed effects; regressions by Ekaterina Oparina

coefficients are exaggerated through reverse causality. Thus we would suggest that a figure of 0.30 is a useful benchmark.[13]

This gives us straight away two vital pieces of information. The first is the marginal utility of income (meaning the change in WELLBYs for an extra dollar of annual income). As we explained earlier, this is given by a/Y. So if annual income per head is $30,000, the marginal utility of income is 1/100,000.[14] And 1 extra WELLBY is equivalent to some $100,000 (spread across a group of people).

Second, we can measure the direct impact of inequality on average wellbeing. As Box 13.1 explains, in the typical country this is of the order of 0.12 points (out of 10) – that is how much average wellbeing would rise if average income remained the same but income inequality was abolished. It is a surprisingly small figure.

Box 13.1 The direct effect of income inequality on average wellbeing

We are interested here in the difference between average wellbeing as it now is and average wellbeing as it would be if everyone received the current average level of income. This difference equals[15]

$$0.3 \left(\frac{\sum \log Y_i}{N} - \log \bar{Y} \right).$$

Using a quadratic Taylor's series expansion of $\log Y_i$ this becomes

$$0.3 \left(\log \bar{Y} + \frac{1}{\bar{Y}}(\bar{Y} - \bar{Y}) - \frac{1}{2} \frac{\sum (Y_i - \bar{Y})^2}{N\bar{Y}^2} - \log \bar{Y} \right) = \frac{-0.3}{2} \frac{\text{Var}(Y)}{\bar{Y}^2}.$$

In a typical advanced country, Var$(Y)/\bar{Y}^2$ is around 0.8,[16] so the direct cost of inequality is 0.12 points (out of 10). There are also of course indirect effects through the pattern of human relationships and so on.

---

[13] The high-income country average in Table 13.3 is unaffected if we remove countries in the Middle East.

[14] This would mean that the **statistical value of a life-year** with wellbeing of 7.5 points is $750,000 – higher than is usually allowed for in rich countries.

[15] This is analogous to the Atkinson (1970) income inequality index. If $W = a \log Y$, the Atkinson index of income inequality is given by Var$(Y)/2\bar{Y}^2$.

[16] See A. E. Clark et al. (2018) annex, Tables D1–5.

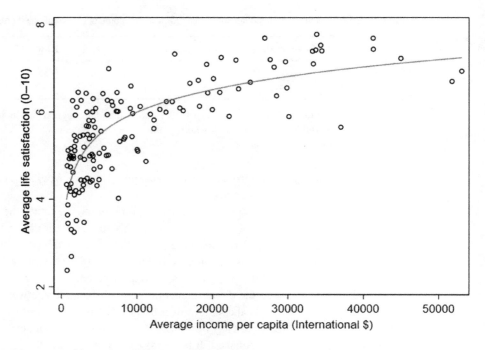

Figure 13.2 Average life satisfaction and household income per head: across countries
Source: Gallup World Poll (2019)

Differences Between Countries

We can turn now to differences in income between countries and how these are reflected in the country's average level of wellbeing. Figure 13.2 shows the scatter diagram of countries together with the line of best fit.

As with individuals, there is overwhelming evidence of diminishing marginal utility of income, and the line of best fit has been estimated using the logarithmic formulation. If no other variables are included, the effect of log income is very substantial. But, as we argued in Chapter 8, this is partly because high income is correlated with many other cultural variables including trust, social support, freedom and generosity. We do not know how far these other characteristics have been caused by national income. But suppose we are asking How much would it help if households were given more income? Then clearly we should be holding these other things constant. In that case, when estimated across countries, the coefficient of wellbeing on log income is 0.33 (se = 0.07).[17] This is conveniently similar to the coefficient across individuals.[18]

---

[17] See Chapter 8. With nothing held constant, the coefficient is rather over double this.

[18] This does not logically prove that social comparisons are unimportant. For example, it might logically be the case that $W_{ic} = b_1(log\, Y_{ic} - log\, \bar{Y}_c) + b_2(log\, \bar{Y}_c - log\, \bar{Y}_{world})$ and $b_1 = b_2$.

Time-Series for Countries

We turn now to the second part of the Easterlin paradox. His claim is that, as time passes, higher national income does not produce higher national wellbeing. In the cross-section of individuals we have found that

$$W = a log Y + \text{etc.}$$

One would therefore expect that over time at the country level

$$\Delta \overline{W} = a\Delta \overline{log Y} + \text{etc.}$$

But Easterlin says it does not.

So what are the facts? The most striking fact supporting Easterlin is the story of the United States. As Figure 13.3 shows, average happiness has not increased there since the 1950s, despite rapid economic growth that was widely shared at least till the 1970s.

However, Figure 13.3 does not prove that in the United States higher income did not improve wellbeing. It might have done so, with other factors offsetting this effect. In any case, the experience of one country can prove little. So the first step is to see whether countries with higher long-term economic growth have had higher growth in wellbeing. It is important to stress the word long-term because there is no doubt that happiness rises in booms and falls in slumps (for all kinds of reasons we shall come to). But do countries with high long-term growth do better in terms of happiness?

Long-term growth and wellbeing

To investigate this, the best available long time-series is for European countries, where the Eurobarometer survey has been conducted regularly in many countries since the

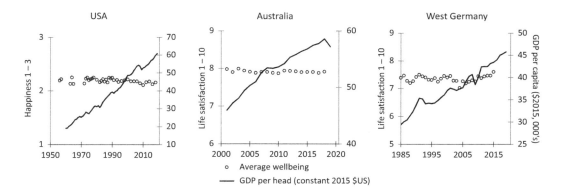

Figure 13.3 Happiness and income per head in the United States, Australia and West Germany
Sources: United States: AIPO, NORC and GSS grafted together using overlapping data; Australia: HILDA; Germany: https://tinyurl.com/3jyjaw4x, based on SOEP.

early 1970s.[19] To investigate the effect of long-term growth, it is of course necessary to control for booms and slumps (which drive wellbeing up and then down). This is done in the following equation, by including percentage unemployed (u) and annual percentage inflation (π), as well as GDP per head and country fixed effects.

$$\bar{W}_{ct} = a_1 + \underset{(.17)}{0.29} \, \log \bar{Y}_{ct} - \underset{(.02)}{0.06} \, u - \underset{(.004)}{0.007} \, \pi + f_c.$$

As the equation shows, income is estimated to have a positive effect but with a huge standard error.[20] This is typical of multi-country time-series – reflecting in part the very different growth rates of wellbeing in different countries with similar rates of income growth.[21] Thus, the conclusion on the second part of the Easterlin hypothesis has to be 'sometimes yes and sometimes no'. But for citizens of the United States there is a particular challenge – of why they are no happier on average than people were in the 1950s.

The Role of Income Comparisons and Adaptation

There is one obvious reason why national increases in income over time might produce lower changes in wellbeing than individual increases in income at one point in time. It is **social comparisons**.

   Suppose that each of us has a comparator group with whom we compare our incomes and that much of our concern about income is focused on our **relative income** rather than our absolute income. Then a person's wellbeing depends positively on her wellbeing but negatively on the income of her comparators. The relationship could be[22]

$$W_i = a_1 \log Y_i - a_2 \log \bar{Y}_i + \text{etc.} \qquad (a_1, a_2 > 0) \tag{5}$$

where $\bar{Y}_i$ is the average income in the person's comparator group. This can also be written as the sum of the effects of absolute income (Y_i) and of relative income ($Y_i / \bar{Y}_i$):

$$W_i = (a_1 - a_2) \log \, Y_i + a_2 \log \left(\frac{Y_i}{\bar{Y}_i} \right) + \text{etc.}$$

Absolute income	Relative income

---

[19] The countries covered below are Austria, Belgium, Denmark, Finland, France, Germany, Greece, Ireland, Italy, Netherlands, Portugal, Spain, Sweden and the UK.

[20] Analysis by Ekaterina Oparina. Splitting the coefficient into trend and cycle makes no difference once unemployment is included. And including time dummies as well reduces 0.29–0.08. An identical equation to the one in the text, but using World Values Survey for all waves 1981–2019, gives the following coefficients: −0.11 (.20), −0.04 (.01), −0.02 (.00).

[21] An analogous way to study the data is to estimate for each country the trend in wellbeing and the trend in log GDP per head and then regress one on the other (across countries). This is the approach in Easterlin and O'Connor (2020). See Annex 13.1.

[22] In this formulation $\bar{Y}$ has no effect on individual i's choice of hours. There is some evidence that it does (see A. E. Clark et al. [2008]), which raises an even bigger policy problem – that people are working harder simply because others are doing so (the rat-race).

Table 13.4 Effect of log own income and log comparator income on life satisfaction (0–10) (pooled cross-sections)

	Britain	Germany	Australia	United States
Own income	**0.16** (.01)	**0.26** (.01)	**0.16** (.01)	**0.31** (.01)
Comparator income	**−0.23** (.07)	**−0.25** (.04)	**−0.17** (.06)	**−0.19** (.03)

Source: A. E. Clark et al. (2018) Table 2.3; Britain, Understanding Society (1996–2014); Germany, SOEP (1984–2015); Australia, HILDA (2001–2015); United States, BRFSS (2006–14)
Note: Standard errors in brackets. 'controls' include all those in Figure 8.1.

If a_2 is substantial, comparators' income is a substantial force reducing our happiness.

So what is the evidence on the effect of comparator income? In the great majority of studies, it is negative and large.[23] But the findings sometimes depend on what group people are assumed to compare themselves with – very local (such as neighbours or colleagues) or people from the same region, age group and gender.[24] In the cross-sectional study reported in Table 13.1, we used the latter definition. The results are shown in Table 13.4.

In these countries, the effects of comparator income are negative and large. Thus, the effects of relative income are positive and large. Meanwhile, the effects of absolute average income, which is the sum of the two rows in Table 13.4, are small. If these numbers are anywhere near right, they provide an obvious explanation of the Easterlin paradox:

- When an individual has a higher income, holding $\bar{Y}$ constant, she is happier. This is mainly because her relative income is higher.
- But when the whole society becomes richer, $\bar{Y}$ rises and relative incomes do not change. (Some people may go up in relative terms and others down but the average of relative income remains constant.) So at the level of society the only effect of economic growth is the weaker effect of absolute income.

There is much other evidence that people care about relative income as well as absolute income. Some of it comes from neuroscience, led by Armin Falk of the University of Bonn.[25] His team organised an experiment where participants had to undertake a task while undergoing a functional MRI measurement of brain activity in the brain's reward centre, the ventral striatum. Those who successfully completed the task were given a financial reward, which was varied randomly. They were also told of the reward, if any, received by the person with whom they were paired. The findings were remarkable. The measure of activity in the ventral striatum increased by 0.92

[23] A. E. Clark et al. (2008).
[24] In local comparisons, the coefficient is sometimes positive. This is probably because neighbours' incomes are taken as a forecast of our own incomes ('light at the end of the tunnel'). Graham (2012); Ifcher et al. (2018).
[25] Dohmen et al. (2011).

Table 13.5 Effect of own income, comparator income and own lagged income on life satisfaction (0–10) (with fixed effects)

	Britain	Germany	Australia
Log own income	**0.06** (.01)	**0.19** (.01)	**0.06** (.01)
Log comparator income	−**0.09** (.06)	−**0.12** (.04)	**0.01** (.04)
Log previous 3 yrs' income	−**0.02** (.02)	−**0.08** (.01)	−**0.01** (0.01)

Source: A. E. Clark et al. (2018) Table 2.4; Britain, Understanding Society (1996–2014); Germany, SOEP (1984–2015); Australia, HILDA (2001–2015).
Note: Standard errors in brackets. 'Controls' include all those in Figure 8.1. Note that comparator income has little movement except for people who move regions.

units for every €100 they themselves received and fell by 0.67 units for every €100 their pair received. So, relative income had double the effect of absolute income.

In another ingenious experiment, David Card (another winner of the Nobel Prize) and his colleagues examined the effect of knowing the incomes of your colleagues. It happened that the University of California, where he works, had recently put all faculty salaries online. But most people did not know about it. So Card informed a random selection of the faculty members that these data existed. He also measured the wellbeing of the treatment and control group before and after he did this. Those who learned about colleagues' salaries became on average less satisfied.[26] So relative income clearly matters.[27]

Adaptation

However, some psychologists favour a different explanation of the Easterlin paradox – **adaptation**. According to this, people may enjoy an increase in income for a time but then they get used to the higher income and their wellbeing reverts to its former level. Unfortunately, not many studies have tested the effect of social comparisons and adaptation simultaneously. In Table 13.5 we do this, using the same panel data that was used cross-sectionally in Table 13.4. But this time we include a fixed effect for each individual, and we include not only social comparison income but also the lagged values of own income:

$$W_{it} = \alpha_1 \log Y_{it} - \alpha_2 \log \bar{Y}_{it} + \alpha_3 \log Y_{i,t-1} + \alpha_4 \log Y_{i,t-2} + \text{etc} + v_t + f_i + e_{it}. \quad (6)$$

When this fixed effects model is run, the effect of one's own income is lower than in cross-section (as discussed earlier). But the negative effect of comparator income is

[26] Card et al. (2012).
[27] Similarly, Perez-Truglia (2020) found that, since Norwegian tax records became publicly available in 2001, the gap in life satisfaction between rich and poor people increased by 21%. Many psychologists, like Nicholas Chater and Gordon D. A. Brown, argue that people care more about their position in the rank order of income than they care about relative income. The broad implications of both views are similar.

much more substantial than of lagged income from the previous three years. In any case, adaptation cannot be the main reason for the Easterlin paradox: in any community, most richer people have always been richer and poorer people have been poorer, and yet the richer people are on average happier.[28]

Policy Implications of Income Comparisons

The analysis in this chapter has major implications. First, as we have said, diminishing marginal utility is a powerful argument for the redistribution of income to the point where it ceases to raise average wellbeing. This point has been understood for many years. But the role of social comparisons introduces a completely new argument in favour of taxation (not based on the diminishing marginal utility of income nor on the need to fund public goods).[29]

To see this, assume a world in which everybody is equal. It will still be the case that when someone works longer and therefore earns more, she increases the income level against which everyone else compares their income. This is a **negative externality**, and it leads to an inefficient scale of work unless something is done. What level of tax would suffice? Let us suppose that there are $(N + 1)$ identical individuals each paid (for simplicity) a salary of one unit per hour worked – meaning that a person's earnings equal the hours she works. So suppose that individual wellbeing depends additively on own log income, log comparator income and the cost of work effort. Then, if there are no taxes,

$$W_i = \alpha_1 \log H_i - a_2 \log \bar{H} - C(H_i) \quad (C' > 0) \tag{7}$$

where $\bar{H}$ is the average income of the other N people, and the last term is the psychic cost of working H_i hours.[30]

When anyone works longer to improve their own income, they also raise the average income $(\bar{H})$ against which others compare their income. In the absence of a tax, the individual chooses H_i to maximise W_i, ignoring the effect this has on $\bar{H}$. So the **individual optimum** in the absence of a tax is found by setting dW/dH_i equal to zero, which gives

$$\frac{\alpha_1}{H_i} = \frac{dC}{dH}(H_i) \tag{8}$$

The value of marginal income is equated to the psychic cost of obtaining the marginal income.

But the **social optimum** would also allow for the negative effect of increased H_i on the wellbeing of the other N people. When H_i goes up by one unit, $\bar{H}$ goes up by 1/N.

---

[28] This is not because their position in the distribution is temporary – it is mainly 'permanent'.

[29] Layard (1980, 2006).

[30] If the leisure time of comparators also had a negative effect, the distortion would be less. But there is evidence that people do not compare their leisure with that of others. See Solnick and Hemenway (1998).

This in turn reduces the wellbeing of each of the other N people by $(\alpha_2/\bar{H}_i)(1/N)$. But there are N people who are affected in this way, so the total loss of wellbeing is $(\alpha_2/\bar{H}_i)$. The **social optimum** takes this into account and is therefore given by[31]

$$\frac{a_1 - a_2}{\bar{H}_i} = \frac{dC}{dH}(\bar{H}_i). \tag{9}$$

This implies fewer hours of work.

So what is the optimum corrective tax?[32] Suppose it is structured as a linear tax with a constant marginal tax rate (t) and the yield is returned to the workers in lump-sum form. Then the **individual optimum** is now

$$\frac{a_1(1-t)}{H_i} = \frac{dC}{dH}(H_i). \tag{10}$$

We now want to find that value of t that ensures that the individual optimum is the same as the social optimum. This requires

$$a_1(1-t) = a_1 - a_2.$$

So the optimum marginal tax rate is α_2/α_1 – the ratio of the pollution effect to the own income effect. Given the estimated values of α_2, this could justify quite high marginal tax rates on grounds of efficiency. At the very least, this externality argument should be put against the traditional argument that taxation has an 'excess burden' – because it inefficiently discourages work.[33] If when people earn more they are imposing a cost on others, this should be taken into account in any argument about what is efficient.

Similarly, with cost-benefit analysis. If a project is paid for out of higher taxes paid by everybody, any loss of wellbeing from the tax will be partially softened by the fact that everybody else is losing as well.

It is sometimes said that this argument is less forceful if people only compare themselves with small numbers of other people. But, as our reasoning earlier about N showed, the argument applies whatever the size of the group.[34]

Another important implication of social comparisons is for us as individuals. People who make fewer comparisons are on average happier.[35] So we should train our tastes, as far as we can, to reduce α_2. Libertarians argue that, if we don't do this, that is our lookout, and governments should ignore human failings. But this approach is inconsistent with an evidence-based approach to ethical questions.

---

[31] Another way to arrive at this conclusion is simply to find the level of H, which, if everybody worked that long, would yield the social optimum. Differentiating equation (7) by H and setting $dW/dH = 0$ yields (9) straight away.

[32] Boskin and Sheshinski (1978). They solve this problem for a world in which wage rates differ between people.

[33] In the economic jargon, the 'excess burden' compares the cost of the tax with the cost of a lump sum tax. The excess is due to the effect of the tax in making people substitute income for leisure. See Layard and Walters (1978) p. 87.

[34] This assumes that α_2 is independent of N.   [35] For example, White et al. (2006).

A second argument in support of corrective taxation comes from unforeseen adaptation. If people work harder to increase their income but overestimate the effects of this on their own wellbeing,[36] that is another reason why some marginal taxation could be good for efficiency.

Economic Fluctuations

We turn finally to fluctuations of income over the business cycle. What is certain is that wellbeing rises in booms and falls in slumps. Two processes are at work here. The first is **adaptation**. Morale is higher when income is high relative to previous income and low in recessions (when the reverse applies). And the second is **loss-aversion**. This time we are talking about ex post loss aversion (not the ex ante loss aversion that affects decisions). There is powerful evidence that the loss of wellbeing when income falls by a given amount is roughly double the increase in wellbeing when income rises by the same amount.[37] This has profound implications.

- First, it helps to explain the weak long-term relationship between income and wellbeing, since the years of income decline have such strong negative effects.
- Second, in terms of policy, it argues strongly for the importance of economic stability. In his famous Presidential Address to the American Economic Association, the neo-classical economist Robert Lucas argued that economic cycles were unimportant compared with the rate of long-term economic growth. Cycles could therefore be tolerated if they increased long-term growth. The implication of wellbeing research is the opposite: higher long-term growth ought not to be pursued if it leads to economic instability. Humans like stability and it is the job of policy to provide it.

Conclusions

- The Easterlin paradox states that
  (1) in a given context richer people are on average happier than poorer people,
  (2) but over time greater national income per head does not cause greater national happiness.
- Statement (1) is certainly true. We reviewed a mass of evidence and concluded that, as a benchmark, a unit increase in log income raises wellbeing by 0.3 points (out of 10). The share of the within country variance in wellbeing explained by income inequality is 3% or less. So income is in no sense a proxy for wellbeing.
- Across countries, the effect of a unit change in log income per capita (other things equal) is also around 0.3 points of wellbeing.

---

[36] Loewenstein, O'Donoghue and Rabin (2003).
[37] One such study uses country data (De Neve et al. [2018]). Another uses individual data (Boyce et al. [2013]).

- Over time, wellbeing has increased with income in some countries but not in others. Thus statement (2) is still the subject of ongoing research.
- From direct studies on individual data, it is clear that in most cases a rise in other people's income reduces your own wellbeing. This means that the effect of one person's income on that individual's wellbeing overestimates the effect of economic growth on the overall wellbeing of society.
- From a policy point of view, income comparisons mean that when a person earns more she imposes a cost on other people. This is a negative externality and one way to control it would be by corrective taxation. If the externality is as large as our estimates suggest, this could mean that quite high rates of marginal tax are efficient.
- The final issue is economic fluctuations. Wellbeing rises in booms and falls in slumps. One important reason is loss-aversion – people dislike a loss of income twice as much as they like a gain of equal size (both likes and dislikes being measured in units of ex post wellbeing). This may be a partial explanation of the Easterlin paradox. In terms of policy, it means that economic stability is enormously important and ought not to be sacrificed in pursuit of small increases in long-term economic growth.

Questions for discussion

(1) Are the estimated effects of income plausible?
(2) Why do they not differ between rich and poor countries?
(3) Are national time-series estimates of the effect of income consistent with within-country estimates based on individuals?
(4) How important are social comparisons and what are their policy implications?
(5) How important is adaptation?

Further Reading

Clark, A. E., et al. (2008). Relative income, happiness, and utility: An explanation for the Easterlin paradox and other puzzles. *Journal of Economic Literature*, 46(1), 95–144.

Clark, A. E., et al. (2018). *The Origins of Happiness: The Science of Wellbeing over the Life Course*. Princeton University Press.

Easterlin, R. A. (1974). Does economic growth improve the human lot? Some empirical evidence. In *Nations and Households in Economic Growth* (pp. 89–125). Academic Press.

Layard, R. (2006). Happiness and public policy: A challenge to the profession. *Economic Journal*, 116 (March), C24–C33.

WE NEED EACH OTHER

14 Community

When I is replaced with We, illness becomes wellness.

Malcolm X

Social Connections

As Aristotle observed, human beings are social animals. In prehistory, it was our ability to cooperate that ensured our survival. And we still rely on other people to satisfy most of our needs. We need them for objective support but also for much more. We need them for affection and our very sense of who we are (our identity). And, to have a sense of meaning and belonging in our lives, we need to be needed by others.[1]

Most of us have a wide range of social connections. We have family and other intimate relationships. We have friends. We have colleagues through work. And we may have a wide range of other contacts through sports clubs, cultural organisations, community centres (for the young and old), parents' associations, political parties, trades unions and voluntary organisations of all kinds. So, to begin with, you might like to list all your main social connections of all kinds, in the order of their importance for your wellbeing.

To show how important these relationships are, many researchers have taken a sample of people, measured their initial characteristics, and then followed them for 10 years or so to see who lived and who died. The initial characteristics they measured included the respondents' health and their social relationships. And it turned out that having 'poor or insufficient' relationships, compared with 'adequate' relationships is as likely to kill you as smoking cigarettes is. In each of these cases, (other things equal) you become 50% more likely to die in the next 10 years or so.[2]

This is the result of a meta-analysis of 148 different studies and focuses on all forms of social relationships. Other studies focus just on loneliness. **Loneliness** is surprisingly common. As Vivek Murthy reported after serving as US Surgeon General: 'To

---

[1] For an excellent survey of the main issues in this chapter, see Helliwell et al. (2018a). On the physiology of social connections see Lieberman (2013).

[2] Holt-Lunstad et al. (2010). See also the original Grant and Glueck Study from Harvard University: www .adultdevelopmentstudy.org/grantandglueckstudy.

my surprise, the topic of ... loneliness ... received the strongest response from the public of any issue that I worked on.'[3] In the United States, 22% of adults say they often or always feel lonely or socially isolated.[4] It is a growing problem as more and more people worldwide live on their own.

Loneliness is a killer.[5] Compared with others, those who feel lonely are 26% more likely to die, those who feel isolated are 26% more likely and those who live on their own are 30% more likely to die. They lead less healthy lives, have higher blood pressure and weaker immune systems.

So what is the effect of social connections on wellbeing (rather than on life-expectancy and physical health)? Perhaps the simplest question of all about social connections is 'If you were in trouble, do you have relatives or friends you can count on to help you whenever you need them?' This question is asked in the Gallup World Poll, and in Chapter 8 we have seen its key role in explaining differences in wellbeing across countries. In the Central African Republic, 29% say Yes to this question (the lowest proportion of any country) while in Iceland 99% say Yes (the highest propor-tion). This difference of itself causes an estimated difference in average wellbeing of 1.4 points (out of 10) between the two countries.[6]

Similarly, family relationships (having a partner) increase wellbeing and so do high-quality working relationships (see Chapter 8). But we have not so far looked at the importance of relationships that people have **in the community**. That is what this chapter is about.

We are concerned here with the whole network of social relationships outside the family and the workplace. We are also concerned with the norms and values embed-ded in these relationships. Together, these phenomena comprise the '**social capital**' of a community. So we shall examine

- community networks (sometimes also called 'civil society'),
- trust and social norms and
- some specific community activities – culture, sport and religious worship.

We shall look at the following issues:

- How important are social networks and volunteering?
- How important is a culture of trustworthy behaviour?
- The importance of inequality, crime, diversity and immigration.
- How do cultural, sporting and religious activities affect wellbeing?

Community Networks

The idea that social networks matter is hardly new. It was central to the founders of sociology including de Tocqueville (who described their importance in

---

[3] Murthy (2020).   [4] DiJulio et al. (2018).   [5] Holt-Lunstad et al. (2015).
[6] Helliwell et al. (2017).

nineteenth-century America), as well as Durkheim, Dewey and Weber. But in recent times, their importance has been highlighted above all by **Robert Putnam** of Harvard University. In *Bowling Alone* (2000) he contrasted a society where people do most things with other people (including going bowling) to a society where people do more on their own. He showed that in the United States, membership of group associations was in sharp decline.

He then, working with John Helliwell, showed that this was bad for people's wellbeing. In a seminal article the two of them studied what determined life satisfaction among the 84,000 people covered in the early waves of the World Values Survey.[7] They studied both individual and national influences upon life satisfaction. And they showed that an increase of one in the average number of organisations that people belonged to raised average wellbeing in a country by 0.3 points (on a scale of 0–10). Trust also had a strong effect (see 'Trust' section below). Similar results have been found in many subsequent studies. These later studies have also shown how social connections have buffered people against the negative effects of recession and natural disasters, by being of greater help the greater the disaster.[8]

Volunteering

All the networks we have been considering depend on **volunteering**. The governing committees are often volunteers, and most of the work is done by volunteers. This is true whether the organisation operates for the benefit of its members or to help others who are more disadvantaged. In the latter case, the activity is twice blessed – it blesses those being helped, but it also blesses the helpers. ('It is in giving that we receive.')

A good example of these two-way benefits is the Experience Corps that flourishes in many American cities and enables old people to feel needed by giving meaningful support to children. The volunteers must be at least fifty and they deliver literacy support to primary school children up to the third grade. Most of the volunteers have high school education only, and they get two weeks' training in how to deliver the literacy support. They then work in schools delivering this support for fifteen hours a week. In Baltimore, the volunteers have been carefully followed up in a controlled trial, lasting on average for six months. Compared with a wait-list control group, the volunteers who participated in the trial found they had increased 'the number of people they could turn to for help', as well as their level of physical activity.[9] Over two years, when compared with controls, they were found to have increased their brain volume in both the hippocampal and cortical areas.[10] This makes good sense: contacts between young and old not only advance the young, but they rejuvenate the old.

Another clear example of the benefits of volunteering comes from the experience of East Germany after reunification with the West. During reunification, much of the

---

[7] Helliwell and Putnam (2004).   [8] Helliwell et al. (2018c).   [9] Tan et al. (2006).
[10] Carlson et al. (2015).

voluntary activity that had prevailed under Communism collapsed, and the wellbeing of the previous volunteers fell much more than that of other East Germans.[11]

Social networks serve many functions. Some of these are very practical services for their members, while others reach out to the wider community. Through all forms of social connection, the happiness of one person affects the happiness of others. This is demonstrated clearly by the Framingham Heart Study. The connections it studied included not only what we have called community networks but also relatives, friends and colleagues. For each member of the sample, it repeatedly measured their happiness and that of their close contacts. It found that if your relative, friend or neighbour became happier, you became significantly more likely to be happy – and thus to make others happy in your network. This effect was then passed on through two further waves of contacts.[12]

But networks can also of course transmit negative outcomes. The sociologist Nicolas Christakis, who showed how networks spread happiness, also showed how they can spread obesity.[13] So the message that a network transmits is hugely important. One key message is about trust.

Trust

'Do you think that most people can be trusted (or alternatively, that you can't be too careful in dealing with people)?' You might like to try giving your own answer to this question. At the national level, the proportion of people saying Yes to this question is an obvious measure of the extent of trustworthy behaviour in the community. The proportion who say Yes varies hugely from 5% in Brazil to 64% in Norway.[14] And, as we saw in Chapter 8, it has a substantial impact on average wellbeing in the country – a rise of 60% in the population saying Yes (corresponding to the difference between Brazil and Norway) increases average wellbeing by some 0.6 points (out of 10). This is similar to the gap between employed and unemployed people.

But how accurately do these answers on trust really reflect actual behaviour in a country? Fortunately, there is a simple experiment, first conducted by the Reader's Digest. **Actual wallets** were dropped in the street, containing significant amounts of money as well as the name and address of the wallet's owner. In one experiment, this was done in 20 cities in Europe and in 12 cities in the United States.[15] The experimenters counted what proportion of the wallets were returned. In Oslo and Copenhagen, all the wallets were returned, but the proportion varied greatly across

---

[11] Meier and Stutzer (2008). On the benefits of volunteering, see also Binder and Freytag (2013); and Dolan et al. (2021).

[12] Fowler and Christakis (2008).

[13] Christakis and Fowler (2007). The obesity problem may have been accentuated by social media – see Chapter 9.

[14] World Values Survey, www.worldvaluessurvey.org/wvs.jsp.   [15] Knack (2001).

the other cities.[16] And, importantly for the research, the proportion of wallets that were returned was highly correlated with the answers to the question about trust given in the same country. So we can indeed place some credence on the answers about trust.

We can also examine the effect of trust at the individual level.[17] In one survey, people were asked whether they would expect a lost wallet containing $200 to be returned. Those who said 'Very likely' were experiencing (other things equal) an extra one point of wellbeing (out of 10) compared with those who said 'Very unlikely'.[18]

One of the most remarkable findings about the wallet experiments is this: the more money a wallet contains, the more likely it is to be returned. This is contrary to most models of human nature. But it comes from a study in the largest cities in 40 countries, rich and poor, involving 17,000 wallets.[19] In virtually all countries, a wallet was more likely to be returned to the owner if it included some money. And the more money there was the more likely the wallet was to be returned (see Figure 14.1).

Moreover, higher trust has another important effect – it not only raises average wellbeing, but it also reduces the inequality of wellbeing. This is because high trust raises wellbeing more for those who are initially disadvantaged.[20] Using the European Social Survey, it is possible to simulate the distribution of wellbeing in two cases.

(i)   Where everyone has a low level of trust, both in others and in institutions.
(ii) Where everyone has a high level of trust.

In the latter case, average wellbeing is much higher. But wellbeing is also much less widely dispersed, because people with the lowest wellbeing have improved their wellbeing the most.

In some countries, trust has fallen sharply since the 1960s (e.g., in the United States) while in others it has risen (e.g., Denmark and Italy). This may help to explain why life satisfaction has not risen in the United States since the 1960s while it has risen in many European countries.[21]

In many countries, low levels of trust are associated with **corrupt behaviour** both among public officials (police, judges, railway clerks) and in business. So the wellbeing equation in Figure 8.5 looks very similar if trust is replaced by averaging the answers to the following questions: 'Is corruption widespread throughout the government or not?' and 'Is corruption widespread within business or not?' None of this is surprising. For, if we reflect on our own experience, we can see how clearly our own wellbeing has been affected by how well others around us behave.[22]

In the debate on social capital, critics have complained that these results were driven by high levels of trust and social networks in Scandinavia and claimed that Scandinavia was also well known for its high rate of suicide. However, in fact,

---

[16] Higher than people forecast – as so often when people are asked to guess about others' behaviour. See Helliwell and Wang (2010); and Helliwell et al. (2021).

[17] For a study showing its importance in rural China, see Yip et al. (2007).   [18] Helliwell et al. (2021).

[19] Cohn et al. (2019). The experimenters handed in the wallets at a bank or public building and asked the recipient to 'take care of it'. (There was a business card in each wallet.) The money was in local currency.

[20] Helliwell et al. (2020).   [21] Bartolini et al. (2016).   [22] Helliwell et al. (2019) Table 2.1.

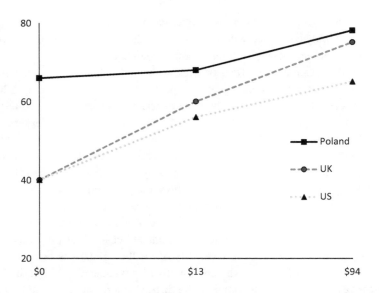

Figure 14.1 Percentage of wallets returned: By amount of money in wallet
Source: Cohn et al. (2019)

Scandinavian suicide rates are similar to the European average.[23] Moreover, similar equations explain both national suicide rates and national wellbeing (and indeed the rate of road accident deaths).[24]

Inequality

As many people have pointed out, the countries with the highest levels of trust (like those in Scandinavia) also tend to have the highest levels of income equality.[25] So how does income equality affect community wellbeing?

First, there is the immediate effect of the diminishing marginal utility of income. This means that countries with a given average level of income will on average be happier the more equal the distribution of income. But this effect is not large.[26] A second effect can be through the impact of income inequality on the pattern of human relationships. The basic idea is that people feel most comfortable with people like themselves. So the greater the differences in income between individuals, the greater the social distance and the less the sense of ease.

However, despite both these points, few researchers have found any substantial correlation between income inequality and average national wellbeing. This may be surprising given the correlations between income inequality and social trust (and many other good things) so powerfully demonstrated by Wilkinson and Pickett.[27]

---

[23] On Scandinavian exceptionalism, see Martela et al. (2020).   [24] Helliwell (2007).
[25] For example, see Wilkinson and Pickett (2009, 2018).   [26] See Chapter 13.
[27] Wilkinson and Pickett (2009, 2018).

Table 14.1 Equations to explain individual life satisfaction (0–10) – partial correlation coefficients

	European Social Survey	World Values Survey	Gallup World Poll
National standard deviation of wellbeing	−0.20	−0.17	−0.10
National Gini coefficient of income	−0.02	−0.01	−0.04
National log GDP per head	0.18	0.21	0.39
Controls for gender, age, education, employment and mental states	√	√	√
N	301,960	243,875	1,133,621

Source: Goff et al. (2018) Tables 2, 3, and 4

But John Helliwell and his colleagues have provided evidence that looks like an explanation.[28] In their view (evidenced below), what really matters is the **inequality of wellbeing**. This will reflect the 'spirit of equality' in a country, which affects the equality of everything (the distribution of social services and the codes of behaviour, as well as household income inequality). And this general equality (best proxied by the equality of wellbeing) will then affect the **average** levels of wellbeing.

Table 14.1 provides the evidence for this approach. It uses the European Social Survey (2006–15), the World Values Survey (waves 1–6) and the Gallup World Poll (2008–14). In each of these surveys, it is the wellbeing inequality in their country that has a strong effect on the wellbeing of the citizens. Income inequality (measured by Gini) has a small and often insignificant effect. Even if wellbeing inequality is dropped from the equation, the partial correlation coefficient on Gini does not rise above 0.07 in absolute magnitude. So we should take the issue of equality very seriously, but just tackling income inequality alone will not be enough to make a huge difference.

Crime

As we have seen, trustworthy behaviour is a key ingredient of a happy society. And one variant of untrustworthy behaviour is crime. Crime affects community wellbeing in two ways: it hurts the victims and it spreads the fear of crime even more widely. To capture both these effects, one can estimate an equation in which the average wellbeing in each community is explained by the logarithm of its annual crime rate (after allowing for many controls and a fixed effect for each community). When this is done in Britain, the coefficient is substantial (0.14).[29]

But crime is also not great for most of the criminals. In one study of people in mid-life, the number of self-reported crimes they have committed explained as much of the

[28] Goff et al. (2018) annex 14.1 shows the level of inequality of wellbeing in each country, as well as the proportion of the population with life satisfaction of 4 or below.

[29] Dustmann and Fasani (2016).

dispersion of wellbeing (other things equal) as did income.[30] A high proportion of criminals have mental health problems and need treatment. But also crucial for prisoners is their lack of supportive social connections. When people come out of prison, connections can be crucial in determining whether they re-offend. In Los Angeles, the Anti-Recidivism Coalition's mission is to help them re-establish connections (including to employment and education). In 2018, 11% of those helped returned to prison, compared with an average of 50% for the state of California.

By contrast, people who are more satisfied with their lives are much less likely to commit crime. This is true even after controlling for a large range of other factors. Happiness is a strong predictor of good behaviour.[31]

Ethnic Diversity and Immigration

We come now to a troubling aspect of human nature. As we have said, most people feel more comfortable with people like themselves. That is why in his analysis of social capital, Robert Putnam distinguished between **'bonding' capital** (networks that bring together people who are naturally close to each other) and **'bridging' capital** (which bring together people who are naturally more different and less close).

A healthy society needs both types, including bridging capital. For, at least in the United States, there is strong evidence that trust is lower in areas of greater ethnic diversity. In such cases, people are not only less trustful of other ethnic groups but also less trustful of their own group; they tend to withdraw and to participate less in the life of the community.[32] There is similar evidence in Britain that diversity in a local area reduces somewhat your satisfaction with your area.[33] In Europe, the evidence is less clear-cut, but for many people diversity is certainly an issue.[34] However, even in the United States and Canada, there are many individuals for whom diversity is not an issue – especially those people who regularly talk to their neighbours.[35]

A somewhat different issue, though related, is immigration – the flow of people into a country from outside. This has become a major political issue. We now know a considerable amount about the impact of immigration upon all those involved.

About 3% of the world's population live in a different country from where they were born. Today's levels of global migration are unprecedented and reflect the greater ease of travel and communication. Economists tend to favour migration

---

[30] A. E. Clark et al. (2018) Fig 1.1. In this study, wellbeing is measured after the crimes, and wellbeing before the crimes is included as a control.

[31] Hanniball et al. (2021).

[32] Alesina and La Ferrara (2000, 2002); Glaeser et al. (2000); Alesina and Glaeser (2004); Putnam (2007); For a different view, see Uslaner (2012).

[33] Langella and Manning (2016). See also Longhi (2014), who finds that this result applies only to the white British population. It also differs for different groups. For example, if we look only at the effects of immigrants coming from Eastern Europe, Ivlevs and Veliziotis (2018) find that life-satisfaction is actually increased for residents who are younger or employed or on higher incomes but reduced for people who are older or unemployed or on lower incomes.

[34] Akay et al. (2014); Betz and Simpson (2013).   [35] Stolle et al. (2008).

because world output increases when people move to more productive environments. But what does the wellbeing approach say about the gains and losses from migration?

Three lots of people are affected.[36] The first is the people who move. On average, international migrants increase their happiness when they move by 0.6 points (out of 10). This is a lot. Most migration is to happier countries and, after moving, migrants become on average about as happy as the existing residents in the country where they end up.[37] This change happens very quickly; and second-generation immigrants are on average as happy as their parents were after they moved.

The second group affected is the family that the migrants left behind. According to the evidence, they remain as satisfied with life as they were before, partly because they often receive very large financial remittances from their migrant relative.

Finally, there are the original residents of the country to which the migrants migrate. Resentment against immigrants is particularly common among less-skilled workers, who feel that migrants undermine their bargaining power in the labour market. This can clearly reduce their wellbeing. But there is little persuasive evidence of large effects, and there is no evidence across countries that those with high proportions of immigrants are less happy because of it. In fact, the happiest ten countries in the world include on average 17% of their population who were born abroad.

This said, immigration has become a huge political issue and, as Chapter 17 shows, it has fuelled populism and undermined the stability of politics in many countries. Whatever the findings of wellbeing science, Paul Collier is surely right when he argues that migration flows would be highly destabilising if they were not effectively managed.[38]

Culture, Sport and Religion

Finally, let's look at some of the most enjoyable things we do in the company of others: the arts, sports and (for some) religious worship.

By the arts we mean mainly music, dance, drama, cinema, visual arts, museums and book clubs. In most of these, we can either perform actively or we can be attendees while others are performing. In each case, there is normally a social element and the activity is also intrinsically uplifting.

To study the wellbeing effects of these activities is not easy. There is obviously a short-run effect, but if we want to study the longer-term effect there is a problem of timing. In one study, the researchers investigated the effect of attending music events.[39] They studied the long-run effects on life satisfaction by taking two standard social surveys and (including a fixed effect for each person) they asked 'How much

---

[36] On this and the next two paragraphs, see Helliwell, Layard and Sachs (2018) chapters 2 and 3.
[37] Interestingly, their happiness is also marginally affected by the happiness in the country they left.
[38] Collier (2013).   [39] Dolan and Testoni (2017a). On music, see also Daykin, Mansfield et al. (2017).

was a person's life satisfaction increased by attending at least one of each type of music event in the last year?' The average effect of each type of event was about 0.1 points of life satisfaction (out of 10). On the other hand, when the researchers used time-use studies and looked at the contemporaneous effect over a shorter time, the effect on happiness (a hedonic measure) was nearer to 0.8 points (out of 10). The effects were strongest when group activities are involved.

A more comprehensive enquiry looked at all the arts and evaluated separately the effects of **participating** in any activity at least once a week or of **attending** at least once a year. The analysis used Britain's Understanding Society sample, with a fixed effect for each person. Participation (as defined) raised life satisfaction by around 0.1 points (out of 10), as did attendance.[40]

When it comes to **sports and exercise**, we shall only look at participation.[41] (Attending matches is much more like watching them on TV). Again it is useful to distinguish between long-run effects on life satisfaction and short-run effects on positive emotion. Most of the existing studies have been cross-sectional, and these show good associations between exercise and life satisfaction.[42] But an association has been more difficult to establish in panel studies of annual time-series. As for the short-run effects on mood, these are strong and reliably established. Given this evidence, there is now a strong movement among doctors in favour of **social prescribing**. In other words, patients are encouraged to engage in a form of cultural activity or exercise that suits them.

Religious worship is one of the oldest forms of human group activity. Religion can play at least three major roles: to instil values, to provide valuable social interaction and to offer comfort. We have discussed the general importance of the first two elements in different parts of the book. But what of the specific effect of religion?

The Gallup World Poll provides important evidence;[43] 68% of adults in the world say that 'religion is important in their daily lives'. Religious belief and practice is more common in countries where life is harder (low income, life expectancy, education and personal safety). But, after controlling crudely for those factors, there is no difference in life satisfaction between more and less religious countries. Nor, within countries where life is less hard, are religious individuals in the Gallup World Poll systematically more satisfied with life than less religious people.

The position is somewhat different if we focus exclusively on the United States, using the Gallup Daily Poll. And, allowing for other factors, people in more religious US states are on average more satisfied with life.[44] And so are more religious people. In comparisons between individuals, there is always the problem that people who are naturally happier in given circumstances may be more willing to believe that there is a benevolent deity. However, meta-analysis concludes that greater religiosity is mildly

---

[40] Wang et al. (2020).   [41] Dolan and Testoni (2017b).

[42] For a literature survey, see appendix A.1. to Dolan and Testoni (2017b).

[43] See Diener et al. (2011). In this context Buddhists normally report themselves as religious, even if others question this use of words.

[44] Diener et al. (2011).

associated with fewer depressive symptoms[45] and 75% of studies find at least some positive effect of religion on wellbeing.[46] This effect is particularly prevalent in very high-loss situations, such as bereavement (and weaker after less severe losses, such as job loss or marital problems). Thus, religion can reduce the wellbeing consequences of stressful events, via its stress-buffering role.[47] There is some longitudinal evidence suggesting that it is the friendship and social support that result from religious attendance that do most to enhance wellbeing.[48]

In Europe, another large study of individuals (the European Social Survey) also found small but statistically significant effects on life satisfaction of 'ever attending religious services' and 'ever praying'.[49] And interestingly, the religiosity of others in the region was also found to have positive benefits both on those who are religious and on those who are not.

Conclusions

- We are social animals. Social connections are vital to our wellbeing, not only for practical reasons but also for mutual affection, a sense of being needed and a source of identity. This applies not only to connections within the family and the workplace but also within the community ('community networks').
- Community networks raise the average wellbeing in a society. Such networks depend heavily on volunteering, and volunteering benefits both the members of the community who are served but also the volunteers themselves.
- The norms of a society are crucial to its wellbeing. If everyone feels they can trust the other members of society, their wellbeing increases by 1 whole point compared with a position of zero trust. High levels of trust benefit especially those who are more disadvantaged, so trust is a force for equalising wellbeing.
- Societies where wellbeing is more equal also tend to have higher average wellbeing. This works through many channels, and higher income equality on its own has a very small impact on overall wellbeing.
- Crime is a breach of trust, and the prevalence of crime reduces average wellbeing.
- Immigration may cause political tensions but it has no measurable impact on the wellbeing of the existing residents and it confers huge wellbeing gains on the immigrants. But political stability requires controls on immigration.
- Some of the most rewarding things that people do together involve the arts (music, dance, drama, cinema, visual arts, museums and book clubs). Sport and exercise also have important benefits. Religion has also been shown to raise individual wellbeing, especially in countries where life is hard or for individuals experiencing loss.

---

[45] Smith et al. (2003).   [46] Pargament (2002).   [47] Ellison (1991).
[48] By comparison with the private intensity of faith, see Lim and Putnam (2010).
[49] A. E. Clark and Lelkes (2009).

The physical environment and planning policy also have huge effects on community wellbeing. This is the next topic for us to examine.

Questions for discussion

(1) Is there convincing evidence that higher trust **causes** higher wellbeing (i) across countries (ii) across individuals?
(2) What can be done to increase social capital (community networks and trust)?
(3) In what way or ways does inequality influence the average wellbeing in a society?
(4) Is there convincing evidence that one person's happiness affects the happiness of other people?
(5) Compare the arguments in favour of immigration when the criterion is world GDP and when it is world wellbeing.

Further Reading

Cohn, A., Maréchal, M. A., Tannenbaum, D., and Zünd, C. L. (2019). Civic honesty around the globe. *Science*, 365(6448), 70–73.

Diener, E., Tay, L., and Myers, D. G. (2011). The religion paradox: If religion makes people happy, why are so many dropping out? *Journal of Personality and Social Psychology*, 101 (6), 1278.

Goff, L., Helliwell, J. F., and Mayraz, G. (2018). Inequality of subjective well-being as a comprehensive measure of inequality. *Economic Inquiry*, 56(4), 2177–2194. doi:10.1111/ecin.12582.

Helliwell, J. F., Aknin, L. B., Shiplett, H., Huang, H., and Wang, S. (2018c). Social capital and prosocial behaviour as sources of well-being. In E. Diener, S. Oishi and L. Tay (Eds.). *Handbook of Well-Being* (pp. 528–543). DEF.

Helliwell, J. F., Layard, R., and Sachs, J. (Eds.). (2018d). *World Happiness Report 2018*. Sustainable Development Solutions Network, chapters 2 and 3.

Holt-Lunstad, J., Smith, T. B., and Layton, J. B. (2010). Social relationships and mortality risk: A meta-analytic review. *PLoS Medicine*, 7(7), n.p.

Meier, S., and Stutzer, A. (2008). Is volunteering rewarding in itself? *Economica*, 75(297), 39–59.

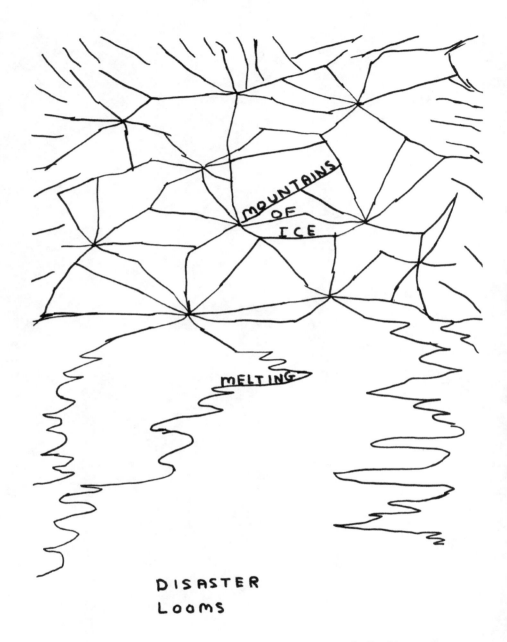

DISASTER
Looms

WE IGNORE IT

15 The Physical Environment and the Planet

> I felt my lungs inflate with the onrush of scenery – air, mountains, trees, people.
> I thought, 'This is what it is to be happy'.
>
> Sylvia Plath

Human life is a recent arrival on this planet. Homo sapiens evolved about 200,000 years ago, and for most of the time since then we humans have moved around in nature and lived off wild plants and animals. About 12,000 years ago, the first villages developed; and about 6,000 years ago, the first major towns emerged. But we remain massively dependent for our wellbeing upon nature (including the ways in which we have modified it).

In this chapter, we shall examine the following issues.

(1) How important for our wellbeing is direct experience of the natural world?
(2) How do different aspects of the man-made environment affect our wellbeing?
(3) How should we respond when climate change threatens the wellbeing of future generations?

To set the scene for the first two questions, we can begin with an ambitious study of human experience in Britain using the app called **Mappiness**.[1] People who use this app are beeped three times a day and asked to record how happy they feel, using a slider along a 'visual analogue scale'. They are also asked what they are doing and with whom.

The GPS system also records their location. This tells us three things – whether they are in an urban or rural environment, whether they are in an area covered with buildings or not (as in a park) and, finally, how scenic the area is (as judged by an independent panel viewing photographs of the area). It also tells us the prevailing weather at the moment when they reply.

The strength of the study is that each individual records many experiences, so that by including a 'fixed effect' we are tracing how different experiences affect the same person – the results being averaged across all of the people studied. All the experiences are measured as either 0 or 1, except for 'scenic quality', heat, sun and rain

---

[1] www.mappiness.org.uk/.

Table 15.1 Effect of real-time experience on real-time happiness (0–10) (UK)

Activity	Points (0–10)
Sports	0.72
Fishing	0.48
Socialising	0.42
Gardening	0.40
Walking	0.39
Resting	0.11
Commuting	−0.22
Working	−0.32
Weather	
Heat (0–1)	0.40
Sun (0–1)	0.12
Rain (0–1)	−1.11
Environment	
Natural habitat	0.06
Rural (v. urban)	0.09
Scenic (0–1)	0.28

Source: Seresinhe et al. (2019) Table 1. The coefficient on scenic has been adjusted using the discussion in the text; all activity effects are measured relative to the average; controls include who you are with

which are continuous variables, where the lowest value scores 0 and the highest value scores 1. Happiness is measured 0–10.

The results for the UK are striking (see Table 15.1). First, we look at the importance of which **activity** a person is engaged in. People don't like working or commuting as much as they like exercising or socialising. We have already documented similar effects in Chapter 1.

Next come the effects of the **weather**. British people are happier when it is hotter, when the sun shines and when it is not raining. These are instantaneous measures of how people are affected by today's weather. A quite different question is how people are affected by the year-round weather (or 'climate') where they live. Research on this produces a somewhat confusing picture. For example, Daniel Kahneman astonished many people by showing that people are as happy in Minnesota, which is subject to weather extremes, as in sunny California.[2] More systematic research suggests that the climate that is best for wellbeing has an average temperature of 18 degrees centigrade (64 degrees Fahrenheit). Anything less than that reduces wellbeing and so does anything greater.[3] This means that climate change will have much worse direct effects on wellbeing in tropical countries than in those with more temperate climates.

[2] Schkade and Kahneman (1998).

[3] Maddison and Rehdanz (2011). They used World Values Survey waves between 1981 and 2008 with regional but not country fixed effects. The effect of a 1 degree centigrade deviation (from 18 degrees

Finally, in Table 15.1, there is the impact of the local **physical environment**. People prefer being in a natural habitat, be it in the countryside or in an urban park or garden. (From other research 'blue' environments with water are as appealing as those that are 'green'). They also, on average, dislike being in towns. And finally, they value the beauty of the environment, whether it is rural or urban.

How Nature Affects Us

So let's look at the impact of the **natural environment**. There is abundant evidence that people value nature, whether it is the countryside or green spaces in towns. For some time, we have known about the effects of nature upon health, generosity, aggression and crime, and now we have similarly powerful evidence of its effects on wellbeing.

We can begin with health. A classic early study reports the results of a specific **'natural experiment'** – a difference in how people are treated, which is essentially random. In this case, after operations for gall bladder, some patients were placed in rooms that faced trees, while others were placed in rooms that faced brick walls. The patients facing trees needed fewer painkillers and recovered faster.[4] In another study in hospitals, it was found that even pictures of nature made a difference – people recovered faster when they were surrounded by pictures of landscapes than when they were surrounded by abstract art.[5] Similarly, having plants in your hospital room affected patients' recovery – in a study of 90 patients who had a haemorrhoidectomy, those in rooms with plants experienced less pain, anxiety and fatigue and they had lower blood pressure.[6]

Contact with nature also makes people behave better. In a simple **lab experiment**, 85 students were shown four slides, either of nature or of an urban landscape (2 minutes for each slide).[7] Allocation was random. The students then participated in a game in which they were given $5. They then had to choose between the following:

- Keep $5 or
- Give it to another student, who will also then receive another $5 from the organisers (and can dispose of the $5 as she likes).

Those exposed to nature were significantly more generous with their money. The same happened if, instead of seeing different slides, one group of students were in rooms with plants and the others in rooms without. These results are remarkable, and

centigrade) upon annual wellbeing was approximately 0.01 points (out of 10) for each 1 degree deviation for each month of such deviation. However, within countries, there is no strong seasonal variation in wellbeing except that up to 5% of people suffer seasonal depression in winter (Seasonal Affective Disorder, SAD). Counter-intuitively, suicide tends to be high in late spring and summer when 'other people' are more visibly enjoying themselves.

[4] Ulrich (1984).   [5] Montgomery (2013).   [6] Park and Mattison (2009).
[7] Weinstein et al. (2009).

they suggest that people will also behave better in real life if there is more nature around.

And so they do. The Ida B. Wells public housing development is in a poor section of Chicago and includes 98 similar apartment blocks. But some of these blocks are surrounded by trees, while others are surrounded by asphalt, and others lie in between. In path-breaking research, the degree of green cover was analysed by helicopter and scored at between 0 and 4. The number of crimes reported by residents in each building was also recorded. It turned out that more trees were associated with less crime.[8]

Why was this? The researchers hypothesised that criminal aggression resulted from 'mental fatigue' – the inability to concentrate and the associated irritability and impulsivity. They then showed (in another housing project) that tree cover did indeed improve people's measured ability to concentrate, and it also reduced their aggression.[9] Thus, they claimed, nature improves our behaviour by calming our minds.

However, the ultimate test is how **green space** affects wellbeing, rather than behaviour. In a number of studies, researchers have traced the same individuals when they move to a new house that is nearer or further from green space. The results of these studies again show clearly how urban green space improves wellbeing.[10]

One study of Germany used the panel data from the Socio-Economic Panel (SOEP), which measures the life satisfaction (and much else) of panel members, year by year. From the respondent's address,, it is also possible to measure the amount of urban green space there is within 1 kilometre of the respondent's home. Fixed effects regression then shows that, for each extra hectare of green space within 1 kilometre, wellbeing goes up by 0.007 points (out of 10).[11]

It is interesting to see what this implies for the value of additional green space. In German cities, the average number of adults living within a kilometre of any spot is 6,000. Thus, if an extra hectare of green space is provided for one year, the gain in wellbeing is 0.007 times 6,000 which is 42 WELLBYs. As we have seen in Chapter 13, the monetary equivalent of a wellbeing-year (WELLBY) is about €100,000. So it would be worthwhile to provide an extra hectare of green space if it cost less that €4.2 million a year in terms of upkeep and the alternative rental value of the land.

There is, of course, a totally different way of valuing an urban amenity or disamenity, which has been used by economists for many decades. This is based on the theory of '**spatial equilibrium**'. This says that people of a given income and characteristics will distribute themselves between areas (or between houses) in such a way that no one could become happier by moving. In other words, at the margin people of given income and characteristics are equally happy wherever they live.

---

[8] Kuo and Sullivan (2001a).   [9] Kuo and Sullivan (2001b).
[10] For example, in the UK, see White et al. (2013); and Alcock et al. (2014).
[11] Krekel et al. (2016). The study controlled for the quality of housing (type, rooms per person) but not for the price of houses.

If they live in a nicer place, then they must be paying for it. Typically, they will be paying through higher house prices. Thus, we can find out the value of an amenity (like green space) by seeing how much it affects house prices. We simply estimate a **'hedonic' price equation** where we regress house prices on the amenities of the area (and, of course, the quality of the house). The coefficient on each amenity is its hedonic price.[12]

But these 'hedonic prices' only capture the full value of the green space if the assumption is true. And the assumption is that people who live near green space are (at the margin) no happier than those who live further away – because they are having to pay for whatever the green space is worth to them. But we have already seen that in Germany they are in fact happier if they live near green space. So, there is clearly an excess value of the green space on top of what people are actually paying for it.[13]

More generally, it has been shown that, contrary to the theory of spatial equilibrium, the happiness of people of given income and characteristics varies widely between US counties – and this variation is related to many aspects of the environment and local public goods.[14] People do tend to move to places that will make them happier,[15] but the result is not full spatial equilibrium and hedonic prices do not therefore reflect the true value of different amenities.

A quite separate question is why nature matters to us. In 1984, the great biologist Edward O. Wilson advanced the hypothesis of **biophilia** (love of living things). According to this hypothesis, humans evolved in close contact with nature and we therefore experience a strong attraction towards both plants and trees, as well as other mammals (especially when they are young). Others have hypothesised that there is a huge comfort to be got from a world not governed by humans but by the huge forces of nature.

But, whatever the explanation, there is ample evidence that nature is good for our wellbeing. This is an important argument for national parks. It is also an important principle for urban design. But there are many other aspects of the built environment which are also crucial for wellbeing.

---

[12] One British study (Gibbons, Mourato and Resende [2014]) found that a 1% point rise in the share of green space in your ward raised the value of your house by about £2,000. This extra 1% of green space would average 10 hectares (since there are about 1,000 hectares per ward). So the value of each extra hectare to one household is £200. Since the average number of households per ward is 3,000, the total social value of each hectare is £600k. And this is a stock value – the annual value will be a tenth of that or lower. This is an order of magnitude below the German estimate of annual value quoted earlier.

Another study by the ONS estimated that the green space and water in Britain raised house prices by on average £4,800, or in total by £135 billion. Since there are about 40 million hectares of urban green space, a maximum value per hectare is £34,000. (There are 8,000 wards of roughly 1,000 hectares each, 50% of which is green.) This is a substantially lower figure than the previous one. (ONS [2018]).

[13] The total willingness to pay should reflect this excess plus the hedonic price that residents are already paying. We can find the excess value from a wellbeing equation that does not include the house price on the right-hand side of the regression. If, alternatively, one estimates $W = a_1$ Green Space $+ a_2 \log$ (Income-House Cost Value), then a_1 includes the full value of the green space.

[14] Ahmadiani and Ferreira (2019).   [15] Goetzke and Islam (2017).

The Built Environment and Urban Design

Over half the world's population now live in urban areas (56%) and this is increasing every year.[16] Towns and cities exist mainly because people can work more productively if they work closer to each other – the benefits of '**agglomeration**'. In early stages of development, these advantages may not be fully exploited and people in cities may have higher wellbeing than other people. But, when development is more advanced, one might expect a situation closer to equilibrium – with people equally happy in cities and elsewhere. Broadly, this is what we observe (see Figure 15.1) – in less developed countries, people in cities are happier on average than other people, but in more developed countries there is no difference. There is less disequilibrium.

Civilised city life requires major collective decisions about zoning (of houses and workplaces), housing (standards and provision) and the outdoor environment. So in this section, we shall examine the zoning of houses and workplaces, the regulation and the provision of housing and the control of air pollution and noise.

Some things are obvious from what we have said already. People want spaces that provide social connections. This argues for quiet, unpolluted residential streets and attractive pedestrianised local centres where people congregate within walking distance of their homes.[17] But people also want safety from unwanted social connections. In an interesting experiment, shielding ground-floor flats from strangers walking outside them reduced mental illness by at least 25%.[18] And people also like a 'scenic' environment that includes greenery and nice-looking buildings.

But there are other issues that are not so obvious:

- How bad is commuting?
- How important is the size and quality of homes?
- What are the effects of polluted air and of noise?

Let us take these issues in turn.

Commuting time

Workplaces in a city tend to be congregated near the centre (to get the benefits of agglomeration). So if you live further out, you probably travel further to work. There is plenty of evidence that this commuting is one of the experiences people enjoy least (see Table 15.1), and it costs money. But people are willing to commute because the rental value of housing is cheaper the further you go from the centre. In standard economic theory, this lower rental value must be low enough to compensate for the increased cost and bother of commuting, so that in equilibrium the marginal person is

---

[16] United Nations (2018).   [17] Appleyard and Lintell (1972).   [18] Halpern (1995).

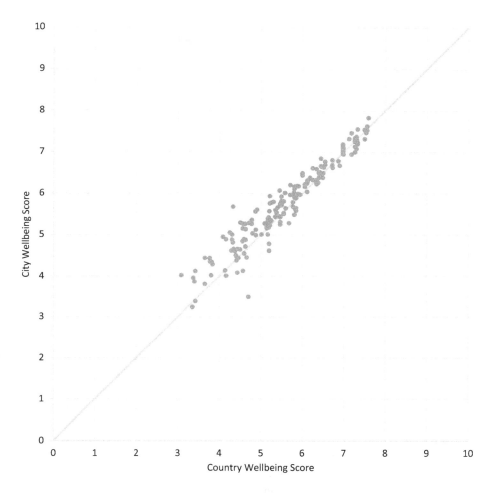

Figure 15.1 Subjective wellbeing in cities worldwide
Source: De Neve and Krekel (2020); Gallup World Poll, Gallup US Poll
Notes: The scatterplot takes into account all cities worldwide with at least 300 observations of individuals in the Gallup World Poll during the period 2014–2018, as well as the ten largest cities in the United States using data from the Gallup US Poll.

indifferent about where to live. Thus, life satisfaction should be independent of commuting time. But as Stutzer and Frey showed, in a notable paper, this is not the case in Germany – the overall situation is shown in Figure 15.2.[19] And, in a multiple regression, it was found that the average commuter (who spends 46 minutes a day

---

[19] Stutzer and Frey (2008). For results for England, see ONS (2014); and B. Clark et al. (2020) – both are mainly supportive.

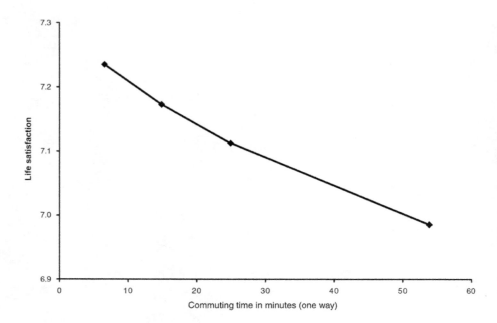

Figure 15.2 Commuting time and average life satisfaction, Germany
Source: Stutzer and Frey (2008); GSOEP 1985–2003; average life satisfaction for each quartile of commuting time

commuting) is 0.08 points (out of 10) worse off than a similar person who has no commute.[20]

This pattern cannot be explained by standard economics but wellbeing science offers a clue. The big commuters probably overestimate the benefits of the higher pay they get (compared with if they worked more locally). And they probably overestimate the benefits of the better supply of housing in the suburbs. So let us turn to the housing market.

Housing quality

In the United States, people in larger houses are more satisfied with their house. And over time houses have become bigger – since 1945 they have doubled in size. Yet, despite this, people are no more satisfied with their houses than they were in the 1980s when measurement began (see Figure 15.3).

Clearly, this is the Easterlin paradox again, but this time relating to houses rather than income. And once again the main explanation seems to be social comparisons, plus a bit of adaptation.

---

[20] This is from a fixed effects regression which contains education but not wages or rents. Rents should be compensating for the commute. Thus 0.09 is a minimum estimate of the true psychic cost of commuting.

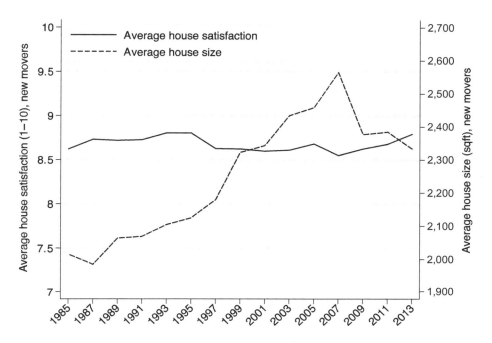

Figure 15.3 House sizes and house satisfaction, United States 1985–2013, new movers
Source: Bellet (2019) Figure 2
Notes: New movers are defined as homeowners who bought their house within the last 2 years before being surveyed (N = 22,772).

In a study of single-family houses in US suburbs, a 1% rise in the size of your house increased your satisfaction with your home by 0.08%. But at the same time, a 1% rise in the size of other houses in your area decreased your satisfaction with your home by 0.07%. And the longer you had lived in your house, the less satisfied you were.[21] Clearly Karl Marx was on to something when he wrote:

A house may be large or small: as long as the neighbouring houses are likewise small, it satisfies all social requirements for a residence. But let there arise next to the little house a palace, and the little house shrinks to a hut.[22]

But doesn't this whole analysis underestimate the importance of housing for our wellbeing? To investigate this issue, the British government used its regular English National Housing Survey to find out how far people's life satisfaction depended on their housing, other things being equal.[23] Surprisingly, the answer was: little. When

---

[21] Bellet (2019) Tables 2 and 10. The comparator house size is at the 90th percentile. Panel data from the American Housing Survey (AHS).

[22] Marx (1947).

[23] Department of Housing, Communities and Local Government (2014). In the analysis, income was held constant.

life satisfaction was regressed on the standard control variables and housing variables were then introduced, the only really important new influence came from the finance of housing. If you were in arrears on your rent or mortgage, this reduced your life satisfaction by a big 0.60 points (out of 10). But no variables within the home had any significant influence (including overcrowding, damp, disrepair and poor heating). However, people did dislike living in high-rise apartments (-0.32 points compared with terraced housing). And people in social housing were as content as outright homeowners.

A recent study of house moves in Germany also found that housing has a small or zero impact on life satisfaction.[24] But in the US, a rather different impression comes from a targeted intervention known as Moving to Opportunity. Here people in poor, run-down housing estates were randomly offered housing vouchers to enable them to live in less disadvantaged areas. Fifteen years later, those who used the vouchers were 0.4 points (out of 10) happier than the controls. But it was not clear what aspect of their new life had made them happier.[25]

Air pollution and noise

Finally, pollution. There have been many studies of the effects of **air pollution** and noise. One careful study used longitudinal data from the German Socio-Economic Panel (SOEP) together with data on sulphur dioxide levels, county by county.[26] This showed that, where the sulphur dioxide level was reduced by 1 microgram per cubic metre, wellbeing rose by 0.005–0.008 points (out of 10). This implies that the reductions in sulphur dioxide achieved in Germany from 1985 to 2003 raised average wellbeing by 0.25–0.40 points. That is a lot. To bring about the same change in wellbeing would require a doubling of income. By contrast, when the cost of pollution is estimated by looking at differential house prices, the effect is under one-tenth of that estimated by the wellbeing method.[27]

A similar difference in costs is found in relation to **airport noise**. A classic study looked at the wellbeing of people living near Amsterdam's Schiphol Airport. It estimated that the median resident affected by significant noise would need compensation for the noise equal to nearly 4% of her income.[28] But noise had no detectable influence on house prices.

---

[24] A. E. Clark and Díaz Serrano (2020).

[25] Kling, Ludwig and Katz (2005); Ludwig et al. (2012, 2013); Chetty, Hendren and Katz (2016). The study was not of course able to trace any external effects on the remaining residents in the poor areas nor on the existing residents in the 'better' areas.

[26] Luechinger (2009). There was the risk that, when they are happier, people choose to live in less polluted counties. So the pollution level was instrumented by the extent to which local pollution had been reduced by mandated scrubbing of power plants. See also Welsch (2006); and Dolan and Laffan (2016).

[27] A parallel wellbeing study in the United States, using a cross-section of individuals and the particulate density in their county, found that a 1 standard deviation of particulate density was equivalent to roughly a 1/3 fall in income per head. Levinson (2012).

[28] Van Praag and Baarsma (2005).

Though these studies are far from perfect, they cast obvious doubt on the use of house prices to value environmental harms. They also remind us that pollution is an important problem outcome of uncontrolled economic growth.

Climate Change

A bigger problem still is **climate change**. If you care about wellbeing, it is natural to care about climate change. For the first principle in the wellbeing approach is that everybody matters equally, wherever they are born and whenever they are born. So the wellbeing of future generations matters as much as our own wellbeing – subject to a small discount (as we shall see later).

The climate change problem is a classic case (perhaps the biggest ever) of a **public good problem**, that is, one that affects everyone. Such problems can only be solved by collective action. In the case of climate change, the action has to be international. Every tonne of CO_2 that is emitted locally joins the body of greenhouse gasses surrounding the world and it affects every country in the world. To resolve the problem, the UN organises an annual Conference of the Parties (or CoP) meeting to reach agreement on the action that is needed.

The nature of the problem is well-known.[29] At present, the earth is warming by an extra 0.2°C each decade. And the rate of warming is not slowing down, because greenhouse gas emissions worldwide are not falling. The earth is already 1°C hotter than it was 100 years ago, and the impact on sea levels, fires, floods and hurricanes is already apparent. At higher temperatures, there would inevitably be major droughts and floods causing millions or even billions to move. The sea level would rise – threatening the security of the one billion people who live lower than 10 metres above sea level. Conflict would be inevitable, and wellbeing in many hotter and lower-lying parts of the world would fall.[30] Warming is also killing off many species of plants and animals. The reduction of biodiversity reduces the opportunities of future generations to find new ways to fight disease, increase food production and experience the wonders of nature.[31] To prevent unacceptable climate warming will require rapid action, because the CO_2 that is emitted today will stay in the atmosphere for a hundred years or more.[32] To limit the temperature rise to 1.5°C above nineteenth-century levels requires emissions to fall to net-zero by 2050.

However, there are sceptics who challenge this mainstream view. They argue that it will impose unreasonable costs on the present generation for the sake of future generations. There are two elements of this argument: the discount rate to be used and the actual scale of the costs.

---

[29] Stern (2015).

[30] Extra heat also increases aggression and reduces wellbeing; see Carleton and Hsiang (2016); and Krekel and MacKerron (2020).

[31] Dasgupta (2021). Some people would also give wider, non-human reasons for preserving biodiversity and the planet as it is.

[32] This assumes that no economic way is discovered for removing the CO_2 once it is out in the atmosphere.

The discount rate

There has to be **some discounting** of the future. Distant benefits are inherently less certain than ones that come sooner. Moreover if there were no discounting, any way in which we benefitted all future generations would be infinitely valuable. But, as we argued in Chapter 2, the rate at which we discount future wellbeing should be quite low. The official British 'pure social time-preference rate' is 1.5%:[33]

$$\text{Discount rate for wellbeing} = 1.5\% \text{ a year.}$$

By contrast, when economists think about discounting, it is income they are planning to discount, not wellbeing. And when discounting income, you also have to take into account the fact that income is likely to rise in future, and (as we have seen) the impact of additional income on wellbeing declines as income rises. For example, suppose that wellbeing is a linear function of log income. Then the marginal utility of income is inversely proportional to income – it falls at the same rate as income rises. So, if real income is expected to rise at 2% a year,

$$\text{Discount rate for real income} = 1.5\% + 2\% = 3.5\%.$$

This 3.5% discount rate makes the future much less important than the present. For example, a loss of $1 in 2100 is only worth averting if it costs less than $0.06 today to do so. Thus, when economists measure the impact of climate change in units of GDP, some of them question the importance of incurring costs today to avert future losses due to climate change – simply because the losses are so distant.

However, the wellbeing approach differs from the standard economic approach, in three ways. First, the discount rate applied to those effects is much smaller – 1.5% a year. At a rate of 1.5%, a loss of 1 WELLBY in 2100 is always worth avoiding, so long as it costs less than 0.33 WELLBYs today to avoid it. Second, the wellbeing approach looks at the impact of climate change in much wider terms than GDP. It includes the wellbeing impact of conflict, the uprooting of communities and the sheer fact of loss aversion (meaning that $1 lost makes a bigger impact than $1 gained). Finally, it takes into account the fact that those who lose will mainly live in countries with low initial levels of wellbeing.

How big are the costs?

This immediately raises the issue of how big are the costs of limiting climate change to 1.5°C? Some years ago, the costs seemed dauntingly high. But today it is apparent that the costs are less. The biggest change is in the costs of clean electricity. By now, onshore wind, offshore wind and solar energy are close to competitive in terms of cost with fossil fuels. And there are now real possibilities of expanding the use of electricity (or hydrogen made from electricity) as a power source for all forms of transport and for heating buildings.

---

[33] HM Treasury (2020). The Stern Review (Stern et al. [2010]) argues for a lower rate.

The key issue is the **cost of clean energy** compared with dirty energy. Once clean energy is cheaper than dirty energy, the dirty sources of energy will be abandoned and the coal, oil and gas will stay underground.[34] Reductions in the cost of clean energy have been driven partly by private investment but they have been (and remain) hugely dependent on publicly funded research and development, which in the last 100 years has been central to most technological change.[35] In addition, the behaviour of consumers has to change toward low-energy transport and low-energy housing. Thus, we have the possibility of a Green Revolution (including energy generation and energy saving) that will be largely self-funding. But it will also require some regulations that impose costs on consumers and business, some extra public expenditure on research and development and some subsidies. The total annual cost of reaching net zero by 2050 is expected to be between 1 and 2% of world GDP each year.

Who should bear the cost? As regards costs borne by present generations, the richer countries should clearly bear the greater part of the cost since their marginal utility of income is lower.[36] But it is difficult to persuade anyone to bear the cost. To see this, it is illuminating to regress the wellbeing differences between countries on their differential performance on each of the 17 UN Sustainable Development Goals (SDGs).[37] This regression shows that, for most of the goals, good performance predicts higher measured wellbeing. But for two of them it does not, and those are 'climate action' and 'responsible consumption and production'. People don't like making these sacrifices. No wonder it is a proving so difficult to secure adequate and binding international agreements in this field.

There is, however, an obvious way out – let future generations contribute, as well as us.[38] If today's government borrows to finance green expenditures, this will (probably) reduce investment of other kinds. This in turn will reduce the amount of capital available to future generations and thus reduce their national income to below what it would have been. But in return for that the future generations will be spared excessive climate change – and they will probably also be richer than us anyway due to technological progress.

So which countries are doing best in providing wellbeing to the present generation, while at the same time protecting future generations against climate change? The New Economics Foundation provides an interesting approach to this analysis, through the **Happy Planet Index**. This measures the ratio between WELLBYs experienced by the current generation and the country's ecological footprint (i.e., its impact on the future).[39]

[34] King et al. (2015).

[35] Mazzucato (2015).The key international partnership for developing cheap ways of producing clean energy is Mission Innovation – a partnership of some 20 countries who pledged to double their public expenditure on clean energy research and development. Annual expenditure at present is about $25 billion.

[36] Budolfson et al. (2021).   [37] De Neve and Sachs (2020).   [38] Sachs (2014).

[39] See Happy Planet Index (2016). In this index, WELLBYs are adjusted for inequality (the adjusted measure is essentially $\sum_i \log WELLBY_i$ per person born). The ecological footprint is a measure of land needed per person to sustain the current pattern of consumption and to absorb the CO_2 produced in the process.

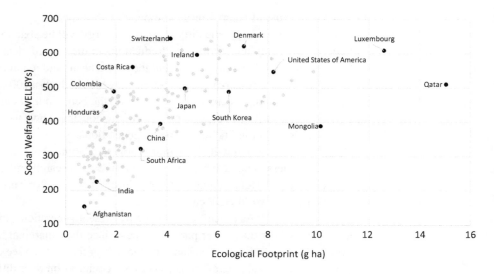

Figure 15.4 The Happy Planet Index: Happy life-years against ecological footprint
Source: Happy Planet Index (2016) Figure 3

In Figure 15.4, WELLBYs are measured on the vertical axis and the ecological footprint on the horizontal axis. So a country is doing well and scores highly on the index if it has a high value on the vertical axis relative to the horizontal axis. (The index is the ratio of one to the other). The country doing worst is Qatar and the countries doing best are Honduras, Colombia and Costa Rica.

As this analysis shows, there is a natural alliance between those who care about wellbeing and those who care about climate change. For climate change is the biggest threat to the wellbeing of future generations. At the very least, policy-makers should be able to deliver a **sustainable** future – meaning that wellbeing does not fall.

Conclusions

(1) Being exposed to nature (trees, plants, green space and water) has demonstrable effects on our physical health, our behaviour (including crime) and our wellbeing. Quantifying this can improve the design of our lifestyle and our cities.
(2) House price differences underestimate the wellbeing effect of green space and other aspects of the environment (like air pollution and noise).
(3) People with **longer** commutes experience less wellbeing.
(4) The quantity and quality of housing has a relatively small effect on wellbeing. This is partly because people compare their houses with those of their neighbours. But being in arrears on your mortgage or rent has a really negative effect.
(5) Climate change is a clear threat to the wellbeing of future generations. The wellbeing approach invites us to value the wellbeing of future generations as much as we value our own (subject only to a very small discount rate).

(6) Climate change is a classic public good problem, since CO_2 emitted anywhere affects people living everywhere. Every country has an incentive to free ride on the costs incurred by others. Only international agreement can overcome this problem.

Questions for discussion

(1) How convincing it the valuation of urban green space in Germany that is reported in the chapter?
(2) Why do house price differences so strikingly underestimate the effects of the external environment on wellbeing?
(3) Do people overvalue the importance of housing and, if so, why?
(4) How important is the wellbeing of future generations relative to our own?
(5) How can the costs of controlling greenhouse gas emissions be shared most fairly between those countries which are already rich and poorer countries which are trying to catch up?

Further Reading

Happy Planet Index: https://neweconomics.org/2006/07/happy-planet-index.

Krekel, C., Kolbe, J., and Wüstemann, H. (2016). The greener, the happier? The effect of urban land use on residential well-being. *Ecological Economics*, 121, 117–127.

Luechinger, S. (2009). Valuing air quality using the life satisfaction approach. *Economic Journal*, 119, 482–515.

Seresinhe, C. I., Preis, T., MacKerron, G., and Moat, H. S. (2019). Happiness is greater in more scenic locations. *Scientific reports*, 9(1), 1–11.

Stutzer, A., and Frey, B. S. (2008). Stress that doesn't pay: The commuting paradox. *Scandinavian Journal of Economics*, 110(2), 339–366.

Part IV

Government and Wellbeing

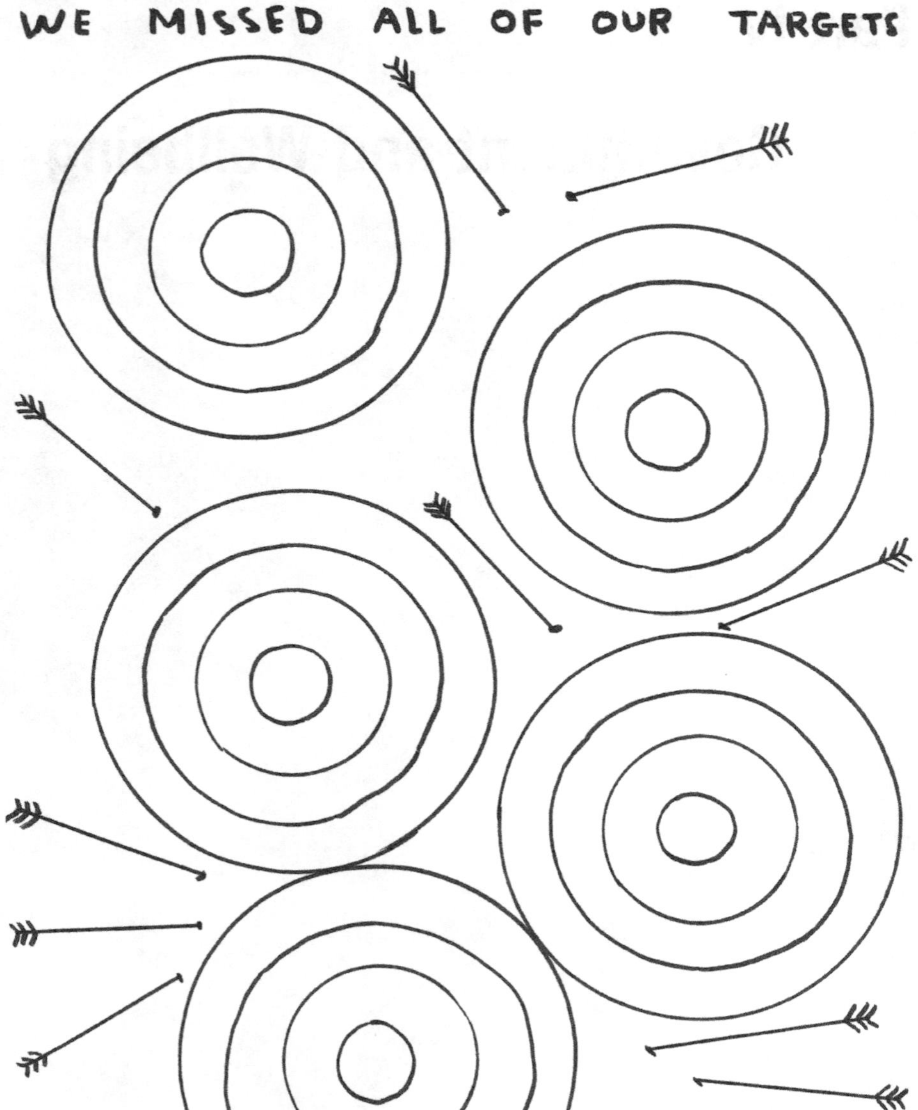
WE MISSED ALL OF OUR TARGETS
TO HELL WITH OUR TARGETS

16 How Government Affects Wellbeing

The care of human life and happiness and not their destruction is the only legitimate object of good government.

Thomas Jefferson (1809)

Introduction

In this chapter, we will turn to the interaction between wellbeing and governance. We will look at the extent to which differences in government institutions can explain differences in wellbeing around the world. In doing so, we will consider wellbeing as the outcome or 'output' of government. In econometric terms, we will consider wellbeing as the dependent variable. Here we are interested not only in whether or not governments fulfil their basic functions – provide for public safety, establish and enforce laws, etc. – but also in the effects of government size and the scope of public programs. Are citizens happier in countries with larger welfare states, or do larger tax burdens threaten wellbeing? Are democracies more conducive to happy lives, or are government services even more important? These questions can be difficult to untangle. Throughout the discussion, we will summarise the various ways researchers have attempted to answer them and comment on the advantages and disadvantages of each approach.

How Do Political Institutions, Processes, and Politics Shape Wellbeing?

Every year, the UN Sustainable Development Solutions Network publishes the World Happiness Report. What often makes headlines is the country that earned the title of happiest country in the world.[1] Yet what is perhaps even more newsworthy is that there should be any World Happiness Report to publish in the first place. It is not unreasonable to imagine that happiness would be evenly distributed in all countries.

---

[1] Since 2012, only four countries have topped the list: Denmark three times, Norway once, Switzerland once, and Finland four times.

If so, there would be no international average differences in wellbeing to speak of. As it turns out, this is not the case. About one-fifth of the global variation in wellbeing is between countries.[2] The average difference in life satisfaction between the highest ranked country (Finland) and the lowest (Afghanistan) in the latest report is 7.8 to 2.5 on a scale from 0 to 10 (see Table 1.1).[3] This represents a huge variation in the quality of life around the world. What accounts for it?

Throughout this textbook, we have focused on a variety of factors at the individual level – genes, income, employment status, family, health, etc. Yet much of what determines the quality of our lives is also shaped by the broader structures of our society. Governments play central roles in determining life outcomes and opportunities. Understanding differences in public institutional design and effectiveness is therefore essential to understanding global differences in wellbeing. In the next section, we will touch on two key differences in particular: government conduct and democratic quality. Later on, we will consider the importance of government size and political affiliation.

Government conduct and democratic quality

One of the most basic questions to ask about a government is whether or not it works. If we look at a particular country, is the government capable of performing its essential functions well? To Adam Smith, the responsibilities of government could be boiled down to three elements: 'peace, easy taxes, and a tolerable administration of justice'. All the rest, he argued, flows naturally.[4] Modern theories of government have continued to stress the importance of peace-making, fiscal and legal capacities. These, according to political economists Tim Besley and Torsten Persson, are the three pillars of prosperous states.[5] In recent years, an emerging literature has begun to consider the extent to which differences in these government capacities around the world are also capable of predicting cross-country differences in wellbeing. In this section, we will review the results of these endeavours. Specifically, we will consider the role of government conduct and democratic quality.

Over the last two decades, the World Bank has evaluated governments around the world in terms of six fundamental characteristics: (1) ability to enforce rule of law, (2) effectiveness of service delivery, (3), regulatory quality, (4) control of corruption, (5) political stability and absence of violence and (6) voice and accountability.[6] Each dimension is itself composed of a broad set of individual indicators drawn from international databases on government performance. In the empirical literature, the first four are often aggregated to provide an overall assessment of government conduct

---

[2] See Table 2.1 in Helliwell and Wang (2012).   [3] Helliwell et al. (2021).
[4] Quoted from Besley et al. (2021).
[5] Besley and Persson (2011). In a recent test, Besley et al. (2021) show that governments with strong capacities in each area, those in the 'highest developmental cluster' are also those with the highest average levels of life satisfaction.
[6] For more information, visit: https://info.worldbank.org/governance/wgi.

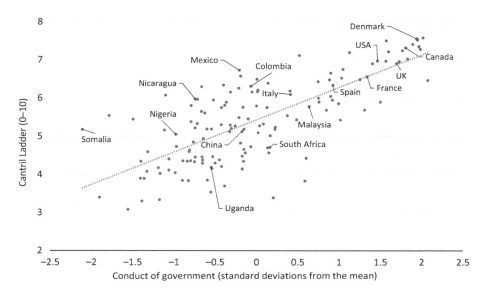

Figure 16.1 Correlation between government conduct and wellbeing
Source: Gallup World Poll and Worldwide Governance Indicators
Note: Average life evaluations measured using responses to the Cantril ladder question.
Government conduct measure drawn from the Worldwide Governance Indicators and evaluated
in terms of (1) rule of law, (2) government effectiveness, (3), regulatory quality and (4) control
of corruption. Data from 2005 to 2019. Linear trendline displayed and selected
countries highlighted.

while the latter two are considered to be indicators of democratic quality.[7] It is
important to note that these features are not necessarily fixed across time. States and
government institutions are constantly in flux. Governments can certainly become
more or less effective or democratic over time, and in some cases even collapse
entirely. Nevertheless, the fundamental quality of institutions tends to remain relatively stable,[8] allowing for broadly reliable cross-country comparisons.

Let's start with **government conduct**. When we look around the world, government conduct proves to be highly related to average country life satisfaction.[9] In
Figure 16.1, this relationship is shown for a diverse set of 60 countries using data from
the Gallup World Poll. With few exceptions, the trendline is clear: countries with
higher performing governments have happier citizens. The overall correlation is
roughly 0.7. Yet as we've seen many times already, correlation does not necessarily
imply causation. Countries with better performing governments are also generally
richer and able to afford the provision of essential goods and services. To truly isolate

---

[7] These are generally calculated as simple means of each group of variables. See Helliwell and Huang
(2008); Ott (2010, 2011); Helliwell et al. (2018b).
[8] See, for example, Besley et al. (2021).   [9] This result is again reflected in Besley et al. (2021).

the effect of good governance on wellbeing, we need to control for these sorts of potentially confounding variables.

In the literature, many studies have continued to find strong and significant relationships between government conduct and wellbeing across countries, even after controlling for other influences. In one of the first studies of its kind, the economist John Helliwell found a significant relationship between life satisfaction and good governance using data from 46 countries from 1990 to 1998.[10] Control variables were included at the individual-level for age, gender, marital status and employment status, among others, as well as societal-level variables including level of economic development, social capital and region were also added. More recent studies have expanded on this result by including additional years and countries and considered indicators of democratic quality and government conduct separately. Most of these generally continue to find a strong and significant relationship between government conduct and life satisfaction.[11] In one study, even after controlling for income, trust, religiosity and democratic quality, a one standard deviation increase in government conduct predicted a 0.74-point increase in life satisfaction.[12] Some researchers have also found that higher levels of government conduct predict lower levels of happiness inequality.[13]

These results are typically obtained by comparing different countries to one another. Another way to consider this relationship is to look at the impact of changes in government conduct over time. Readers will recall that this type of longitudinal analysis has the benefit of controlling for time-invariant fixed effects. On an individual level, these could be genes or affective predispositions. On a societal level, variables such as norms, culture and geography may begin to play a role. With the emergence of new waves of international happiness and governance data over time, these types of studies have recently become more feasible. In one recent test of 157 countries using data from the Gallup World Poll and World Bank, a one standard deviation increase in government conduct predicted a subsequent increase in life satisfaction of 0.6 points on a scale from 0 to 10.[14] This effect held after controlling for changes in economic development, health outcomes, social support, freedom to make life choices, generosity and democratic quality, as well as country and year fixed effects. Perhaps even most importantly, these effects were observed over the short period of seven years, suggesting that improvements in government functions can have meaningful impacts on wellbeing within policy-relevant timespans.

What about **democratic quality**? It is perhaps first worth noting that any analysis of the link between democracy and wellbeing is bound to face challenges. In its simplest form, democracy means that citizens have rights and reasonable opportunities to influence legislation or elect representatives to do so on their behalf. Yet even this relatively simple definition defies precise measurement. Relying on any one indicator of democratic quality is likely to present an oversimplified account. At the same time, evaluating degrees of democracy between countries using multiple indicators can

---

[10] Helliwell (2003).   [11] Bjørnskov et al. (2010); Ott (2010, 2011).   [12] Helliwell and Huang (2008).
[13] Ott (2010).   [14] Helliwell et al. (2018b).

become quite a complicated endeavour. Nevertheless, over the last several decades, a number of international organisations and research teams have made impressive attempts to do just that. As mentioned earlier, governance indicators developed by the World Bank for voice and accountability, as well as political stability and lack of violence, are often grouped together to provide an overall assessment of democratic quality. Since 2006, the Economist Intelligence Unit has also published a yearly Democracy Index in which countries are evaluated and ranked as full democracies, flawed democracies, hybrid regimes or authoritarian regimes.[15] In the most comprehensive effort to date, the Varieties of Democracy project has rated the degree of democracy in almost every society in the world going back to the late eighteenth century.[16]

Unfortunately, wellbeing data does not extend so far back.[17] Nevertheless, many researchers have linked more recent estimates of democratic governance to average reported levels of wellbeing between and within countries. As it turns out, the relationship is not quite as straightforward as one might expect. The general takeaway from this body of work is represented in Figure 16.2. Average life satisfaction (measured using the Cantril ladder and provided by the Gallup World Poll) is given on the y-axis, while democratic quality (measured in terms of political instability and violence, as well as voice and accountability) is given on the x-axis. Here again we see that both variables are strongly associated, with an overall correlation of 0.7.

However, the association between democratic quality and wellbeing tends to be stronger in more developed countries. One study found that the effect of democratic quality is insignificant in countries with incomes below the global average, even after controlling for societal trust and religiosity.[18] Using an alternative set of democratic indicators, another study also found the quality of legal institutions to be more predictive of life satisfaction than democracy in low-income countries. The reverse was true in high-income countries.[19] In a longitudinal within-country analysis controlling for country fixed effects, John Helliwell and colleagues also found that increases in democratic quality significantly predicted increases in Cantril ladder scores in countries with high government conduct but not in countries with low government conduct.[20]

These results are suggestive of increasing marginal returns to democratic institutions at higher levels of socioeconomic development. For countries with less advanced economies, citizens may be more reliant on government for basic and essential services. In these regions, it may therefore be unsurprising that government

---

[15] For more information, visit www.eiu.com/n/campaigns/democracy-index-2020.

[16] For more information, visit www.v-dem.net/en.

[17] Although some researchers have used creative analytical techniques to find proxies. See Hills et al. (2019).

[18] In fact, the authors also find that the relationship between government conduct and wellbeing flips by income level. For higher income countries, the impact of government conduct become insignificant, while the impact of democratic quality becomes significant. The reverse is true for lower income countries. For more information, see Helliwell and Huang (2008).

[19] Bjørnskov et al. (2010). Similar results were obtained by Ott (2010).   [20] Helliwell et al. (2018b).

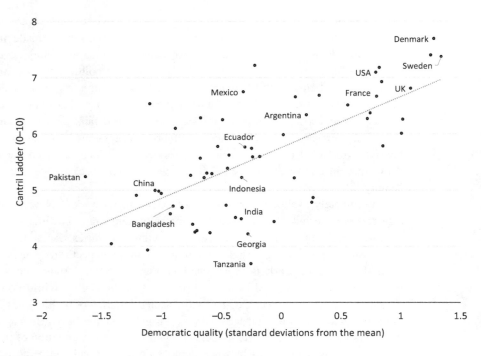

Figure 16.2 Correlation between democratic quality and wellbeing
Source: Gallup World Poll and Worldwide Governance Indicators.
Note: Average life evaluations measured using average responses to the Cantril ladder question.
Democratic quality measured in terms of (1) voice and accountability and (2) political stability.
Data from 2005 to 2019. Linear trendlines displayed.

conduct and service delivery would supersede the importance of democratic quality
for wellbeing. Yet, past a certain threshold of development, democratic quality
appears to play a more important role in determining national happiness.

However, it is also important to keep in mind the limitations of this body of work.
For one, macro-level analyses generally have much greater data limitations. In
previous chapters, when we considered the impact of employment status on wellbeing,
for example, we could evaluate hundreds of thousands or even millions of individual
respondents per year. When making cross-country comparisons, we often only have
data on roughly 150 countries to compare in any given year. At the same time,
institutional change generally happens very slowly, or all at once. Both of these
limitations can make cross-sectional and longitudinal comparisons of national governments somewhat difficult to make.

At the same time, governments do not evolve in a vacuum. Even with the inclusion
of fixed effects in longitudinal models, separating out the individual effect of good
government from economic development or democratic quality is not only empirically
difficult but also hard to meaningfully interpret. Given the interplay and even interde-
pendence of all of these dynamic processes, knowing what to control for and what not

to control in a regression is not always obvious. For example, given the substantial correlation between absence of violence and effective delivery of public services, it can be difficult to determine what percentage of citizens' wellbeing is attributable to either one, independent of the other. Using linear regressions, the standard approach is to include both indicators as right-hand-side independent variables in a regression equation; yet because they are so interrelated, doing so can make it difficult to interpret what the resulting coefficients actually represent.[21]

A separate strand of research has investigated the relationship between democratic processes and wellbeing by looking at institutional differences **within country borders**. This can be somewhat challenging in countries where similar democratic rules govern the entire society. But this is not always the case. In Switzerland, for example, democratic processes and procedures vary considerably between the 26 cantons (states) that make up the country. This fact, coupled with the availability of large-scale wellbeing data, has made Switzerland a uniquely suitable environment for micro-level research into the relationship between democracy and wellbeing.

In one widely cited study, the political economists Alois Stutzer and Bruno Frey created an index of political participation across Swiss cantons.[22] Cantons were rated on a scale from 1 to 6 depending on the degree of decision-making that relies on public referenda.[23] In a cross-sectional regression controlling for a number of individual characteristics including age, gender, income, marital status, citizenship and health, among others, the authors found that residents of cantons with higher levels of public political participation were significantly more satisfied with their lives than counterparts in less democratic cantons. This benefit also accrued almost entirely to Swiss citizens and not foreigners, suggesting that opportunities for political participation are more likely to positively affect those who are able to directly take advantage of them. Overall, a one-point increase in the index of political participation possibilities predicted an increase in the number of people reporting high life satisfaction (10 out of 10) by 3.4 percentage points. Controlling for other factors, the difference in wellbeing between the most and least democratic cantons was 1.2 points on a 10-point scale.

Because these effects are estimated for residents of the same country, the potential for confounding variable bias is expected to be much smaller than in international comparison studies. Nevertheless, cross-sectional comparisons between cantons may still leave out important regional differences and time invariant fixed effects.

Another study attempted to overcome these concerns by considering the impact of political reforms that centralised political decision-making within different Swiss

---

[21] In econometric terms, this can lead to 'multicollinearity' problems in which explanatory variables are themselves linearly related to each other. In this situation, the resulting coefficient estimates become unreliable.

[22] Stutzer and Frey (2006).

[23] More specifically, the index is based on four components: 'Popular initiative to change the canton's constitution; the popular initiative to change the canton's law; the compulsory and optional referendum to prevent new law or changing law; and the compulsory and optional referendum to prevent new state expenditure.' (Stutzer and Frey [2006] p. 413).

cantons.[24] These reforms meant that democratic referenda at more local (municipality) levels lost some degree of influence as more decisions were passed up to political processes at the level of the canton itself. They were intended to increase government efficiency but also had the effect of reducing direct opportunities for political participation.

Importantly, reforms were also adopted by different cantons at different times, resulting in something of a **natural experiment**. By comparing changes in life satisfaction following reforms in some cantons to life satisfaction levels in cantons where reforms were not adopted, the causal effect of centralisation on wellbeing could be estimated. In the empirical literature, this is referred to as a **difference-in-difference** approach, since changes (or differences) in wellbeing arising from an intervention in one place are compared to changes (or differences) in wellbeing over time in another place where no intervention took place. By implication, for this empirical approach to get off the ground, there has to first be evidence of parallel trends prior to the event in question. In this case, before a given reform, life satisfaction levels in the reforming canton and comparison canton should have been following similar trajectories. If wellbeing levels were already decreasing in the former before the reforms, attempting to estimate their effects on wellbeing by comparing cantons would produce biased results.

Using this method, the study found a small but significant negative effect of centralisation reforms on wellbeing. Relative to those living in cantons in which reforms were not introduced, residents of cantons where democratic decision-making became more centralised experienced a decline in life satisfaction of 0.06 points on a 0 to 10-point scale.[25] This effect was twice as severe in cantons with relatively low levels of direct democracy to begin with.

How are we to explain these results? To be clear, the above analyses suggest that (at least in more developed countries) increased opportunities for democratic involvement in decision-making have a positive effect on wellbeing, regardless of the actual decisions made. This implies that the benefits of democracy extend beyond simply producing better outcomes for citizens. Rather, there appears to be inherent value in being able to participate in the democratic process – what Bruno Frey and Alois Stutzer have called 'procedural utility'.[26] This has crucial implications for politics and government but also in domains outside of the public sector. Affording people more agency and voice in work and educational settings, for example, may also help to promote and support wellbeing. Put simply, it is not only the *what*, but also the *how* that matters.[27]

---

[24] Flèche (2017).

[25] These effects were significant after a host of control variables including individual- and municipality-level fixed effects.

[26] Frey et al. (2004); Frey (2010). This idea is also in line with a number of theoretical understandings of human wellbeing in psychology including self-determination theory (Ryan and Deci [2000]), personal control theory (Ryff and Singer [1998]) and related theories of human potential (Peterson [1999]).

[27] Frey et al. (2004).

The size of government

We now turn from the nature of government to the size of government. The debate over 'small' or 'big' government has dominated political conversations for centuries. Despite the impressive array of opinions on this issue, the debate often centres around the same fundamental questions. At what size is the state best equipped to provide for better lives? Are larger and more activist governments better able to support societal welfare? Does the route to prosperity demand reducing the size and scale of government interventions? In this section, we will consider the answers to these questions emanating from empirical wellbeing science.

To begin, we should first define what we mean by the size of government. There are two components to consider. The first is the scale of welfare expenditures (as a share of GDP). These include state pensions, unemployment benefits, family allowances and the like – all of them cash transfers of various kinds. The second element is government expenditure on goods and services (like education, healthcare, law and order and defence – otherwise known as government consumption). We can now investigate how these measures affect wellbeing, both across countries and within countries over time. In doing so, we shall hold constant things like the educational level and health of the population, thereby somewhat underestimating the total effects of government activity.

Let's begin with **welfare expenditures**. One early study used WVS data from 1981 to 2001.[28] It found significant effects of welfare expenditures upon average wellbeing in a country. In addition, governments were also rated in terms of the ease by which citizens can access these expenditures.[29] If we combine these two ratings, the gap in life satisfaction between the highest and lowest rated country was found to be 1.8 points out of 10.[30] Over time, countries that expanded their welfare states also experienced subsequent increases in average life satisfaction.

Other more recent studies have extended these results. One again found positive wellbeing effects of welfare expenditures.[31] Specifically, a 1% point increase in welfare expenditures (as a share of GDP) raised average wellbeing by 0.03 points

[28] The World Values Survey (WVS) has become one of the most widely used datasets in this literature. The worldwide survey is typically conducted over the course of three to four years, with seven waves of data available as of 2021.

[29] This index was originally proposed by Gøsta Esping-Andersen and defined as 'labour being decommodified to the degree to which individuals or families can uphold a socially acceptable standard of living independent of market participation' (Esping-Andersen [1990] p. 37). A more specific definition is provided by Messner and Rosenfeld (1997) p. 1399 and quoted in Radcliff (2013) p. 117: 'Esping-Andersen's measure of decommodification encompasses three primary dimensions of the underlying concept: the ease of access to welfare benefits, their income-replacement values, and the expansiveness of coverage across different statuses and circumstances. A complex scoring system is used to assess [the amount of decommodification provided by] the three most important social welfare programs: pensions, sickness benefits, and unemployment compensation. The scoring system reflects the 'prohibitiveness' of conditions for eligibility [e.g., means testing], the distinctiveness for and duration of entitlements [e.g., maximum duration of benefits], and the degree to which benefits replace normal levels of earnings. The indices for these three types of ... programs are then aggregated into a combined [additive] index.'

[30] Pacek and Radcliff (2008).   [31] Flavin et al. (2011).

(out of 10). Moreover, this effect was found to hold for rich people as much as for those who are poorer and therefore more likely to benefit.[32]

However, one potential limitation of the early literature is the small number of observations it relies on. Given this, a handful of potential outliers – for example, the Nordic countries with high happiness levels and large welfare states – can skew the estimated relationships. One recent study dealt with this worry by expanding the sample to 107 countries using the Gallup World Poll, including many low income and lower-income countries. Even in this expanded sample, positive and significant relationships between welfare expenditures and life satisfaction remained apparent, after controlling for a host of potentially confounding variables.[33] These effects were still significant after Nordic countries and other potential outliers were dropped from the sample. This would appear to suggest that welfare spending can benefit not only those in the most developed countries but also those in developing regions. More cautiously, the results of this literature indicate that countries with very limited welfare expenditures may struggle to promote social welfare.

So what about **government expenditure on goods and services**? Most studies considering the relationship between government consumption and national wellbeing find a positive relationship. One analysis showed that a 1percentage-point increase in the share of government consumption in GDP increases average wellbeing by 0.04 points (out of 10);[34] and a 1percentage-point increase in the share of taxes in GDP increases average wellbeing by 0.03 points (out of 10). Another analysis using data from the Gallup World Poll found a positive and significant relationship between wellbeing and the level of progressive taxation.[35]

Like those in the previous section, some of these results may seem surprising. In almost all of the papers discussed, control variables were included for health, trust, economic stability, employment status and a host of other personal characteristics and societal conditions. One could argue that these are in fact some of the most important channels by which the state can impact wellbeing. In this section, we have left them mostly aside. Yet even after controlling for many of the most fundamental ways in which governments are presumed to positively impact citizens lives, most studies continue to find positive effects of government programs on wellbeing. At the very least, the evidence would seem to suggest that forgoing or severely limiting public expenditures seems unlikely to promote wellbeing.

Political orientation

A natural question arising from the discussion so far is which political program is most conducive to wellbeing. In a majority of countries around the world, including almost all high-income countries, governments are elected by some form of democratic political process in which political parties compete for the popular vote. The spectrum of political ideas tends to be represented as a continuum from left to right. The

---

[32] Flavin et al. (2014).   [33] O'Connor (2017).   [34] Flavin et al. (2011).   [35] Oishi et al. (2012).

specifics vary between countries, although many of the most fundamental political viewpoints and policy goals of these two opposing sides are common around the world. While there are numerous ethical and philosophical differences between proponents of each position that cannot be easily adjudicated with data, some disagreements do lend themselves to empirical analysis. Here again, the tools of empirical wellbeing science can help shed light on which political project is more likely to succeed at making people happier. That question will be the focus of this section.

There are a few ways we can go about trying to answer this question. One way would be to simply look at differences in wellbeing between **people** who identify as left-wing or right-wing. This task is easy enough to accomplish. Many large-scale datasets used in happiness research including the European Social Survey and Gallup World Poll also contain information on political ideology. The findings of this body of research constitute an impressively large literature.[36] The results are remarkably consistent: conservatives (right-wing) are generally happier than liberals (left-wing).[37] A number of possible explanations have been put forth to explain these gaps. They have included conservatives' higher levels of perceived personal agency, more transcendent moral beliefs, greater perceptions of the fairness of the world and more positive life-outlooks.[38] Other studies have qualified these relationships, noting that conservatism only predicts higher levels of wellbeing in the most developed countries[39] or in countries with higher levels of perceived national threat.[40] Relative to liberals, conservatives are also generally less likely to be unemployed, more satisfied with their finances and more likely to own homes.[41] Part of the reason they are happier may therefore be because prevailing societal institutions in many countries are relatively supportive of their interests.[42] Along similar lines, some research has shown that the wellbeing of partisans is also dependent on whichever party is in power.[43] However, as interesting as these results are, they are somewhat unhelpful for our present purposes. Observing that proponents of one set of political ideas are happier than those of another tells us little about whether or not the political program they put forth is conducive to wellbeing on a societal scale.

Another route would be to look at whether or not citizens of **countries** with more left-leaning governments are happier than those in countries with right-leaning governments. In one of the first and most cited studies conducted along these lines, Benjamin Radcliff analysed the extent to which cross-country differences in socialist, liberal or conservative welfare regimes, as well as the degree of left-dominance in national parliaments, predict national wellbeing levels, using World Values Survey data.[44] Control variables were included for GDP and overall unemployment. Both

---

[36] Onraet et al. (2013).   [37] Carroll (2007); Napier and Jost (2008); Butz et al. (2017).

[38] Schlenker et al. (2012).   [39] Napier and Jost (2008).   [40] Onraet et al. (2017).

[41] Pew Research Center (2017).

[42] An important exception in this regard is the growing proportion of new conservatives supporting populist candidates including Donald Trump and Marine Le Pen. This group tends to be worse off economically than core conservatives (Pew Research Center [2017]), and as we will see in Chapter 17, more likely to be dissatisfied than other groups.

[43] Di Tella and MacCulloch (2005); Tavits (2008).   [44] Radcliff (2001).

higher levels of socialism and left-dominance predicted higher levels of wellbeing. However, this result was potentially limited by familiar problems of scale (only 15 countries and one year of data was included), cross-country comparability, and confounding variable bias.

In a more recent test, a team of researchers looked at whether political differences between state governments in the United States predicted differences in wellbeing.[45] The authors relied on representative life satisfaction data collected throughout the country from 1985 to 1998. The two key variables of political interest in this case were (a) the ideological leaning of the state government as determined by an independent rating system and (b) the percentage of the state legislature controlled by the Democratic party. A host of individual, state and regional control variables were included, including region and year fixed effects. The authors found that more left-leaning state governments predicted higher levels of life satisfaction. The effect of Democratic party control was positive but statistically insignificant.[46] The magnitude of the former was also relatively modest. The impact of moving across the full range of the political spectrum from right to left was associated with an increase in life satisfaction equivalent to about half of the magnitude of the individual effect of unemployment.

The results of these studies suggest that left-leaning political programs are (slightly) more conducive to wellbeing than countervailing programs on the right. Nevertheless, even these results seem somewhat uninformative. Given the large diversity of policies put forth by left- and right-wing political programmes, it remains somewhat unclear why or which particular policies are conducive to happiness. The modest size of the coefficients in both studies may suggest that some left-wing policies have stronger effects than others.

Conclusions

- Both government conduct and government quality are significantly related to wellbeing levels around the world.
- The impact of democratic quality appears to be more important for wellbeing in high-income countries. This could suggest that residents of low-income countries are more affected by their governments' provision of basic goods and services, while residents of high-income countries place a higher value on democratic influence.
- It is often difficult to make reliable comparisons between countries. As a result, other researchers have looked at within-country variation in democratic processes and procedures to predict wellbeing. The results of these studies generally show that decreased opportunities for democratic involvement in politics decrease wellbeing. This has led some researchers to suggest that wellbeing – or 'procedural utility' – is

---

[45] Alvarez-Diaz et al. (2010).
[46] However, this latter effect was only barely statistically insignificant at a 10% level (p = 0.12).

inherently derived from democratic participation, regardless of the actual outcome of democratic decisions.

- While the results can vary depending on the definition, government size (measured in terms of both welfare expenditures and government consumption) is generally positively associated with wellbeing. In particular, both the level of social benefits, as well as the ease by which citizens can access them predict higher levels of national happiness.
- In terms of political orientation, right-leaning individuals are generally happier than left-leaning individuals. But residents of countries with left-leaning governments are generally happier than those living in countries with right-leaning governments. In the United States, adoption of left-leaning state policies has also been associated with increases in wellbeing over time.

Questions for discussion

(1) Is there a contradiction between maximising wellbeing and promoting procedural utility?
(2) There is some evidence to suggest that democratic quality is more strongly related to wellbeing in high-income countries. Does this imply that governments in low-income countries should not prioritise democracy?
(3) What are two primary limitations of making cross-country comparisons when conducting wellbeing research?
(4) How can these limitations be overcome using natural experiments?

Further Reading

Alvarez-Diaz, A., Gonzalez, L., and Radcliff, B. (2010). The politics of happiness: On the political determinants of quality of life in the American states. *The Journal of Politics*, 72(3), 894–905.

Flavin, P., Pacek, A. C., and Radcliff, B. (2011). State intervention and subjective well-being in advanced industrial democracies. *Politics & Policy*, 39(2), 251–269.

Flèche, S. (2017). The welfare consequences of centralization: Evidence from a quasi-natural experiment in Switzerland. *Review of Economics and Statistics*, 103 (4), 621–635.

Pacek, A. C., and Radcliff, B. (2008). Welfare policy and subjective well-being across nations: An individual-level assessment. *Social Indicators Research*, 89(1), 179–191.

FIGHT THE NONSENSE

17 How Wellbeing Affects Voting

It's the economy, stupid.

Aide to Bill Clinton

Introduction

Thus far, most of the discussion in this textbook has focused on the determinants of wellbeing. We have focused on what makes us happy and what could make us happier. As a result, we have largely considered wellbeing as an output (a dependent variable). Yet we can also flip this equation around and consider wellbeing an input (an independent variable). In doing so, we can ask what sorts of behaviours flow downstream from wellbeing. This will be our perspective for this chapter. In particular, we will consider the extent to which (un)happiness can help explain political behaviour, voter preferences and the rise of populism. While we will focus primarily on evaluative measures of wellbeing, we will also briefly comment on the role of negative emotions in determining political actions and outcomes.

Does Wellbeing Shape Political Behaviour and Voter Preferences?[1]

The first question we can ask is whether or not happy people are more likely to be politically engaged. Intuitions may cut in different directions. On the one hand, it is possible to imagine that as people become more satisfied with their lives, they would also become less politically engaged. Some commentators have even worried that too much happiness could lead to an 'emptying of democracy'.[2] On the other hand, research suggests that those with higher levels of wellbeing are also more socially engaged in their communities. Happy people are, for example, more likely to volunteer and donate to charity.[3] As a result, they may also be more likely participate in national elections or political movements.

[1] This chapter relies largely on Ward (2019).   [2] Veenhoven (1988).   [3] De Neve et al. (2013).

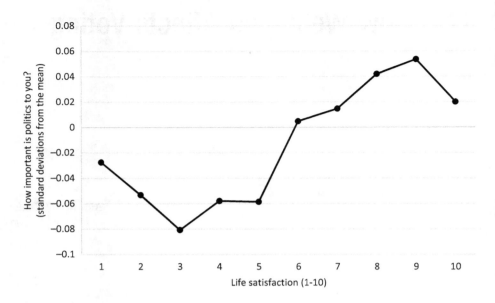

Figure 17.1 Relationship between the importance of politics and life satisfaction
Source: World Values Survey
Note: Average importance of politics depending on life satisfaction. Importance of politics measured on an individual level using a 4-point scale from 'not at all important' to 'very important'. Sample includes 392,757 respondents in 104 countries from 1989–2020.

The effect of *un*happiness on political participation is also not immediately obvious. If unhappiness is taken to be indicative of anger or fear, it's possible to imagine that unhappiness would be highly predictive of political engagement. Inasmuch as they hold the state responsible for their circumstances, the least well-off members of any given society may be the most motivated to change it. On the other hand, if unhappiness is indicative of depression or lethargy, the opposite could be true. Some studies have indeed shown that both loneliness[4] and depression[5] predict lower levels of voter turnout.

To begin parsing these dynamics, we can first look at the relationship between life satisfaction and political interest on a global scale. In Figure 17.1, using World Values Survey data on roughly 393,000 respondents from 1981 to 2020, we plot the raw association between both variables. In fact, we can see some preliminary evidence for all of the intuitions above. The most important takeaway from this graph is that happier people seem to be more interested in politics overall. Even the most satisfied people in the world are more engaged than the least satisfied. However, at the tail ends of the distribution, there may be motivational tipping points where satisfaction turns into disengagement and dissatisfaction turns into political action. The happiest people in the world (those reporting 10 out of 10 life satisfaction) seem less politically

---

[4] Langenkamp (2021).   [5] Ojeda (2015).

engaged than slightly less satisfied people. At the other the end of the spectrum, the least satisfied respondents are more interested in politics than those slightly less happy than they are.

These relationships are of course just correlations, although a growing body of research is beginning to provide causal support for them. One of the first such large-scale analyses in the United States looked at the 2000 wave of the American National Election Study (ANES), which contained indicators of life satisfaction, political engagement and voter turnout.[6] Relative to those who considered their lives to be 'very unsatisfying', respondents who were 'completely satisfied' were 7 percentage points more likely to have voted in the last election, an effect roughly on par with the difference between high school and college graduates. This result also held after controlling for personal characteristics including age, gender, race, partisanship, trust and more. Happier people were also more likely to engage in a variety of other political behaviours including working for a political campaign, contributing funds to political candidates and attending political meetings or rallies.

However, due to data limitations, this study only considered one year of observations. Other studies since have taken a longer-term perspective. One in particular used longitudinal panel data in the United Kingdom and found that life satisfaction significantly increased the propensity to vote but only in some specifications.[7] The relationship became much weaker once control variables for party affiliation and past voting behaviour were included. Another analysis using three years of panel data in Germany found that life satisfaction was not significantly related to broad measures of political participation.[8] A related study in Switzerland using fixed effects analysis of panel data found that neither life satisfaction, nor positive affect, nor negative affect was significantly predictive of voting behaviour. On the other hand, another analysis of large-scale data in Latin America found a strong and significant relationship between life satisfaction and voting behaviour.[9] These authors concluded the significant association between both variables was most likely explained in terms of happiness driving people to vote and not the other way around. Other research has found evidence of a link between happiness and voting in local elections in China.[10]

Overall, the existing evidence does not offer conclusive evidence in either direction. Some evidence is broadly suggestive that happier people are more likely to vote in local and national elections, although these results have not been replicated across contexts or in more robust methodologies. As we will see in the final section of this chapter, counterevidence of negative affect and low wellbeing driving voting behaviour has also been observed, which may further complicate the story.

[6] Flavin and Keane (2012).   [7] Dolan et al. (2008).   [8] Pirralha (2018).
[9] The researchers also found that voting did not seem to make people happier later on, regardless of party affiliation or electoral outcomes (Weitz-Shapiro and Winters [2011]).
[10] Zhong and Chen (2002).

Before moving on, it is worth considering one more form of political participation: protest. In this case, the intuition seems more straightforward. Almost by definition, protest movements are presumed to be driven by dissatisfaction. It may therefore be reasonable to expect that low levels of wellbeing would be highly predictive of participation in political protest. However, at the same time, if protesting is accompanied by feelings of social support, solidarity and purpose, it could also have positive impacts on wellbeing.

In this case too, existing studies point in different directions, particularly when affective and evaluative measures of wellbeing are considered separately. In the United States, the relationship between life satisfaction and protest was found to be insignificant in ANES data.[11] Dissatisfied adults were not more or less likely to engage in political protest than happier counterparts. In Switzerland, after carefully considering a number of possible causal pathways, it was negative emotions, not low life satisfaction, that were found to significantly increase protest intentions.[12] This could suggest that the affective dimension of wellbeing is a more important predictor of protest behaviour than evaluative wellbeing. However, in another study of employed young people, lower life satisfaction was associated with protest behaviour, while the reverse was true for unemployed young people.[13]

These relationships can also depend on the regional context. An emerging body of work has begun to examine the causes and effects of protest movements and peaceful uprisings across the Arab world in the early 2010s, commonly known as the Arab Spring. The results suggest a powerful and important role of declining wellbeing as an impetus to protest. In three separate studies using data from the Gallup World Poll, low levels of wellbeing proved to be significant predictors of protest movements and demonstrations, in some cases even more so than standard economic and political indicators.[14] Two studies found that worsening levels of life satisfaction in some countries in the years preceding the Arab spring significantly predicted more frequent protests later on and that declines in life satisfaction were largely explained by dissatisfaction with living standards.[15]

One other study focusing specifically on the case of Syria noted that life satisfaction, as well as affective wellbeing indicators including hope, negative affect and positive affect worsened significantly in the years leading up to the civil war.[16] These results are all the more striking, as many related indicators of economic development were trending upwards in the Arab world around the same time. These dynamics are presented for Egypt and Syria in Figure 17.2. In both countries, life satisfaction began to sharply decline as early as three years before the start of the uprisings, while GDP per capita continued to increase.[17]

---

[11] Flavin and Keane (2012).   [12] Lindholm (2020).   [13] Lorenzini (2015).
[14] Arampatzi et al. (2018); Witte et al. (2019); Cheung et al. (2020).
[15] Arampatzi et al. (2018); Witte et al. (2019).   [16] Cheung et al. (2020).
[17] In the time since the Arab Spring uprisings, wellbeing levels have stagnated or even continued to decline in many Arab countries. As of 2015 in Syria, the most recent year data was collected, average life satisfaction levels stood at 3.5 out of 10, down from 5.4 in 2008. In Egypt, average life satisfaction was 4.3 in 2019, down from 5.2 in 2007.

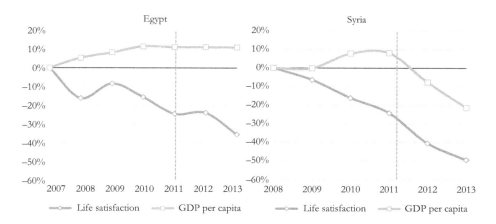

Figure 17.2 Change in life satisfaction and GDP leading up to the Arab Spring
Source: Gallup World Poll
Note: Changes in life satisfaction (measured using the Cantril ladder) and GDP per capita shown are normalised to a baseline level in 2007. Vertical lines indicate the start of the Egyptian revolution (15 January 2011) and Syrian civil war (15 March 2011).

More recent developments in Hong Kong are also reflective of this general story. Beginning on 15 March 2019, protests erupted in response to a proposed bill in the Hong Kong legislature that would allow for the extradition of fugitives to mainland China. The initial government sit-in evolved into months of heated conflict between protesters – primarily young people and university students – and Hong Kong police. This period of civil unrest represented the greatest political crisis the city had faced in decades. However, to someone looking only at economic indicators in the time leading up to the protests, this would have come as quite a shock. From 2010 to 2019, GDP per capita in Hong Kong had increased by a staggering 50%. Nevertheless, indicators of young people's wellbeing tell quite a different story. Over the same period, young people's satisfaction with life and expected satisfaction with life in five years' time had been in consistent decline. These trends are represented in Figure 17.3 using data from the Gallup World Poll. In the years leading up to the protests, both indicators steeply declined. Future life satisfaction in particular declined by 0.68 points on a scale from 0 to 10, an effect roughly on a par with becoming unemployed.[18]

Overall, the results of this section are somewhat mixed. Wellbeing appears to be predictive of political engagement, voting behaviour and political protests in some countries but not others. These relationships appear to be complex and context-dependent, which may help to explain the variety of results. Isolating the causal effect of happiness on political behaviour also requires careful analytical designs and high-frequency data, which is often difficult or unavailable at large-scales. Natural experiments and quasi-experimental designs may help shed light on these dynamics in the years to come. For now though, let's turn our attention to voter preferences.

[18] See Chapter 11.

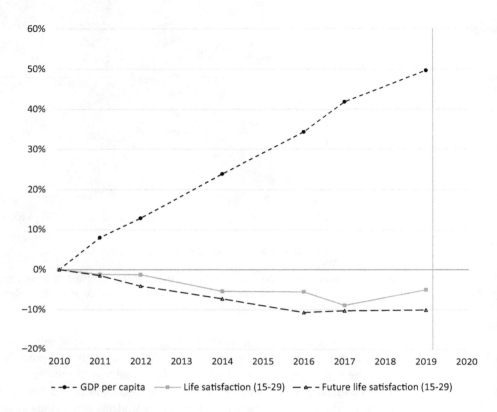

Figure 17.3 Changes in GDP per capita and young people's wellbeing in Hong Kong before the protests
Source: Gallup World Poll
Note: Changes in young people's life satisfaction (measured using the Cantril ladder), expected future life satisfaction in five years and GDP per capita shown and normalised to a baseline level in 2010. Vertical line indicates the start of the Hong Kong protests on March 15, 2019.

Voter preferences

In this section, we move from political participation to voter preferences. Our discussion will centre around the following question: does wellbeing play a role in determining how people vote? Before tackling this question head-on, it is worth underscoring its importance. Throughout this textbook, we have highlighted the limitations of relying on economic indicators as proxies for wellbeing. Even the inventor of GDP, Simon Kuznets, himself once remarked: 'The welfare of a nation can scarcely be inferred from a measurement of national income.'[19] Yet in democratic countries, sceptics could argue that the prime goal of politicians is not necessarily to make people happy but to get (re)elected. If, as a democratic strategist for Bill Clinton famously noted, the most important predictor of political success is 'the economy,

[19] Kuznets (1934).

stupid' after all, perhaps politicians could be justified, or at least excused for focusing primarily on economics. Several theories of voter behaviour in political science do suggest that voters support or oppose politicians in accordance with their rational economic self-interest, and these theories have been supported by a considerable degree of evidence.[20] Overall, governing parties tend to have greater electoral success when the economy is doing well. As a result, while there may very well be strong moral reasons to care about wellbeing, if wellbeing does not affect voting, there may not be as strong political reasons to do so. Fortunately for our purposes, this is precisely the kind of question that lends itself to empirical analysis.

In the literature, this relationship is generally framed in terms of the vote share of the incumbent government. The intuition here is that successful governments would raise wellbeing and therefore be rewarded at the polls. On the other hand, if governments are performing badly and wellbeing is low, incumbents would be more likely to lose elections. These assumptions underlie a number of theoretical models of political behaviour, although relatively few consider the direct influence of wellbeing.[21]

One of the largest studies of these dynamics to date looked at Eurobarometer data covering 139 elections in 15 **European countries** from 1973 to 2014.[22] In the first set of analyses, the study considered whether national life satisfaction data collected at the time of the Eurobarometer surveys explained outcomes in the next national election.[23] The main results are presented in Figure 17.4. Overall, national happiness levels explained roughly 9% of the variance of the incumbent vote share in the European countries surveyed, while leading economic indicators including the GDP growth rate and unemployment rate explained 7% and 4%, respectively. Voters who were most satisfied with their lives (on a 4-point scale) were also found to be roughly 50% more likely to say they would vote for the governing party in the next election than those who were least satisfied.

From a political perspective, these results alone provide strong reasons for elected officials to care about the wellbeing of their constituents. For our purposes though, it is worth pressing on. While these results are at least suggestive of causal dynamics – in that pre-existing happiness levels are used to predict future election outcomes – there may still be a number of confounding variables at play. In later specifications, the study also controlled for societal-level variables including incumbent party seat share and party system fractionalisation, as well as individual-level variables including past voting behaviour and personal finances. Even after accounting for all of these effects, wellbeing levels continued to emerge as meaningful and significant predictors of both incumbent vote shares at the national level and voter preferences at the individual level. In one analysis in particular, an increase in national wellbeing of one standard deviation predicted an increase in the incumbent vote share of 6 percentage points in

---

[20] For reviews, see Lewis-Beck and Nadeau (2011); Healy and Malhotra (2013); Lewis-Beck and Stegmaier (2018).

[21] These are typically called 'political agency' models. For standard examples and reviews, see Ferejohn (1986); Besley and Burgess (2002); Persson and Tabellini (2002).

[22] Ward (2020).   [23] Elections occurred, on average, four months after surveys were administered.

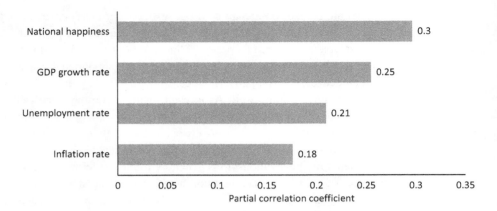

Figure 17.4 Predictors of government vote share in Europe
Source: Adapted from Ward (2020)
Note: Each bar represents the correlation coefficient for four indicators, estimated in separate bivariate regressions with cabinet vote share as the dependent variable using Eurobarometer data. Country fixed effects were also included as controls. National happiness is the average country life satisfaction at the closest year prior to the election. Macroeconomic variables are drawn from the OECD and refer to the country-year of each election. The sample is 139 elections in 15 European countries, 1973–2014.

the next election, while the same increase in the economic growth rate predicted an increase of 3 percentage points. Taken together, these results strongly suggest that wellbeing plays an important role in determining election outcomes.

An analysis in the **United Kingdom** provides additional evidence of this relationship.[24] The authors in this case relied on 18 years of panel data from 1991 to 2008 collected by the British Household Panel Survey (BHPS), a period covering four national elections. The dataset also contained yearly information on respondents' voting intentions 'if the general election were held tomorrow'. Because the same respondents are interviewed every year, the authors are able to control for time-invariant individual fixed effects. Overall, being more than averagely satisfied with life predicted an increase in incumbent party support of 1.6%. This effect held even after controlling for personal financial situation – widely considered to be a fundamental driver of voting behaviour. For comparison, a 10% increase in family income predicted an increase in incumbent support of only 0.18%.

However, these results may be at least partially attributable to **reverse causation.** As discussed earlier, voters tend to be happier when the party they support is in power.[25] The positive effect of wellbeing on voter preferences may therefore simply be a side-effect of political partisanship. In other words, even if happier voters are more likely to support the incumbent party, they may also be happier because the party they support is in power in the first place. In this case it wouldn't necessarily be

[24] Liberini et al. (2017a).   [25] Di Tella and MacCulloch (2005); Tavits (2008).

wellbeing that drives voter preferences but rather voter preferences that drive wellbeing.

To account for this potential bias, the UK study ran two additional empirical tests. In the first, the authors limited their sample to swing voters, defined as (a) those declaring that they do not favour one particular political party over the other or (b) those who consistently voted for different parties in various elections. Even within these groups, wellbeing still proved to be a significant predictor of incumbent support. In fact, this effect among swing voters was even stronger than it was in the full sample.[26] In the second test, the authors split their sample not in terms of partisanship but in terms of exogenous shocks to wellbeing. They first selected out respondents who recently became **widowed**, and then used **propensity score matching** techniques to compare the voting preferences of these respondents to those who are similar to them in all other relevant respects, except for the fact that they did not recently become widowed. This approach is intended to resemble a randomised control trial, though in this case the treated and control groups are divided by (presumably random) variation in the recent death of a spouse and not by random assignment on the part of researchers. Using this procedure, 'treated' respondents who recently became widowed were 8% less likely to support the incumbent party than controls.

A third analysis related to the **United States**. It used county-level data from the Gallup Daily Poll and found that wellbeing levels were significantly predictive of incumbent party support in the 2012 and 2016 US elections.[27] In 2016, low life satisfaction today and low expected life satisfaction in five years explained 28% and 61% of the variation in Donald Trump's vote share, respectively. The effect of the latter proved to be larger than any other variable under consideration, including race, age, racial animus, education or population density. In subsequent regressions, a one standard deviation increase in life satisfaction was associated with a 7-percentage-point reduction in Trump voter support in 2016, while a similar increase in expected future life satisfaction was associated with a 12-percentage-point decrease. The authors also found similar results for the 2012 election, in which present and expected future life satisfaction scores predicted decreases in support for Mitt Romney, the Republican challenger to Barack Obama, of 6 and 10 percentage points respectively.

A handful of other analyses have used other forms of exogenous shocks to wellbeing to explain voting outcomes. In one of the most entertaining tests of this sort, election outcomes in counties across the United States were linked to the outcome of local sports games.[28] The authors found that counties in which local college football teams had won games in the ten days leading up to the election were 1.6 percentage points more likely to support incumbent parties in Senate, gubernatorial and national elections. The authors suggested that this result was likely explainable in terms of

---

[26] Among swing voters, high life satisfaction increased support for incumbent parties by 2.4%, relative to 1.6% in the full sample.

[27] Ward et al. (2020).   [28] Healy et al. (2010).

higher levels of wellbeing in counties with victorious teams, although the analysis did not contain a direct measure of wellbeing.

Overall, the results of this section imply a strong link between happiness levels and incumbent party support. While all of these results are representative of effects in high-income countries, some analyses have also found wellbeing to be a significant predictor of incumbent party support in Latin America[29] and in Malaysia.[30] While this literature is still very much in its infancy, these findings underscore the important role that voter wellbeing can play in determining election outcomes. In this section, we have focused on the role of wellbeing and incumbent support, though there are of course many more lenses through which this relationship could be analysed. In the next and final section of this chapter, we will consider one more of those perspectives in particular: the association between wellbeing and populism.

Populism

In the previous section, we introduced evidence indicating that US voters with lower wellbeing were more likely to vote for Donald Trump in the 2016 election. These results are largely in line with related evidence showing dissatisfaction as a predictor of non-incumbent party support. Yet they may also be indicative of another phenomenon: the rise of **populism**. While populist political parties are nothing new;[31] in recent years, many of them have gained traction in Western countries. In Europe, populist parties have more than doubled their share of the vote in national elections since 1960, from 5% to 13%, while their share of parliamentary seats has tripled.[32] A number of explanations have been put forward to explain these developments, though perhaps the most common narrative in popular discourse has been the rise of 'discontent'.[33] In this section, we will look at the empirical evidence for this relationship in greater detail. Specifically, we will consider whether or not low wellbeing predicts support for populism.

Populist movements have sprung out of both left-wing and right-wing political movements, making them somewhat difficult to classify. Settling on a universally agreed-upon definition can be challenging. Nevertheless, most researchers generally agree on certain key shared features between all populist movements. Three in particular are: (1) valuing 'the people' in opposition to 'the elite', (2) opposition to the political establishment and (3) support for popular sovereignty.[34] Using these characteristics as a starting point, several classifications of European political parties have been developed to rate their degree of populist rhetoric, platforms and policies.[35] Armed with these data, some researchers have begun examining the extent to which wellbeing is predictive of populist party support.

In one recent analysis of roughly 180,000 **European adults** across 29 countries, lower levels of wellbeing were significantly associated with higher levels of populist

[29] Bravo (2016).   [30] Ng et al. (2017).   [31] Von Beyme (1985).   [32] Inglehart and Norris (2016).
[33] For example, see Sorkin (2016).   [34] Mudde (2007); Inglehart and Norris (2016, 2017).
[35] Van Kessel (2015); Inglehart and Norris (2016).

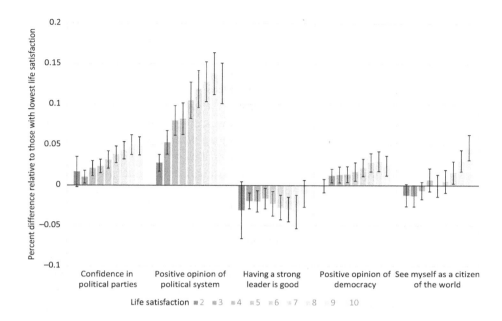

Figure 17.5 Difference in political attitudes depending on life satisfaction
Source: World Values Survey
Note: Based on results from Ward (2019). Bars represent percent differences in political opinion
from those with the lowest life satisfaction level Estimated using OLS linear regressions
controlling for household income (quintiles), education level, marital status, gender, age and its
square; 95% confidence intervals displayed.

support.[36] After controlling for a number of personal characteristics including age,
gender, race, education, employment status, income, residential area and other related
variables, respondents who were the most satisfied with their lives were 3.7 percentage
points less likely to have voted for a populist party in the previous election than those
who were least satisfied with their lives. To put this figure into context, it was larger
than the effect of anti-immigrant sentiment on populist support.[37]

Another approach is to consider populist support not in terms of voting preferences
but in terms of political attitudes. An analysis of this sort used representative data on
more than 350,000 respondents in **100 countries** and estimated the extent to which
life satisfaction is predictive of political attitudes associated with populism, after
controlling for age, gender, income, education, marital status and country fixed
effects.[38] The results are presented in Figure 17.5. Overall, wellbeing proves to be
highly related to political attitudes across the board. Happier voters are more likely to
have confidence in political parties, faith in the political system, maintain a positive
opinion of democracy and consider themselves to be citizens of the world. They are

---

[36] Nowakowski (2021).
[37] This was measured as opposition to immigration from outside the European Union specifically.
[38] Ward (2019).

also less likely to view having a strong leader as a good thing for their country. The starkest differences relate to political institutions. Compared with the least satisfied respondents, those reporting a 10 out of 10 on a life satisfaction scale are roughly 5% more likely to have confidence in the political parties and 13% more likely to have a positive opinion of the political system.

Both of the analyses thus far suggest that the rise of populism in Western countries is at least partly related to unhappiness. A separate strand of literature has sought to address this issue by closely examining notable **political successes for populists** in recent years, including the 2017 national elections in France, the Brexit referendum in the United Kingdom, and Donald Trump's presidential victory in the United States. Here, the results tend to be less straightforward.

In France, Marine Le Pen's populist National Front party outperformed traditional left- and right-wing political rivals to reach the final round of the runoff national election in 2017 against Emmanuel Macron. Macron eventually won by a comfortable margin, but the stark rise and success of Le Pen's party platform, which was partially fuelled by populist anti-establishment and elite-opposition sentiment, warrants further attention. One study sought to examine the drivers of French populist support using a unique dataset of roughly 17,000 surveys of voters in the lead-up to the election.[39] The authors found that lower levels of life satisfaction were strongly predictive of votes in favour of Marine Le Pen. Her voters were less satisfied with their lives than supporters of any other candidate. Even after controlling for income, education, ethnicity and other sociodemographic variables, low life satisfaction remained significantly predictive of populist support, while high life satisfaction predicted support for the eventual winner Emmanuel Macron. At the same time, Le Pen voters were also less trusting of others (including their family and neighbours) and less optimistic about their future than any other group across the political spectrum.

While Marine Le Pen did not win the French national election in 2017, populist movements for Brexit in the United Kingdom and Donald Trump's presidential candidacy in the United States proved successful. However, in both cases, the evidence seems to be somewhat mixed. In the United Kingdom, two studies in particular have examined the link between support for leaving the European Union and dissatisfaction. While both studies find dissatisfaction with income in particular to be strongly predictive of Brexit support – in fact, even more predictive than the actual level of income itself – life satisfaction was found to have a much smaller and largely insignificant effect.[40]

One study in the United States also looked at county-level data on wellbeing and voting patterns for Donald Trump and Bernie Sanders in the Republican and Democratic primaries.[41] Because both candidates promoted populist messages and policies, we might expect that dissatisfaction would be predictive of support for both. The authors do in fact observe this to be the case. In two separate regressions controlling for income, employment status, religion, economic growth, residential

---

[39] Algan et al. (2018).   [40] Liberini et al. (2017b); Alabrese et al. (2019).   [41] Ward et al. (2020).

area population density, and region fixed effects, Republican voters with low life satisfaction today or low expectations for future life satisfaction in five years were more likely to vote for Donald Trump in the primary, while Democratic voters with the same characteristics were more likely to vote for Bernie Sanders.

A related study also relied on high-frequency Gallup data to examine the extent to which changes in wellbeing from 2012 to 2016 could explain electoral swings in favour of Donald Trump.[42] The authors compiled information on life satisfaction, future predicted life satisfaction and affective wellbeing[43] for roughly 177,000 US respondents in 2012 and 353,000 respondents in 2016. The study found that counties that swung from supporting Barack Obama in 2012 to supporting Donald Trump in 2016 were significantly more likely to have experienced average declines in wellbeing over the same period. Specifically, in counties in which the vote share from Democrats to Republicans swung by at least 10%, the rate of respondents reporting severely low life satisfaction (1 to 4) had more than doubled from 3.4% to 7.1%, while the rate of respondents reporting high life satisfaction (7 to 10) had declined from 73% to 61%. Similar trends were observed for future expected life satisfaction and satisfaction with the area in which the respondent lived. Residents of these counties were also significantly more likely to report feeling sadness and less likely to report feelings of happiness and enjoyment. For comparison, changes in income over the same time were not significantly predictive of vote shifts.

Finally, another study found that, controlling for other factors, both feelings of worry and racial animus significantly predict higher levels of Trump support. However, once a measure of relatedness (social connection to others) was introduced, the effect of worry becomes significantly weaker, while the effect of racial animus becomes insignificant. The authors interpreted this result as an indication that Trump support in the 2016 election was driven primarily by a desire for in-group affiliation to buffer against the economic and cultural anxieties that had led to unhappiness. In other words, voters who felt disconnected from their communities channelled their anxieties towards Trump support. These dynamics echo those observed among Marine Le Pen's supporters in France.

All of these studies provide suggestive evidence that dissatisfaction and disconnectedness precede and predict populist victories. Taken together, they underscore the role of social connection and general wellbeing in explaining the recent resurgence of populism in Western countries. However, it is also important to recognise the limitations of these results. While the longitudinal dynamics observed in these latter studies are suggestive that unhappiness drives populist support, the issue does not easily lend itself to causal inference. As of yet, no studies to our knowledge have sought to run randomised controlled experiments in which treated respondents are induced to feel more or less happy and then asked about their level of populist support. Exploiting natural experiments or quasi-experimental designs in the future to predict populist party vote shares may prove fruitful.

---

[42] Herrin (2018).
[43] Measures of affect include feeling happy, stress, enjoyment, worry, smile, sadness, anger.

However, overall time series cast some doubt on the interpretation that the rise of populism can be entirely explained by declining wellbeing. As discussed in previous chapters, in many countries around the world, including those in Europe and North America, average levels of life satisfaction have remained remarkably flat.[44] Given the dramatic increase in populist party support over recent years, one might expect similarly dramatic declines in life satisfaction. This does not appear to be the case. At the same time, in many countries, social isolation and negative affect (a sense of 'worry' in particular) have been on the rise.[45] Inasmuch as this phenomenon reflects growing disconnectedness and anxieties about the future, it could help to explain populists' appeal to voters. These issues remain open to future research.

Overall, the results of this section call out for further research and experimentation. Despite a handful of recent electoral defeats in both Europe and the United States, populist political parties on both the left and right of the political spectrum retain considerable influence in mainstream politics. Understanding the primary drivers of their support, and in particular the role of wellbeing in explaining them, will remain a central and urgent challenge for social scientists in the years to come.

Conclusions

- Happier voters are generally more likely to be politically engaged than less happy voters.
- Despite these broad correlations, causal studies on the relationship between wellbeing and political participation have produced mixed results. Happier voters are found to be more engaged in some contexts but not in others.
- In the Arab world, lower wellbeing was a strong precedent and predictor of future uprisings. This relationship appears to be slightly weaker in Western countries.
- Overall, there is strong evidence that happiness predicts higher levels of support for the incumbent political party. This effect has been found in a number of countries and using a variety of different analytic methodologies, including propensity score matching techniques and natural experiments. In many cases, this effect is even stronger than standard economic models of voter preferences.
- Around the world, unhappier voters are also more likely to vote for populist parties and identify with populist ideologies. However, studies performed on elections in France, the United Kingdom and the United States have found mostly mixed results regarding the extent to which life satisfaction in particular is predictive of populist electoral victories.
- Nevertheless, dissatisfaction with income, and social disconnectedness in particular, proved to be strong predictors of Marine Le Pen's support in France,

---

[44] See Chapter 13.
[45] For negative affect, see Helliwell et al. (2021). For loneliness and social isolation, see Ortiz-Ospina and Roser (2020).

votes to leave the European Union in the United Kingdom and Donald Trump's presidential victory in the United States.

Questions for discussion

(1) Research has shown that wellbeing predicts incumbent party support. If you were advising an elected official, how would you make use of this knowledge?
(2) So far, there has been limited experimental research to examine whether or not low wellbeing leads to populist support. Can you think of an experimental design (either in the lab or in the real world) to test this assumption? What are the main benefits and drawbacks of your approach?

Further Reading

Arampatzi, E., Burger, M., Ianchovichina, E., Röhricht, T., and Veenhoven, R. (2018). Unhappy development: Dissatisfaction with life on the eve of the Arab Spring. *Review of Income and Wealth*, 64, S80–S113.

Liberini, F., Redoano, M., and Proto, E. (2017a). Happy voters. *Journal of Public Economics*, 146, 41–57.

Ward, G. (2020). Happiness and voting: Evidence from four decades of elections in Europe. *American Journal of Political Science*, 64(3), 504–518.

Ward, G., De Neve, J. E., Ungar, L. H., and Eichstaedt, J. C. (2020). (Un) happiness and voting in US presidential elections. *Journal of Personality and Social Psychology*, 120(2), 370–383.

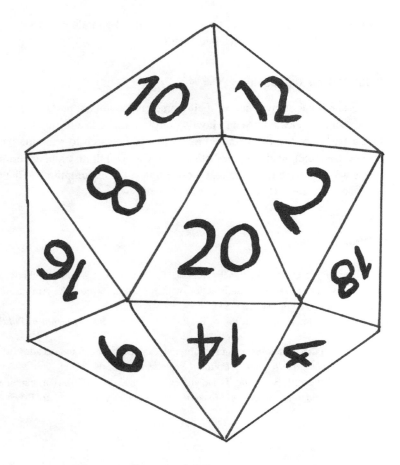

MANY-SIDED DICE

THE GOVERNMENT USE THEM
TO MAKE DIFFICULT DECISIONS

18 Cost-Effectiveness and Policy Choice

The ultimate purpose of economics, of course, is to understand and promote the enhancement of wellbeing.

Ben Bernanke, former Chairman, US Federal Reserve

The ultimate purpose of wellbeing science is to help us increase wellbeing. Hopefully, readers of this book will by now have learned a little more about themselves, which they can use to improve their own wellbeing and that of others. But what about policy-makers, be they in central or local government, or in NGOs big and small? Are there steps by which wellbeing science could help them improve their contribution to human wellbeing?[1]

In this chapter we ask the following questions

- How would policy-makers spend their money if they wanted to maximise wellbeing? How can we measure cost-effectiveness when benefits are measured in units of wellbeing?
- How does this approach compare with traditional cost-benefit analysis where benefits are measured in units of money? Which approach is better?
- If policy-makers wanted especially to reduce misery, how would they proceed?
- How far are central policy-makers using the new approach?

The Goal

First, policy-makers would need to be clear that wellbeing is their overarching goal. At present most organisations have **multiple goals**. But when they decide how much effort to devote to each of these goals, they are implicitly balancing one goal against another. Ultimately there can be no rationale for such decisions unless it is based on some overarching goal, against which the importance of the different subsidiary goals can be assessed.

---

[1] This chapter draws heavily on A. E. Clark et al. (2018) chapter 15. For a formal statement of the argument of this chapter, see Annex 18.1.

In Part I, we already set out the argument for wellbeing as the overarching goal. So, in this vision every organisation would be contributing in whatever way it could to the goal of maximising the **sum of future WELLBYs** (suitably discounted).[2]

For example, every nation's finance minister would say to each cabinet colleague 'When you make the case for your department's budget, please estimate how much each of your main proposed expenditures (new and old) will increase the wellbeing of the community. Tell us their effect on wellbeing and how much they will cost'. And the leaders of any organisation, large or small, would ask the same questions of its different branches.

Cost-Effectiveness Analysis

The decision on these proposals would then proceed as follows.[3] Realistically, we can assume that any typical public organisation has an overall budget constraint – the total amount of overall expenditure it can incur on all its policies. Thus, for each policy the key issue is how much wellbeing it produces per dollar of cost – **the cost-effectiveness of the policy**. So policies would be ranked according to the (discounted) WELLBYs they will generate per dollar of net (discounted) expenditure.

Once they are ranked in order of their cost-effectiveness, we would choose those that were the most cost-effective until the available budget was exhausted. There would thus be a **cut-off level** (λ) of cost-effectiveness above which policies were approved and below which they were rejected. Thus, the criterion for approving policy would be[4]

$$\frac{\sum\sum W_{it}(1-\delta)^t}{\sum C_t(1-\delta)^t} > \text{Cut} - \text{off value} = \lambda \qquad (1)$$

where C_t is the net cost in year t.

The appropriate **critical value** (λ) could be found by trial and error. An alternative approach would be to start with values of λ already used in more limited areas of life. For example, the WELLBY approach is similar in many ways to the approach already followed in some healthcare systems. As we have noted in Chapter 10, England's National Institute of Health and Care Excellence (NICE) evaluates a proposed treatment according to the number of QALYs (Quality Adjusted Life Years) that it produces relative to its cost. A treatment is only approved if the ratio of cost to benefit is low enough. Currently, NICE require the cost per QALY to be below around $40,000. But this applies only to health expenditures and to the health-related benefits to the individuals who are treated in the healthcare system. The WELLBY approach

---

[2] Assuming for the moment that we ignore who gains and who loses.

[3] For an early discussion of this whole approach, see O'Donnell et al. (2013). For more recent applications, see De Neve et al. (2020); and Frijters and Krekel (2021).

[4] The same δ is used for wellbeing and for cost, on the assumption that the rate at which expenditure produces wellbeing is constant over time.

would relate to all government expenditure and to the wellbeing effects on all the individuals affected. It would be the standard way in which all public expenditures are decided.

Relation to traditional cost-benefit analysis

A natural question is, How does this approach compare with traditional economic cost-benefit analysis, where benefits are measured in units of money (rather than of wellbeing)? The answer is that the results of existing **cost-benefit analysis** can be incorporated very easily into the wellbeing framework. For we know the impact that money income has on wellbeing, and we can always therefore convert any benefits measured in money into benefits that are measured in units of wellbeing. To be precise, if income is Y and X is a policy variable, the effect of the policy on wellbeing is given by

$$\frac{dW}{dX} = \frac{dY}{dX} \cdot \frac{dW}{dY} \tag{2}$$

where dY/dX is the effect of X on income, and dW/dY is the marginal utility of money.

This approach is often very useful, because for some policies it is easier to measure their effects initially in monetary units. This applies not just to direct effects on wages or other incomes (due, for example, to educational investment), but also to intangible benefits (like reduced journey times). These intangible benefits are in this case valued by what people's behaviour shows they would be willing to pay for them (by their **revealed preference**).[5]

But **willingness to pay** works only when people can show by their choices how much they value different outcomes. Sometimes they can do this, but very often they cannot. They can do it for things like transport, industrial production, education and some aspects of the environment. But many outcomes are not things that people can choose – they are things that just happen to people through outside influences – what economists call external effects. People fall sick, children get abused, elderly people get abandoned and people get mugged. We cannot learn about how much people value these experiences by observing choices. So how are we to evaluate policies like vaccination, or child protection, or family courts, or elderly care, or police protection? Measuring benefits in units of wellbeing is an obvious solution.

Critics might argue that, even though people can't show their values by their choices, we can ask them **hypothetical questions** about how much they would in principle be willing to pay to promote these goods? Unfortunately, however, it has been shown repeatedly that asking people hypothetical questions about how they value things produces nonsensical answers.[6]

So data on the happiness effects of activities may offer a better route to evidence-based policy making. But why not then translate those wellbeing estimates back into

---

[5] Layard and Glaister (1994).   [6] Kahneman, Ritov and Schadke (2000).

units of money? Thus, suppose we know the effect of a policy upon wellbeing. We could compute the equivalent gain in income that would increase wellbeing as much as the policy would. This **equivalent variation** in income could be computed by dividing the change in wellbeing by the marginal utility of income. Thus, if policy X improves wellbeing by dW/dX, the equivalent variation in income is given by

$$\frac{dY}{dX} = \frac{dW}{dX} \bigg/ \frac{dW}{dY}. \tag{3}$$

This is the reverse operation to that in equation (2). The resulting aggregate benefit measured in units of money could then be compared with the cost.

There are, however, two overwhelming objections to this approach. First, it automatically makes changes in happiness less important if they occur to poor people – it treats a dollar as the same whether it belongs to a Trump or a tramp. To avoid this, the results could be analysed separately for different income groups, applying a different marginal utility of income to each group. This re-establishes wellbeing as the measure of benefit, so why not simply stay with it in the first place?

Second, we might not want to simply add the ΔWs, but rather to give extra weight to those with low initial happiness. If the monetary valuation procedure is followed, there is no way to do this, since the happiness level of each individual has become invisible. We may or may not want to give extra weight to those who are most miserable (see Chapter 2), but it is helpful to retain the ability to do so.

Note that throughout this chapter we assume that the total budget is determined by political considerations. We do not use the wellbeing approach to determine the total of public expenditure. The same thing happens with traditional cost-benefit analysis – projects are often rejected even if their monetary benefits exceed their costs. The reason is that there is not enough public money to finance all projects whose benefits exceed their costs. In consequence, the only projects that get through are those with a high enough ratio B/C, with the cut-off value being frequently higher than 1.

The alternative approach would be to allow wellbeing cost-effectiveness analysis to determine the total of public spending. But this would lead to much higher public expenditure. For example, if $W = 0.3 \log Y$, the value of a healthy life year (with $W = 7.5$) is in England $750,000. But England's NICE does not sanction the expenditure of more than $40,000 per additional life-year.[7]

Taxes and regulations

Going on, there are other important public policy problems besides how to spend a given budget total. There is the issue of how to structure the taxes. The approach here can be straightforward. If we envisage a self-financing tax change, we would simply

---

[7] Moreover, if public money is raised by general taxation, we have to allow for the fact that, when other people pay a tax, that generates a positive externality for the rest of the population. So the equation $W = 0.3 \log Y$ overvalues the cost of reducing incomes generally across the population. A lower coefficient would imply an even higher optimal scale of public expenditure.

evaluate how this alters the happiness of each member of the population and aggregate these changes (assuming we are simply maximising the sum of wellbeing across all members of the population). We should also use wellbeing as the criterion for whether to introduce a new regulation or to abolish an old one.[8]

Five major issues

It is time to address some thorny issues. First, there is the issue of the **discount rate**. We discussed this in Chapter 15, where we suggested something like 1.5% per annum.

Then there is the issue of the **length of life**. If we know the quality of any additional life-year that a policy would produce, we would value the extra life-year by the quality of life it produces. But otherwise we would value changes in life-years by the average level of wellbeing (in the country in question).

Then there is the issue of how we treat the **birth-rate.** If we increase discounted WELLBYS by encouraging the birth of more children, would that count as a benefit? If it did, it would almost certainly be the most cost-effective way of increasing the sum of future wellbeing. For example, by switching expenditure from healthcare to child subsidies, we could surely increase the birth rate by more (in %) than we reduced the length of life. This would increase the number of future WELLBYs. But most people would not support the policy. We would therefore propose that, when evaluating the effect of policies, we ignore any effect on total WELLBYs coming from changes in the number of people born.[9]

Next, there is the issue of **whose wellbeing** counts. In principle, it should cover at least the whole of humanity. Every person is equally important. But for private ethics, there are some people who are easier for us to help than others. So, in practice, human society works through a division of labour. People take especial care of people close to them, and this also satisfies the need that humans have for a kind of affection they can only give to a small number of people.

But, when it comes to public policy or charitable activity, the **circle of concern** has to be widened to include people we do not know, including people in far-off parts of the world.[10] Ideally, each government would choose to do whatever it could for the good of humanity. In practice, democratic governments inevitably feel that their main responsibility is for their own electorates. But this responsibility would hopefully include two other important considerations:

---

[8] In practice, a regulation may also have a net cost to the organisation making it. To allow for this we need to rewrite the decision criterion in equation (1) as $\sum\sum W_{it}(1-\delta)^t > \lambda\sum C_t(1-\delta)^t$

On regulation, one obvious issue is 'Do smoking bans improve human wellbeing?' This has been studied using data on more than half a million Europeans since 1990. Odermatt and Stutzer (2015). The conclusion is that the ban increased the life satisfaction of those smokers who wanted to quit, without significant negative effects on any other group. See also Gruber and Mullainathan (2005).

[9] In other words, we treat the number of people born as exogenous. But if it changes, we still look at the average wellbeing of all those born. For an extensive discussion of this issue, see Meade (1955); Parfit (1984); and Broome (2004).

[10] Singer (1981).

- the altruistic desire to help less happy nations and
- the necessity of collaborating with other countries to secure global public goods like fighting climate change and securing world peace.

And what about the wellbeing of **other sentient beings,** besides humans? They must surely count. There is ample evidence that birds and mammals (at least) have feelings of pleasure and pain. For example, researchers have offered injured birds or mammals the choice between food that includes standard pain-killers and food that does not. Injured animals prefer the food with pain-killers. And, even more important, when they've taken the painkiller, they stop whimpering or calling out. This shows that the choice of the painkiller is not simply an automatic reaction to a wound but a reaction to an emotional feeling.[11]

Finally, there is the issue of **equity.** As we said in Chapter 2, the starting point for public policy analysis could be the Benthamite approach of adding up all changes in WELLBYs, regardless of who they accrue to. But most people would probably wish to give extra weight to improving the wellbeing of those who are least happy. The problem is how to secure agreement on the weights. One obvious approach is to conduct a representative survey of the views of the public, and this is a high priority for future research. In the meantime, one natural approach is through sensitivity analysis, examining how far the results are reversed when different weights are used. Equally, when considering new policy initiatives, it seems natural to focus on those areas of life that account for the greatest amount of total misery.

Developing New Policies

The natural starting point in this search for new policies is to ask two very similar questions.

- What aspects of life do most to explain the inequality of wellbeing?
- What aspects of life do most to explain the proportion of people who have low wellbeing?

In practice, the answers to the two questions are very similar.[12] As we saw in Chapter 7, the answer to the first question comes from the following standardised regression equation:

$$\frac{W_i}{\sigma_w} = \sum \beta_j \frac{X_{ij}}{\sigma_j} + e_i \tag{4}$$

where β_j^2 measures the independent contribution of each variable X_j to the overall inequality (variance) of W.

---

[11] Singer (1995). To apply the WELLBY approach to non-humans remains however a major quantitative challenge.

[12] See A. E. Clark et al. (2018) and the comparison of our Figures 8.2 and 8.3. This result would be expected if, for example, all the right-hand variables were jointly normally distributed.

Table 18.1 What explains the variation in life satisfaction in adults over 25? (United Kingdom) – partial correlation coefficients

	β
Physical health	0.11 (0.01)
Mental health	0.19 (0.05)
Work (not unemployed)	0.06 (0.04)
Quality of work	0.16 (0.04)
Partnered	0.11 (0.03)
Income	0.09 (0.01)
Education	0.02 (0.01)

Source: See Figure 8.2. Standard errors in brackets.

Alternatively, we could focus on misery and ask what explains it. We could, for example, define misery as a level of life satisfaction below 6. Then the dummy variable for misery takes the following values

$$1 \; if \; W < 6$$

$$0 \; if \; W \geq 6.$$

If we run a regression equation of this dummy variable on our usual explanatory factors, the β_j^2 measure the independent contribution of each variable X_j to the presence or absence of misery.[13]

Empirically, it turns out that the pattern of β_j^2 obtained from estimating equation (4) are very similar to those obtained from the regression explaining misery, except that in the latter case the β_js are all slightly smaller (because a binary variable is more difficult to explain).[14] Given this similarity, it is enough to focus on equation (4) and search for policies in areas with high β, knowing that reducing the inequality in those areas would make a big impact on the prevalence of misery.[15]

In Table 18.1, we repeat the βs that we saw in Chapter 8. For each factor X_j, β_j^2 represents the share of inequality explained by the independent variation of X_j. Top is mental illness, with physical illness also important. Then comes the quality of work and personal relationships, and only then comes income. These are data for the UK, but similar rankings apply in other advanced countries.[16]

---

[13] The variance of misery is $p_m(1\text{-}p_m)$, which for small values of p_m is close to p_m. If the right-hand variable is also a dummy variable (X) then (if it were the only independent variable) we could write $M_i = a X_i + b + e_i$, and $\bar{M} = a\bar{X} + b$. If instead, $\bar{X}$ were zero, we could say that X had increased the proportion of people in misery by a p_x, where p_x is the proportion for whom X has the value of 1. By contrast $\beta^2 = \frac{a^2 p_x(1-p_x)}{p_m(1-p_m)}$. This is clearly related to ap_x.

[14] See Figures 8.2 and 8.3.

[15] This is obvious when the factor is essentially a binary 'bad', e.g., mental or physical illness, lack of a partner or unemployment. When the factor is continuous, it is important **how** the inequality is reduced – for example, it would reduce misery if we increased low income but not if we reduced high income.

[16] A. E. Clark et al. (2018) Table 6.3.

But the basic message of the wellbeing approach is clear. Policy-makers would not focus too heavily on economic issues. To support wellbeing, they would also give at least as much serious, evidence-based attention to

- mental health (treatment and promotion),
- physical health (treatment and promotion),
- the quality of work,
- support for families and
- community building.

Experiments

But this is only the beginning of the search for new policies. The next step is to identify specific policy changes that might be considered. Once a plausible policy option has been identified, it would ideally be the subject of a proper randomised experiment in the field. Where it is impractical or unethical to randomise across individuals, it is often possible to randomise across areas or across institutions (schools, hospitals, etc.). From such an experiment would come information on the short-run wellbeing benefits and budgetary costs of the experiment – and then it can ideally be projected into the longer term using a model.

The final result of such an evaluation would be an estimate of the change in WELLBYs per dollar of expenditure – or alternatively the number of people removed from misery per dollar. Or these estimates can be expressed the other way round – as the cost per WELLBY or the cost per person removed from misery. Table 18.2 is a crude illustration of the latter approach. It is a back-of-the-envelope calculation and we only include it to provoke thought and discussion and to encourage the reader to do better. In the table, we have taken four standard methods proposed in the UK for reducing misery. We then estimate what public costs would need to be incurred each year to ensure that there was one less person in misery. (The assumptions are in Annex 18.2.) The outcome is somewhat surprising. Better mental health care is the most cost-effective of the four polices, followed by active labour market policy and physical health care, with income redistribution the least effective. Because redistribution is so expensive and relatively few of those in misery are also poor, it is often more effective to spend public money on services in kind – helping people to help themselves.

Table 18.2 Average cost of reducing the numbers in misery, by one person

	£k per year
Poverty. Raising more people above the poverty line	180
Unemployment. Reducing unemployment by active labour market policy	30
Physical health. Raising more people from the worst 20% of health	100
Mental health. Treating more people for depression and anxiety	10

Source: A. E. Clark et al. (2017)

So in this analysis, the top priority is building up the social infrastructure (health care, skills development, employment, and community services).

Who Is Doing What?

So how many policy-makers worldwide now view wellbeing as their goal and act accordingly? Many express support for the idea, but many fewer are yet implementing it. Both the European Union's Council of Ministers and the OECD in Paris have requested their members to 'put people and their wellbeing at the centre of policy design'.[17] They favour an 'economy of wellbeing', where wellbeing is the goal that the economy serves; but at the same time, wellbeing is valued for its positive effect on the economy.[18] In China, President Xi has repeatedly stated that 'the wellbeing of the people is the fundamental goal of development'.[19]

But the country that has gone furthest in making wellbeing their goal is New Zealand. In 2019, the Labour government there announced its first Wellbeing Budget, which attracted worldwide interest. Its novel feature was to focus any new additional expenditure on things that increase wellbeing in a cost-effective way (mental health services, reduction of child poverty and domestic violence, Maori wellbeing and climate change). The rest of the budget was justified in terms of its effect on four pillars (physical capital, human capital, social capital and natural capital), which were seen as contributing to the sustainability of wellbeing – but that contribution was not quantified.

The New Zealand approach is one way in which change may come about. But one day governments (central and local) and NGOs may go further and evaluate their **whole** operation through the quantitative lens of wellbeing.[20] This is increasingly authorised in official manuals on evaluation,[21] but most policy-makers have yet to use these tools. If they wanted to, they would need to establish their own Wellbeing Analysis Units that could scrutinise more and more of the policies they funded in terms of their effects on wellbeing.

And they would take urgent action to improve the knowledge base. This requires, as we have said, literally thousands of experiments in which one policy is compared with a counterfactual for its effects upon wellbeing and upon costs. And, of course, all experiments ever conducted would measure wellbeing as one of the outcomes, whatever else they measured.

---

[17] EU Council (2019).

[18] This has also been pushed strongly by the Wellbeing Economy Alliance (based in Scotland) and by the Wellbeing Economy Governments which include Scotland, Iceland, Wales, Finland and New Zealand.

[19] Speech on 18 October 2017 to the 19th National Congress of the Chinese Communist Party. There are 12 mentions of wellbeing in his speech.

[20] Local governments actively targeting wellbeing include Bristol, England; Jalisco, Mexico; Andra Pradesh, India. NGOs can receive advice on this approach from the Happier Lives Institute, from Effective Altruism and from Give Well.

[21] For example, HM Treasury (2020, 2021) in the United Kingdom.

The follow-up period for most experiments is quite short, even though the actual effects may be quite long-lived. To simulate the longer effects requires a model of how wellbeing evolves from year to year over the lifespan. So we need quantitative models of how wellbeing evolves over the lifespan – and of the claims which people in different circumstances impose on the public finances. Building these models is a priority for research.

We already know many of the coefficients that would apply in such models.[22] But the better the knowledge base, the better the chances that policy-makers would use it. The wellbeing revolution would only happen through granular knowledge about the causes of wellbeing. Such knowledge would also become a central feature of modern social science.

Conclusions

If wellbeing were to be at the heart of policy-making, some major changes would be needed.

(1) Every organisation would try in whatever way it could to generate the largest number of future WELLBYs (appropriately discounted).

(2) Wherever there is a budget constraint, the available funds would go to those policies that generate the most WELLBYs (discounted) per dollar of expenditure (discounted).

(3) Where traditional cost-benefit analysis measures benefits in units of money (rather than of wellbeing), these benefits could be readily changed into units of wellbeing by multiplying them by the marginal utility of money.

(4) Because monetary cost-benefit is not able to capture more than a fraction of the benefits of public policy, it would be better to convert monetary benefits into wellbeing benefits rather than the reverse. Moreover, converting everything into money would sacrifice information since the marginal utility of income varies so much between people.

(5) Policy-makers would not count as a benefit any effects of a policy change that affects the birth rate and through that the number of future WELLBYs.

(6) Policy-makers would develop new policies in areas which are causing the largest numbers of people to live in misery (low wellbeing). This means areas with high βs. New Zealand has followed this approach. But, having developed the specific policies proposed, the next step would be to estimate their effect on total WELLBYs – subject to sensitivity analysis using differential equity-weights.

(7) Thousands of experiments would be essential to evaluate possible specific policies. We would also need better models of the determinants of wellbeing over the life-course. The explanation of wellbeing would become a central aim of all the social sciences.

---

[22] See, for example, A. E. Clark et al. (2018); Frijters et al. (2020); and Frijters and Krekel (2021).

Questions for discussion

(1) How if at all does the wellbeing approach to public expenditure improve on traditional cost-benefit analysis. Can the two approaches be reconciled? How?
(2) How can equity considerations be best incorporated in the design of policies aimed at wellbeing?
(3) Would we ignore effects on the number of births?
(4) What is your reaction to Table 18.2? How could you improve the analysis?

Further Reading

Frijters, P., Clark, A. E., Krekel, C., and Layard, R. (2020). A happy choice: Wellbeing as the goal of government. *Behavioural Public Policy*, 4(2), 126–165.

O'Donnell, G., Deaton, A., Durand, M., Halpern, D., and Layard, R. (2014). *Wellbeing and Policy*. Legatum Institute.

Singer, P. (1995). *Animal Liberation*. Random House.

Our Thanks

We have had invaluable help in writing this book. We are extremely grateful to Maria Cotofan, Micah Kaats and Ekaterina Oparina for their skillful research support, and to Jo Cantlay for her brilliant management of the manuscript from beginning to end.

The first draft of this book was subjected to a two-day chapter-by-chapter review in July 2021 in the beautiful setting of Magdalen College, Oxford. The reviewers were: Christopher Barrington-Leigh, Meike Bartels, Timothy Besley, Andrew Clark, Paul Dolan, Sarah Fleche, Philip Good, Carol Graham, Claire Haworth, John Helliwell, Christian Krekel, Stephen Machin, Alan Manning, George MacKerron, Andrew Oswald, Michael Plant and Laurie Santos.

Many others have also given us valuable help and advice, including Lucy Bailey, Lucy Bowes, David Clark, Thalia Eley, Peter Fonagy, David Halpern, Daniel Kahneman, Grace Lordan, Alistair McGuire, Geoff Mulgan, Stephen Nickell, Steve Pischke, Robert Plomin, Robert Putnam, Andrew Steptoe, Graham Thornicroft and Lovis Wentworth.

We would like to thank the many generous donors who have supported our recent research programmes at the LSE Centre for Economic Performance and the Wellbeing Research Centre at the University of Oxford and, through that, this book. They include the ESRC, the What Works Centre for Wellbeing, the Illy Foundation, Rishi Khosla, Pavel Teplukhin, Sushil Wadhwani, Andrew Barnes, KSI Education, Wellbeing for Planet Earth Foundation, Victor Pinchuk Foundation, and the Robert Wood Johnson Foundation.

Finally, we are hugely indebted to our colleagues at the Cambridge University Press (CUP), especially our editor Philip Good, and to our agent Caroline Dawnay who arranged our marriage to CUP.

Thank you all.

Richard and Jan

List of Annexes

Available on the Cambridge University Press website

References

Adler, A. (2016). Teaching well-being increases academic performance: evidence from Bhutan, Mexico, and Peru. *Publicly Accessible Penn Dissertations*, University of Pennsylvania.

Adler, M. D., Dolan, P., and Kavetsos, G. (2017). Would you choose to be happy? Tradeoffs between happiness and the other dimensions of life in a large population survey. *Journal of Economic Behavior & Organization*, 139, 60–73.

Ahmadiani, M., and Ferreira, S. (2019). Environmental amenities and quality of life across the United States. *Ecological Economics*, 164, 106341.

Ahmedani, B. K., Peterson, E. L., Wells, K. E., and Williams, L. K. (2013). Examining the relationship between depression and asthma exacerbations in a prospective follow-up study. *Psychosomatic Medicine*, 75(3), 305–310.

Akay, A., Constant, A., and Giulietti, C. (2014). The impact of immigration on the well-being of natives. *Journal of Economic Behavior & Organization*, 103(C), 72–92.

Aknin, L. B., Barrington-Leigh, C. P., Dunn, J. F., Helliwell, J. F., Burns, J., Biswas-Diener, R., . . . and Norton, M. I. (2013). Prosocial spending and well-being: Cross-cultural evidence for a psychological universal. *Journal of Personality and Social Psychology*, 104(4), 635.

Aknin, L. B., Broesch, T., Hamlin, J. K., and Van de Vondervoort, J. W. (2015). Prosocial behavior leads to happiness in a small-scale rural society. *Journal of Experimental Psychology: General*, 144(4), 788.

Aknin, L. B., Hamlin, J. K., and Dunn, E. W. (2012). Giving leads to happiness in young children. *PLoS ONE*, 7(6), e39211.

Aknin, L. B., Whillans, A. V., Norton, M. I., and Dunn, E. W. (2019). Happiness and prosocial behavior: an evaluation of the evidence. In J. E. De Neve, J. F. Helliwell, R. Layard and J. Sachs (Eds.). *World Happiness Report 2019* (pp. 67–86). Sustainable Development Solutions Network.

Alabrese, E., Becker, S. O., Fetzer, T., and Novy, D. (2019). Who voted for Brexit? Individual and regional data combined. *European Journal of Political Economy*, 56, 132–150.

Albertsen, K., Garde, A. H., Nabe-Nielsen, K., Hansen, Å. M., Lund, H., and Hvid, H. (2014). Work-life balance among shift workers: Results from an intervention study about self-rostering. *International Archives of Occupational and Environmental Health*, 87(3), 265–274.

Alcock, I., White, M. P., Wheeler, B. W., Fleming, L. E., and Depledge, M. H. (2014). Longitudinal effects on mental health of moving to greener and less green urban areas. *Environmental Science & Technology*, 48(2), 1247–1255.

Alesina, A., and Glaeser, E. (2004). *Fighting Poverty in the US and Europe: A World of Difference*: Oxford University Press.

Alesina, A., and La Ferrara, E. (2000). Participation in heterogeneous communities. *The Quarterly Journal of Economics*, 115(3), 847–904.

Alesina, A., and La Ferrara, E. (2002). Who trusts others? *Journal of Public Economics*, 85(2), 207–234.

Algan, Y., Beasley, E., Cohen, D., and Foucault, M. (2018). The rise of populism and the collapse of the left-right paradigm: lessons from the 2017 French presidential election. CEPR Discussion Paper 13103. CEPR, London, UK.

Allcott, H., Braghieri, L., Eichmeyer, S., and Gentzkow, M. (2020). The welfare effects of social media. *American Economic Review*, 110(3), 629–676.

Alvarez-Diaz, A., Gonzalez, L., and Radcliff, B. (2010). The politics of happiness: On the political determinants of quality of life in the American states. *The Journal of Politics*, 72(3), 894–905.

Amabile, T. M., Barsade, S. G., Mueller, J. S., and Staw, B. M. (2005). Affect and creativity at work. *Administrative Science Quarterly*, 50(3), 367–403.

Amato, P.R., and Bruce K.(1991) Parental divorce and the well-being of children: A meta-analysis. *Psychological Bulletin*, 110(1), 26–46.

Andersson, G. (2016). Internet-delivered psychological treatments. *Annual Review of Clinical Psychology*, 12, 157–179.

Andrews, F. M., and Withey, S. B. (1976). Measuring global well-being. *Social Indicators of Well-Being* (pp. 63–106). Springer.

Angrave, D., and Charlwood, A. (2015). What is the relationship between long working hours, over-employment, under-employment and the subjective well-being of workers? Longitudinal evidence from the UK. *Human Relations*, 68(9), 1491–1515.

Angrist, J. D., and Levy, V. (1999). Using Maimonides' Rule to estimate the effect of class size on scholastic achievement. *Quarterly Journal of Economics*, 114(2), 533–575.

Angrist, J. D., and Pischke, J. S. (2008). *Mostly Harmless Econometrics*. Princeton University Press.

Anisman, H., Zaharia, M. D., Meaney, M. J., and Merali, Z. (1998). Do early-life events permanently alter behavioral and hormonal responses to stressors? *International Journal of Developmental Neuroscience*, 16(3–4), 149–164.

Anusic, I., Yap, S. C., and Lucas, R. E. (2014). Testing set-point theory in a Swiss national sample: Reaction and adaptation to major life events. *Social Indicators Research*, 119(3), 1265–1288.

Appleyard, D., and Lintell, M. (1972). The environmental quality of city streets: The residents' viewpoint. *Journal of the American Institute of Planners*, 38(2), 84–101.

Arampatzi, E., Burger, M., Ianchovichina, E., Röhricht, T., and Veenhoven, R. (2018). Unhappy development: Dissatisfaction with life on the eve of the Arab Spring. *Review of Income and Wealth*, 64, S80–S113.

Artz, B. M., Goodall, A. H., and Oswald, A. J. (2017). Boss competence and worker well-being. *IlR Review*, 70(2), 419–450.

Atkinson, A. B. (1970). On the measurement of inequality. *Journal of Economic Theory*, 2(3), 244–263.

Ayuso-Mateos, J. L., Miret, M., Caballero, F. F., Olaya, B., Haro, J. M., Kowal, P., and Chatterji, S. (2013). Multi-country evaluation of affective experience: Validation of an abbreviated version of the day reconstruction method in seven countries. *PLoS One*, 8(4), e61534.

Ayuso-Mateos, J. L., Nuevo, R., Verdes, E., Naidoo, N., and Chatterji, S. (2010). From depressive symptoms to depressive disorders: The relevance of thresholds. *British Journal of Psychiatry*, 196, 365–371. doi:10.1192/bjp.bp.109.071191.

Azeez, R. O., Jayeoba, F., and Adeoye, A. O. (2016). Job satisfaction, turnover intention and organizational commitment. *Journal of Management Research*, 8(2), 102–114.

Baer, R. A. (2003). Mindfulness training as a clinical intervention: A conceptual and empirical review. *Clinical Psychology: Science and Practice* 10(2): 125–143.

Bakosh, L. S., Snow, R. M., Tobias, J. M., Houlihan, J. L., and Barbosa-Leiker, C. (2016). Maximizing mindful learning: Mindful awareness intervention improves elementary school students' quarterly grades. *Mindfulness*, 7(1), 59–67.

Bandiera, O., Fischer, G., Prat, A., and Ytsma, E. (2017). Do women respond less to performance pay? Building evidence from multiple experiments. CEPR Discussion Paper (11724). Centre for Economic Policy Research.

Banerjee, R., Weare, K., and Farr, W. (2014). Working with 'social and emotional aspects of learning' (SEAL): Associations with school ethos, pupil social experiences, attendance, and attainment. *British Educational Research Journal*, 40(4), 718–742.

Barlow, D. H., and Durand, V. M. (2009). *Abnormal Psychology: An Integrative Approach*. Wadsworth Cengage Learning.

Barraclough, B., Bunch, J., Nelson, B., and Sainsbury, P. (1974). A hundred cases of suicide: Clinical aspects. *British Journal of Psychiatry*, 125, 355–373.

Barrington-Leigh, C. (2022). Trends in conceptions of progress and well-being. In J. F. Helliwell, R. Layard, J. Sachs and J. E. S (Eds.). *World Happiness Report 2022* (n.p.). Sustainable Development.

Bartels, M. (2015). Genetics of wellbeing and its components satisfaction with life, happiness, and quality of life: A review and meta-analysis of heritability studies. *Behavior Genetics*, 45 (2), 137–156.

Bartels, M., and Boomsma, D. I. (2009). Born to be happy? The etiology of subjective well-being. *Behavior Genetics*, 39(6), 605–615.

Bartolini, S., Bilancini, E., and Sarracino, F. (2016). Social capital predicts happiness over time. In S. Bartolini, E. Bilancini, L. Bruni and P. L. Porta (Eds). *Policies for Happiness* (pp. 175–198). Oxford University Press.

Baselmans, B. M., Jansen, R., Ip, H. F., van Dongen, J., Abdellaoui, A., van de Weijer, M. P., ... and Bartels, M. (2019). Multivariate genome-wide analyses of the well-being spectrum. *Nature Genetics*, 51(3), 445–451.

Baumeister, D., Akhtar, R., Ciufolini, S., Pariante, C. M., and Mondelli, V. (2016). Childhood trauma and adulthood inflammation: A meta-analysis of peripheral C-reactive protein, interleukin-6 and tumour necrosis factor-α. *Molecular Psychiatry*, 21(5), 642–649.

Beck, A. T. (Ed.). (1979). *Cognitive Therapy of Depression*. Guilford Press.

Beck, A. T. (2006). How an anomalous finding led to a new system of psychotherapy. *Nature Medicine* 12(10): 1139–1141.

Beck, J. S., and Beck, A. T. (2011). *Cognitive Behavior Therapy*. Guilford Press.

Beck, R., and Harter, J. (2014). Why great managers are so rare. *Gallup Business Journal*, 25.

Bell, D. N., and Blanchflower, D. G. (2011). Young people and the Great Recession. *Oxford Review of Economic Policy*, 27(2), 241–267.

Bellet, C. (2019). The McMansion effect: Top house size and positional externalities in US suburbs. SSRN 3378131.

Bellet, C., De Neve, J. E., and Ward, G. (2020). Does employee happiness have an impact on productivity? Saïd Business School WP. WP 2019-13.

Belsky, J. (2016). The differential susceptibility hypothesis: Sensitivity to the environment for better and for worse. *JAMA Pediatrics*, 170(4), 321–322.

Benjamin, D. J., Heffetz, O., Kimball, M. S., and Rees-Jones, A. (2012). What do you think would make you happier? What do you think you would choose? *American Economic Review*, 102 (1), 2083–2110.

Bennett, K., and Dorjee, D. (2016). The impact of a Mindfulness-Based Stress Reduction Course (MBSR) on well-being and academic attainment of sixth-form students. *Mindfulness* 7, 105–114.

Ben-Shahar, T. (2007). *Happier: Learn the Secrets to Daily Joy and Lasting Fulfillment*. McGraw-Hill.

Bentham, J. (1970). *An Introduction to the Principles of Morals and Legislation (1789)*. J. H Burns and H. L. A. Hart (Eds.). T. Payne & Son.

Bentham, J. (2002). *Rights, Representation, and Reform: Nonsense upon Stilts and Other Writings on the French Revolution* (Vol. 15). Oxford University Press.

Berg, J. M., Dutton, J. E., and Wrzesniewski, A. (2013). Job crafting and meaningful work. In B. J. Dik, Z. S. Byrne and M. F. Steger (Eds.). *Purpose and meaning in the workplace* (pp. 81–104). American Psychological Association.

Berniell, M. I., and Bietenbeck, J. (2017). The effect of working hours on health. SSRN. IZA Discussion Paper No. 10524.

Besley, T., and Burgess, R. (2002). The political economy of government responsiveness: Theory and evidence from India. *The Quarterly Journal of Economics*, 117(4), 1415–1451.

Besley, T., and Persson, T. (2011). *Pillars of Prosperity*. Princeton University Press.

Besley, T., Dann, C., and Persson, T. (2021). State capacity and development clusters. *VoxEU CEPR*. www.voxeu.org/article/state-capacity-and-development-clusters.

Bessa, I., Charlwood, A., and Valizade, D. (2020). Do unions cause job dissatisfaction? Evidence from a quasi-experiment in the United Kingdom, *British Journal of Industrial Relations*, 1–29.

Betz, W., and Simpson, N. (2013). The effects of international migration on the well-being of native populations in Europe. *IZA Journal of Migration*, 2(1), 1–21.

Binder, M., and Freytag, A. (2013). Volunteering, subjective well-being and public policy. *Journal of Economic Psychology*, 34, 97–119.

Birkjær M., and Kaats M. (2019). in Er sociale Medier Faktisk en Truss for Unges Trivsel? [Does Social Media Really Pose a Threat to Young People's Well-Being?]. N.M.H.R. Institute (Eds.). Nordic Co-operation.

Biswas-Diener, R., Vittersø, J., and Diener, E. (2005). Most people are pretty happy, but there is cultural variation: The Inughuit, the Amish, and the Maasai. *Journal of Happiness Studies*, 6 (3), 205–226.

Bjørnskov, C., Dreher, A., and Fischer, J. A. (2010). Formal institutions and subjective well-being: Revisiting the cross-country evidence. *European Journal of Political Economy*, 26(4), 419–430.

Blakemore, S. J. (2018). *Inventing Ourselves: The Secret Life of the Teenage Brain*. Black Swan.

Blanchflower, D. G., and Bryson, A. (2020). Now unions increase job satisfaction and well-being (No. w27720). National Bureau of Economic Research.

Blanchflower, D. G., and Oswald, A. J. (2004). Money, sex and happiness: An empirical study. *Scandinavian Journal of Economics*, 106(3), 393–415.

Blanchflower, D. G., and Oswald, A. J. (2019a). Do humans suffer a psychological low in midlife? Two approaches (with and without controls) in seven data sets. In M. Rojas (Ed). *The Economics of Happiness* (pp. 439–453). Springer.

Blanchflower, D. G., and Oswald, A. J. (2019b). Unhappiness and pain in modern America: A review essay, and further evidence, on Carol Graham's Happiness for All? *Journal of Economic Literature*, 57(2), 385–402.

Blasi, J., Freeman, R., and Kruse, D. (2016). Do broad-based employee ownership, profit sharing and stock options help the best firms do even better? *British Journal of Industrial Relations*, 54(1), 55–82.

Bloom, N., Liang, J., Roberts, J., and Ying, Z. J. (2015). Does working from home work? Evidence from a Chinese experiment. *The Quarterly Journal of Economics*, 130(1), 165–218.

Bloom, N., and Van Reenen, J. (2010). Why do management practices differ across firms and countries? *Journal of Economic Perspectives*, 24(1), 203–224. doi: 10.1257/jep.24.1.203.

Blumenthal, S. J. (1988). Suicide: A guide to risk factors, assessment, and treatment of suicidal patients. *Medical Clinics of North America*, 72, 937–971.

Blundell, R., Dias, M. C., Meghir, C., and Van Reenen, J. (2004). Evaluating the employment impact of a mandatory job search program. *Journal of the European Economic Association*, 2(4), 569–606.

Böckerman, P., Bryson, A., Kauhanen, A., and Kangasniemi, M. (2016). Does job support make workers happy? Working Paper No. 16-16. Department of Quantitative Social Science-UCL Institute of Education, University College London.

Böckerman, P., and Ilmakunnas, P. (2012). The job satisfaction-productivity nexus: A study using matched survey and register data. *ILR Review*, 65(2), 244–262.

Bond, T. N., and Lang, K. (2019). The sad truth about happiness scales. *Journal of Political Economy*, 127(4), 1629–1640.

Borjas, G. (1979). Job satisfaction, wages, and unions. *Journal of Human Resources*, 14(1), 21–40.

Boskin, M. J., and Sheshinski, E. (1978). Optimal redistributive taxation when individual welfare depends upon relative income. *The Quarterly Journal of Economics*, 589–601.

Bouckenooghe, D., Raja, U., and Butt, A. N. (2013). Combined effects of positive and negative affectivity and job satisfaction on job performance and turnover intentions. *The Journal of Psychology*, 147(2), 105–123.

Bowlby, J. (1969). *Attachment and Loss: Attachment*. Basic Books.

Boyce, C. J., Wood, A. M., Banks, J., Clark, A. E., and Brown, G. D. (2013). Money, well-being, and loss aversion: Does an income loss have a greater effect on well-being than an equivalent income gain? *Psychological Science*, 24(12), 2557–2562.

Bradburn, N. M. (1969). *The Structure of Psychological Well-Being*. Aldine.

Bravo, I. M. (2016). The usefulness of subjective well-being to predict electoral results in Latin America. In *Handbook of Happiness Research in Latin America* (pp. 613–632). Springer.

Brayfield, A. H., and Crockett, W. H. (1955). Employee attitudes and employee performance. *Psychological Bulletin*, 52(5), 396.

Breza, E., Kaur, S., and Shamdasani, Y. (2018). The morale effects of pay inequality. *The Quarterly Journal of Economics*, 133(2), 611–663.

Brodeur, A., Clark, A. E., Fleche, S., and Powdthavee, N. (2021). COVID-19, lockdowns and well-being: Evidence from Google Trends. *Journal of Public Economics*, 193, 104346.

Broome, J. (2004). *Weighing Lives*. Oxford University Press.

Brough, P., and O'Driscoll, M. P. (2010). Organizational interventions for balancing work and home demands: An overview. *Work & Stress*, 24(3), 280–297.

Brown, D. E. (1991). *Human Universals*. Temple University Press.

Bryson, A., Clark, A. E., Freeman, R. B., and Green, C. P. (2016). Share capitalism and worker wellbeing. *Labour Economics*, 42, 151–158.

Bryson, A., and Davies, R. (2019). Accounting for geographical variance in the union satisfaction gap. *Industrial Relations Journal*, 50(2); 104–125.

Bryson, A., Forth, J., and Stokes, L. (2017). Does employees' subjective well-being affect workplace performance? *Human Relations*, 70(8), 1017–1037.

Bryson, A., and MacKerron, G. (2017). Are you happy while you work? *The Economic Journal*, 127(599), 106–125.

Bubonya, M., Cobb-Clark, D. A., and Wooden, M. (2014). A family affair: Job loss and the mental health of spouses and adolescents (No. 8588). Institute of Labour Economics (IZA).

Budolfson, M. B., Anthoff, D., Dennig, F., Errickson, F., Kuruc, K., Spears, D., and Dubash, N. K. (2021). Utilitarian benchmarks for emissions and pledges promote equity, climate and development. *Nature Climate Change*, 11(10), 827–833.

Bureau of Labor Statistics (2014). American Time Use Survey 2010, 2012, and 2013 Multi-Year Well-Being Module Microdata Files. www.bls.gov/tus/wbdatafiles_1013.htm.

Business Roundtable (2019). Business roundtable redefines the purpose of a corporation to promote 'an economy that serves all Americans'. Business Roundtable. www.businessroundtable.org/business-roundtable-redefines-the-purpose-of-a-corporation-to-promote-an-economy-that-serves-all-americans.

Butz, S., Kieslich, P. J., and Bless, H. (2017). Why are conservatives happier than liberals? Comparing different explanations based on system justification, multiple group membership, and positive adjustment. *European Journal of Social Psychology*, 47(3), 362–372.

Cadoret, R. J., Yates, W. R., Woodworth, G., and Stewart, M. A. (1995). Genetic-environmental interaction in the genesis of aggressivity and conduct disorders. *Archives of general psychiatry*, 52(11), 916–924.

Camerer, C., Babcock, L., Loewenstein, G., and Thaler, R. (1997). Labor supply of New York City cabdrivers: One day at a time. *The Quarterly Journal of Economics*, 112(2), 407–441.

Campbell, A., Converse, P., and Rodgers, W. (1976) *The Quality of American Life: Perceptions, Evaluations, and Satisfactions*. Russell Sage Foundation.

Cantril, H. (1965). *The Pattern of Human Concerns*. Rutgers University Press.

Card, D., Kluve, J., and Weber, A. (2018). What works? A meta-analysis of recent active labour market program evaluations. *Journal of the European Economic Association*, 16(3), 894–931.

Card, D., Mas, A., Moretti, E., and Saez, E. (2012). Inequality at work: The effect of peer salaries on job satisfaction. *American Economic Review*, 102(6), 2981–3003.

Carleton, T. A., and Hsiang, S. M. (2016). Social and economic impacts of climate. *Science*, 353 (6304), 9837-1–9837-15.

Carlson, M. C., Kuo, J. H., Chuang, Y.-F., Varma, V. R., Harris, G., Albert, M. S., Erickson, K. I., Kramer, A. F., Parisi, J. M., and Xue, Q.-L. (2015). Impact of the Baltimore Experience Corps trial on cortical and hippocampal volumes, alzheimer's and dementia: *The Journal of the Alzheimer's Association*, 11(11), 1340–1348.

Carroll, J. (2007). Most Americans 'very satisfied' with their personal lives. Gallup website, 31 December, 389–412.

Carroll, N. (2007). Unemployment and psychological well-being. *Economic Record*, 83(262), 287–302.

Case, A., and Deaton, A. (2020). *Deaths of Despair and the Future of Capitalism*. Princeton University Press.

Caspi, A., McClay, J., Moffitt, T. E., Mill, J., Martin, J., Craig, I. W., . . . and Poulton, R. (2002). Role of genotype in the cycle of violence in maltreated children. *Science*, 297(5582), 851–854.

Chatterjee, K., Chng, S., Clark, B., Davis, A., De Vos, J., Ettema, D., . . . and Reardon, L. (2020). Commuting and wellbeing: A critical overview of the literature with implications for policy and future research. *Transport Reviews*, 40(1), 5–34.

Cheng, T. C., Powdthavee, N., and Oswald, A. J. (2017). Longitudinal evidence for a midlife nadir in human well-being: Results from four data sets. *The Economic Journal*, 127(599), 126–142.

Chetty, R., Hendren, N., and Katz, L. F. (2016). The effects of exposure to better neighborhoods on children: New evidence from the Moving to Opportunity experiment. *American Economic Review*, 106(4), 855–902.

Cheung, F., Kube, A., Tay, L., Diener, E., Jackson, J. J., Lucas, R. E., . . . and Leung, G. M. (2020). The impact of the Syrian conflict on population well-being. *Nature Communications*, 11(1), 1–10.

Chida, Y., Hamer, M., Wardle, J., and Steptoe, A. (2008). Do stress-related psychosocial factors contribute to cancer incidence and survival? *Nature Clinical Practice (Oncology)*, 5(8), 466–475. doi:10.1038/ncponc1134.

Chiles, J. A., Lambert, M. J., and Hatch, A. L. (1999). The impact of psychological interventions on medical cost offset: A meta-analytic review. *Clinical Psychology: Science and Practice*, 6(2), 204–220.

Chilvers, C., Dewey, M., Fielding, K., Gretton, V., Miller, P., Palmer, B., . . . and Harrison, G. (2001). Antidepressant drugs and generic counselling for treatment of major depression in primary care: Randomised trial with patient preference arms. *BMJ*, 322(7289), 772.

Chisholm, D., Sweeny, K., Sheehan, P., Rasmussen, B., Smit, F., Cuijpers, P., and Saxena, S. (2016). Scaling-up treatment of depression and anxiety: A global return on investment analysis. *The Lancet Psychiatry*, 3(5), 415–424.

Choi, J., Laibson, D., and Madrian, B. C. (2006). *Saving for Retirement on the Path of Least Resistance, in Behavioral Public Finance: Toward a New Agenda*. E. McCaffrey and J. Slemrod (Eds.). Russell Sage Foundation.

Christakis, N. A., and Fowler, J. H. (2007). The spread of obesity in a large social network over 32 years. *New England Journal of Medicine*, 357(4), 370–379.

Clark, A. E. (2003). Unemployment as a social norm: Psychological evidence from panel data. *Journal of Labour Economics*, 21(2), 323–351.

Clark, A. E., and Díaz Serrano, L. (2020). The Long-run effects of housing on well-being.

Clark, A. E., Flèche, S., Layard, R., Powdthavee, N., and Ward, G. (2017). The key determinants of happiness and misery. CEP Discussion Paper, London School of Economics.

Clark, A. E., Flèche, S., Layard, R., Powdthavee, N., and Ward, G. (2018). *The Origins of Happiness: The Science of Wellbeing over the Life Course*. Princeton University Press.

Clark, A. E., Frijters, P., and Shields, M. A. (2008). Relative income, happiness, and utility: An explanation for the Easterlin paradox and other puzzles. *Journal of Economic literature*, 46 (1), 95–144.

Clark, A. E., and Georgellis, Y. (2013). Back to baseline in Britain: Adaptation in the British household panel survey. *Economica*, 80(319), 496–512.

Clark, A. E., Layard, R., and Senik, C. (2012). The causes of happiness and misery. In *World Happiness Report 2012*. J. F. Helliwell, R. Layard and J. Sachs (Eds.). Sustainable Development Solutions Network.

Clark, A. E., and Lelkes, O. (2009). Let us pray: Religious interactions in life satisfaction. PSE Working Paper No 2009-01. Paris School of Economics.

Clark, A. E., and Lepinteur, A. (2019). The causes and consequences of early-adult unemployment: Evidence from cohort data. *Journal of Economic Behavior & Organization*, 166, 107–124.

Clark, B., Chatterjee, K., Martin, A., and Davis, A. (2020). How commuting affects subjective wellbeing. *Transportation*, 47(6), 2777–2805.

Clark, D. M. (2018). Realizing the mass public benefit of evidence-based psychological therapies: The IAPT program. *Annual Review of Clinical Psychology*, 14, 159–183.

Clark, D. M., Canvin, L., Green, J., Layard, R., Pilling, S., and Janecka, M. (2018). Transparency about the outcomes of mental health services (IAPT approach): An analysis of public data. *The Lancet*, 391(10121), 679–686.

Clark, D. M., Ehlers, A., Hackmann, A., McManus, F., Fennell, M., Grey, N., . . . and Wild, J. (2006). Cognitive therapy versus exposure and applied relaxation in social phobia: A randomized controlled trial. *Journal of Consulting and Clinical Psychology*, 74(3), 568.

Clark, D. M., Layard, R., and Smithies, R. (2009). Improving access to psychological therapy: Initial evaluation of two UK demonstration sites. CEP Discussion Paper 897. London School of Economics.

Clifton, J., and Harter, J. (2019) *It's the Manager*. Gallup Press.

Coghill, R. C. (2010). Individual differences in the subjective experience of pain: New insights into mechanisms and models. *Headache: The Journal of Head and Face Pain*, 50(9): 1531–1535.

Coghill, R. C., McHaffie, J. G., and Yen, Y. F. (2003). Neural correlates of interindividual differences in the subjective experience of pain. *Proceedings of the National Academy of Sciences*, 100(14), 8538–8542.

Cohen, S., Miller, G. E., and Rabin, B. S. (2001). Psychological stress and antibody response to immunization: A critical review of the human literature. *Psychosomatic Medicine*, 63(1), 7–18.

Cohn, A., Maréchal, M. A., Tannenbaum, D., and Zünd, C. L. (2019). Civic honesty around the globe. *Science*, 365(6448), 70–73.

Cole-King, A., and Harding, K. G. (2001). Psychological factors and delayed healing in chronic wounds. *Psychosomatic Medicine*, 63(2), 216–220.

Collier, P. (2013). *Exodus: How Migration Is Changing Our World*. Oxford University Press.

Cooper, C., and Dewe, P. (2008). Well-being – absenteeism, presenteeism, costs and challenges. *Occupational Medicine*, 58(8), 522–524.

Cotofan, M., Cassar, L., Dur, R., and Meier, S. (2021a). Macroeconomic conditions when young shape job preferences for life. *The Review of Economics and Statistics*. doi.org/10.1162/rest_a_01057.

Cotofan, M., De Neve, J. E., Golin, M., Kaats, M., and Ward, G. (2021b). Work and well-being during COVID-19: Impact, inequalities, resilience, and the future of work. In J. F. Helliwell, R. Layard, J. Sachs and J. E. De Neve (Eds.). *World Happiness Report 2021* (p. 153). The Earth Institute.

Crépon, B., Duflo, E., Gurgand, M., Rathelot, R., and Zamora, P. (2013). Do labour market policies have displacement effects? Evidence from a clustered randomized experiment. *The Quarterly Journal of Economics*, 128(2), 531–580.

Creswell, J. D., Taren, A. A., Lindsay, E. K., Greco, C. M., Gianaros, P. J., Fairgrieve, A., . . . and Ferris, J. L. (2016). Alterations in resting-state functional connectivity link mindfulness meditation with reduced interleukin-6: a randomized controlled trial. *Biological Psychiatry*, 80(1), 53–61.

Dahl, C. J., Wilson-Mendenhall, C. D., and Davidson, R. J. (2020). The plasticity of well-being: A training-based framework for the cultivation of human flourishing. *Proceedings of the National Academy of Sciences*, 117(51), 32197–32206.

Dahl, M. S., and Pierce, L. (2019). Pay-for-performance and employee mental health: Large sample evidence using employee prescription drug usage. Academy of Management Discoveries, 26 February.

Danese, A., and Widom, C. S. (2020). Objective and subjective experiences of child maltreatment and their relationships with psychopathology. *Nature Human Behaviour*, 4(8), 811–818.

Danese, A., Pariante, C. M., Caspi, A., Taylor, A., and Poulton, R. (2007). Childhood maltreatment predicts adult inflammation in a life-course study. *Proceedings of the National Academy of Sciences*, 104(4), 1319–1324.

Danner, D., Snowden, D., and Friesen, W. (2001). Positive emotions in early life and longevity: Findings from the nun study. *Journal of Personality and Social Psychology*, 80, 804–813.

Dasgupta, P., Managi, S., and Kumar, P. (2021). The inclusive wealth index and sustainable development goals. *Sustainability Science*, 1–5.

Davidson, R. J., and Schuyler, B. S. (2015). Neuroscience of happiness. In J. F. Helliwell, R. Layard and J. Sachs (Eds.). *World Happiness Report 2015* (pp. 88–105). Sustainable Development Solutions Network.

Davidson, R. J., Kabat-Zinn, J., Schumacher, J., Rosenkranz, M., Muller, D., Santorelli, S. F., . . . and Sheridan, J. F. (2003). Alterations in brain and immune function produced by mindfulness meditation. *Psychosomatic Medicine*, 65(4), 564–570.

Davis, R. S. (2012) Unionization and work attitudes: How union commitment influences public sector job satisfaction. *Public Administration Review*, 73(1), 74–84.

Daykin, N., Mansfield, L., Payne, A., Kay, T., Meads, C., D'Innocenzo, G., . . . and Victor, C. (2017). What works for wellbeing in culture and sport? Report of a DELPHI process to support coproduction and establish principles and parameters of an evidence review. *Perspectives in Public Health*, 137(5), 281–288.

de Lazari-Radek, K., and Singer, P. (2017). *Utilitarianism: A Very Short Introduction*: Oxford University Press.

De Neve, J. E. (2018). Work and well-being: A global perspective. Global Happiness and Well-Being Policy Report 2018.

De Neve, J. E., Clark, A. E., Krekel, C., Layard, R., and O'donnell, G. (2020). Taking a wellbeing years approach to policy choice. *BMJ*, 371.

De Neve, J. E., Diener, E., Tay, L., and Xuereb, C. (2013). The objective benefits of subjective well-being. In J. F. Helliwell, R. Layard, and J. Sachs (Eds.).*World Happiness Report 2013*. Sustainable Development Solutions Network.

De Neve, J. E., and Krekel, C. (2020). Cities and happiness: a global ranking and analysis. In D. E. Neve, J. F. Helliwell, R. Layard and J. Sachs (Eds.). *World Happiness Report 2020*. Sustainable Development Solutions Network.

De Neve, J. E., and Oswald, A. J. (2012). Estimating the influence of life satisfaction and positive affect on later income using sibling fixed effects. *Proceedings of the National Academy of Sciences*, 109(49), 19953–19958.

De Neve, J. E., and Sachs, J. D. (2020). The SDGs and human well-being: A global analysis of synergies, trade-offs, and regional differences. *Scientific Reports*, 10(1), 1–12.

De Neve, J. E., and Ward, G. (2017). Happiness at work. In J. F. Helliwell, R. Layard and J. Sachs (Eds.). *World Happiness Report 2017*. Sustainable Development Solutions Network.

De Neve, J. E., Ward, G., De Keulenaer, F., Van Landeghem, B., Kavetsos, G., and Norton, M. I. (2018). The asymmetric experience of positive and negative economic growth: Global evidence using subjective well-being data. *Review of Economics and Statistics*, 100(2), 362–375.

Deacon, B. J., and Abramowitz, J. S. (2005). Patients' perceptions of pharmacological and cognitive-behavioral treatments for anxiety disorders. *Behavior Therapy*, 36, 139–145.

Deaton, A., and Cartwright, N. (2018). Understanding and misunderstanding randomized controlled trials. *Social Science & Medicine*, 210, 2–21.

Deci, E. L., and Ryan, R. M. (1985). *Intrinsic Motivation and Self-Determination in Human Behavior*. Plenum.

Deci, E. L., and Ryan, R. M. (2000). The 'what' and 'why' of goal pursuits: Human needs and the self-determination of behavior. *Psychological Inquiry*, 11(4), 227–268.

Dee, T. S., and M. R. West (2011). The non-cognitive returns to class size. *Educational Evaluation and Policy Analysis*, 33(1), 23–46.

Delhey J. (2014) Domain satisfaction. In A.C. Michalos (Ed.). *Encyclopedia of Quality of Life and Well-Being Research*. Springer. doi.org/10.1007/978-94-007-0753-5_769.

Department for Education (DfE) (2012). The impact of Sure Start local programmes on seven year olds and their families. National Evaluation of Sure Start Team, Research Report DFE-RR220. London, Department for Education.

Department of Housing, Communities and Local Government (2014). Housing and well-being report. English Housing Survey 2014. Office for National Statistics.

Deters, F. G., and Mehl, M. R. (2013). Does posting Facebook status updates increase or decrease loneliness? An online social networking experiment. *Social Psychological and Personality Science*, 4(5), 579–586.

Di Tella, R., and MacCulloch, R. (2005). Partisan social happiness. *The Review of Economic Studies*, 72(2), 367–393.

Diener, E. (1984). Subjective well-being. *Psychological Bulletin*, 95(3), 542–575.

Diener, E., Inglehart, R., and Tay, L. (2013). Theory and validity of life satisfaction scales. *Social Indicators Research*, 112(3), 497–527.

Diener, E., and Lucas, R. E. (1999). Personality and subjective well-being. In D. Kahneman, E. Diener and N. Schwarz (Eds.). *Well-Being* (pp. 213–229). Russell Sage Foundation.

Diener, E., Suh, E. M., Smith, H., and Shao, L. (1995). National differences in reported subjective well-being: Why do they occur? *Social Indicators Research*, 34(1), 7–32.

Diener, E., Tay, L., and Myers, D. G. (2011). The religion paradox: If religion makes people happy, why are so many dropping out? *Journal of Personality and Social Psychology*, 101 (6), 1278.

DiJulio B., Hamel, L, Munana C., and Brodie M. (2018). Loneliness and social isolation in the United States, the United Kingdom, and Japan: An international survey. Report to the Kaiser Family Foundation and The Economist.

Dohmen, T., Falk, A., Fliessbach, K., Sunde, U., and Weber, B. (2011). Relative versus absolute income, joy of winning, and gender: Brain imaging evidence. *Journal of Public Economics*, 95(3–4), 279–285.

Dolan, P., and Testoni, S. (2017a). Music, singing and wellbeing. What Works Centre for Wellbeing.

Dolan, P., and Testoni. S. (2017b). The relationship between engagement in sport or physical activity and subjective wellbeing among healthy young adults. What Works Centre for Wellbeing.

Dolan, P. (2014). *Happiness by Design: Finding Pleasure and Purpose in Everyday Life*. Penguin.

Dolan, P. (2019). *Happy Ever After: Escaping the Myth of the Perfect Life*. Penguin.

Dolan, P., and Kahneman, D. (2008). Interpretations of utility and their implications for the valuation of health. *Economic Journal*, 118(525), 215–234.

Dolan, P., Krekel, C., Shreedhar, G., Lee, H., Marshall, C., and Smith, A. (2021). Happy to help: The welfare effects of a nationwide micro-volunteering programme. Centre for Economic Performance DP1772. London School of Economics.

Dolan, P., and Laffan, K. (2016). Bad air days: The effects of air quality on different measures of subjective well-being. *Journal of Benefit-Cost Analysis*, 7(1), 147–195.

Dolan, P., Metcalfe, R., and Powdthavee, N. (2008). Electing happiness: Does happiness affect voting and do elections affect happiness? Department of Economics and Related Studies. University of York.

Donegani, C. P., and McKay S. (2012). Is there a paradox of lower job satisfaction among trade union members? European evidence. *Transfer: European Review of Labour and Research* 18(4), 471–489.

Duncan, G. J., and Brooks-Gunn J. (Eds.). (1999). *Consequences of Growing up Poor*. Russell Sage Foundation.

Dunn, E. W., Aknin, L. B., and Norton, M. I. (2008). Spending money on others promotes happiness. *Science*, 319(5870), 1687–1688.

Dunning, D. L., Griffiths, K., Kuyken, W., Crane, C., Foulkes, L., Parker, J., and Dalgleish, T. (2019). Research review: The effects of mindfulness-based interventions on cognition and mental health in children and adolescents – a meta-analysis of randomized controlled trials. *Journal of Child Psychology and Psychiatry*, 60(3), 244–258.

Durlak, J. A., Weissberg, R. P., Dymnicki, A. B., Taylor, R. D., and Schellinger, K. B. (2011). The impact of enhancing students' social and emotional learning: A meta-analysis of school-based universal interventions. *Child Development*, 82(1), 405–432.

Dustmann, C., and Fasani, F. (2016). The effect of local area crime on mental health. *The Economic Journal*, 126(593), 978–1017.

Dutton, J. E. (2003). *Energize Your Workplace: How to Create and Sustain High-Quality Connections at Work*. Jossey-Bass.

Dutton, J. E., and Ragins, B. R. (2007). *Exploring Positive Relationships at Work*. Lawrence Erlbaum Associates.

Easterlin, R. A. (1974). Does economic growth improve the human lot? Some empirical evidence. In *Nations and Households in Economic Growth* (pp. 89–125). Academic Press.

Easterlin, R. A., and O'Connor, K. (2020). The Easterlin paradox. IZA Discussion Paper No. 13923.

Easterlin, R. A., Wang, F., and Wang, S. (2017). Growth and happiness in China, 1990–2015. In J. F. Helliwell, R. Layard and J. Sachs (Eds.). *World Happiness Report 2017* (pp. 48–83). Sustainable Development Solutions Network.

Edmans, A. (2012). The link between job satisfaction and firm value, with implications for corporate social responsibility. *Academy of Management Perspectives*, 26(4), 1–19.

Eisenberger, N. I., Lieberman, M. D., and Williams, K. D. (2003). Does rejection hurt? An fMRI study of social exclusion. *Science*, 302(5643), 290–292.

Eley, T. C., Hudson, J. L., Creswell, C., Tropeano, M., Lester, K. J., Cooper, P., . . . and Collier, D. A. (2012). Therapygenetics: The 5HTTLPR and response to psychological therapy. *Molecular Psychiatry*, 17(3), 236–237.

Ellison, C. G. (1991). Religious involvement and subjective well-being. *Journal of Health and Social Behavior*, 80–99.

Epstein, N. B., LaTaillade, J. J., Werlinich, C. A. (2015). Couple therapy for partner aggression. In J. L. L. A. S. Gurman, D. K. Snyder (Eds.). *Clinical Handbook of Couple Therapy* (5th ed., pp. 389–411). Guilford Press.

Esping-Andersen, G. (1990). *The Three Worlds of Welfare Capitalism.* Princeton University Press.

EU Council (2019). The economy of wellbeing: Creating opportunites for people's wellbeing and economic growth (13171/19). Brussels: Council of the European Union. https://data .consilium.europa.eu/doc/document/ST-13171-2019-INIT/en/pdf.

Evans, D. (2003). *Placebo: The Belief Effect.* HarperCollins.

Fearon, R. P., and G. I. Roisman (2017). Attachment theory: Progress and future directions. *Current Opinion in Psychology*, 15, 131–136.

Fehr, E., and Fischbacher U. (2003). The nature of human altruism. *Nature* 425(23 October), 785–791.

Feinberg, M. E., Jones, D. E., Kan, M. L., and Goslin, M. C. (2010). Effects of family foundations on parents and children: 3.5 years after baseline. *Journal of Family Psychology*, 24(5), 532.

Ferejohn, J. (1986). Incumbent performance and electoral control. *Public Choice*, 50(1), 5–25.

Ferris, L. J., Jetten, J., Hornsey, M. J., and Bastian, B. (2019). Feeling hurt: Revisiting the relationship between social and physical pain. *Review of General Psychology*, 23(3), 320–335.

Flavin, P. (2019). State government public goods spending and citizens' quality of life. *Social Science Research*, 78, 28–40.

Flavin, P., and Keane, M. J. (2012). Life satisfaction and political participation: Evidence from the United States. *Journal of Happiness Studies*, 13(1), 63–78.

Flavin, P., Pacek, A. C., and Radcliff, B. (2011). State intervention and subjective well-being in advanced industrial democracies. *Politics & Policy*, 39(2), 251–269.

Flavin, P., Pacek, A. C., and Radcliff, B. (2014). Assessing the impact of the size and scope of government on human well-being. *Social Forces*, 92(4), 1241–1258.

Flèche, S. (2017a). Teacher quality, test scores and non-cognitive skills: Evidence from primary school teachers in the UK. CEP Discussion Paper No. 1472. Centre for Economic Performance.

Flèche, S. (2017b). The welfare consequences of centralization: Evidence from a quasi-natural experiment in Switzerland. *Review of Economics and Statistics*, 1–45.

Flèche, S., Clark, A. E., and Lekfuangfu, W. (2021) The long-lasting effects of family and childhood on adult wellbeing: Evidence from British cohort data. *Journal of Economic Behavior & Organization*, 181, 290–311.

Fleurbaey, M., and Schwandt, H. (2015). Do People Seek to Maximize Their Subjective Well-Being? IZA Discussion Paper No.9450.

Fonagy, P. (2015). The effectiveness of psychodynamic psychotherapies: an update. *World Psychiatry*, 14(2), 137–150.

Ford, T., Collishaw, S., Meltzer, H., and Goodman, R. (2007). A prospective study of childhood psychopathology: Independent predictors of change over three years. *Social Psychiatry and Psychiatric Epidemiology*, 42(12), 953–961.

Ford, T., Goodman, R., and Meltzer, H. (2004). The relative importance of child, family, school and neighbourhood correlates of childhood psychiatric disorder. *Social Psychiatry and Psychiatric Epidemiology*, 39(6), 487–496.

Ford, T., Hayes, R., Byford, S., Edwards, V., Fletcher, M., Logan, S., . . . and Ukoumunne, O. C. (2019). The effectiveness and cost-effectiveness of the Incredible Years® Teacher Classroom Management programme in primary school children: Results of the STARS cluster randomised controlled trial. *Psychological Medicine*, 49(5), 828–842.

Foresight Mental Capital and Wellbeing Project (2008). Final project report. The Government Office for Science, London. https://assets.publishing.service.gov.uk/government/uploads/system/uploads/attachment_data/file/292450/mental-capital-wellbeing-report.pdf.

Fortin, N., Helliwell, J. F., and Wang, S. (2015). How does subjective well-being vary around the world by gender and age. In J. F. Helliwell, R. Layard and J. Sachs (Eds.). *World Happiness Report 2015* (pp. 42–75). Sustainable Development Solutions Network.

Fournier, J. C., DeRubeis, R. J., Amsterdam, J., Shelton, R. C., and Hollon, S. D. (2014). Gains in employment status following antidepressant medication or cognitive therapy for depression. *British Journal of Psychiatry*, 206(4), 332–338.

Fowler, J. H., and Christakis, N. A. (2008). Dynamic spread of happiness in a large social network: Longitudinal analysis over 20 years in the Framingham Heart Study. *BMJ*, 337.

Frank, R. H. (1988). *Passions within Reason: The Strategic Role of the Emotions*. Norton.

Fredrickson, B. (2013). *Love 2.0: How Our Supreme Emotion Affects Everything We Feel, Think, Do, and Become*. Avery.

Fredrickson, B. L. (2000). Cultivating positive emotions to optimize health and well-being. *Prevention & Treatment*, 3(1), Article 1.

Fredrickson, B. L. (2004). The broaden–and–build theory of positive emotions. *Philosophical Transactions of the Royal Society of London. Series B: Biological Sciences*, 359(1449), 1367–1377.

Fredrickson, B. L., and C. Branigan (2005). Positive emotions broaden the scope of attention and thought-action repertoires. *Cognition & Emotion* 19(3), 313–332.

Fredriksson, P., Öckert, B., and Oosterbeek, H. (2013). Long-term effects of class size. *The Quarterly Journal of Economics*, 128(1), 249–285.

Freeman, R. B. (1978). Job satisfaction as an economic variable. *American Economic Review*, 68(2), 135–141.

Freeman, R. B., and J. Medoff, (1984). *What Do Unions Do?* Basic Books.

Frey, B. S. (2008). *Happiness: A Revolution in Economics*. MIT Press.

Frey, B. S. (2010). *Happiness: A Revolution in Economics*. MIT Press.

Frey, B. S., Benz, M., and Stutzer, A. (2004). Introducing procedural utility: Not only what, but also how matters. *Journal of Institutional and Theoretical Economics (JITE)/Zeitschrift für die gesamte Staatswissenschaft*, 377–401.

Frijters, P., and Beatton, T. (2012). The mystery of the U-shaped relationship between happiness and age. *Journal of Economic Behavior & Organization*, 82(2–3), 525–542.

Frijters, P., Clark, A. E., Krekel, C., and Layard, R. (2020). A happy choice: Wellbeing as the goal of government. *Behavioural Public Policy*, 4(2), 126–165.

Frijters, P., Geishecker, I., Haisken-DeNew, J. P., and Shields, M. A. (2006). Can the large swings in Russian life satisfaction be explained by ups and downs in real incomes? *Scandinavian Journal of Economics*, 108(3), 433–458.

Frijters, P., Haisken-DeNew, J. P., and Shields, M. A. (2004). Investigating the patterns and determinants of life satisfaction in Germany following reunification. *Journal of Human Resources*, 39(3), 649–674.

Frijters, P., Johnston, D. W., and Shields, M. A. (2011). Happiness dynamics with quarterly life event data. *Scandinavian Journal of Economics*, 113(1), 190–211.

Frijters, P., and Krekel, C. (2021). *A Handbook for Wellbeing Policy-Making in the UK: History, Measurement, Theory, Implementation, and Examples.* Oxford University Press.

Fujita, F., and Diener, E. (2005). Life satisfaction set point: Stability and change. *Journal of Personality and Social Psychology*, 88(1), 158.

Garde, A. H., Albertsen, K., Nabe-Nielsen, K., Carneiro, I. G., Skotte, J., Hansen, S. M., . . . and Hansen, Å. M. (2012). Implementation of self-rostering (the PRIO project): Effects on working hours, recovery, and health. *Scandinavian Journal of Work, Environment & Health*, 314–326.

Gautier, P., Muller, P., van der Klaauw, B., Rosholm, M., and Svarer, M. (2018). Estimating equilibrium effects of job search assistance. *Journal of Labour Economics*, 36(4), 1073–1125.

Genesove, D., and Mayer, C. (2001). Loss aversion and seller behavior: Evidence from the housing market. *The Quarterly Journal of Economics*, 116(4), 1233–1260.

Giattino, C., Ortiz-Ospina, E., and Roser, M. (2013). Working hours. OurWorldInData.org. https://ourworldindata.org/working-hours

Gibbons, S., Mourato, S., and Resende, G. M. (2014). The amenity value of English nature: A hedonic price approach. *Environmental and Resource Economics*, 57(2), 175–196.

Gilbert, D. (2009). *Stumbling on Happiness.* Vintage Canada.

Gilbert, D. T., and Wilson, T. D. (2000). Miswanting: Some problems in the forecasting of future affective states. In J. P. Forgas (Ed.). *Studies in Emotion and Social Interaction, Second Series. Feeling and thinking: The Role of Affect in Social Cognition* (pp. 178–197). Cambridge University Press.

Gimenez-Nadal, J. I., and Sevilla, A. (2012). Trends in time allocation: A cross-country analysis. *European Economic Review*, 56(6), 1338–1359.

Glaeser, E. L., Gottlieb, J. D., and Ziv, O. (2016). Unhappy cities. *Journal of Labor Economics*, 34(S2), S129–S182.

Glaeser, E. L., Laibson, D. I., Scheinkman, J. A., and Soutter, C. L. (2000). Measuring trust. *The Quarterly Journal of Economics*, 115(3), 811–846. doi:10.1162/003355300554926.

Goetzke, F., and Islam, S. (2017). Testing for spatial equilibrium using happiness data. *Journal of Regional Science*, 57(2), 199–217.

Goff, L., Helliwell, J. F., and Mayraz, G. (2018). Inequality of subjective well-being as a comprehensive measure of inequality. *Economic Inquiry*, 56(4), 2177–2194. doi:10.1111/ecin.12582.

Golder, S. A., and Macy, M. W. (2011). Diurnal and seasonal mood vary with work, sleep, and daylength across diverse cultures. *Science*, 333(6051), 1878–1881.

Goleman, D. (1995). *Emotional Intelligence.* Bantam Books.

Goleman, D., and Davidson, R. (2017). *The Science of Meditation: How to Change your Brain, Mind and Body.* Penguin UK.

Goodman, R., and Scott, S. (2012). *Child and Adolescent Psychiatry.* John Wiley & Sons.

Graham, C. (2012). *Happiness around the World: The Paradox of Happy Peasants and Miserable Millionaires.* Oxford University Press.

Grant, A. M. (2008). The significance of task significance: Job performance effects, relational mechanisms, and boundary conditions. *Journal of Applied Psychology*, 93(1), 108.

Groh, A. M., Roisman, G. I., Booth-LaForce, C., Fraley, R. C., Owen, M. T., Cox, M. J., and Burchinal, M. R. (2014). Stability of attachment security from infancy to late adolescence. *Monographs of the Society for Research in Child Development*, 79(3), 51–66.

Gross, J. (2010). SEAL: The big experiment. *Better: Evidence-Based Education*, 2(2): 6–7.

Gruber, J. H., and Mullainathan, S. (2005). Do cigarette taxes make smokers happier. *The BE Journal of Economic Analysis & Policy*, 5(1), n.p.

Gruber, J., Lordan, G., Pilling, S., Propper, C., and Saunders, R. (2019). Quantifying the impact on hospital use of a national psychological treatment programme (IAPT) for patients with long-term chronic conditions: A difference-in-differences analysis. Imperial College Business School. Mimeo.

Hallam, S., Rhamie, J., and Shaw, J. (2006). Evaluation of the primary behaviour and attendance pilot. London. Department for Education and Skills.

Halpern, D. (1995). *Mental Health and the Built Environment: More than Bricks and Mortar?* Taylor & Francis.

Hamermesh, D. S., Kawaguchi, D., and Lee, J. (2017). Does labor legislation benefit workers? Well-being after an hours reduction. *Journal of the Japanese and International Economies*, 44, 1–12.

Hamilton, W. D. (1971). Geometry for the selfish herd. *Journal of Theoretical Biology*, 31(2), 295–311.

Hanh, T. N. (2001). *Anger: Buddhist Wisdom for Cooling the Flames*. Rider.

Hanh, T. N. (2008). *The Miracle Of Mindfulness: The Classic Guide to Meditation* (reprint). Rider.

Hanh, T. N., and K. Weare (2017). *Happy Teachers Change the World: A Guide for Cultivating Mindfulness in Education*. Parallax Press.

Hanniball, K. B., Viljoen, J. L., Shaffer, C. S., Bhatt, G., Tweed, R., Aknin, L. B., ... and Dooley, S. (2021). The role of life satisfaction in predicting youth violence and offending: A prospective examination. *Journal of Interpersonal Violence*, 36(11–12), 5501–5529.

Hanson, R. (2016). *Hardwiring Happiness: The New Brain Science of Contentment, Calm, and Confidence*. Harmony.

Hanushek, E. A. (1999). Some findings from an independent investigation of the Tennessee STAR experiment and from other investigations of class size effects. *Educational Evaluation and Policy Analysis*, 21(2), 143–163.

Happy Planet Index (2016). *A Global Index of Sustainable Wellbeing*. New Economics Foundation.

Harbaugh, W. T., Mayr, U., and Burghart, D. R. (2007). Neural responses to taxation and voluntary giving reveal motives for charitable donations. *Science*, 316(5831), 1622–1625.

Hare, R. M. (1981). *Moral Thinking: Its Levels, Method, and Point*. Clarendon Press; Oxford University Press.

Harju, J., Jäger, S., and Schoefer, B. (2021). Voice at work (No. w28522). National Bureau of Economic Research.

Harsanyi, J. (1955a). Cardinal utility in welfare economics and in the theory of risk-taking. *Journal of Political Economy*, 61(5), 413–433.

Harsanyi, J. (1955b). Cardinal welfare, individualistic ethics, and interpersonal comparisons of utility. *Journal of Political Economy*, 63(4), 309–321.

Harter, J., and Adkins, A. (2015). Employees want a lot more from their managers. Gallup. www.gallup.com/workplace/236570/employees-lot-managers.aspx.

Harter, J. K., Schmidt, F. L., Asplund, J. W., Killham, E. A., and Agrawal, S. (2010). Causal impact of employee work perceptions on the bottom line of organizations. *Perspectives on Psychological Science*, 5(4), 378–389.

Haworth, C. M., and Davis, O. S. (2014). From observational to dynamic genetics. *Frontiers in Genetics*, 5, 6.

Haworth, C. M., Nelson, S. K., Layous, K., Carter, K., Jacobs Bao, K., Lyubomirsky, S., and Plomin, R. (2016). Stability and change in genetic and environmental influences on well-being in response to an intervention. *PlosOne*, 11(5), e0155538.

Headey, B. (2006). *Revising Set-Point Theory and Dynamic Equilibrium Theory to Account for Long-Term Change*. DIW.

Healy, A., and Malhotra, N. (2013). Retrospective voting reconsidered. *Annual Review of Political Science*, 16, 285–306.

Healy, A. J., Malhotra, N., and Mo, C. H. (2010). Irrelevant events affect voters' evaluations of government performance. *Proceedings of the National Academy of Sciences*, 107(29), 12804–12809.

Heatherton, T. F., and Wagner, D. D. (2011). Cognitive neuroscience of self-regulation failure. *Trends in Cognitive Sciences*, 15(3), 132–139.

Heckman, J. J., Moon, S. H., Pinto, R., Savelyev, P. A., and Yavitz, A. (2010). The rate of return to the HighScope Perry Preschool Program. *Journal of public Economics*, 94(1–2), 114–128.

Heller, A. S., Johnstone, T., Light, S. N., Peterson, M. J., Kolden, G. G., Kalin, N. H., and Davidson, R. J. (2013). Relationships between changes in sustained fronto-striatal connect-ivity and positive affect in major depression resulting from antidepressant treatment. *American Journal of Psychiatry*, 170(2), 197–206. doi:10.1176/appi.ajp.2012.12010014.

Helliwell, J. F. (2003). How's life? Combining individual and national variables to explain subjective well-being. *Economic Modelling*, 20(2), 331–360.

Helliwell, J. F. (2007). Well-being and social capital: Does suicide pose a puzzle? *Social Indicators Research*, 81(3), 455–496. doi:10.1007/s11205-006-0022-y.

Helliwell, J. F. (2021). Measuring and using happiness to support public policies. In M. T. Lee, L. D. Kubzansky and T. J. VanderWeele (Eds.), *Measuring Well-Being: Interdisciplinary Perspectives from the Social Sciences and the Humanities* (pp. 20–93). Oxford University Press.

Helliwell, J. F., Aknin, L. B., Shiplett, H., Huang, H., and Wang, S. (2018). Social capital and prosocial behaviour as sources of well-being. In E. Diener, S. Oishi and L. Tay (Eds.), *Handbook of Well-Being*. DEF.

Helliwell, J. F., and Huang, H. (2008). How's your government? International evidence linking good government and well-being. *British Journal of Political Science*, 38(4), 595–619.

Helliwell, J. F., Huang, H., Grover, S., and Wang, S. (2014). Good governance and national well-being: What are the linkages? OECD Working Papers on Public Governance, No. 25.

Helliwell, J. F., Huang, H., Grover, S., and Wang, S. (2018). Empirical linkages between good governance and national well-being. *Journal of Comparative Economics*, 46(4), 1332–1346.

Helliwell, J. F., Huang, H. and Wang, S. (2016). The distribution of world happiness. In J. F. Helliwell, R. Layard and J. Sachs (Eds.). *World Happiness Report 2016* (pp. 8–49). Sustainable Development Solutions Network.

Helliwell, J. F., Huang, H., and Wang, S. (2017). Social Foundations of World Happiness. In J. F. Helliwell, R. Layard and J. Sachs (Eds.), *World Happiness Report 2017* (pp. 8–47). Sustainable Development Solutions Network.

Helliwell, J. F., Huang, H., and Wang, S. (2019). Changing world happiness. In J. F. Helliwell, R. Layard and J. Sachs (Eds.). *World Happiness Report 2019* (pp. 11–46). Sustainable Development Solutions Network.

Helliwell, J. F., Huang, H., Wang, S., and Norton, M. (2020). Social environments for world happiness. In J. F. Helliwell, R. Layard, J. Sachs and J. E. De Neve (Eds.). *World Happiness Report 2020* (pp. 13–45). Sustainable Development Solutions Network.

Helliwell, J. F., Huang, H., Wang, S., and Norton, M. (2021). World happiness, trust and deaths under COVID-19. In J. F. Helliwell, R. Layard, J. Sachs and J. E. De Neve, (Eds.). *World Happiness Report 2021* (pp. 13–56). Sustainable Development Solutions Network.

Helliwell, J. F., Huang, H., Wang, S., and Shiplett, H. (2018). International migration and world happiness. In J. F. Helliwell, R. Layard and J. Sachs (Eds.). *World Happiness Report 2018* (pp. 13–44). Sustainable Development Solutions Network.

Helliwell, J. F., Layard, R., and Sachs, J. (2012). *World Happiness Report*. Sustainable Development Solutions Network.

Helliwell, J. F., Layard, R., and Sachs, J. (Eds.). (2018). *World Happiness Report 2018*. New York: Sustainable Development Solutions Network.

Helliwell, J. F., and Putnam, R. D. (2004). The social context of well–being. *Philosophical Transactions of the Royal Society of London. Series B: Biological Sciences*, 359(1449), 1435–1446.

Helliwell, J. F., and Wang, S. (2010). Trust and well-being (No. w15911). National Bureau of Economic Research.

Helliwell, J. F., and Wang, S. (2012). The state of world happiness. In J. F. Helliwell, R. Layard and J. Sachs (Eds.). *World Happiness Report 2012* (pp. 10–57). Sustainable Development Solutions Network.

Helliwell, J. F., and Wang, S. (2014). Weekends and subjective well-being. *Social Indicators Research*, 116(2), 389–407.

Herrin, J., Witters, D., Roy, B., Riley, C., Liu, D., and Krumholz, H. M. (2018). Population well-being and electoral shifts. *PloSOne*, 13(3), e0193401.

Hetschko, C. (2016). On the misery of losing self-employment. *Small Business Economics*, 47 (2), 461–478.

Hetschko, C., Knabe, A., and Schöb, R. (2019). Looking back in anger? Retirement and unemployment scarring. *Demography*, 56(3), 1105–1129.

Hetschko, C., Knabe, A., and Schöb, R. (2021). Happiness, work, and identity (No. 783). GLO Discussion Paper.

Hicks, J. R. (1940). The valuation of the social income. *Economica*, 7(26), 105–124.

Hills, T. T., Proto, E., Sgroi, D., and Seresinhe, C. I. (2019). Historical analysis of national subjective wellbeing using millions of digitized books. *Nature Human Behaviour*, 3(12), 1271–1275.

HM Treasury (2020). *The Green Book: Central Government Guidance on Appraisal and Evaluation*. OGL Press.

HM Treasury. (2021). *Wellbeing Guidance for Appraisal: Supplementary Green Book Guidance*. OGL Press

Hollon, S. D., and Beck, A. T. (2013). Cognitive and cognitive-behavioral therapies. *Bergin and Garfield's Handbook of Psychotherapy and Behavior Change*, 6, 393–442.

Holt-Lunstad, J., Smith, T. B., and Layton, J. B. (2010). Social relationships and mortality risk: A meta-analytic review. *PLoS Medicine*, 7(7), e1000316.

Holt-Lunstad, J., Smith, T. B., Baker, M., Harris, T., and Stephenson, D. (2015). Loneliness and social isolation as risk factors for mortality: A meta-analytic review. *Perspectives on Psychological Science*, 10(2), 227–237.

Hölzel, B. K., Carmody, J., Vangel, M., Congleton, C., Yerramsetti, S. M., Gard, T., and Lazar, S. W. (2011). Mindfulness practice leads to increases in regional brain gray matter density. *Psychiatry Research: Neuroimaging*, 191(1), 36–43.

Hoxby, C. M. (2000). The effects of class size on student achievement: New evidence from population variation. *Quarterly Journal of Economics*, 115(4), 1239–1285.

Humphrey, N., Lendrum, A., and Wigelsworth, M. (2010). Social and emotional aspects of learning (SEAL) programme in secondary schools: National evaluation. Department for Education. DFE Research Report (RR049).

Huppert, F. A. (2009). Psychological well-being: Evidence regarding its causes and consequences. *Applied Psychology: Health and Well-Being*, 1(2), 137–164.

Hutter, N., Schnurr, A., and Baumeister, H. (2010). Healthcare costs in patients with diabetes mellitus and comorbid mental disorders – a systematic review. *Diabetologia*, 53, 2470–2479. doi:10.1007/s00125-010-1873-y.

Iaffaldano, M. T., and Muchinsky, P. M. (1985). Job satisfaction and job performance: A meta-analysis. *Psychological Bulletin*, 97(2), 251.

Ialongo, N. S., Werthamer, L., Kellam, S. G., Brown, C. H., Wang, S., and Lin, Y. (1999). Proximal impact of two first-grade preventive interventions on the early risk behaviors for later substance abuse, depression, and antisocial behavior. *American Journal of Community Psychology*, 27(5), 599–641.

Idstad, M., Torvik, F. A., Borren, I., Rognmo, K., Røysamb, E., and Tambs, K. (2015). Mental distress predicts divorce over 16 years: The HUNT study. *BMC Public Health*, 15(1), 1–10.

Ifcher, J., Zarghamee, H., and Graham, C. (2018). Local neighbors as positives, regional neighbors as negatives: Competing channels in the relationship between others' income, health, and happiness. *Journal of Health Economics*, 57, 263–276.

Inglehart, R. F., and Norris, P. (2016). Trump, Brexit, and the rise of populism: Economic have-nots and cultural backlash. SSRN Papers.

Inglehart, R. F., and Norris, P. (2017). Trump and the populist authoritarian parties: The silent revolution in reverse. *Perspectives on Politics*, 15(2), 443–454.

International Labour Organization (2018). *Women and Men in the Informal Economy: A Statistical Picture*, 3rd ed. International Labour Organization.

Isen, A. M., Daubman, K. A., and Nowicki, G. P. (1987). Positive affect facilitates creative problem solving. *Journal of Personality and Social Psychology*, 52(6), 1122.

Ivlevs, A., and Veliziotis, M. (2018). Local-level immigration and life satisfaction: The EU enlargement experience in England and Wales. *Environment and Planning A: Economy and Space*, 50(1), 175–193.

Jacobs, T. L., Epel, E. S., Lin, J., Blackburn, E. H., Wolkowitz, O. M., Bridwell, D. A., . . . and Saron, C. D. (2011). Intensive meditation training, immune cell telomerase activity, and psychological mediators. *Psychoneuroendocrinology*, 36(5), 664–681.

Jahoda, M. (1981). Work, employment, and unemployment: Values, theories, and approaches in social research. *American Psychologist*, 36(2), 184.

Jaidka, K., Giorgi, S., Schwartz, H. A., Kern, M. L., Ungar, L. H., and Eichstaedt, J. C. (2020). Estimating geographic subjective well-being from Twitter: A comparison of dictionary and data-driven language methods. *Proceedings of the National Academy of Sciences*, 117(19), 10165–10171.

Jakobsson, N., Persson, M., and Svensson, M. (2013). Class-size effects on adolescents' mental health and well-being in Swedish schools. *Education Economics*, 21(3), 248–263.

Jamshidi, J., Williams, L. M., Schofield, P. R., Park, H. R., Montalto, A., Chilver, M. R., . . . and Gatt, J. M. (2020). Diverse phenotypic measurements of wellbeing: Heritability, temporal stability and the variance explained by polygenic scores. *Genes, Brain and Behavior*, 19(8), e12694.

Jebb, A. T., Tay, L., Diener, E., and Oishi, S. (2018). Happiness, income satiation and turning points around the world. *Nature Human Behaviour*, 2(1), 33–38.

Jefferson, T. (1809). Thomas Jefferson to the Republicans of Washington County, Maryland, 31 March 1809. Founders Online. https://founders.archives.gov/documents/Jefferson/03-01-02-0088.

Jennings, P. A., and Greenberg, M. T. (2009). The prosocial classroom: Teacher social and emotional competence in relation to student and classroom outcomes. *Review of Educational Research*, 79(1), 491–525.

Judge, T. A., Thoresen, C. J., Bono, J. E., and Patton, G. K. (2001). The job satisfaction–job performance relationship: A qualitative and quantitative review. *Psychological Bulletin*, 127(3), 376.

Kahneman, D. (2011). *Thinking, Fast and Slow*. Allen Lane.

Kahneman, D., Knetsch, J. L., and Thaler, R. H. (1990). Experimental tests of the endowment effect and the Coase theorem. *Journal of Political Economy*, 98(6), 1325–1348.

Kahneman, D., Krueger, A. B., Schkade, D. A., Schwarz, N., and Stone, A. A. (2004). A survey method for characterizing daily life experience: The day reconstruction method. *Science*, 306 (5702), 1776–1780.

Kahneman, D., Ritov, I., and Schkade, D. A. (2000). Economic preferences or attitude expressions? An analysis of dollar responses to public issues. In D. Kahneman and A. Tversky (Eds.). *Choices, Values and Frames*. Cambridge University Press; Russell Sage Foundation.

Kaiser, C., and Vendrik, M. C. M. (2020). How threatening are transformations of happiness scales to subjective wellbeing research? INET Oxford Working Paper No. 2020-19.

Kaldor, N. (1939). Welfare propositions of economics and interpersonal comparisons of utility. *The Economic Journal*, 549–552.

Kamerāde, D., Wang, S., Burchell, B., Balderson, S. U., and Coutts, A. (2019). A shorter working week for everyone: How much paid work is needed for mental health and well-being? *Social Science & Medicine*, 241, 112353.

Katon, W. J. (2003). Clinical and health services relationships between major depression, depressive symptoms, and general medical illness. *Society of Biological Psychiatry*, 54, 216–226. doi:10.1016/S0006-3223903)00273-7.

Katz, L. F., and Krueger, A. B. (2019). The rise and nature of alternative work arrangements in the United States, 1995–2015. *ILR Review*, 72(2), 382–416.

Kellam, S. G., Mackenzie, A. C., Brown, C. H., Poduska, J. M., Wang, W., Petras, H., and Wilcox, H. C. (2011). The good behavior game and the future of prevention and treatment. *Addiction Science & Clinical Practice*, 6(1), 73.

Kelly, E. L., Moen, P., Oakes, J. M., Fan, W., Okechukwu, C., Davis, K. D., . . . and Casper, L. M. (2014). Changing work and work-family conflict: Evidence from the work, family, and health network. *American Sociological Review*, 79(3), 485–516.

Kendler, K. S., Walters, E. E., Neale, M. C., Kessler, R. C., Heath, A. C., and Eaves, L. J. (1995). The structure of the genetic and environmental risk factors for six major psychiatric disorders in women: Phobia, generalized anxiety disorder, panic disorder, bulimia, major depression, and alcoholism. *Archives of General Psychiatry*, 52(5), 374–383.

Kessler, J. B., McClellan, A., Nesbit, J., and Schotter, A. (2021). Short-term fluctuations in incidental happiness and economic decision-making: Experimental evidence from a sports bar. *Experimental Economics*, 1–29.

Kessler, R. C., Berglund, P., Demler, O., Jin, R., Merikangas, K. R., and Walters, E. E. (2005a). Lifetime prevalence and age-of-onset distributions of DSM-IV disorders in the National Comorbidity Survey Replication. *Archives of General Psychiatry*, 62, 593–602.

Kessler, R. C., Chiu, W. T., Demler, O., Merikangas, K. R., and Walters, E. E. (2005b). Prevalence, severity, and comorbidity of 12-month DSM-IV disorders in the National Comorbidity Survey Replication. *Archives of General Psychiatry*, 62(6), 617–627.

Keyes, C. L., Shmotkin, D., and Ryff, C. D. (2002). Optimizing well-being: The empirical encounter of two traditions. *Journal of Personality and Social Psychology*, 82(6), 1007–1022.

Kiecolt-Glaser, J. K., Marucha, P.T., Malarkey, W.B., Mercado, A. M., Glaser R. (1995). Slowing of wound healing by psychological stress. *Lancet*. 346 (8984): 1194–1196.

Kim-Cohen, J., Caspi, A., Moffitt, T. E., Harrington, H., Milne, B. J., and Poulton, R. (2003). Prior juvenile diagnoses in adults with mental disorder: Developmental follow-back of a prospective-longitudinal cohort. *Archives of General Psychiatry*, 60, 709–17.

Kind, M., and Haisken-DeNew, J. P. (2012). Unexpected victims: How parents' unemployment affects their children's life satisfaction (No. wp2012n02). Melbourne Institute of Applied Economic and Social Research. The University of Melbourne.

King, D., Browne, J., Layard, R., O'Donnell, G., Rees, M., Stern, N., and Turner, A. (2015). A Global Apollo Programme to combat climate change.

King, V. (2016). *10 Keys to Happier Living*. Headline.

Kirby, J. N., Tellegen, C. L., and Steindl, S. R. (2017). A meta-analysis of compassion-based interventions: Current state of knowledge and future directions. *Behavior Therapy*, 48(6), 778–792.

Kling, J., Ludwig, J., and Katz, L. (2005). Neighborhood effects on crime for female and male youth: Evidence from a randomized housing voucher experiment. *Quarterly Journal of Economics*, 120(1), 87–130.

Knabe, A., and Rätzel, S. (2011). Quantifying the psychological costs of unemployment: The role of permanent income. *Applied Economics*, 43(21), 2751–2763.

Knabe, A., Schöb, R., and Weimann, J. (2017). The subjective well-being of workfare participants: Insights from a day reconstruction survey. *Applied Economics*, 49(13), 1311–1325.

Knack, S. (2001). Trust, associational life and economic performance. In J. Helliwell and A. Bonikowska (Eds.), *The Contribution of Human and Social Capital to Sustained Economic Growth and Well-Being*. HRDC; OECD.

Knies, G. (2012). Life satisfaction and material well-being of children in the UK (No. 2012-15). ISER working paper series.

Kok, B. E., Coffey, K. A., Cohn, M. A., Catalino, L. I., Vacharkulksemsuk, T., Algoe, S. B., . . . and Fredrickson, B. L. (2013). How positive emotions build physical health: Perceived positive social connections account for the upward spiral between positive emotions and vagal tone. *Psychological Science*, 24(7), 1123–1132.

Kral, T. R., Davis, K., Korponay, C., Hirshberg, M. J., Hoel, R., Tello, L. Y., . . . and Davidson, R. J. (2022). Absence of structural brain changes from mindfulness-based stress reduction: Tow combined randomized controlled trials. *Science Advances*, 8(20), n.p.

Krekel, C., De Neve, J. E., Fancourt, D., and Layard, R. (2020) A local community course that raises mental wellbeing and pro-sociality. CEP Discussion Papers (1671). Centre for Economic Performance, London School of Economics.

Krekel, C., Kolbe, J., and Wüstemann, H. (2016). The greener, the happier? The effect of urban land use on residential well-being. *Ecological Economics*, 121, 117–127.

Krekel, C., and MacKerron, G. (2020). How environmental quality affects our happiness. In D. E. Neve, J. F. Helliwell, R. Layard and J. Sachs (Eds.). *World Happiness Report 2020*. Sustainable Development Solutions Network.

Krekel, C., Ward, G., and De Neve, J. E. (2019). Employee well-being, productivity, and firm performance: evidence and case studies. In Global Happiness and Well-Being Policy Report.

Krueger, A. B. (2003). Economic considerations and class size. *Economic Journal* 113(485), F34–F63.

Krueger, A. B. (2007). Are we having fun yet? Categorizing and evaluating changes in time allocation. Brookings Papers on Economic Activity. No. 2, 193–217.

Krueger, A. B. (Ed.). (2009). *Measuring the Subjective Well-Being of Nations: National Accounts of Time Use and Well-Being*. University of Chicago Press.

Krueger, A. B., and Stone, A. A. (2008). Assessment of pain: A community-based diary survey in the USA. *The Lancet*, 371(9623), 1519–1525.

Krueger, A. B., and D. Schkade (2008). The reliability of subjective well-being measures. *Journal of Public Economics*, 92, 1833–1845.

Kruse, D. L., Freeman, R. B., and Blasi, J. R. (2010). *Shared Capitalism at Work: Employee Ownership, Profit and Gain Sharing, and Broad-Based Stock Options*. University of Chicago Press.

Kubzansky, L. D., Huffman, J. C., Boehm, J. K., Hernandez, R., Kim, E. S., Koga, H. K., ... and Labarthe, D. R. (2018). Positive psychological well-being and cardiovascular disease: JACC health promotion series. *Journal of the American College of Cardiology*, 72(12), 1382–1396

Kuo, F. E., and Sullivan, W. C. (2001b). Aggression and violence in the inner city: Effect.s of environment via mental fatigue. *Environment and Behavior*, 33(4), 543–571.

Kuo, F. E., and Sullivan, W. C. (2001b). Environment and crime in the inner city: Does vegetation reduce crime? *Environment and Behavior*, 33(3), 343–367.

Kuyken, W., Ball, S., Crane, S., Canuli, P., Jones, B., Montero-Marin, J., ... MYRIAD Team. (2022). Effectiveness of universal school-based mindfulness training compared with normal school provision on teacher mental health and school climate: Results of the MYRIAD cluster randomised controlled trial. *Evidence-Based Mental Health*, 25(3), 125–134.

Kuznets, S. (1934). *National Income, 1929–1932*. NBER.

Lades, L. K., Laffan, K., Daly, M., and Delaney, L. (2020). Daily emotional well-being during the COVID-19 pandemic. *British Journal of Health Psychology*, 25(4), 902–911.

Laibson, D. (1998). Life-cycle Consumption and hyperbolic discount functions. *European Economic Review Papers and Proceedings* 42(3–5), 861–871.

Lane, T. (2017). How does happiness relate to economic behaviour? A review of the literature. *Journal of Behavioral and Experimental Economics* 68, 62–78.

Langella, M., and Manning, A. (2016). Diversity and neighbourhood satisfaction. *Economic Journal*, 129(624), 3219–3255.

Langenkamp, A. (2021). Lonely hearts, empty booths? The relationship between loneliness, reported voting behavior and boting as civic duty. *Social Science Quarterly*, 102(4), 1239–1254.

Layard, R. (1980). Human satisfactions and public policy. *The Economic Journal*, 90(360), 737–750.

Layard, R. (2006). Happiness and public policy: A challenge to the profession. *Economic Journal*, 116(March), C24–C33.

Layard, R., and Clark, D. M. (2014). *Thrive: The Power of Evidence-Based Psychological Therapies*. Penguin.

Layard, R., and Dunn, J., (2009). *A Good Childhood: Searching for Values in a Competitive Age*. Penguin UK.

Layard, R., and Glaister, S. (1994). *Cost-Benefit Analysis*. Cambridge University Press.

Layard, R., Nickell, S., and Jackman, R. (1991). *Unemployment: Macroeconomic Performance and the Labour Market*. Oxford University Press.

Layard, R., Nickell, S., and Jackman, R. (2005). *Unemployment: Macroeconomic Performance and the Labour Market*. Oxford University Press.

Layard, R., Mayraz, G., and Nickell, S. J. (2008). The marginal utility of income. *Journal of Public Economics*, 92(8–9), 1846–1857.

Layard, R., Mayraz, G., and Nickell, S. J. (2010). Does relative income matter? Are the critics right? In E. Diener, J. F. Helliwell and D. Kahneman (Eds.). *International Differences in Well-Being* (pp. 139–165). Oxford University Press.

Layard, R., and Oparina, E. (2021). Living long and living well: The WELLBY approach. In J. F. Helliwell, R. Layard, J. Sachs and J. E. De. Neve (Eds.). *World Happiness Report 2021* (p. 191). Sustainable Development Solutions Network.

Layard, R., and Walters, A. A. (1978). *Microeconomic Theory*. McGraw-Hill.

Layard, R., and Ward, G. (2020). *Can We Be happier? Evidence and Ethics*. Penguin UK.

Lazear, E. P. (2000). Performance pay and productivity. *American Economic Review*, 90(5), 1346–1361. doi: 10.1257/aer.90.5.1346.

Lazear, E. P., Shaw, K. L., and Stanton, C. T. (2015). The value of bosses. *Journal of Labor Economics*, 33(4), 823–861.

Lee, H., and Singh, G. K. (2020). Inequalities in life expectancy and all-cause mortality in the United States by levels of happiness and life satisfaction: A longitudinal study. *International Journal of Maternal and Child Health and AIDS*, 9(3), 305.

Leichsenring F., Salzer, S., Jaeger, U., Kächele, H., Kreische, R., Leweke, F., . . . and Leibing E. (2010). Short-term psychodynamic psychotherapy and cognitive-behavioral therapy in generalized anxiety disorder: A randomized, controlled trial. *Focus*, 8(1), 66–74.

LePine, J. A., Podsakoff, N. P., and LePine, M. A. (2005). A meta-analytic test of the challenge stressor–hindrance stressor framework: An explanation for inconsistent relationships among stressors and performance. *Academy of Management Journal*, 48(5), 764–775.

Lepinteur, A. (2019). The shorter workweek and worker wellbeing: Evidence from Portugal and France. *Labour Economics*, 58, 204–220.

Levinson, A. (2012). Valuing public goods using happiness data: The case of air quality. *Journal of Public Economics*, 96(9–10), 869–880.

Lewis-Beck, M. S., and Nadeau, R. (2011). Economic voting theory: Testing new dimensions. *Electoral Studies*, 30(2), 288–294.

Lewis-Beck, M. S., and Stegmaier, M. (2018). Economic voting. In R. D. Congelton, B. Grofman and S. Voigt (Eds.). *The Oxford Handbook of Public Choice* (vol. 1, p. 247). Oxford University Press.

Liberini, F., Oswald, A. J., Proto, E., and Redoano, M. (2017b). Was Brexit caused by the unhappy and the old? (No. 11059). Institute of Labor Economics (IZA).

Liberini, F., Redoano, M., and Proto, E. (2017a). Happy voters. *Journal of Public Economics*, 146, 41–57.

Lieberman, M. D. (2013). *Social: Why Our Brains Are Wired to Connect*. Oxford University Press.

Lim, C., and Putnam, R. D. (2010). Religion, social networks, and life satisfaction. *American Sociological Review*, 75(6), 914–933.

Lim, L., Radua, J., and Rubia, K. (2014). Gray matter abnormalities in childhood maltreatment: A voxel-wise meta-analysis. *American Journal of Psychiatry*, 171(8), 854–863.

Lindholm, A. (2020). Does subjective well-being affect political participation? *Swiss Journal of Sociology*, 46(3), 467–488.

Lindqvist, E., Östling, R., and Cesarini, D. (2020). Long-run effects of lottery wealth on psychological well-being. *The Review of Economic Studies*, 87(6), 2703–2726.

List, J. A. (2003). Does market experience eliminate market anomalies? *The Quarterly Journal of Economics*, 118(1), 41–71.

Loewenstein, G., O'Donoghue, T., and Rabin, M. (2003). Projection bias in predicting future utility. *The Quarterly Journal of Economics*, 118(4), 1209–1248.

Loewenstein, G., and Schkade, D. (1999). Wouldn't it be nice? Predicting future feelings. In D. Kahneman, R. Diener and N. Schwarz (Eds). *Well-Being: The Foundations of Hedonic Psychology* (pp. 85–105). Russell Sage Foundation.

Longhi, S. (2014). Cultural diversity and subjective well-being. *IZA Journal of Migration*, 3(1), 13.

Lordan, G., and McGuire, A. J. (2019). Widening the high school curriculum to include soft skill training: Impacts on health, behaviour, emotional wellbeing and occupational aspirations. CEP Discussion Paper 1630, Centre for Economic Performance, London School of Economics.

Lorenzini, J. (2015). Subjective well-being and political participation: A comparison of unemployed and employed youth. *Journal of Happiness Studies*, 16(2), 381–404.

Ludwig, J., Duncan, G. J., Gennetian, L. A., Katz, L. F., Kessler, R. C., Kling, J. R., and Sanbonmatsu, L. (2012). Neighborhood effects on the long-term well-being of low-income adults. *Science*, 337(6101), 1505–1510.

Ludwig, J., Duncan, G. J., Gennetian, L. A., Katz, L. F., Kessler, R. C., Kling, J. R., and Sanbonmatsu, L. (2013). Long-term neighborhood effects on low-income families: Evidence from moving to opportunity. *American Economic Review*, 103(3), 226–231.

Luechinger, S. (2009). Valuing air quality using the life satisfaction approach. *Economic Journal*, 119, 482–515.

Lykken, D., and Tellegen, A. (1996). Happiness is a stochastic phenomenon. *Psychological Science*, 7(3), 186–189.

Lyubomirsky, S. (2008). *The How of Happiness: A Scientific Approach to Getting the Life You Want*. Penguin Press.

Lyubomirsky, S., King, L., and Diener, E. (2005a). The benefits of frequent positive affect: Does happiness lead to success? *Psychological Bulletin*, 131(6), 803.

Lyubomirsky, S., Sheldon, K. M., and Schkade, D. (2005b). Pursuing happiness: The architecture of sustainable change. *Review of General Psychology*, 9(2), 111–131.

Macchia, L., and Oswald, A. J. (2021). Physical pain, gender, and the state of the economy in 146 nations. *Social Science & Medicine*, 287, 114332.

Maddison, D., and Rehdanz, K. (2011). The impact of climate on life satisfaction. *Ecological Economics*, 70(12), 2437–2445.

Maguire, E. A., Gadian, D. G., Johnsrude, I. S., Good, C. D., Ashburner, J., Frackowiak, R. S., and Frith, C. D. (2000). Navigation-related structural change in the hippocampi of taxi drivers. *Proceedings of the National Academy of Sciences*, 97(8), 4398–4403.

Marcus, J. (2013). The effect of unemployment on the mental health of spouses: Evidence from plant closures in Germany. *Journal of Health Economics*, 32(3), 546–558.

Martela, F., Greve, B., Rothstein, B., and Saari, J. (2020). The Nordic exceptionalism: what explains why the Nordic Countries are constantly among the happiest in the world. J. F. Helliwell, R. Layard, J. D. Sachs and J. E. De Neve (Eds.). *World Happiness Report* (pp. 128–145). Sustainable Development Solutions Network.

Martela, F., and Riekki, T. J. (2018). Autonomy, competence, relatedness, and beneficence: A multicultural comparison of the four pathways to meaningful work. *Frontiers in Psychology*, 9, 1157.

Marx, K. (1947). Wage-labour and capital. Lecture to the German Workingmen's Club of Brussels in 1847.

Mas, A., and Pallais, A. (2017). Valuing alternative work arrangements. *American Economic Review*, 107(12), 3722–3759.

Maslow, A. H. (1948). 'Higher' and 'lower' needs. *The Journal of Psychology*, 25(2), 433–436.

Maslow, A. H. (1954). The instinctoid nature of basic needs. *Journal of Personality*, 22, 326–347.

Mazzucato, M. (2015). *The Entrepreneurial State: Debunking Public vs. Private Sector Myths* (Vol. 1): Anthem Press.

McHugh, R. K., Whitton, S. W., Peckham, A. D., Welge, J. A., and Otto, M. W. (2013). Patient preference for psychological versus pharmacologic treatment of psychiatric disorders: a meta-analytic review. *Journal of Clinical Psychiatry*, 74(6), 595–602.

McManus, S., Bebbington, P., Jenkins, R., and Brugha, T. (2016). Mental health and wellbeing in England. Adult Psychiatric Morbidity Survey 2014.

Meade, J. (1955). *Theory of International Economic Policy (Vol. 2): Trade and Welfare*. Oxford University Press.

Meier, S., and Stutzer, A. (2008). Is volunteering rewarding in itself? *Economica*, 75(1), 39–59.

Melhuish, E., Belsky, J., Leyland, A. H., Barnes, J., and National Evaluation of Sure Start Research Team. (2008). Effects of fully-established Sure Start Local Programmes on 3-year-old children and their families living in England: a quasi-experimental observational study. *The Lancet*, 372(9650), 1641–1647.

Mellor-Marsá, B., Miret, M., Abad, F. J., Chatterji, S., Olaya, B., Tobiasz-Adamczyk, B., . . . and Caballero, F. F. (2016). Measurement invariance of the day reconstruction method: Results from the COURAGE in Europe project. *Journal of Happiness Studies*, 17(5), 1769–1787.

Mendolia, S. (2014). The impact of husband's job loss on partners' mental health. *Review of Economics of the Household*, 12(2), 277–294.

Menesini, E., and Salmivalli, C. (2017). Bullying in schools: The state of knowledge and effective interventions. *Psychology, Health & Medicine*, 22(supp. 1), 240–253.

Messner, S. F., and Rosenfeld, R. (1997). Political restraint of the market and levels of criminal homicide: A cross-national application of institutional-anomie theory. *Social Forces*, 75(4), 1393–1416.

Methot, J. R., Lepine, J. A., Podsakoff, N. P., and Christian, J. S. (2016). Are workplace friendships a mixed blessing? Exploring tradeoffs of multiplex relationships and their associations with job performance. *Personnel Psychology*, 69(2), 311–355.

Metzler, H., Rimé, B., Pellert, M., Niederkrotenthaler, T., Di Natale, A., and Garcia, D. (2021). Collective emotions during the COVID-19 outbreak. doi.org/10.31234/osf.io/qejxv.

Michel, C., Sovinsky, M., Proto, E., and Oswald, A. J. (2019). Advertising as a major source of human dissatisfaction: Cross-national evidence on one million Europeans. In M. Rojas (Ed.). *The Economics of Happiness* (pp. 217–239). Springer.

Michel, J.-B., Shen, Y. K., Aiden, A. P., Veres, A., Gray, M. K., Pickett, J. P., . . . and Aiden, E. L. (2011). *Quantitative Analysis of Culture Using Millions of Digitized Books*. 331(6014), 176–182. doi:10.1126/science.1199644.

Michels, N., Van de Wiele, T., Fouhy, F., O'Mahony, S., Clarke, G., & Keane, J. (2019). Gut microbiome patterns depending on children's psychosocial stress: Reports versus biomarkers. *Brain, Behavior, and Immunity*, 80, 751–762.

Mistry, R. S., Vandewater, E. A., Huston, A. C., and McLoyd, V. C. (2002). Economic well-being and children's social adjustment: The role of family process in an ethnically diverse low-income sample. *Child Development*, 73(3), 935–951.

Moen, P., Kelly, E. L., Fan, W., Lee, S. R., Almeida, D., Kossek, E. E., and Buxton, O. M. (2016). Does a flexibility/support organizational initiative improve high-tech employees' well-being? Evidence from the work, family, and health network. *American Sociological Review*, 81(1), 134–164.

Moen, P., Kelly, E. L., Lee, S. R., Oakes, J. M., Fan, W., Bray, J., . . . and Buxton, O. (2017). Can a flexibility/support initiative reduce turnover intentions and exits? Results from the work, family, and health network. *Social Problems*, 64(1), 53–85.

Montgomery, C. (2013). *Happy City: Transforming Our Lives through Urban Design*. Macmillan.

Moore, D., Benham-Clarke, S., Kenchington, R., Boyle, C., Ford, T., Hayes, R., and Rogers, M. (2019). Improving behaviour in schools. Evidence Review. Education Endowment Foundation. London.

Moore, S. E., Norman, R. E., Suetani, S., Thomas, H. J., Sly, P. D., and Scott, J. G. (2017). Consequences of bullying victimization in childhood and adolescence: A systematic review and meta-analysis. *World Journal of Psychiatry*, 7(1), 60.

Mudde, C. (2007). *Populist Radical Right Parties in Europe*. Cambridge University Press.

Muldoon, J. (2012). The Hawthorne legacy: A reassessment of the impact of the Hawthorne studies on management scholarship, 1930–1958. *Journal of Management History*, 18(1), 105–119.

Murabito, J. M., Zhao, Q., Larson, M. G., Rong, J., Lin, H., Benjamin, E. J., . . . and Lunetta, K. L. (2018). Measures of biologic age in a community sample predict mortality and age-related disease: The Framingham Offspring Study. *The Journals of Gerontology: Series A*, 73(6), 757–762.

Murthy, V. H. (2020). *Together: The Healing Power of Human Connection in a Sometimes Lonely World*. Harper Wave.

Mykletun, A., Bjerkeset, O., Prince, M., Dewey, M., and Stewart, R. (2009). Levels of anxiety and depression as predictors of mortality: the HUNT study. *The British Journal of Psychiatry*, 195(2), 118–125.

Napier, J. L., and Jost, J. T. (2008). Why are conservatives happier than liberals? *Psychological Science*, 19(6), 565–572.

Naylor, C., Parsonage, M., McDaid, D., Knapp, M., Fossey, M., and Galea, A. (2012). Long-term conditions and mental health: The cost of co-morbidities. www.kingsfund.org.uk/sites/files/kf/field/field_publication_file/long-term-conditions-mental-health-cost-comorbidities-naylor-feb12.pdf.

Nelson, C. A., Zeanah, C. H., Fox, N. A., Marshall, P. J., Smyke, A. T., and Guthrie, D. (2007). Cognitive recovery in socially deprived young children: The Bucharest Early Intervention Project. *Science*, 318(5858), 1937–1940.

Ng, J. W. J., Vaithilingam, S., and Rangel, G. J. (2017). The role of life satisfaction on election voting preferences in Malaysia. *Asian Journal of Social Science*, 45(1–2), 149–175.

NHS Digital (2021). Annual Report on IAPT services for 2020/21. UK. https://digital.nhs.uk/data-and-information/publications/statistical/psychological-therapies-annual-reports-on-the-use-of-iapt-services/annual-report-2020-21.

Nicholson, A., Kuper, H., and Hemingway, H. (2006). Depression as an aetiologic and prognostic factor in coronary heart disease: A meta-analysis of 6,362 events among 146,538 participants in 54 observational studies. *European Heart Journal*, 27, 2763–2774. doi:10.1093/eurheartj/ehl338.

Nikolova, M., and Ayhan, S. H. (2019). Your spouse is fired! How much do you care? *Journal of Population Economics*, 32(3), 799–844.

Nikolova, M., and Nikolaev, B. N. (2021). Family matters: The effects of parental unemployment in early childhood and adolescence on subjective well-being later in life. *Journal of Economic Behavior & Organization*, 181, 312–331.

Nowakowski, A. (2021). Do unhappy citizens vote for populism? *European Journal of Political Economy*, 68, 101985.

Nozick, R. (1974). *Anarchy, State, and Utopia*. Basic Books.

Nussbaum, M., and Sen, A. (Eds.). (1993). *The Quality of Life*. Clarendon Press.

O'Connor, K. J. (2017). Happiness and welfare state policy around the world. *Review of Behavioral Economics*, 4(4), 397–420.

Ochsen, C., and Welsch, H. (2012). Who benefits from labor market institutions? Evidence from surveys of life satisfaction. *Journal of Economic Psychology*, 33(1), 112–124.

Odean, T. (1998). Are investors reluctant to realize their losses? *The Journal of Finance*, 53(5), 1775–1798.

Odermatt, R., and Stutzer, A. (2015). Smoking bans, cigarette prices and life satisfaction. *Journal of Health Economics*, 44, 176–194.

Odermatt, R., and Stutzer, A. (2019). (Mis-) predicted subjective well-being following life events. *Journal of the European Economic Association*, 17(1), 245–283.

O'Donnell, G., Deaton, A., Durand, M., Halpern, D., and Layard, R. (2014). Wellbeing and policy. Legatum Institute, London.

OECD (2013). OECD Guidelines on measuring subjective well-being.

OECD (2017). PISA 2015 Results (Volume III. Wellbeing).

OECD (2018). PISA 2018 Results (Volume III).

OECD (2020). Job retention schemes during the COVID-19 lockdown and beyond. Paris: Organization for Economic Co-operation and Development. www.oecd.org/coronavirus/policy-responses/job-retention-schemes-during-the-covid-19-lockdown-and-beyond-0853ba1d.

Ogbonnaya, C., and Daniels, K. (2017). Good work, wellbeing and changes in performance outcomes: Illustrating the effects of good people management practices with an analysis of the National Health Service.

Oishi, S., Schimmack, U., and Diener, E. (2012). Progressive taxation and the subjective well-being of nations. *Psychological Science*, 23(1), 86–92.

Ojeda, C. (2015). Depression and political participation. *Social Science Quarterly*, 96(5), 1226–1243.

Okbay, A., Baselmans, B. M., De Neve, J. E., Turley, P., Nivard, M. G., Fontana, M. A., ... and Rich, S. S. (2016). Genetic variants associated with subjective well-being, depressive symptoms, and neuroticism identified through genome-wide analyses. *Nature Genetics*, 48(6), 624–633.

Onraet, E., Van Assche, J., Roets, A., Haesevoets, T., and Van Hiel, A. (2017). The happiness gap between conservatives and liberals depends on country-level threat: A worldwide multilevel study. *Social Psychological and Personality Science*, 8(1), 11–19.

Onraet, E., Van Hiel, A., & Dhont, K. (2013). The relationship between right-wing ideological attitudes and psychological well-being. *Personality and Social Psychology Bulletin*, 39(4), 509–522.

ONS (2018). Estimating the impact urban green space has on property prices. www.ons.gov.uk/economy/nationalaccounts/uksectoraccounts/compendium/economicreview/july2018/estimatingtheimpacturbangreenspacehasonpropertyprice.

Orben, A. (2020). Teenagers, screens and social media: A narrative review of reviews and key studies. *Social Psychiatry and Psychiatric Epidemiology*, 55(4), 407–414.

Ortiz-Ospina, E., and Roser, M. (2020). Loneliness and Social Connections. OurWorldInData.org. www.ourworldindata.org/social-connections-and-loneliness.

Oswald, A. J. (2008). On the curvature of the reporting function from objective reality to subjective feelings. *Economics Letters*, 100(3), 369–372.

Oswald, A. J., Proto, E., and Sgroi, D. (2015). Happiness and productivity. *Journal of Labour Economics*, 33(4), 789–822.

Otake, K., Shimai, S., Tanaka-Matsumi, J., Otsui, K., and Fredrickson, B. L. (2006). Happy people become happier through kindness: A counting kindnesses intervention. *Journal of Happiness Studies*, 7(3), 361–375.

Ott, J. C. (2010). Good governance and happiness in nations: Technical quality precedes democracy and quality beats size. *Journal of Happiness Studies*, 11(3), 353–368.

Ott, J. C. (2011). Government and happiness in 130 nations: Good governance fosters higher level and more equality of happiness. *Social Indicators Research*, 102(1), 3–22.

Pacek, A. C., and Radcliff, B. (2008). Welfare policy and subjective well-being across nations: An individual-level assessment. *Social Indicators Research*, 89(1), 179–191.

Pan, A., Sun, Q., Okereke, O. I., Rexrode, K. M., and Hu, F. B. (2011). Depression and risk of stroke morbidity and mortality: A meta-analysis and systematic review. *JAMA*, 306(11), 1241–1249.

Parfit, D. (1984). *Reasons and Persons*. Oxford University Press.

Pargament, K. I. (2002). The bitter and the sweet: An evaluation of the costs and benefits of religiousness. *Psychological Inquiry*, 13(3), 168–181.

Park, S., and Mattison, R. (2009). Therapeutic influences of plants in hospital rooms on surgical recovery. *Hortscience*, 44, 102–105.

Parks, G. (2000). The High/Scope Perry Preschool Project. Office of Juvenile Justice and Delinquency Prevention. Washington, DC, U.S. Department of Justice. October.

Patten, S. B., Williams, J. V. A., Lavorato, D. H., Modgill, G., Jetté, N., and Eliasziw, M. (2008). Major depression as a risk factor for chronic disease incidence: Longitudinal analyses in a general population cohort. *General Hospital Psychiatry*, 30, 407–413. doi:10.1016/j.genhosppsych.2008.05.001.

Paul, G. L. (1966). *Insight vs. Desensitisation in Psychotherapy: An Experiment in Anxiety Reduction*. Stanford University Press.

Perez-Truglia, R. (2015). A Samuelsonian validation test for happiness data. *Journal of Economic Psychology*, 49, 74–83.

Perez-Truglia, R. (2020). The effects of income transparency on well-being: Evidence from a natural experiment. *American Economic Review*, 110(4), 1019–1054.

Persson, T., and Tabellini, G. (2002). *Political Economics: Explaining Economic Policy*. MIT Press.

Peterson, C. (1999). Personal control and well-being. In D. Kahneman, E. Diener and N. Schwarz (Eds.). *Well-Being: The Foundation of Hedonic Psychology*. Russell Sage Foundation.

Pew Research Center (2017). Political typology reveals deep fissures on the Right and Left. Pew Research Center. www.pewresearch.org/politics/2017/10/24/political-typology-reveals-deep-fissures-on-the-right-and-left.

Pfeffer, J., and Davis-Blake, A. (1990). Unions and job satisfaction: An alternative view. *Work and Occupations*, 17(3): 259–283.

Pinker, S. (2011). *The Better Angels of Our Nature: The Decline of Violence in History and Its Causes*. Penguin Books.

Pinker, S. (2018). *Enlightenment Now: The Case for Reason, Science, Humanism, and Progress*. Viking.

Pirralha, A. (2018). The link between political participation and life satisfaction: A three wave causal analysis of the German SOEP household panel. *Social Indicators Research*, 138(2), 793–807.

Pleck, J. H., and Masciadrelli B. P. (2004). Paternal involvement by US residential fathers: Levels, sources, and consequences. In M. E. Lamb (Ed.), *The Role of the Father in Child Development* (pp. 222–271). John Wiley & Sons.

Plomin, R., DeFries, J. C., McClearn, G. E., and McGuffin, P. (2013). *Behavioral Genetics* (6th ed.). Worth.

Pluess, M. (Ed.). (2015). *Genetics of Psychological Well-Being: The Role of Heritability and Genetics in Positive Psychology*. Series in Positive Psychology. Oxford University Press.

Powdthavee, N., and Vernoit, J. (2013). Parental unemployment and children's happiness: A longitudinal study of young people's well-being in unemployed households. *Labour Economics*, 24, 253–263.

Pryce, J., Albertsen, K., and Nielsen, K. (2006). Evaluation of an open-rota system in a Danish psychiatric hospital: A mechanism for improving job satisfaction and work–life balance. *Journal of Nursing Management*, 14(4), 282–288.

Przybylski, A. K., and L. Bowes (2017). Cyberbullying and adolescent well-being in England: A population-based cross-sectional study. *The Lancet Child & Adolescent Health*, 1(1), 19–26.

Putnam, R. D. (2007). E Pluribus Unum: Diversity and community in the twenty-first century. The 2006 Johan Skytte Prize Lecture. *Scandinavian Political Studies*, 30(2), 137–174. doi:10.1111/j.1467-9477.2007.00176.x.

Rabin, M. (1998). Psychology and cconomics. *Journal of Economic Literature* 36: 11–46.

Rabin, M. (2000). Risk aversion and expected-utility theory: A calibration theorem. *Econometrica*, 68(5), 1281–1292.

Radcliff, B. (2001). Politics, markets, and life satisfaction: The political economy of human happiness. *American Political Science Review*, 939–952.

Radcliff, B. (2013). *The Political Economy of Human Happiness: How Voters' Choices Determine the Quality of Life*. Cambridge University Press.

Raichle, M. E., MacLeod, A. M., Snyder, A. Z., Powers, W. J., Gusnard, D. A., and Shulman, G. L. (2001). A default mode of brain function. *Proceedings of the National Academy of Sciences*, 98(2), 676–682.

Raphael, D. D. (1969). *British Moralists 1650–1800*. Clarendon Press.

Rath, T. (2006). *Vital Friends: The People You Can't Afford to Live Without*. Gallup Press.

Rawls, J. (1971). *A Theory of Justice*. Harvard University Press.

Ricard, M. (2015). *Altruism: The Power of Compassion to Change Yourself and the World*. Little, Brown and Company.

Rietveld, C. A., Cesarini, D., Benjamin, D. J., Koellinger, P. D., De Neve, J. E., Tiemeier, H., . . . and Bartels, M. (2013). Molecular genetics and subjective well-being. *Proceedings of the National Academy of Sciences*, 110(24), 9692–9697.

Riketta, M. (2008). The causal relation between job attitudes and performance: A meta-analysis of panel studies. *Journal of Applied Psychology*, 93(2), 472.

Rilling, J. K., Gutman, D. A., Zeh, T. R., Pagnoni, G., Berns, G. S., and Kilts, C. D. (2002). A neural basis for social cooperation. *Neuron*, 35(2), 395–405.

Robbins, L. (1932). The nature and significance of economic science. *The Philosophy of Economics: An Anthology*, 1, 73–99.

Roest, A. M., Martens, E. J., Denollet, J., and De Jonge, P. (2010). Prognostic association of anxiety post myocardial infarction with mortality and new cardiac events: A meta-analysis. *Psychosomatic Medicine*, 72, 563–569. doi:10.1097/PSY.0b013e181dbff97.

Rollman, B. L., Belnap, B. H., Mazumdar, S., Houck, P. R., Zhu, F., Gardner, W., . . . and Shear, M. K. (2005). A randomized trial to improve the quality of treatment for panic and generalized anxiety disorders in primary care. *Archives of General Psychiatry*, 62(12), 13321341.

Rosling, H. (2019). *Factfulness*. Flammarion.

Roth, A., and Fonagy, P. (Eds.). (2005). *What Works for Whom? A Critical Review of Psychotherapy Research*. 2nd ed. Guilford Press.

Rothbard, N. P., and Wilk, S. L. (2011). Waking up on the right or wrong side of the bed: Start-of-workday mood, work events, employee affect, and performance. *Academy of Management Journal*, 54(5), 959–980.

Røysamb, E., and Nes, R. B. (2018). The genetics of wellbeing. In E. Diener, S. Oishi and L. Tay. (Eds.). *Handbook of Well-Being*. DEF.

Røysamb, E., Nes, R. B., Czajkowski, N. O., and Vassend, O. (2018). Genetics, personality and wellbeing. A twin study of traits, facets and life satisfaction. *Scientific Reports*, 8(1), 1–13.

Rudolf, R., and Kang, S. J. (2015). Lags and leads in life satisfaction in Korea: When gender matters. *Feminist Economics*, 21(1), 136–163.

Runciman, W. G. (1966). *Relative Deprivation and Social Justice*. Routledge; Kegan Paul.

Rush, A. J., Beck, A. T., Kovacs, M., and Hollon, S. (1977). Comparative efficacy of cognitive therapy and pharmacotherapy in the treatment of depressed outpatients. *Cognitive Therapy and Research*, 1(1), 17–37.

Ryan, R. M., and Deci, E. L. (2000). Self-determination theory and the facilitation of intrinsic motivation, social development, and well-being. *American Psychologist*, 55, 68–78.

Ryff, C. D. (1989). Happiness is everything, or is it? Explorations on the meaning of psychological well-being. *Journal of Personality and Social Psychology*, 57, 1069–1081.

Ryff, C. D., and Keyes, C. L. M. (1995). The structure of psychological well-being revisited. *Journal of Personality and Social Psychology*, 69(4), 719.

Ryff, C. D., and Singer, B. (1998). The contours of positive human health. *Psychological Inquiry*, 9, 1–28.

Ryff, C. D., and Singer, B. (2003). The role of emotion on pathways to positive health. *Handbook of Affective Sciences*, 1083–1104.

Sachs, J. D. (2014). Climate change and intergenerational well-being. *The Oxford Handbook of the Macroeconomics of Global Warming*, 248–259.

Sacks, D. W., Stevenson, B., and Wolfers, J. (2010). Subjective well-being, income, economic development and growth (Working Paper No. 16441). www.nber.org/papers/w16441.

Sacks, D. W., Stevenson, B., and Wolfers, J. (2012). The new stylized facts about income and subjective well-being. *Emotion*, 12(6), 1181.

Sadler, K., Vizard, T., Ford, T., Marcheselli, F., Pearce, N., Mandalia, D., . . . and McManus, S. (2018). Mental Health of Children and Young People in England, 2017. Trends and characteristics. Leeds, UK: NHS Digital.

Salmivalli, C., and E. Poskiparta (2012). KiVa antibullying program: Overview of evaluation studies based on a randomized controlled trial and national rollout in Finland. *International Journal of Conflict and Violence (IJCV)*, 6(2), 293–301.

SAMHSA (2019). 2017 National Survey of Drug Use and Health (NSDUH). www.samhsa.gov/data/data-we-collect/nsduh-national-survey-drug-use-and-health.

Satin, J. R., Linden, W., and Phillips, M. J. (2009). Depression as a predictor of disease progression and mortality in cancer patients: A meta-analysis. *Cancer*, 115, 5349–5361. doi:10.1002/cncr.24561.

Schkade, D. A., and Kahneman, D. (1998). Does living in California make people happy? A focusing illusion in judgments of life satisfaction. *Psychological Science*, 9(5), 340–346.

Schlenker, B. R., Chambers, J. R., and Le, B. M. (2012). Conservatives are happier than liberals, but why? Political ideology, personality, and life satisfaction. *Journal of Research in Personality*, 46(2), 127–146.

Schneider, D., and Harknett, K. (2019). Consequences of routine work-schedule instability for worker health and well-being. *American Sociological Review*, 84(1), 82–114.

Schoon, I., Hansson, L., and Salmela-Aro, K. (2005). Combining work and family life: Life satisfaction among married and divorced men and women in Estonia, Finland, and the UK. *European Psychologist*, 10(4), 309.

Schutte, N. S., and Malouff, J. M. (2014). A meta-analytic review of the effects of mindfulness meditation on telomerase activity. *Psychoneuroendocrinology*, 42, 45–48.

Schwartz, S. (1970). Elicitation of moral obligation and self-sacrificing behaviour: An experimental study of volunteering to be a bone marrow donor. *Journal of Personality and Social Psychology*, 15, 283–93.

Scruton, R. (1982). *Kant, Oxford Paperbacks*. Oxford University Press.

Seligman, M. E. P. (2002). *Authentic Happiness: Using the New Positive Psychology to Realize Your Potential for Lasting Fulfilment*. Free Press.

Seligman, M. E. P. (2011). *Flourish: A Visionary New Understanding of Happiness and Well-Being*. Free Press.

Semrau, M., Evans-Lacko, S., Alem, A., Ayuso-Mateos, J. L., Chisholm, D., Gureje, O., . . . and Thornicroft, G. (2015). Strengthening mental health systems in low- and middle-income countries: The Emerald programme. *BMC Medicine*, 13(1), 79.

Sen, A. (1970). *Collective Choice and Social Welfare*. North-Holland.

Sen, A. (1999). *Development as Freedom*. Knopf

Sen, A. (2009). *The Idea of Justice*. Allen Lane.

Sen, A., and Williams, B. (Eds.). (1982). *Utilitarianism and Beyond*. Cambridge University Press.

Seresinhe, C. I., Preis, T., MacKerron, G., and Moat, H. S. (2019). Happiness is greater in more scenic locations. *Scientific Reports*, 9(1), 1–11.

Shakya, H. B., and Christakis, N. A. (2017). Association of Facebook use with compromised well-being: A longitudinal study. *American Journal of Epidemiology*, 185(3), 203–211.

Singer, P. (1981). *The Expanding Circle: Ethics and Sociobiology*. Oxford University Press.

Singer, P. (1995). *Animal Liberation*. Random House.

Singla, D. R., Kohrt, B. A., Murray, L. K., Anand, A., Chorpita, B. F., and Patel, V. (2017). Psychological treatments for the world: Lessons from low- and middle-income countries. *Annual Review of Clinical Psychology*, 13, 149–181.

Smart, J. J. C., and Williams, B. (1973). *Utilitarianism: For and Against*. Cambridge University Press.

Smith, T. B., McCullough, M. E., and Poll, J. (2003). Religiousness and depression: Evidence for a main effect and the moderating influence of stressful life events. *Psychological Bulletin*, 129(4), 614.

Soares, S., Bonnet, F., and Berg, J. (2021). Working from home during the COVID-19 pandemic: Updating global estimates using household survey data. VOX, CEPR Policy Portal. www.voxeu.org/article/working-home-during-covid-19-pandemic-updated-estimates.

Solnick, S. J., and Hemenway, D. (1998). Is more always better? A survey on positional concerns. *Journal of Economic Behavior & Organization*, 37(3), 373–383.

Sorkin, A. R. (2016) 'Brexit' vote and Donald Trump's surge reflect discontent. *The New York Times*. www.nytimes.com/2016/03/01/business/dealbook/brexit-vote-and-donald-trumps-surge-reflect-discontent.html.

Specht, J., Egloff, B., and Schmukle, S. C. (2011). Stability and change of personality across the life course: The impact of age and major life events on mean-level and rank-order stability of the Big Five. *Journal of Personality and Social Psychology*, 101(4), 862.

Steptoe, A., Hamer, M., and Chida, Y. (2007). The effects of acute psychological stress on circulating inflammatory factors in humans: a review and meta-analysis. *Brain, Behavior, and Immunity*, 21(7), 901–912.

Steptoe, A., and J. Wardle (2012). Enjoying life and living longer. *Archives of Internal Medicine*, 172(3), 273–275.

Steptoe, A., Wardle, J., and Marmot, M. (2005). Positive affect and health-related neuroendocrine, cardiovascular, and inflammatory processes. *Proceedings of the National Academy of Sciences*, 102(18), 6508–6512.

Stern, N. (2015). *Why Are We Waiting? The Logic, Urgency, and Promise of Tackling Climate Change*. MIT Press.

Stern, N., Peters, S., and Bakhshi, V. (2010). The Stern Review: Government Equalities Office, Home Office.

Stevenson, B., and Wolfers, J. (2008). Happiness inequality in the United States. *The Journal of Legal Studies*, 37(S2), S33–S79.

Stevenson, B., and Wolfers, J. (2009). The paradox of declining female happiness. *American Economic Journal: Economic Policy*, 1(2), 190–225.

Stigler, G. J., and Becker, G. S. (1977). De gustibus non est disputandum. *The American Economic Review*, 67(2), 76–90.

Stolle, D., Soroka, S., and Johnston, R. (2008). When does diversity erode trust? Neighborhood diversity, interpersonal trust and the mediating effect of social interactions. *Political Studies*, 56(1), 57–75.

Stutzer, A., and Frey, B. S. (2006). Political participation and procedural utility: An empirical study. *European Journal of Political Research*, 45(3), 391–418.

Stutzer, A., and Frey, B. S. (2008). Stress that doesn't pay: The commuting paradox. *Scandinavian Journal of Economics*, 110(2), 339–366.

Suchak, M., Eppley, T. M., Campbell, M. W., Feldman, R. A., Quarles, L. F., and de Waal, F. B. (2016). How chimpanzees cooperate in a competitive world. *Proceedings of the National Academy of Sciences*, 113(36), 10215–10220.

Suomi, S. J. (1997). Early determinants of behaviour: Evidence from primate studies. *British Medical Bulletin*, 53(1), 170–184.

Suppa, N. (2021). Unemployment and subjective well-being (No. 760). GLO Discussion Paper.

Tan, E. J., Xue, Q.-L., Li, T., Carlson, M. C., and Fried, L. P. (2006). Volunteering: A physical activity intervention for older adults – the experience Corps program in Baltimore. *Journal of Urban Health*, 83(5), 954–969.

Tavits, M. (2008). Representation, corruption, and subjective well-being. *Comparative Political Studies*, 41(12), 1607–1630.

Tay, L., and Diener, E. (2011). Needs and subjective well-being around the world. *Journal of Personality and Social Psychology*, 101(2), 354.

Tellegen, A., Lykken, D. T., Bouchard, T. J., Wilcox, K. J., Segal, N. L., and Rich, S. (1988). Personality similarity in twins reared apart and together. *Journal of Personality and Social Psychology*, 54(6), 1031.

Tenney, E. R., Poole, J. M., and Diener, E. (2016). Does positivity enhance work performance? Why, when, and what we don't know. *Research in Organizational Behavior*, 36, 27–46.

Tett, R. P., and Meyer, J. P. (1993). Job satisfaction, organizational commitment, turnover intention, and turnover: Path analyses based on meta-analytic findings. *Personnel Psychology*, 46(2), 259–293.

Thaler, R. H. (2015). *Misbehaving: The Making of Behavioural Economics*. Penguin Books.

Thaler, R. H., and Sunstein, C. R. (2008). *Nudge: Improving Decisions about Health, Wealth, and Happiness*. Yale University Press.

Theodossiou, I. (1998). The effects of low-pay and unemployment on psychological well-being: A logistic regression approach. *Journal of Health Economics*, 17(1), 85–104.

Tims, M., Derks, D., and Bakker, A. B. (2016). Job crafting and its relationships with person – job fit and meaningfulness: A three-wave study. *Journal of Vocational Behavior*, 92, 44–53.

Toffolutti, V., McKee, M., Clark, D. M., and Stuckler, D. (2019). The economic and mental health impact of IAPT: Pragmatic trial in three English regions. *European Journal of Public Health*, 29(Supp. 4), 185–047.

Tromholt, M. (2016). The Facebook experiment: Quitting Facebook leads to higher levels of well-being. *Cyberpsychology, Behavior, and Social Networking*, 19(11), 661–666.

Tversky, A., and Kahneman, D. (1992). Advances in prospect theory: Cumulative representation of uncertainty. *Journal of Risk and Uncertainty*, 5(4), 297–323.

Twenge, J. M. (2017). *IGen: Why Today's Super-Connected Kids Are Growing up Less Rebellious, More Tolerant, Less Happy – and Completely Unprepared for Adulthood – and What That Means for the Rest of Us*. Atria Books.

Ulrich, R. S. (1984). View through a window may influence recovery from surgery. *Science*, 224(4647), 420–421.

United Nations, Department of Economic and Social Affairs, Population Division (2018). World Urbanization Prospects: The 2018 Revision, Online Edition. https://population.un .org/wup/.

US Business Roundtable (2019). Statement on the purpose of a corporation. https://opportunity .businessroundtable.org/ourcommitment.

Uslaner, E. M. (2012). *Segregation and Mistrust: Diversity, Isolation, and Social Cohesion*. Cambridge University Press.

Van de Weijer, M., de Vries, L., and Bartels, M. (2020). *Happiness and Wellbeing: The Value and Findings from Genetic Studies*. Mimeo.

Van Kessel, S. (2015). *Populist Parties in Europe: Agents of Discontent?* Springer.

Van Praag, B. M. S., and Baarsma, B. E. (2005). Using happiness surveys to value intangibles: The case of airport noise. *Economic Journal*, 115(500), 224–246.

van Schaik, D. J. F., Klijn, A. F. J., van Hout, H. P. J., van Marwijk, H. W. J., Beekman, A. T. F., de Haan, M., and van Dyck, R. (2004). Patients' preferences in the treatment of depressive disorder in primary care. *General Hospital Psychiatry*, 26, 184–189.

Van Wingerden, J., Bakker, A. B., and Derks, D. (2017). Fostering employee well-being via a job crafting intervention. *Journal of Vocational Behavior*, 100, 164–174.

Veenhoven, R. (1988). The utility of happiness. *Social Indicators Research*, 20(4), 333–353.

Veenhoven, R. (2012). Cross-national differences in happiness: Cultural measurement bias or effect of culture? *International Journal of Wellbeing*, 2(4), 333–353.

Veldkamp, S. A., Boomsma, D. I., de Zeeuw, E. L., van Beijsterveldt, C. E., Bartels, M., Dolan, C. V., and van Bergen, E. (2019). Genetic and environmental influences on different forms of bullying perpetration, bullying victimization, and their co-occurrence. *Behavior Genetics*, 49(5), 432–443.

Verduyn, P., Ybarra, O., Résibois, M., Jonides, J., and Kross, E (2017). Do social network sites enhance or undermine subjective well-being? A critical review. *Social Issues and Policy Review*, 11(1), 274–302.

Volkow, N. D., Tomasi, D., Wang, G.-J., Fowler, J. S., Telang, F., Goldstein, R. Z., . . . and Alexoff, D. (2011). Positive emotionality is associated with baseline metabolism in orbito-frontal cortex and in regions of the default network. *Molecular Psychiatry*, 16(8), 818–825. doi:10.1038/mp.2011.30.

Von Beyme, K. (1985). *Political Parties in Western Democracies*. Gower.

Wang, P. S., Berglund, P., Olfson, M., Pincus, H. A., Wells, K. B., and Kessler, R. C. (2005). Failure and delay in initial treatment contact after first onset of mental disorders in the National Comorbidity Survey Replication. *Archives of General Psychiatry*, 62, 603–613.

Wang, S., Mak, H. W., and Fancourt, D. (2020). Arts, mental distress, mental health functioning and life satisfaction: Fixed-effects analyses of a nationally-representative panel study. *BMC Public Health*, 20(1), 1–9.

Ward, G. (2019). Happiness and voting behaviour. In J. F. Helliwell, R. Layard and J. Sachs (Eds.). *World Happiness Report 2019* (pp. 46–65). Sustainable Development Solutions Network.

Ward, G. (2020). Happiness and voting: Evidence from four decades of elections in Europe. *American Journal of Political Science*, 64(3), 504–518.

Ward, G. (2022). Happiness at Work: Essays on subjective wellbeing in the workplace and labor market. *Doctoral dissertation*. Massachusetts Institute of Technology.

Ward, G., De Neve, J. E., Ungar, L. H., and Eichstaedt, J. C. (2020). (Un) happiness and voting in US presidential elections. *Journal of Personality and Social Psychology*, 120(2), 370–383.

Washbrook, E., Gregg, P., and Propper, C. (2014). A decomposition analysis of the relationship between parental income and multiple child outcomes. *Journal of the Royal Statistical Society*. Series A (Statistics in Society), 757–782.

Weare, K. (2000). *Promoting Mental, Emotional, and Social Health: A Whole School Approach*. Psychology Press.

Weinstein, N. D. (1982). Community noise problems: Evidence against adaptation. *Journal of Environmental Psychology*, 2(2), 87–97.

Weinstein, N. D., Przybylski, A. K., and Ryan, R. M. (2009). Can nature make us more caring? Effects of immersion in nature on intrinsic aspirations and generosity. *Personality and Social Psychology Bulletin*, 35(10), 1315–1329.

Weitz-Shapiro, R., and Winters, M. S. (2011). The link between voting and life satisfaction in Latin America. *Latin American Politics and Society*, 53(4), 101–126.

Wellcome Global Monitor (2021). The role of science in mental health. https://wellcome.org/news/what-role-science-mental-health-insights-wellcome-global-monitor.

Wells, K. B., Sherbourne, C., Schoenbaum, M., Duan, N., Meredith, L., Unutzer, J., . . . and Rubenstein, L. V. (2000). Impact of disseminating quality improvement programs for depression in managed primary care: A randomized controlled trial. *JAMA*, 283(2), 212–220.

Welsch, H. (2006). Environment and happiness: Valuation of air pollution using life satisfaction data. *Ecological Economics*, 58(4), 801–813.

White, J. B., Langer, E. J., Yariv, L., and Welch, J. C. (2006). Frequent social comparisons and destructive emotions and behaviors: The dark side of social comparisons. *Journal of Adult Development*, 13(1), 36–44.

White, M. P., Alcock, I., Wheeler, B. W., and Depledge, M. H. (2013). Would you be happier living in a greener urban area? A fixed-effects analysis of panel data. *Psychological Science*, 24(6), 920–928.

Wilkinson, R., and Pickett, K. (2009). *The Spirit Level: Why More Equal Societies Almost Always Do Better*. Allen Lane.

Wilkinson, R., and Pickett, K. (2018). *The Inner Level: How More Equal Societies Reduce Stress, Restore Sanity and Improve Everybody's Wellbeing*: Penguin.

Williams, J. M. G. (2001). *Suicide and Attempted Suicide*. Penguin.

Williams, J. M. G., and Penman, D. (2011). *Mindfulness: A Practical Guide to Finding Peace in a Frantic World*. Piatkus.

Williams, J. M. G., and Kabat-Zinn, J. (Eds.). (2013). *Mindfulness: Diverse Perspectives on Its Meaning, Origins and Applications*. Routledge.

Wilson, S. J., and Lipsey, M. W. (2007). School-based interventions for aggressive and disruptive behavior: Update of a meta-analysis. *American Journal of Preventive Medicine*, 33(2), S130–S143.

Wilson, S. J., Woody, A., and Kiecolt-Glaser, J. K. (2018). Inflammation as a Biomarker Method in Lifespan Developmental Methodology. In O. Raddick (Ed.), *Oxford Research Encyclopedia of Psychology*. Oxford University Press, n.p.

Wilson, T. (2011). *Redirect: The Surprising New Science of Psychological Change*. Penguin UK.

Winkelmann, L., and Winkelmann, R. (1995). Happiness and unemployment: A panel data analysis for Germany. *Applied Economics Quarterly*, 41(4), 293–307.

Winkelmann, L., and Winkelmann, R. (1998). Why are the unemployed so unhappy? Evidence from panel data. *Economica*, 65(257), 1–15.

Witte, C. T., Burger, M. J., and Ianchovichina, E. (2019). Subjective well-being and peaceful uprisings. The World Bank.

Wolke, D., Copeland, W. E., Angold, A., and Costello, E. J. (2013). Impact of bullying in childhood on adult health, wealth, crime, and social outcomes. *Psychological Science*, 24(10), 1958–1970.

Wootton, R. E., Davis, O. S., Mottershaw, A. L., Wang, R. A. H., and Haworth, C. M. (2017). Genetic and environmental correlations between subjective wellbeing and experience of life events in adolescence. *European Child & Adolescent Psychiatry*, 26(9), 1119–1127.

World Health Organisation (WHO). (2009). Promoting gender equality to prevent violence against women. World Health Organization. https://apps.who.int/iris/bitstream/handle/10665/44098/9789241597883_eng.pdf?sequence=1&isAllowed=y.

World Health Organisation (WHO) (2014). Preventing suicide: a global imperative. Geneva. https://apps.who.int/iris/bitstream/handle/10665/131056/9789241564779_eng.pdf.

World Health Organisation (WHO). (2017). Depression and other common mental disorders: Global health estimates. http://apps.who.int/iris/bitstream/handle/10665/254610/WHO-MSD-MER-2017.2-eng.pdf?sequence=1.

Yeung, W. J., Linver, M. R., and Brooks–Gunn, J. (2002). How money matters for young children's development: Parental investment and family processes. *Child Development*, 73 (6), 1861–1879.

Yip, W., Subramanian, S. V., Mitchell, A. D., Lee, D. T., Wang, J., and Kawachi, I. (2007). Does social capital enhance health and well-being? Evidence from rural China. *Social Science & Medicine*, 64(1), 35–49.

Zaccaro, A., Piarulli, A., Laurino, M., Garbella, E., Menicucci, D., Neri, B., and Gemignani, A. (2018). How breath-control can change your life: A systematic review on psycho-physiological correlates of slow breathing. *Frontiers in Human Neuroscience*, 12, 353.

Zajonc, R. B. (1968). Attitudinal effects of mere exposure. *Journal of Personality and Social Psychology*, 9(2p2), 1.

Zhong, Y., and Chen, J. (2002). To vote or not to vote: An analysis of peasants' participation in Chinese village elections. *Comparative Political Studies*, 35(6), 686–712.

Index

CPSIA information can be obtained
at www.ICGtesting.com
Printed in the USA
BVHW020014220223
658979BV00003B/20